DIVIDED LIVES

*The Untold Stories of
Jewish-Christian Women
in Nazi Germany*

CYNTHIA CRANE

*To Joy—This book carries
many Hyde Park Library
memories! Best to you—
Cynthia*

St. Martin's Press
New York

ISBN 0-312-21953-9

Library of Congress Cataloging-in-Publication Data
is available from the Library of Congress.

Design by Acme Art, Inc.

First edition: December 2000
10 9 8 7 6 5 4 3 2 1

There is tremendous elasticity of autobiographical forms, a fact that we discover in any perusal of bookstores, and libraries. There seems an endless variety to personal writings, autobiographical novels, personal essays, journals, diaries, collections of letters, travel literature, oral histories, ethnographies, testimonials, and prison narratives. Autobiographical subjects are everywhere. And the cacophony of autobiographical voices invigorates autobiographical narrative. In fact, it is a wonderful time of autobiographical experimentation as well as autobiographical traditionalism. Fractures in the old forms generate new modes of self-narratives.

—Sidonie Smith, *Subjectivity, Identity, and the Body*

All autobiographic memory is true. It is up to the interpreter to discover in which sense, where, for which purpose.

—Luisa Passerini, *Interpreting Women's Lives*

Even in our world of printed facts and impersonal mass media, we consciously and unconsciously absorb knowledge of the world and how it works through exchanges of life stories. We constantly test reality against such stories, asserting and modifying our own perceptions in light of them.

—Personal Narratives Group, *Interpreting Women's Lives*

TABLE OF CONTENTS

ACKNOWLEDGMENTS

I want to begin with a note that a friend sent to me in Germany that motivated me whenever I felt that I was tilling in questionable soil or planting seeds that might not bear fruit: "I think you must also realize (using a botanical analogy) that you plant seeds and wait. Often one thinks the seeds are no good because they don't do anything. Are they sterile? Is the soil tainted? Then suddenly the cotyledons appear, almost overnight the seeds planted weeks before show life. After weeks of doubt and worry the real work and responsibility begins. It is often overwhelming. I know you are up to it." And so it happened. With such a great army of people behind me, I had every reason to march forward. After nearly ten years of planning and working on this project there are numerous people to thank.

My thank yous start six years back in Germany. I'd like to give special thanks to the following people: All of the women who allowed me to come into their homes to record their stories. My two dear Hamburg friends, K. Ernst Dohnke and Almuth Dittmar-Kolb, for your unending faith and immeasurable assistance—schönen Dank! Your depth of knowledge of German history, in particular, Hamburg's history, strengthened every block in the structure. Claudia Kirschner for providing a safe haven for me when I was suffering from culture shock. My committed helpers and friends in Germany: Candace Barlow, Heather Duke, Inga Nevermann, Kitty Otto, Katharina Kramer, Heike Prahl, and my "savior landlords," Karen and Horst Moeller. Dr. Norbert Finzsch for such a warm welcome—dinner at your home, a work-out at your health club, and guidance through the mazes at the University of Hamburg. The late Dr. Günter Moltmann, who started the ball rolling that made this book possible. Priv.Doz. Dr. Büttner and Frau Baumbach at the Research Center for the

Study of National Socialism; Monika Richarz; and Herr Peter Jaffé, Member, Board of Directors, Vorstandsmitglied der Jüdischen Gemeinde in Hamburg, who gave me a contact to Herr Gerhard Wundermacher, Notgemeinschaft der durch die Nürnberger Gesetze Betroffenen, who led me to Ruth Yost and then Ruth Wilmschen. Stuten and Fridolin Ertz, friend's of my family when they lived in Germany, who led me to the engaging Dr. Ursula Levy Becker in Aachen; Frau Goldman at the Christian-Jewish Society; Erika Hirsch at the Gedenk-und Bildungsstätte Israelitische Töchterschule, who hooked me up with Pastor Ralf Meister-Karanikas, and Ursel Hochmuth. Karanikas led me to the engaging Hans Hermann Mack, who led me to Ingeborg Hecht in Freiburg, and Dr. Ursula Randt; Frau Carola Meinhardt at the Senatskanzlei, who provided me with information about people who had emigrated and been in touch with her office and who played a part when my father decided to return to Hamburg for a visit.

Thank you to the *Eppendorfer Wochenblatt,* a weekly paper that ran an announcement from which I received remarkable feedback, including a contact to Ilse B., and from which I found a great talent and friend, Gisela Gross Seifert, a professional photographer who graciously volunteered to take black and white photographs of the women. Thank you to the *Hamburger Abendblatt* and Renate Schneider, editor of the column *Von Mensch zu Mensch.* Your announcement generated letters from people who had known my grandparents on both sides—Bahlsen and Cohn—to *Mischlinge* who contacted me, including Margot Wetzel, Ingrid Wecker, and Sigrid and Gretel Lorenzen. Also the newspaper *Die Allgemeine Jüdische Wochenzeitung,* which led Ursula Bosselmann to me.

My doctoral committee: Jim Wilson, Don Bogen, and Gila Safran Naveh. You were all superb, keen readers. Mark Schardine, Daniella Bartha, Ina Remus, Christoph Haertel, and Alison Owings—your help was greatly appreciated. All of the groups that invited me to speak and the following organizations and institutes: United States and German Fulbright Commission, University Research Council, University of Cincinnati, PEO, and the Hamburg State Archives.

Dr. John Dolibois for your letters, emails, and phone calls—many years ago you were enthusiastic but realistic about applying for the

Fulbright. I treasure our continuing friendship. Jim Tent, Professor of History and University Scholar at Alabama. What can I say? You were a godsend. Claudia Koonz, with whom I communicated before any of this material was started. Thank you for all the advice. Marion Kaplan, thank you for your help with contacts and your continued interest. Ann Milan, for your knowledge and bibliography. Thanks to Katinka Matson at Brockman, Inc., who, years ago, took the time to give me invaluable feedback on my nascent manuscript.

Monica Davis, translator and friend, to whom I am indebted. Your infectious optimism and meticulousness added to our teamwork. Also a thank you to others who assisted with translation of difficult passages: Dr. Jerry Glenn, from the University of Cincinnati, and Gerhard Christ. All those who supported me at Raymond Walters College, including Pete Bender in Media Services for making slides and reproducing photos and Debbie Gage for your help with specific passages. My 1999 Topics III class, a group of engaging and thoughtful students who taught me about my own work: Renee Angel, Tara Boehner, Krissy Carovillano, Kim Conn, Patrice Flowers, Michelle Harrison, Jennifer Hoffman, Pat Jackson, Kim Janson, Tim Kroeger, Stacy Major, Julie Montgomery, Cari Moreland, Eric Neefus, Brian Thacker, Kristy Thompson, Allyson Vonnida, Sharon Ward, Stephanie Wuest, Cara Young. Also thanks to other students, including Lisa Simpson and Mary Katherine Ramsey, who inquired about my progress.

Dr. Patricia Cramer, my mentor in graduate school at Xavier University, who many years ago gave me the courage, support, and "tough love" that I needed to pursue my path. Lise Williams, my "soul friend," Andreas Drath, and Dr. John Cussen, who provided me with so much love and inspiration over the years, it would take a book to list all your contributions. The late Kay Peters, librarian and great friend, whose presence is all around me, and who I miss every day. This book was as much her dream as it is mine. Al Gavin, ace pilot and pal. Thanks for listening, for flying adventures, for your own stories of family and friends, for intriguing shopping and dining ventures, and your knowledge of World War II military operations. You make me feel like a million bucks. As does Craig Seaver. Thanks for your pep talks, help with the schedule, marketing strategies, blading and biking, the sports club, and all the e-mail, especially from the hypothetical New York fan. Jennifer Callewaert, my childhood best friend, and Jim Soupene. We are irrevocably a part of each other's lives. I hope you know how much our ties mean to me. Gary Wollenweber. Thank you. For the walks and talks, the great food, the jaunts, shaving Isak, working miracles in design, for having the patience of a saint and a superb heart. Susan Macintyre, math teacher *extraordinaire* and dearest friend. Teachers like you are far and few between. Thanks for being at my side through *everything,* and for reading and editing ad nauseum. Your cartoon series is nonpareil and kept me laughing. I will never forget that rainstorm on Main. I know a place is reserved for you in heaven. Special thanks to Barb Schumacher for your constant encouragement, friendship, and creating the index. Special embraces for Scott Goebel, a sensitive and caring confidant. You saw me "keep going" through the degrees, and for years, your shoulder and truck never failed me. Other people who played a major role: Dan Miller, hair designer *par excellence;* Monte Davis, master web designer and great morale booster; Bill Pofahl, heart-felt reader and hilarious friend; Joe Raphael, talented photographer; RL, astute reader of my stories, and "wcyn" founder—you know the rest of the spiel; Dr. Kathy Grant, Steve Deiters, Griff Murphey, Barb Brady, Kristin Dietsche, Steve Hirschberg, and Fred Anderson. Thanks to Scott Selley and Actionfront.com, wizards of technology for coming to my rescue and recovering important data.

Thanks to my top-notch editor, Karen Wolny, who had faith in this book from its inception. How lucky I am to have worked with you. Thank you to Ella Pearce for trouble-shooting and Alan Bradshaw for keeping everything on schedule, and to all the other professional hard workers at St. Martin's who assisted me.

While in Germany, I was told homesickness is a feeling of thankful-ness that you have so many people left behind that you love. That would be my family! Thank you to my cherished, brilliant brothers, George and Andrew (Bud) Crane, who, each in your own way, urged me on. Thanks to George who plays devil's advocate to razz me. Thanks to Bud for marking up the early preface and introduction, providing feedback on the stories, for your sharp wit and laughter, for lifting me up, and keeping me on my toes. And to my parents, Joan and Carl, who have always, unfailingly, cheerleaded at the sidelines. Thank you for instilling in us a love for books and inquiry and for dropping me off, at a very young age, to live at the library. With your constant example of love, commitment, and strong values, our family is tightly knit. Also thanks to those hometown friends of my parents who *still* watch over me. Thanks to Uncle Johann for important dates and family history that made the digging process less arduous.

Thank you to my extended family. We are blessed to have such an enduring connection. Those in my family who are no longer with us: My grandfather George Clyne Cummins (Oley), a superb historian and lawyer, from whom my brothers and I certainly inherited a love of history. My grandfather Dr. Felix Gustav Cohn, his brothers, and sister, and his father, Senator Carl Cohn, whose lives were the basis for this book.

This book raises a glass of fine champagne in toast to the spirit of women—the lives they follow, pursue, or endure and the varied tasks they must manage and balance. The women I know are incredible magicians and jugglers. I am indebted to my paternal grandmother, Herta Bahlsen Cohn, whose courage, tenacity, and independent spirit held together her family, got them out of Nazi Germany, and sustained them in America. Without your indomitable spirit, your memoir, and your stories of Nazi Germany, none of this work would have started or meant half as much. And my maternal grandmother, the late Alma Bender Cummins, an angel and great beauty who held us all lovingly in the palm of her hand, kept us in line, and gave generously of her time and energy. Both grandmothers grew up with strong matrilineal lines that continue through the generations. To the women who under fascism had yet another noose around their necks, to those whose spirit shattered under the memories and was never healed. To women of all races, classes, and ethnicities who are or have been "outsiders," unwittingly or unwillingly forced into outsider status, enduring traumas that no one should have to endure, this book is also for you.

PART I

THE SPIRIT

History took hold of me
and never let me go thereafter.

—*Simone de Beauvoir*

Growing up, I myself do not remember ever feeling like anything but an "outsider." Something deep in my stomach told me, somewhere stretched across the ocean was a piece of myself. I do not remember the exact moment that my family's history began to unravel. People always asked me if I was related to this Crane or that one, and I would smile and say No. As I grew older, it became more irritating, "No, none of my relatives live near here," I would all but shout to the inquisitor. I wondered where all of my relatives were. I always knew my name was different from my grandmother's, but I did not know why. Something was amiss, but when I attempted to ask my father, his face paled and I retreated. My paternal descendants, I discerned, were twilight zone people. I always felt as if I belonged in another place, that there was a dormant world embedded in me via my grandparents and father. Shreds of stories leaked out in whispers when I was young, until my grandmother started to toss out one story at a time, until she broke down and confessed to me that she had written a book. It took me some time to persuade her to retrieve the manuscript out of her basement, where it had been hidden away. Through her stories, I allowed my grandmother to reweave my life, to put back in the original stitches. But not until I was awarded a Fulbright Scholarship to Hamburg, Germany, and was sitting in the Hamburg State Archives (after having waited weeks for my file requests to be fulfilled, and now having all eyes upon me as I checked out the folders) looking through my family's immigration files, housing inane letters my grandmother had to write to the Gestapo just to keep her husband's stethoscope, lists of all the beautiful family heirlooms the Nazis would "pick up," as well as papers regarding the Aryanization[1] of the company Arndt and Cohn, owned by my great-grandfather and great-uncle, did I realize the enormity of what had been missing from my identity, a history that, once seemingly daunting, vivified me the longer I stayed in Germany.

My father and his family, like the women in this book, survived the Third Reich. They are here to talk about it, but millions of others are not. My own family's experiences parallel many of the women's stories recounted here, and because of my relatives' persecution, the women felt a kinship to me and I to them. The subject matter is not only tragic but also reaffirming of the human spirit and its ability to persevere. I have attempted to illuminate for all readers universal stories of human strength and weakness, of hope and survival, that transcend time, race, religion, class, and gender. This is not the story of my family, but it begins with them.

My paternal family, the Cohns, has been traced to 1755 in Germany. In the eighteenth and nineteenth centuries, they resided in Neustrelitz, now a part of the defunct German Democratic Republic (DDR), and then gravitated to Hamburg in northern Germany.[2] My grandfather Felix Cohn was a private practitioner and also a prison doctor in Hamburg when Hitler came to power. His medical license was revoked under Hitler's laws in 1938.[3] As a designated Jew, he could no longer practice medicine. He was supposedly fired from the Grosshamburger Gefängnis (prison), where he served as prison doctor from 1922 to 1934; there he had entered on the prison records the factual reasons for injuries to some of the prisoners, namely that they were beaten. My grandfather endangered his life by helping prisoners to escape who had wrongfully been imprisoned. He also helped "enemies of the state"—Socialists and Jews—by misdiagnosing them or claiming they needed certain medicines and sending them to hospitals from which they could then flee. He also drove ostensibly ill people to the edge of the Baltic near Travemünde, where they fled in boats. Informants tipped off my grandfather that he was on a Gestapo list to be rounded up and most certainly tortured.

He escaped Nazi Germany to the United States in 1938 before Kristallnacht, "the night of broken glass,"[4] thanks to an affidavit from his younger brother, Rudolph, who lived in the United States. My grandfather was not Jewish but was considered a Jew because of his Jewish "blood": his grandparents had been tied socially to Jewish culture but were not observant, religious Jews. My grandmother, Herta Bahlsen

Cohn, was considered "Aryan," or pure German. She was pressured, unsuccessfully, by the Gestapo to divorce my grandfather — "Why would a beautiful young woman like you stay married to a Jew?" Before he left Germany, my grandfather insisted that his children be baptized immediately to protect them. They had been attending Sunday School at a Lutheran church. Nevertheless, because of my grandfather's "blood-line," my father and his siblings were considered *Mischlinge,* Hitler's derogatory term denoting "half-breeds," or "hybrids," those that were "outsiders," not fully German or "Aryan" or even human. Hitler referred to the racially "impure" as "monstrosities halfway between man and ape."[5] After Hitler's rise to power, their lives became a struggle for survival, hanging precariously between life and uncertain death. My book is about *Mischlinge* and their divided lives.

Like many of the *Mischlinge* and their families, my grandfather did not want to leave Germany. He loved his country and was a nationalistic German. He had served in World War I as a doctor in the trenches in France, ran an evacuation hospital, and was rewarded for his bravery with a first and second Iron Cross. He could not fathom that his country would renounce him. He did not think of himself as a Jew. He thought of himself as a German, the son of a famous Hamburg finance senator, Carl Cohn. He could not turn his back on his history very easily. Had my grandmother not been so strong-willed, he might never have made it out of Germany. She had been talking about leaving for years. As early as 1922, at age nineteen, she could see the growing movement of the National Socialists, the Nazi party. My grandfather had merely silenced her. I think, deep down, that he knew she was right. At the time he left, he was fifty years old and my grandmother thirty-five, quite a generation gap when one is thinking of starting over one's life in a foreign land. My grandmother mentioned that he wrote her letters from the United States in the year after he left Germany. She still has these letters. My grandfather later told her she did not need to keep them because they were all lies. He had said everything in the United States was fine to try to keep her spirits up, when, in reality, nothing had been fine with him. Nor was life fine for her. My grandmother claims that once he got to the United States he forgot about her fighting for all of them in Germany. He thought she and the children could remain yet another year. In her view, he had no idea how hopeless life was in Germany and how difficult it had become to get out.

Before my grandmother left Germany, she attempted to help my grandfather's brothers, Carl August and Werner Cohn, who had been rounded up on Kristallnacht. Because she was "Aryan," blonde with blue eyes, she could maneuver through Germany more readily. Carl August was not sent to a camp; instead he was cast into the prison in Fuhlsbüttel.[6] Carl August was more protected; perhaps he was important to the Nazis because he was a partner of Arndt and Cohn, an import/export business that accorded him many connections, and the Nazis could not afford to lose German business. My grandmother became aware that he had plenty of help and did not need hers. They had a cordial, but not close relationship, and Carl's wife, who was "Aryan" and quite alert to the political situation, was in a position to exercise some influence through friends and family. Carl did not remain in prison long after Kristallnacht. On the other hand, Werner, who had never even been in military service, was taken to either Osnabruck or Marinberg, camps north of Berlin. Utterly traumatized by his camp experience, he refused to talk or write about it before he died a few years ago in South Africa.

Indicative of the pervasive secrecy of these times, my grandmother found out about the men's capture in a round-about way. The nephew of a neighbor of my great-grand-mother told his aunt, who told my grandmother, that Werner was on a truck to Berlin. To help him, my grandmother went to the Fuhlsbüttel prison director's home in the middle of the night. The director lived in a five-story apartment building in Eppendorf, a refined suburb in Hamburg. My grandmother remembers climbing all of the stairs in the dark, concentrating on appearing serious. The director had recently come from southwest Africa, where my grandmother's sister lived with one of the first settler's families who were very well known. During the meeting with the director, my grandmother cleverly dropped their names, and he agreed to tell her the official procedure for getting men out of the camps. He could have told her nothing. Within his limits, he tried to be helpful. The wives were supposed to appeal for the release of the men. They needed to gather all of the men's official papers, and then the men had to leave the country immediately. Mausi, Werner's wife, did not believe any of this; nor did others who could not fathom the Nazis' actions. She said if her husband, a lawyer, could not get himself out, she did not know who could. Like some of the women whose husbands had been rounded up, she was in denial. Because she did not believe my grandmother, Mausi went to an elderly Jewish lawyer, who confirmed the truth of what my grandmother had said. Mausi went to Berlin, where she and other friends were hidden in a house. Through a tedious, bureaucratic process, my grandmother managed to get Werner released. When he returned, his clothes needed disinfecting and his head had been shaved. Werner mentioned that the men had been forced to march out of the camp and many had collapsed. Both Werner and Carl emigrated at different times and settled in South Africa. Werner told my grandmother that if she ever needed help getting herself and the children out of the country, he would help. And he, among others, did.

On January 30, 1939, more than a year after my grandfather left, my grandmother and my father, Carl, ten years old, along with his siblings, left Hamburg for the United States on the SS *Washington*, part of the United States Line and the largest steamer ever built in America. They were only allowed to leave with DM 10 per person, which was equivalent to 4.59 in U.S. dollars. After stopping in Le Havre and South Hampton, the ship arrived in New York on February 9, 1939. My father recalled hellish seas, but the children found a way to have fun, sliding by the force of the seas from corner to corner on the ship deck. My grandmother equated America with guaranteed, irreversible freedom. When she arrived in the United States, she ran down the streets in New York, never glancing behind her because no one's eyes were upon her anymore. The youngest children, Johann and Anna, lived with my grandmother at a house in upstate New York where she worked as a maid. Immediately after disembarking the boat in New York, my father and his other sister left for a farm in Doylstown, Pennsylvania, owned by my grandmother's friend from Hamburg, Berta Schroeder. They remained there until my grandfather passed his medical exams and moved everyone to Hamilton, Ohio, to start again in medicine.

Over the years, the German government sent my grandfather information about collecting monies owed him. Like most of the *Mischlinge*, he had a legitimate claim to social security (for his prison work) and for *Wiedergutmachung* ("to make good again"), reparations given to German-Jewish victims of the Third Reich. But my grandfather never wanted to deal with Germany again. Before he could throw out the unopened letters, my grandmother answered them and took care of any future correspondence from Germany.

In the 1950s because of continued adversity, my father, at age twenty-five, changed his last name from Cohn to Crane but did not explain it to me until I was a teenager, and even then he preferred that I not discuss it with anyone as "It's no one's business." Many of the women in this book talked about their

Jewish or "Aryan" name that either marked them for or protected them from persecution. Although we in the United States may think that all this was "only in Germany," the fact is that anti-Semitism was everywhere. Even though my father's identity was a German Christian and, later, an American Christian, his past, which identified him as a *Mischling*, as a "race" that did not in reality exist and that he never understood, followed him. My father's own tormenters haunted him: the Nazi teacher, Herr Stolp, who, in 1938 beat him mercilessly everyday in front of the class (causing permanent hearing loss) to prove what a Jew hater and good Nazi he was; the Americans who saw him as the enemy because he was German and who banned him from walking down certain Midwestern streets; the American high school principal who told him he was not mature enough for college (despite my father's lengthy resumé of jobs and responsibilities) and that, anyway, Michigan State was the only college that took Jewish students (this despite the fact that all of my father's school records classified him as Protestant, which he had always been); and his employer on the West Coast, Long-Bell Lumber Company, in 1954, who would not promote him because, he said, "We can't put a salesman with a Jewish name into the Midwest calling on lumber yards and expect him to meet sales goals. He would not be accepted by his customers!"

Two weeks after the job incident, my father changed his name legally to Crane, and the company promoted and transferred him to Kansas City. My mother, Joan Cummins, had married my father despite some protests from her mother. My mother was only twenty-one, obviously in love, and not too concerned about what was "in a name." My father had talked with his father about changing his name, which my grandfather understood was necessary, as other family members had done the same. My parents sat down with the phone book, and because in those days all their towels and silver were monogrammed, they wanted the last name to remain a C and be monosyllabic like Cohn. They decided that Crane sounded okay. Later, when he returned to his hometown in Ohio as a Crane and not a Cohn, my father sensed that the Zion Lutheran church to which he formerly belonged and the Jewish community alike were miffed. Yet my father was tired of the discrimination he had faced, and he did not want his soon-to-arrive children (who would be raised and baptized Presbyterian, like his wife) to face any unnecessary hassles because of a last name. Interestingly enough, many parents of the *Mischlinge* in this book also had done this. They may not have changed their names, but they baptized their children and were adamantly Christian. They severed all Jewish roots so that they could be "officially" assimilated into German culture. For my father, there was nothing inherently wrong with being Jewish, nor was it a religion to scoff at, but the only remnant of my paternal family's "Jewishness" was a last name that prior to Hitler had no major significance. This identity of "being Jewish" was imposed on them. With the rise of Hitler, their name and bloodline marked them, changing all of their lives forever.

In 1994 when I received the Fulbright to Hamburg, Germany, I could not envision how it would change my life. I was pursuing a project that encompassed my primary field of study in graduate school, personal narratives, which centered on the contextualizing of my grandmother's manuscript that I had retrieved from the basement, a twenty-four chapter historical memoir that discussed her life, hardships, and philosophy in the years from 1915 to 1939 in Austria and Hamburg before her emigration to the United States. I proofread and edited her original manuscript, which had been compiled from nineteen years of journal notes and typed at her kitchen table in Hamilton, Ohio. Although later she published her original manuscript, at the time I applied for the Fulbright, a definitive version had not been written.[7] Therefore, initially my research was to provide additional information and to expand on the foundations of this manuscript. My grandmother's work touches on the specific political, social, and religious upheavals originating in the Weimar period that, she believes, transformed the Germany she had known. My grandmother had a degree from a business school, and had worked at a young age, treasuring her independence. Ironically, my grandmother had worked for my great-grandfather, Senator Carl Cohn, a formidable figure, years before she met my grandfather in a housing community where she was the bookkeeper and he the resident doctor. What interested me most, and what later became my focus, was her role as a middle-class Austrian Lutheran, an "Aryan," married to my grandfather, an upper-class German of Jewish descent, a "non-Aryan." Their marriage, considered a Jewish-Christian one, was labeled a *Mischehe* ("mixed marriage") and denounced as illegal under Hitler's laws.

To better understand "mixed-marriage" situations, I conducted research in the Hamburg State Archives, locating my family's emigration documents that once had been overseen by an arm of the Gestapo. Ironically, these files had reappeared recently after years of being "lost." Because of laws governing these archives, I was not able to see these files until my family granted the archive permission to give them to me. Via a loophole in the laws, I obtained permission from the archives' director.

This feeling of "Let's not speak of it" extended to all groups: Jews, *Mischlinge*, Germans, and the government. My own experiences of secrecy were directly related to what had occurred during the Third Reich. My study of these files helped me later in my interviews because I better understood the horrendous rigmarole, the endless, ubiquitous tracking system of the Nazis. Similarly, many of the women in their stories talk about the endless bureaucracy, and the letters of pleading and "proving" one's "Aryan" heritage. Seeing my family's names listed in an index pertaining to the records of an arm of the Gestapo, Oberfinanzpräsident (OFP), the head of finance, was harrowing. There had been many offices around Hamburg that were simply awful where one had to go to ask to leave the country. This meant that no one got out "illegally," as they went through this long, grueling process to leave. After 1939 it was nearly impossible to get out through "legal" means. I was fascinated by all the calculations of possessions. There were letters back and forth between the wicked OFP and the family. In every one of my family's files were documents from MM Warburg and Co. Family members sold jewelry to the company, which also had my family's Konto (bank) number; which means Warburg and Co. controlled their banking. Their official letters ended with *Heil Hitler!* which is what most people had to write, as if they were being watched. Other letters closed with *Mit Deutschen Grüssen!* (with German greetings), which today has been replaced with *Mit Freundlichen Grüssen!* (with friendly greetings). These signatures were imperative to show the writer's nationalism. I nearly had to get up and leave at times because I could feel the interrogation of the Nazis and the frustration of my grandmother in the letters, and the immensity of the endless calculations of the family's worth. There were letters begging that they be allowed to keep some of their possessions. For instance, my grandmother *asked* to take her typewriter. The official letters had her categorized as "Aryan," and when my grandfather was mentioned, "nicht Aryan" was written in parentheses. The mention of their status as divided from each other was shocking but certainly helped her get out of the country. The *Mischling* women, in their stories that follow, also repeatedly mentioned this pervasive classification system that was on every document in the Third Reich.

In the files of Carl August, my great-uncle, the selling of
his house, to every single item he owned, is listed. There are
letters he wrote to the OFP pleading, "Please, can I keep this?"
The Nazis had marks or circles around some of his words,
analyzing them for falsehoods. One of the Gestapo's replies
said that the points he argued in his last letter were not solid
enough. The last name, Cohn, was always underlined with red
pencil, and the correspondents refer to him as Jewish. Curi-
ously, copies of the anti-Jewish laws prohibiting his family
from this or that were attached to one of his letters. My great-
grandfather, a Hamburg senator from 1921 to 1929, also had
a large file containing numerous articles about his death and
funeral in 1931, and newspaper articles he had written.[8] My
grandmother was thankful that he died before he could see
what his homeland would become. The *Mischling* women also
mentioned how they were glad an elderly relative had died
before Hitler's time, so they did not have to live through it. In
another file, there was a list of all the people who contributed
money to make my grandmother's exit possible. It was a lot of
money by my calculations. I *knew* all about these events, but to
see them in these official documents where entire lives were
determined is something again. Not only sheer tension drove
me from the archives, but also my grandmother's concerns
about digging into the past. After I had been trekking to the
archives for a while, I returned to the United States briefly.
Talks with my grandmother started to steer me away from
dead documents. Once again, just like the *Mischlinge* in their
stories, the need to be secret and protective surfaced in my
grandmother's personality.

So I turned my gaze away from the family and searched
for personal documents of Jewish women who had married
German men, or, like my grandmother, German women who
had married Jewish men. Women's lives at that time had been
more of a private than a public matter; thus few documents
mentioned women, no matter what their background. Because

of the missing women's lives, the hunting quickly became a daunting task. In the archives, I was not only burdened with language barriers but also with gender barriers. It was telling that I found hardly any information on women at all, and I wanted to know why. Because life outside the archives had to be more invigorating, I decided to interview surviving *Mischlinge*. As I interacted daily with more Germans, it became apparent that speaking with *living* women was more immediate, despite the fact that I was told "you won't find anyone," as so many Jewish survivors were deceased. And, indeed, among the survivors, there was not a long line of anxious interviewees ready to disclose their traumatic experiences. Interrogation, violence, spying, mistrust, and silence constituted the sphere of "normal" behavior in the 1930s and 1940s. These women had learned how to dodge their oppressors, to lie, to protect themselves and their families. They were living peacefully with a hidden past. Nevertheless, I continued my search for women who were partners in or were daughters of a "mixed marriage." The "half-Jew" women had a higher survival rate than "full Jews," primarily because one of their parents had been classified "Aryan."

Knowing that my father (who is of the same generation as the women I interviewed) vehemently opposed ever returning to Germany, I was curious as to why and how it happened that some *Mischlinge* never left. Why would those who were persecuted by their own people remain (even after the war), or if they *had* left temporarily, why would they return? As I maneuvered within Hamburg, a city of nearly 2 million people, it was no surprise that my investigations continued for six months. Curious listeners have asked me repeatedly, "How did you find the women?" "It wasn't easy" is my standard reply, and the digging process was lengthy. I began to receive letters from women who were potential interviewees after I developed contacts with community leaders, other researchers, and research institutions, and after a notice about my research was published in a popular weekend column, *Von Mensch zu Mensch* (from person to person), in the city newspaper on March 5, 1995. Once the first contact was tapped, all the subsequent contacts started to fall like dominoes.

Despite their willingness to present themselves through letters and phone calls, most of the *Mischling* women were tentative about being tape recorded and became reticent when I arrived to interview them; they suddenly realized the enormity of disclosing their lives. Nevertheless, by the time I left Germany, I had twenty taped interviews, primarily with *Mischling* daughters, the products of Jewish/Christian "mixed marriages." As historian Claudia Koonz mentioned in *Mothers in the Fatherland*, "perhaps children felt the impact of anti-Semitism most strongly and earlier than their parents. Children of Protestant parents considered themselves Protestants even if they had Jewish grandparents. Suddenly, their Jewish heritage mattered."[9]

I created a collection of voices distinguished thematically. These voices recall the same historical experience with variations and with parts of the stories left concealed: All of the women are victims, but we get ten stories—distinct, varied personalities—out of possible hundreds. The women's stories can be likened to Samuel Barber's "Adagio for Strings, Opus 11," a quiet poignancy with strength. Variances of solitude and intense living are woven throughout their lives. Most stories end, as the piece does, with calm resolution, a slice of peace. As I cannot claim to be an objective, nonparticipatory viewer, my own personal odyssey—the experience itself and the resultant questioning of values and beliefs—surfaces throughout the book. My nomadic journey within Hamburg (with one satchel, wandering from lead to lead, moving from house to house) was more than an academic one; it was a quest for identity, a striving to become, in theorist Maria Lugones's words, a "world-traveller."[10] The knowledge thrust upon me that I was "Other" bound me to the *Mischlinge* and enabled me to hear their stories judiciously; however, my connection also occluded any totalizing, integrative experience. I too felt a nagging, persistent suspicion of Germans.

I was in Germany at a time of "new unrest." Although the country was unified, those not living in the East insinuated that "the East" was a needy, unwanted stepchild draining the economy—divergent political and economic philosophies and views of Germany's history could not be bridged. In addition, the fifty-year commemoration of the concentration camps'[11] liberations had begun. Nonstop TV and public programs and gatherings and newspaper articles threw the 1930s and 40s into the present. When I arrived, talk of the Third Reich was everywhere in the media, but not on many citizens' lips. I heard moans of "not again" from my landlady when the topic appeared on the news night after night. I certainly knew what it felt like to have old wounds reopened, but I could not imagine the deepness of this cut.

If you were to ask the average Jew in America the question, "Do you think of yourself as a Jew first, or an American?" what would the answer be? Many in the Jewish community in America, especially those who emigrated from Germany, will say they are Jews first, primarily because of the persecution. I had this discussion with the women I interviewed, and they think Jews in America identify much more with their Jewishness. More progressive Judaic practices abound in the United States. In Germany, many of the Jews are Orthodox, which has alienated them from more progressive Jews there. As a few of the women mentioned, some Jews will not attend the synagogue in Hamburg, as it is too conservative and strict. A few interviewees commented on the large number of European Jews living in the United States who escaped from or survived the Third Reich. A number of the interviewees questioned if perhaps American Jews are not as forgiving as Israeli Jews, or if they are more disconnected from their origins. The women answered that many Jews in Israel still speak German and are tied to their former culture through the language; thus, they harbor, even nurse, a connection to Germany. The Jews in America have gained a physical and psychological distance from the past, which does not foster nostalgia. Often, for them, the German language and culture are dead, and quantified anger and the reality of what happened to them and their family stands in its place. Esther Bejarano, a survivor of Auschwitz with whom I talked, returned from Israel to live in Germany after having barely made it out alive from Auschwitz. Why return? The answer seems to relate, in part, to money. The persecuted returnees receive pensions, and, compared to Israel, the cost of living is better in Germany. Otherwise, as Jews, they may not have returned. After the war my great-uncle, Werner Cohn, and his wife returned to Germany. They lived in Hamburg only one year, then claimed they could not stand the climate and had to return to South Africa. Not many of the formerly persecuted people could return and remain. I am sure many Germans are proud to be Germans, whether Jew or Gentile. However, it is nearly impossible for Germans to display their pride in Germany. Certain acts of nationalism are against the law because this is part of what led Germany into difficulty in the 1920s and 1930s.

My father called Germany his "graveyard," pondering why he should return for a visit. He readily recalled how he was beaten by Herr Stolp—day in and day out—as an example to the other school children of an "inferior." Did these children not understand, as my father did not? He just wanted to wear a uniform (forbidden to him) like all the other boys—to belong to whatever they belonged to. He was an outsider but he did not understand why. The schoolchildren were told *he* was the cause of Germany's ailments. They could tell their parents "a 'half Jew' was put in his place today." From what source does this mentality derive? Perhaps the Third Reich is still a historical aberration. Primo Levi states in regard to the isolation of the Jews and the concentration camp system,

> At no other place or time has one seen a phenomenon so unexpected and so complex: never have so many human lives been extinguished in so short a time, and with so lucid a combination of technological ingenuity, fanaticism, and cruelty. No one wants to absolve the Spanish conquistadors of the massacres perpetrated in the Americas throughout the sixteenth century. It seems they brought about the death of at least sixty million Indios; but they acted on their own, without or against the directives of their government.[12]

My father reluctantly came back to Hamburg when I was living there. One day, as we walked down Rothenbaumchaussee, a long street in Hamburg, he turned to me and said, "I feel afraid." He also was consternated when we went by his former house in Fuhlsbüttel and he noticed the name plate on his neighbor's home: The same family who had "spied" on his family, offering reportage about his family's comings and goings to the Gestapo, still lived next door. As he was waiting at the airport to return to the United States, three hours before his departure, his name was called over the loudspeaker. His face blanched, his breathing slowed, and his eyes appeared distant, "Now what could they want with me? Are they going to keep me here?" I too felt alarmed. It was an anachronistic moment; both of us, for our own reasons, were thrown back in time. Slowly, he walked down the stairs to the appropriate counter and, of course, it was merely a mix-up with his bags. He explained to me that when they tried to leave Germany in 1939, he and his siblings sat on trains, ready to board a boat to leave the country, only to find out they needed newly required papers. According to my grandmother, the ante was always upped. Just when she thought she had all the papers, the government changed the laws. In order to leave Germany, my grandmother needed approximately twelve official documents. On and off the trains, waiting and waiting, week after week, my father feared they would never get to the United States. Would they always watch the boats leaving without them? To this day, he has fears about missing flights, and if you travel with my father, you are guaranteed a long airport wait.

The Lutheran minister who preached in my father's former church, St. Lukas, while he was visiting during the fifty-year remembrance ceremonies, said that evil resides in the world. It is man's creation. God gave man freedom to act and make decisions. Otherwise we would be mere marionettes with God pulling the strings. One can give up on mankind, but one must not give up on God. An answer, but not so easy to accept. My father accepts it only because the Quakers sponsored him with money that helped to save his life. The Quakers took up a collection and turned it over to the family in whose house my father and his sister would live and work. This money was a guarantee from the American side that these foreign children would be subsidized. The guarantee came just days before they left the country. My father wrote to me on December 13, 1994:

> The Quakers made it possible for my sister and me to immigrate and made it possible with their money to put your grandfather back into the doctor business. The kind of money they came up with in the late 30s was great Christian love and should not be forgotten. That is why I will always give to the church and its mission work just like your grandfather did all his life in gratitude, and to make sure others have the same chance. It's like Woody Hayes told it, "You can't pay people back, but you can pay them forward."

It is good to ask oneself, "Would I honestly have been a hero at that time? Would I really have taken the chance to lose my life to save others?" Not everyone is a hero, and how can any of us know how we would conduct ourselves in such circumstances? We cannot know. We can all only say "I hope that I would have been one of those who were brave and kept my morals intact." There were also *Mischlinge* who spoke in the rhetoric of the Third Reich even though they themselves were persecuted, which made my skin crawl. Somehow, they felt so German that they did or said anything they could to keep their German identity intact. I can imagine that my grandfather went through this agonizing internal struggle as well—all the questions and musings—"Ah, it will pass over. Hitler will be just a fly in the bucket." Or, "I am German and cannot go elsewhere." It is sad to think of my grandfather's emigration because I know he loved his country. This I can understand. It was easier for my grandmother as far as "nationalistic" feelings because she was truly Austrian and so much younger. It was hard on the children, as the stories in this book show. I lived with these ponderings and questions everyday that I was in Germany.

Finally, for me, this book is a personal journey. Christa Wolf, in her book *Patterns of Childhood*, tried to resurrect a curiosity that was squelched during Hitler's reign by allowing her curiosity to lead her through the past, back to her home-town, ultimately to explain her family's role and their guilt as Aryan "bystanders." So too have I followed my curiosity to Germany, back to my father's hometown, to uncover atrocities against his family and other *Mischlinge* that undeniably marred their collective psyches. As theorist Paul John Eakin writes, "to write history and finally autobiography is not merely to recover the lost content of the past; it is to perform metaphorically a work of personal restoration."[13]

PART II

THE LAW

You shall know them by their fruits.

—*Matt. 8:16*

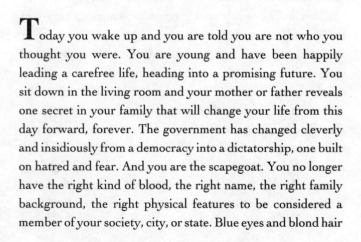

Today you wake up and you are told you are not who you thought you were. You are young and have been happily leading a carefree life, heading into a promising future. You sit down in the living room and your mother or father reveals one secret in your family that will change your life from this day forward, forever. The government has changed cleverly and insidiously from a democracy into a dictatorship, one built on hatred and fear. And you are the scapegoat. You no longer have the right kind of blood, the right name, the right family background, the right physical features to be considered a member of your society, city, or state. Blue eyes and blond hair are favored, and you have neither. According to new laws, you had better be "Aryan," but by definition, you no longer are. You have always been an insider, but you are now an outsider. You have never been a victim, but now you are victimized. You can no longer attend school, see your familiar friends, have a profession, or marry anyone of your choosing. Nothing and no one is to be trusted. The world you've been living in has metamorphosed into an incomprehensible labyrinth. What goes through your mind? Why is this happening to me? Is this true? I want to die. By degrees, your family is torn apart in ways that are irreparable and irreversible. Like having a love, a passion, the likes of which you will never again see, once you have passed through it, your identity is altered. As with a broken heart, some healed, and some did not. You cannot explain to others how your soul and heart have been defiled; the nails have left invisible marks that only God can see, although you try to show the marks when someone you trust asks. But there is always a sense that another breach of faith or of confidence will follow, that someone will pick up the hammer again and hit the nails. This is not make-believe, but happened in this century to people in this book. When we hear someone talk about a divided life today, it usually refers to a division between work and family, or work and social life, or children and spouse. It does not readily conjure up images of the Third Reich and the Holocaust, of people who were torn between a German and a Jewish identity. Through the ten stories of women's voices here, we receive a clearer picture of *Mischlinge* and what they endured under Hitler's laws. In the Lübeck memorial chapel, iron bells had fallen in 1942 during the Allied bombings and they lay there still, badly broken and melted on the smashed floor. It is astonishing to see. Later these bells haunted me and became a symbol of the *Mischling* women: A witness, a survivor, something left behind, but no longer in its original form. And the fall itself had altered the piece forever.

With the onset of the Third Reich in January 1933, Jews were no longer defined under religious or cultural terms, but as a race. The ensuing nomenclature that defined the Jews signaled an emphasis that was racist rather than religious. A specific lexicon illustrated by key terms was used to define and separate Jews from "normal" or *Deutschblütig* (pure German) society. Hitler's regime hoped that by marking and placing people into degrading categories, their spirits would be crushed by the separation from their fellow Germans. Hitler perverted the German language and effectively manipulated it as a psyche breaker. Thus, today, certain terms such as *Ehre* (honor), *Blut* (blood), and *Vaterland* (fatherland) are not used with the patriotic fervor that is still possible in other countries. There are no illegal terms in Germany today, just words that have a certain aura about them, words that older or "conscious" people who still remember have trouble listening to or using. Certain symbols, such as the swastika, indicative of National Socialism, are illegal in public, on flags, on medals of honor from the war, and on book covers.[1] Hitler's book *Mein Kampf* (My Struggle) is not allowed to be sold secondhand unless for "scientific reasons."[2]

Language, especially through Nazi propaganda minister Joseph Goebbels's pervasive propaganda strategies, and violence were effective means to control the people, and propaganda slogans, such as *Juda Verrecke!* (Judah croak!), *Juden sind hier nicht erwünscht* (Jews not wanted here!), *Deutsches Volk! Wehr dich! Kauft nicht beim Juden!* (German people, defend yourselves, do not buy from Jews!), *Die Juden sind unser Unglück* (The Jews are our misfortune) were widely propagated. Nazi publications like *Der Stürmer*[3] and others tried to show through repetition of certain words—*Judenschwein,* (Jewish pig), *Ungeziefer* (vermin), *Schmarotzer* (parasite), *Parasiten* (parasites)—that Jews and other "outcasts" were subhuman. Terms such as *ausmerzen* (eliminate), *ausrotten* (exterminate), and *vernichten* (extinguish) lowered inhibitions to the idea of Jews being treated like vermin or animals. These words today are taboo among politically correct people.

The *Mischling* women talk about the impact of these words, the cause and effect of Hitler's evil, and the confusion that abounded over where they stood within the chaos. Suddenly, these women did not fit an ordained visage — an *Aryan* image. This was a betrayal for the *Mischlinge* — being told they were members of a Jewish "race," but having little or no idea what being Jewish meant. This takeover of their identity was the beginning of their duality of Christian and Jew, German and Jew. Formerly, their identity was constructed to a degree for the purposes of nationalism and national unity, and one day this changed. This *was* betrayal. With whom do they identify now? The women were left with a complex set of emotions, such as an internalized hatred of themselves, often played out in "death wishes;" hatred of the Jewish family member; of their newfound identity; and of those Germans who had relabeled them. They were victim/victimizer, Jew/Christian, outsider/insider. How could a twentieth century, modern society make such laws? How could they then exterminate people? A complex question that the women uttered. "How could *they* determine a "race"? *Where was God*, one woman wondered.

I found the persecutors and the persecuted were often embodied in one — a disquieting phenomenon. This is the horror of the big picture. This division is at the heart of divided lives: split identities and torn loyalties, to which many people in contemporary society can relate. Although these women *were* the persecuted, they sometimes thought, and today think, the same as the persecutors. Was the victims' silence as dangerous as that of the German perpetrators? Did victim and oppressor alike suppress the horror in order to move beyond this chapter in history? Or did only the victims bury their pain and anger temporarily, waiting for the day to speak? After the war, many Nazi officials lived on comfortably in Austria, Germany, and South and North America, having found a way to rationalize their actions. Many former Nazis, such as Nazi Women's League leader Gertrud Scholz-Klink, expressed no qualms about their role in Hitler's Reich. They still believe today that those twelve years bonded the German *Volk* into a golden nationalism. Perhaps they fail to see that today a German can scarcely show partiality to his country. Patriotism is a *Schimpfwort,* dirty word. If acted upon it could again lead to a frenetic nationalism. Germans are divided by their history. Surprisingly, some *Mischling* women harbored anti-Semitic views. It would be absurd to suggest, however, that undeserved, legalized persecution was needed in order to "straighten these women out." (That is similar to saying that someone who managed to survive the camps was "stronger for the experience.") But their endurance of racial persecution altered all of these women's lives to varying degrees. They never saw themselves as *Jewish*: More often than not, their Jewish parent or spouse was fully assimilated into German culture, was not religious, or had been baptized Christian. Today, these women remain *zwischen allen Stühlen* (straddling the fence) to various degrees, although it appears that this "racial" identity forced some of the women in later life to reevaluate their own nationalistic attitudes and their position within society. Could they risk hard-won security of having reattained their German status and relative anonymity, to talk to me, to draw attention to themselves once again, to dabble in the past? Their fear of discussing their twelve years of persecution, when they were Jews and no longer Germans, was great.

The group of women that I interviewed is one about which we rarely hear. These German women who were a part of or were products of a Jewish-Christian "mixed marriage" were persecuted under the Nuremberg Laws[4]; however, they have often been passed over in studies of the Holocaust. Why is this? Perhaps it is because they are not considered "really Jewish"; their families had cut their Jewish ties, and, for the most part, they were not practicing Jews. These women are still struggling with the nightmares of the Third Reich and the Holocaust, the loss of family in concentration camps, and whether or not they are Jewish or Christian. Often, their Jewish background was disclosed to them only after Hitler's laws were passed, and in some cases was not revealed for years after the laws were in place. For some of these women, this Jewish identity was their buttress in post–World War II Germany, as they had to separate themselves from the Germans who were looked upon as Nazis. Although one would think that they could not in good conscience reclaim their German heritage, today some of them have.

Many Germans, including my paternal family, escaped in time; however, many of their relatives and friends did not. The following stories look at the plight of the people who remained behind. At speeches I have given, I am often asked how these women manage to live in a country that once had been their refuge but had betrayed them. These women are often likened to other "mixed" people in the United States. As we become more interracial as a society, questions of cultural and ethnic identity arise. Although obviously we do not live under a totalitarian regime, those of us who are "hyphenated" Americans wrestle with issues of loyalty and identity to one group or another. Most of the interviewees in my book are still searching for a cultural, religious, or national identity as a result of their persecution.

German historian Ursula Büttner mentions that "apart from the Jews themselves, several hundreds of thousands of people, a number originally perhaps just short of 400,000, suffered as a result of the National Socialist racial lunacy because they were spouses, children or grandchildren of Jews."[5] Between 1935 and 1945 those who lived in "mixed marriages" as well as "half Jews" were persecuted as "non-Aryans." After the instatement of the April Laws (Civil Service Law) of 1933, Jews were cast out from the civil service and prohibited from taking up certain professions (legal and medical) and enrolling in particular schools and universities. On September 15, 1935, the Nuremberg Laws took away German citizenship from those who were not of "German or related blood." Marriages and sexual relations were also prohibited between Jews and "pure Germans." Jews and Germans were prohibited from "mixing"; doing so was an act of *Rassenschande* (racial defilement), and was punishable by law and viewed as treasonous. Although it was illegal to stay married to a Jew if you were German, the authorities found it difficult to enforce this law. When the initial push for divorces of "mixed marriages" did not show the desired results, the Gestapo put pressure on the "Aryan" wife or husband to file for divorce; very few left their Jewish partners. Oftentimes, the marriage continued inconspicuously while the couple lived apart. It would have been dangerous for the couple had the Gestapo detected that the bonds between them were intact. For the "Aryan" man, maintaining a marriage with a woman of Jewish origin meant that he could be fired or at least face disadvantages in his profession. An "Aryan" woman married to a man of Jewish origin primarily had to face harassment and often had to use her "Aryan" privileges to rescue members of her husband's family from camps. The major consequence for a Jewish partner in a "mixed marriage" who left (or was left) was more discrimination—fewer food and clothes stamps—and later, instant deportation and death. For the Jewish partner married to an "Aryan," it was crucial that the marriage not end. Government pressure and harassment to divorce was difficult for couples to withstand. There was no discernable legal difference between Jewish men or Jewish women who left their marriages, as both were considered enemies of the state. In the interviews with the *Mischlinge* it is worth noting that the "Aryan" men in a "mixed marriage" did not live very long, perhaps because of the emotional and physical trauma of being married to a Jew and their subsequent loss of status and professional position in society. If they returned from concentration camps, the Jewish women to whom these men were married tended to live long lives.

The Nuremberg Laws and the "law of the preservation of German blood and German honor" as well as other orders that regulated behavior, split up the persecuted into two groups: Jews (German nationals) but not citizens, meaning they were not allowed to vote or run for public office, and *Mischlinge*, who were considered temporary citizens. A person was a "full Jew" if he or she had at least three Jewish grandparents. A *Geltungs-jude*, a self-declared or believing Jew, could be a person without Jewish grandparents who was a member of the Jewish community because he or she converted at the time of marriage or had decided to become a Jew for other reasons. Self-declared Jews were dealt with as Jews and deported from 1943 onward. Hitler's objective for the future was to separate "Germans" from Jews and "mixed persons."

Mischlinge were divided into those of first and second degree—*Mischling ersten grades* and *Mischling zweiten grades*. A first-degree "half Jew" was a person with two Jewish grandparents. A second-degree "quarter Jew" had one Jewish grandparent. Both groups remained temporary citizens but were subject to strict marriage restrictions. Eventually, their rights decreased until they had none. Nazi policies were less restrictive toward second-degree *Mischlinge*. First-degree *Mischlinge* were allowed to marry people of German blood only if they received a practically unattainable marriage approval that entailed Gestapo supervision. Second-degree *Mischlinge*, on the other hand, could only marry persons of German stock. First-degree *Mischlinge* were further divided into two groups. The first were the *Geltungsjuden*. Although they fell under the definition of *Mischlinge*, they were treated as "full Jews." They were permitted to marry either Jews or other *Geltungsjuden*. The second group consisted of those who had been baptized

Christian (the majority of women I interviewed). According to historian Nathan Stoltzfus, "Baptized *Mischlinge* outnumbered *Geltungsjuden* by nine to one, since only 11 percent of *Mischlinge* belonged to Jewish communities."[6]

In December 1938, after Kristallnacht, the laws made a distinction between "privileged" and "non-privileged" "mixed marriages." They were "privileged" if the woman was Jewish or if there were children who were raised Christian and were under age eighteen. Hitler created this "mixed marriage" category because he feared alienating the "Aryan" half of these marriages. They were "non-privileged" when the children were considered Jews or when the man was Jewish and the couple had no children. Most of those in "privileged mixed marriages" were not forced to relocate to houses designated for Jews and were not deported until toward the end of the war. The National Socialists concentrated on those marriages in which the man was Jewish. The irony here is that by doing so, they reversed the Jewish concept of lineage. For Jews, the matrilineal is more important in determining who is Jewish in the family as opposed to the German patriarchal, patrilineal definition of Jews as a race.

The majority of marriages between Jews and non-Jews were considered "privileged." Because of centuries of anti-Semitism, most of the German-Jewish parents and their children had been baptized. They feared persecution if they did not distance themselves from the Jewish faith. Most members of "privileged" marriages belonged to the middle class, and they had tried to "make it" by assimilating into German culture. Beginning January 1, 1939 Hitler decreed that on all German-Jewish identification cards, which already bore the letter "J," the name "Sara" would be added for women, and "Israel" for men. A few of the *Mischling* women mentioned the violation they felt for their mothers who were often addressed simply as "Sara." In September 1941 Jews were forced to wear and display the yellow Star of David sewn onto their clothing. The star marked the Jews for deportation. There was an arbitrariness concerning *Mischlinge* wearing stars, as Joseph Goebbels was still uncertain what to do with them. Whether a *Mischlinge* wore a star often depended on the attitude of the local *Gauleiter* (regional Nazi leader)—the more beastly and fanatical he was, the higher the chance a *Mischlinge* might wear a star. Thus, they were forced to wear a star in certain places, but not in others.

To equalize Jews and *Mischlinge*, Nazi leaders at various times, as at a conference in 1941 and at the Wannsee Conference on January 20, 1942, suggested that *Mischlinge* be forcefully sterilized or deported to camps, and even their German spouses be deported with them. However, they did not know how to put this into action without causing public outcry from the German families, and Hitler, and Goebbels, in particular, stalled the issue. Finally, they were hindered by the turn of the war.

In 1940, men who were married to Jews were discharged from the army, with some exceptions. In 1943, men in "mixed marriages" received drafts from the Organization Todt (OT),[7] and a year later were drafted for forced labor. Initially, the group of forced laborers were to be driven east to construct roads, however, in Hamburg they were needed first of all to build up the destroyed infrastructure, to clean-up, and to recover dead bodies and material. In late 1944 women in "mixed marriages" were forced into labor groups. The sporadic, random transports of *Mischlinge* began in February 1945, and those from Hamburg (as seen in many of the stories) and other areas were sent to Theresienstadt, a camp in which people were worked into their graves, rather than gassed, or transferred to extermination camps such as Auschwitz. Several hundred died in the process. Fortunately, the chaos of the war's end interrupted the process or the targeting of *Mischlinge* would have become systematic. They were the next wave of deportees.

identity and gender that arose under the patriarchal machine of National Socialism. Clearly, all of the women's identities were fractured to some degree, but as they spoke of the desolation of their worlds, the crumbling of their formative years, they seemingly either reconstructed or reinvented their lives *as they were speaking*. In the telling of their stories, they each crafted and sometimes gave birth to a "fictional" identity, one that protected them from the pain of their history as victims. In "Authorizing the Autobiographical," theorist Shari Benstock states, "Language, which operates according to the principles of division and separation, is the medium by which and through which the 'self' is constructed."[8] In some sense, I helped them to create this self, this autobiography. My role interviewing these survivors included coming to terms with my own life as a daughter of a *Mischling* and survivor. I dealt with countless language and cultural barriers in my search for stories that validated but also diverged from my own, often nightmarish, family stories. I played the role of listener, recorder, and excavator of long-buried material and memories. I was entrusted with these women's narratives because of my "spiritual" connection to their history. I lived what they had experienced through my grandmother's and father's stories, the confusion of being "outsiders," neither German nor Jewish, and in particular, my father surviving torment as a *Mischling* that has shaped who he is today. I am aware of and have acknowledged my positionality, where I stand as a first-generation American, also torn between my feelings of kinship and enmity toward Germany. It was up to me then to deliver the narratives in a compelling way. There was a transatlantic link between the women and me—a connection to a dysfunction that they knew made me a sympathetic listener. Dr. Dori Laub, psychoanalyst, states, "Bearing witness to a trauma is, in fact, a process that includes the listener. For the testimonial process to take place, there needs to be a bonding, the intimate and total presence of an *other*—in the position of one who hears. Testimonies are not monologues; they cannot take place in solitude. The witnesses are *talking to* somebody; to somebody they have been waiting for for a long time."[9] I think these women's stories have always been there waiting for me.

The following statement, made by author Ingeborg Hecht, best characterizes all of the interviewees' lives: "We were stripped of our rights, denied the opportunity to train for worthwhile professions, prevented from building up a livelihood, forbidden to marry. We shared the fears of those who failed to survive persecution, but we also had to endure the shame of having fared better than our fathers, our relations, our friends. We did not emerge unscathed."[10] These women carry an enormous burden; they live between the extremes, juggling two worlds. They represent a variety of backgrounds, although the majority would be considered, by German measure, to be in the educated middle or upper class, a class most affected by the ban from the civil service, universities, and skilled jobs. All of the women's fathers were professionals. Ruth Wilmschen's and Ingrid Wecker's fathers were classified as *Beamte* (civil servants), because they worked for the state as a teacher and principal, and a policeman, respectively. Most of them were from the northern port city of Hamburg, the second largest city in Germany.

The discrimination against the "mixed" women was, at times, so severe that many of them suffered after-effects similar to those of camp survivors, as psychologist Louise Kaplan documented—physical illness and/or mental dementia that created a wall between the present and past. Kaplan calls this "transposition . . . where the past reality of the parent intrudes into present psychological reality of the child." Even though these women were not deported, they continually created in their minds the suffering of a parent who returned, or the death of a parent who perished in a camp. Kaplan states, "The children of survivors were living out and dreaming out their parents' nightmares. The children were enacting experiences and relating fantasies that could only come from a person who had actually been in a ghetto or extermination camp."[11]

These German women are caught between the Nazi definitions of patriots and "asocials"; their grief, manifested in physical pain and mental anguish, provides a murkier realm of study than the thoroughly researched grief of camp survivors. I found that traumatic ostracization led to repressed memories of the "mixed" women's outsider status, which, in turn, created some real or imagined physical ailments. After the war, it was imperative they "be" German again—having repressed their negative experiences as victims, they were able to function, albeit superficially. After "purging" themselves through hospitalization, therapy, or work, did these women begin to heal— a prerequisite for coming to terms with their position in present-day Germany? Although their footing is precarious at best, these women have reached a point where they can speak openly, but often only with people they have carefully scrutinized. Their split identity—between victim and participant, Jew and Gentile—which they attempted to ignore or repress, appeared to be the cause of physical and mental ailments.

Some of the conversations with the women came from questions that comprised my questionnaire or were questions formed from discussions I had with Monika Richarz, academic director at the Institute for the History of German Jews in Hamburg. Family dynamics from 1933 to after the war— families under stress—was always the central topic of our talks and was an issue in all of the interviews. To what extent a woman's identity was affected or changed often depended on how the family interpreted their situation. The story always began with the marriage of the parents and grandparents. How did the racial laws split the family? Was there pressure to divorce? What were the reactions to that? Did the "Aryan" partner drop or support the Jewish partner? Was there a major split or solidarity? What happened to their identity once they were designated for racial persecution in all its manifestations under the Nuremberg Laws? How did some of them cope with suddenly "being Jewish" when they had never been exposed to Judaism or ever entered a synagogue? Do they "feel" Jewish now as a consequence of their former "stigmatization"? Are they actively "pro-Jewish"? Neutral? Christian? How was Jewish identity transmitted, if at all? How did their experience of persecution affect their psyches? How do they conduct their lives in Germany? Do they cover up or openly talk about the past?

These are some of the issues discussed in the following stories. There are myriad answers. Many women responded to these questions with rather disturbing answers—at times, contradictory to or in denial of their former plight as "outsiders." A few resorted, perhaps unconsciously, to National Socialist words, a vocabulary particular to the Third Reich, when talking about the past. A few of them related brief sections of their stories in English, certainly because of my presence as an American. I was careful to include all of the questions in each interview, but the women chose how they wanted to engage their lives with me. Most of them did not need to be questioned before they began to talk; they simply started with a vivid memory. They spoke primarily in three different modes: stream of consciousness, associative, or linear. By request, a few of the women's last names have been eliminated or changed, and events might not be relayed in their entirety. Necessarily, because of the voluminous oral material, I had to make decisions about what was relevant to this story and to frame their narratives accordingly. Sometimes this entailed moving around some material or excising tangential chitchat, but never changing the stories or factual events. As Israeli author Aharon Appelfeld said, "Life in the Holocaust . . . was so 'rich' one could choke on it. The literary problem is not to pile up fact upon fact, but rather to choose the most necessary ones, the ones that touch the heart of the experience and not its edges."[12] This does not change the "facts" of the stories, which are historically accurate according to the women's memories. History is perceived differently from country to country and from generation to generation. History is not static and diachronic. Many of the women claim to discuss German history as the Germans perceive it and tell it.

The stories of these *Mischling* women — Ingeborg Hecht, Ingrid Wecker, Ruth Yost, Ruth Wilmschen, Gretel and Sigrid Lorenzen, Ursula Randt, Ilse B., Margot Wetzel, and Ursula Bosselmann — display vividly the trauma these women endured during and after the Third Reich, and the coping mechanisms they sought after or adopted. Wilmschen's, Wetzel's, Bierstedt's, and Bosselmann's mothers were deported to camps. Yost's and Randt's fathers escaped Germany, Gretel Lorenzen's father was deported to a camp, Wecker's father was killed by the Nazis, and Hecht's was purportedly exterminated in Auschwitz. Many of the women experienced trauma symptoms that did not necessarily dissipate once they had "purged" their memories. As Laub says,

> The traumatic event, although real, took place outside the parameters of "normal" reality, such as causality, sequence, place and time. The trauma is thus an event that has no beginning, no ending, no before, no during and no after. This absence of categories that define it lends it a quality of "otherness," a salience, a timelessness and a ubiquity *that puts it outside the range of associatively linked experiences,* outside the range of comprehension, of recounting and of mastery. Trauma survivors live not with memories of the past, but with an event that could not and did not proceed through to its completion, has no ending, attained no closure, and therefore, as far as its survivors are concerned, continues into the present and is current in every respect.[13]

Hence, the women repeatedly commented, "I can't describe this," and "you can't imagine" as they attempted to narrate their past lives in the present. They could not escape the fact that they were victims at one time, that the people with whom they lived had been their persecutors. This problem is seen also in the United States, such as with African Americans and Native Americans. It would seem a difficult thing for anyone to live peacefully among her tormenters. This problem exists in many other nations. South Africa, Argentina, and other states have collapsed and been renewed under somewhat less authoritarian conditions. There is a lot of bitterness and inability to forget. We must look at the Mid-East, the Balkans, Rwanda/Botswana, and other regions where these hatreds continue for generations and generations. Perhaps it is just part of the human condition — not really a disease that can be "healed," or a trauma that can be "purged." The issues that the *Mischling* women faced can be bridged to the present in America. In a country verging sometimes on amorality, very often pushed by the media, we grasp at techniques such as dehumanization, stereotypes, and violence to talk about or act against "enemies." Do the same fears still predominate in human nature, a need to exterminate for racial cleansing, and the fear of the unknown?

History is difficult to escape. These *Mischling* women have little, if any, support in Germany today. Silence is preferable to talking to the "wrong" person about their background. Perhaps this is why they still struggle to one degree or another with their identities. Most *Mischlinge* who survived do not have support within the *Jüdische Gemeinde* (Jewish community). The "mixed" women are still "mixed" psychologically and socially. They rarely and cautiously reveal their heritage or their former outcast status so as not to draw attention to themselves. Often they have not disclosed their past to children or grandchildren. For the most part, they want to be included in German society and not be seen as women who were once considered "inferior" or "outsiders" by the majority. Even though now they can speak about their past, they protect their current status. Few involved give another picture of the persecution of that time. That is why a new look at this subject is necessary."[16] What follows is that new look.

PART III

STORIES

~

I look in their faces for signs of this country twisted in their eyes. Sitting in my place around the table amid *Kaffee und Kuchen,* a German woman's hospitality, the microphone black and silver and large rests out of place, a long chord into the recorder. I look around their homes for signs of their stories— a canvas embroidered with a collage of menorahs dangles from the wall, a pen and ink drawing of a death camp victim, an oil painting of a murdered peasant, an uncle. Inevitably, there is some sign. Often, it is books—the Holocaust, the Jewish "situation"—because the women believe they can learn by absorbing others' words and opinions of a time they experienced, books describing or explaining Hitler's reign. They lived it. But they falter to describe it. I look in the women's faces for signs of this country twisted in their eyes. Some cry over their lost childhood, a child contorted to fit into rules that adults could not comprehend nor explain to them. They ask themselves rhetorical questions; "Can I retrieve lost time?" And who can say No. Some play house now—crying over dead or Nazi husbands, choosing the wrong man again and again, too many divorces, no husbands at all, no children, estranged children, no friends—like the beginning of life again but it is towards the end. They kick their feet under the table, stab the traditional rich pastries and cakes with their forks, slurp coffee—all seemingly tasteless. And they rant. And I sympathize. And record. No one will forget what trauma human beings inflict on each other. The women are pulling at their collars; thumbing buttons in and out of buttonholes; twisting their hair, necklaces around their necks, rings around and around their fingers; clacking their dentures; tapping their pencils; rustling then clamping then smudging their notes; pulling down their library shelves full of Third Reich texts or texts about the Third Reich—tossing volumes on the table before me, dragging out old photo albums with black and white or sepia-toned pictures framed by four glued squares that loosely hold these "before Hitler" memories—and then full, framed pictures of their Jewish grandfather or beloved grandparents hidden in boxes under beds, wrapped in multiple layers of brown paper to protect them and themselves from potential scrutiny. Still so much secrecy. Fear flowed through the walls. Women whispered to me, covered the sides of their mouths when recalling Nazi propaganda. One woman asked me if my German friend was a Nazi—*als Sie leben noch, und werden immer, wahrscheinlich* (as they still live, and probably always will). And when extremists blew up a government building in Oklahoma, a fervent voice calls to tell me she has changed her mind; she does not want her picture taken. The "New Right" in the United States might look her up and find her if she appears in my book. And I understand her fear— things break loose, chaos. Reminiscent of the Third Reich. It creeps everywhere.

CHAPTER ONE

INGEBORG HECHT

*"The Germans and the Nazis
were not synonyms for me"*

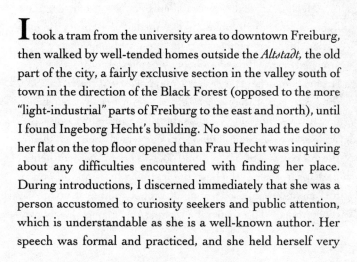

I took a tram from the university area to downtown Freiburg, then walked by well-tended homes outside the *Altstadt,* the old part of the city, a fairly exclusive section in the valley south of town in the direction of the Black Forest (opposed to the more "light-industrial" parts of Freiburg to the east and north), until I found Ingeborg Hecht's building. No sooner had the door to her flat on the top floor opened than Frau Hecht was inquiring about any difficulties encountered with finding her place. During introductions, I discerned immediately that she was a person accustomed to curiosity seekers and public attention, which is understandable as she is a well-known author. Her speech was formal and practiced, and she held herself very erect, sometimes slightly tilting her head to listen. Her clothes were tasteful, nothing overdone. She wore a multicolored wool skirt, a black shirt with a light-gray turtleneck peeking through, and a red wool cardigan in an Austrian style. Her glasses on a gold chain lay elegantly like a necklace over her shirt and capped the conservatism of her dress. She wore no jewelry. Her eyes, which one can see more clearly in photographs, are, like her past, sunken; she would only reveal shadows of her life, through stories she had written down or later had permitted to surface. Her red-lipsticked, pouty mouth always slightly smirking, and her thick, beautifully coifed brunette hair recalled to me the flappers of the 1920s, although her large boned frame did not signify a woman who was light on her feet, dancing the night away. Her life had not been one of constant frivolity. Her apartment was cluttered top to bottom with books, papers, and knickknacks that made the air feel dusty. While pointing out the small rooms in her place, she casually mentioned that her mother was never a good housekeeper but was a good person. This apartment was homier, more lived-in, than any other of the women I had visited. Books were stashed haphazardly in bookshelves—a stereotypical writer's or professor's dwelling.

Hecht's cordiality was undeniable. We sat in her unlit living room, which looked like a nineteenth-century English parlor, in pulpy chairs surrounding an oblong cherry table adorned with Bahlsen chocolate-covered butter cookies, strong, somewhat tasteless tea, and *Stollen*, fruitcake. In 1939, the first year of the war, Hecht wrote in her first book, "To me, tea was not only conversationally stimulating but something akin to an elixir of life."[1] She conversed about teas during the interview. The *Stollen*, she said, was not *richtiger*, authentic; perhaps it was not the best, but it still had raisins and nuts in it. I mention her concern about proper food as it points (as other things did) to her bourgeois upbringing. Hecht was somewhat incapacitated with a bad hip. She sat on a davenport with her back supported against a special electric pad.

Hecht was characteristically reserved, pleasant, slow to reveal, protective of her inner self; she displayed a no-nonsense attitude. She gave me her newest hardback book in German; it centers on her phobia, which kept her a prisoner in her home for nearly thirty years, from 1957 to 1983. Psychologist Louise Kaplan writes, "Not until the late 1970s, when therapists who were treating children of survivors began to share their experiences, did we begin to grasp the meaning of the events that transpired in our consulting rooms. The most common symptom among children and adults we encountered were phobias." For adults it was "agoraphobia, a terror of leaving the house or walking in the streets."[2] During her life, Hecht had suffered incredible losses — her father had been murdered in Auschwitz, her husband and mother died relatively young, and her only child died from a brain tumor. Psychiatrists informed her that the process of writing her first book, *Invisible Walls: A German Family under the Nuremberg Laws,* resulted in her mental recovery and inspired her second book. She was able to go outside accompanied by friends.

Although Hecht's father perished in Auschwitz, somewhere in Hecht's mind he had been a survivor. Her brother more strongly believed this. Hecht reported that her brother stood at incoming train ramps and bus stops waiting for his father to return. Although Hecht overcame her phobia and is able to talk about her life, her nightmares have not lessened in intensity. Hecht mentioned that she often associates present events with the past. Kaplan claims this connotes a child survivor's need to live with a lost parent, to not fully be present in her own time. Although Hecht mentions her father, it is always in passing. It seems she has elided the emotional aspects of her past, sometimes, necessarily, placing herself outside of what happened to her personally.

Hecht mentioned an upcoming Hamburg book promotion in May of 1995. She invited me to breakfast at the "bohemian" *Hotel Pension am Nonnenstieg* where she stays on the Alster Lake. Although she claims not to be an artist, she said that mainly writers and artists frequent this hotel. During our interview, she passed over or dismissed any feminist questions. She repeatedly stressed her lack of education—that she had none—but that her husband taught her much, even how to write better. She writes what she can recount factually, but she cannot describe anything poetically. She claims her work is not literature. Hecht believes she is a "sort-of historian" (more so than an artist) but only an amateur. When asked questions, she often deferred to her book: "I wrote that in my foreword." If she did not want to elaborate on a topic, or if there was a possibility of contradicting herself, she would repeat "it's in my book."

It is necessary to discuss Hecht's first book, *Invisible Walls*, as most *Mischlinge* refer to it and Hecht can be seen as a major spokesperson for this group. In the beginning of that book Hecht sets up the maternal and paternal family interrelations that later sway or collapse under the onus of the Third Reich. Felix, Hecht's father, was born to Jakob Hecht and Hanna Calmann in 1883. He was the oldest of five children. Because he was Jewish, he was transported to Theresienstadt (a work camp) and purportedly murdered in Auschwitz. Her maternal grandparents, Friedrich von Sillich and Fredegonde Ossenkamp, had Edith, Hecht's mother, in 1900. They were Protestant. Both grandfathers died in 1918.

The Hechts owned an antique shop, Rembrandthaus, in the Colonnades at Hamburg that the von Sillichs, who were collectors of pewter, frequented. Felix, the proprietor's son, helped Edith with her homework. Despite the sixteen years age difference, Felix proposed marriage in 1919, shortly before Edith finished her nurse's training. They could not fathom that later their marriage would be labeled a "privileged mixed marriage." Edith and Felix married on May 25, 1920.

On April 1, 1921, Ingeborg was born in a private clinic owned by Adolf Calmann, her grandmother's brother. On November 11, 1923, her brother, Wolfgang, was born. Although they had a normal childhood for a while and played "cowboys and Indians" while growing up, it was not long before the Nuremberg Laws were created for the "protection of German blood and honor." Ingeborg and her brother later would be stamped as "half-breeds of the first degree," and be forcibly divorced from their German heritage.

Hecht had a close friend, "little Inge," whose mother had converted to Judaism when she married, so Inge was a *Geltungsjude*: "a Nazi neologism implying that [one was] technically and formally Jewish."[3] Both Hecht and "little Inge" had been baptized in 1938. Hecht writes, "We existed in a peculiar limbo, torn between fear, suspense, and curiosity. How else could we have endured life, if not as students of the world around us?"[4]

Her book situates her on "the great Germans" side, a rarity to the point of myth. She mentions Frau Flügge, who sacrificed security to help the Jews, "like other courageous Germans."[5] She mentions the ones who risked their lives rather than dwelling on those ordinary Germans who stood by passively and watched. Dreams were lost, but for Hecht, she was a Hamburger first and foremost; she felt protected in her city. She said, "It was only later that I grasped how much I managed to endure for twelve long years, though always buoyed up by a feeling of happiness that I lived in Hamburg. I never wished to be anyone or anything else — not even 'Aryan.'"[6]

In her book, Hecht discusses deportations, in particular, to Theresienstadt. Three other interviewees — Ruth Wilmschen, Margot Wetzel, and Ursula Bosselmann — watched helplessly as their mothers were deported there. Hecht knows her father was sent to this "work camp," but she does not delve

into her father's death in the book, as it must have occurred
on the way to or in Auschwitz. She says, "How people wound
up in Theresienstadt, which was Hitler's attempt to convince
foreigners of his humanity, and how they 'lived,' vegetated,
and died there, is a macabre theme in its own right. There were
no gas chambers, just starvation and disease and harassment
in all its infinitely humiliating forms. For most of the inhabitants, Theresienstadt was a wretched transit camp on the road
to extermination."[7] Hecht, as did Wilmschen and Wecker,
discusses the Jewish people at a home who are gathered up
on the pretense of being moved to a better place. Hecht says,
"Aunt Jenny and the other old ladies from her home were
assigned to a batch of deportees who never arrived. It later
transpired that, in many cases, 'gassing vans' were summarily
put to work en route."[8] There was a promise of a home for
these people when they arrived at Theresienstadt, which was,
of course, a lie. Deeds were collected from Jews, but no houses
existed. Jews had to give up their furs and woolens supposedly
to keep the soldiers warm. In truth, ordinary Germans—the
"Aryans"—received them.

In 1940 Hecht's mother was imprisoned for visiting her
Jewish husband, which was forbidden. Hecht describes what
she said to the Hamburg Reparations Office in September
1961, "in support of a (rejected) claim for compensation."[9]
Imagine being rejected after having been persecuted and still
loving your city. For Hecht, though, only those who were in
concentration camps really have a reason for continued *Haß*,
hate. She writes,

> I began by describing the world in which my mother grew
> up. During her three weeks in custody—over which I
> prefer to draw a veil—she began to feel as if her childhood
> were only a dream. The two worlds seemed so utterly
> incompatible. "That first day," she said, "I met the kinds
> of girls I'd never come up against before . . ." / "Whores,

you mean?"/ She was relieved that I'd absolved her from saying the word. It had never passed her lips before, any more than the girls themselves had formed part of her social environment.[10]

Her mother mentions how kind these women were to her—how any "humane gesture in inhumane surroundings" was appreciated.[11] Those, such as Primo Levi, who were in concentration camps, made a similar statement. One can not categorize horrors, but her mother's imprisonment can not be read in the same way as we read an Auschwitz survivor story. However, someone who is a political prisoner is more familiar to the American experience—it is an occurrence that can be envisioned—but internment in camps for "racial imperfection" is a picture one cannot conjure up, let alone believe, when reading about it. Some horrors are only partially visualized because to encircle the totality of the nightmare is too much for the human heart and mind. In our country, it is always harder for most people to empathize with the already privileged.

Hecht's father pondered emigration to Honduras and Shanghai. His lawyer friends had left, and his partner committed suicide. He did not have the capital to emigrate, and felt that he could not reestablish himself elsewhere. Hecht writes, "Doctors could make a fresh start abroad without too much difficulty, whereas lawyers had no such professional prospects."[12] "'What on earth could I do in a Chinese city?' my father protested, and he had a point. What *could* a Hamburg attorney have done in the Far East, in a city that had been occupied by Japan, an Axis power, since its seizure from the Chinese in 1937?"[13] Privilege allows choosiness of where to emigrate. Many people just emigrated anywhere they could to escape degradation and persecution. They did not ask where they would end up when they climbed aboard a boat. It did not matter. If you have little to lose, should it matter to what foreign land you set out? The privilege of choice. Hecht's relatives did leave for Shanghai in 1940. She writes: "The emigrants were depressed, dispirited, and filled with premature homesickness. Our family had, after all, lived on the banks of the Elbe for two generations. Besides, we all dreaded that some terrible hitch might occur at the last moment, because it went without saying that the permits and papers had to be examined yet again by some official of forbidding mien."[14] Hecht's family experiences parallel those of my grandmother Herta Bahlsen Cohn's, although my grandmother talked about freedom, getting away, escape. To her it did not matter that she left behind a fashionable life. My grandmother simply did what she had to in order to regain freedom, including leaving Europe, her past, behind. Sentimentality and rumination can crush life-saving action. Is Hecht's nostalgia proper? It is certainly difficult to ascertain or theorize such ponderous history.

At age twenty, when Hecht was leaving to join her aunt and uncle in Shanghai, she discovered she was pregnant. An illegitimate child was foreign to her mother's sensibilities, but she was happy her daughter would remain in Hamburg. Hecht says," "I'd grown accustomed to expecting nothing, not even consolation."[15] Her daughter's father was killed in action at the Russian front in 1944.

Hecht mentions that the tone of her book "appropriate to a memoir of this kind" should "strive to be impersonal and objective."[16] I thought this objectivity was precisely the problem with her memoir. She seemed to be missing from it. She wrote her book standing back from the situation, centering on specific laws—factual data—that head each chapter. After these headings, she then writes about her family's specific predicament. Hecht said to me, "I actually avoid emotions because I think that young people who read this want to know facts instead of 'when I cried.' For me, however, an 'I' is absent."

Aharon Appelfeld believes that Holocaust testimonies like Hecht's "are actually repressions, meant to put events in proper chronological order. They are neither introspection nor anything resembling introspection, but rather the careful weaving together of many external facts in order to veil the inner truth . . . . nothing but externalization upon externalization, so that what is within will never be revealed."[17] Many of the interviewees who either knew Hecht or had read her books felt likewise, that Hecht stood back and reported "from a strange distance."[18] The style of Hecht's book allowed her to submerge the self in objectivity; nevertheless the writing of this largely factual first book was what cured her illness. Perhaps the only way to write about atrocities—in this case, racially motivated atrocities—is to distance oneself from the events. By doing so Hecht can speak in classrooms and pass on her stories to younger generations. Objectivity saves her from falling into the stark realities of her text. Hecht is one of the few interviewees who has buried or "stripped down" her split identity—has presented herself as "wholly there, wholly German." Hecht's "factual fiction" of herself as German author, lecturer, and celebrity at times transcends the memories of her former self as an outsider, a Jew, a murdered father's daughter. In essence, she has skillfully cozened herself and her listeners. It seems the return to her childhood city, Hamburg, after decades of absence, was one of the catalysts for the phobia cessation, in addition to her writing of the book. In the interview she stressed her struggle with whether to accept a lecture invitation to Hamburg. Her deep love for her hometown combined with her desire to encounter her history gave her the courage to leave her house and travel to Hamburg. To observers, her exile inside Germany continues; as former victim, she lives within the remnants of the past on a fissured foundation.

I have had many visitors, especially ten years ago. However, fun is not the right word for it. I'm very thankful and happy that the response to my books has been so great. It's a difficult topic. I want to tell people something. People who emigrated from Germany or who lived in America couldn't talk about it. And the children in America don't know and can't speak German.

My first book was published ten years ago. An English translation appeared in America—*Invisible Walls*. Furthermore, the book has been published in France and Denmark, and sold out rapidly because many people are interested in history. But it was very difficult to get good sources [historical data]. My book was dramatized in 1988 and 1989 in a youth theater in Karlsruhe and in Freiburg for a guest production, and in Hamburg, 1988. In these performances the final scenes with the father have been the most horrible for me. In Hamburg a class in the *Jahnschule* [a high school] tried to perform it on its own, but the teacher responsible for the play left the school. The play will be performed only in German because in that language it has such a personal touch.

It is interesting that your grandmother's maiden name is Bahlsen, like the cookies. [I explain my family was part of the cookie business, even though my maternal great-grandfather did not want to be in the business. She laughs.] Bahlsen, *like the cookies!* A Bahlsen edited my husband's first book, *Saturnische Erde,* about Italians, who said "end of cookies—we start culture."[19] This was Bahlsen's catch-phrase when he first founded his publishing house—it actually was his advertising slogan. And you are also Bahlsen.

[Signs her first book] I'd like to sign only my name. I have already signed thirty books this morning at the school. I must take thirty books with me to each school. If I wrote more than my name, my hand would fall off. I have five binders full of letters, all beautiful letters, about my first book and a package of positive reviews. Because the reviews of my first book were so positive, I decided to write a second book, *Von der Heilsamkeit des Erinnerns.*[20] There are only a few books about "mixed marriages" in Hamburg. It started with Ralph Giordano's *Die Bertinis*[21] so I asked him to write the preface to my first book, and we are now friends. Some well-known "mixed" children are Inge Meysel (very famous, even now she shows up often on TV), Dr. Ursula Randt, IngeHutton,[22] and Ida Ehre, the actress. *Not only* an actress but also a theater director—very big. She wore many hats. I know Ursula Gaupp in America and a school friend—no—she's a "full Jew"—in England. You have a long list to get through, but are there *really* that many *halbes* [half Jews] in Hamburg?[23] I got the book *Die Sondergesetze gegen die Juden*[24] *(The Special Laws against the Jews)* compiled by Professor Joseph Walk in Jerusalem, as a gift. I received a letter from Professor Walk in 1985 thanking me for using his material. In 1990 we met for tea. I picked up the book in 1981; it contains all the Nuremberg Laws, and I got the idea to describe the Jewish life in "the mirror of the laws."

Whenever I read a law, I recovered my memory as to how it applied to me. Before I got Walk's book, I didn't have an idea how to do it. When I read *Die Bertinis* I realized no one knew about the "half Jews" and their lives. I explained the relation between these laws and everyday life. I think that this was a fantastic idea, pure chance, and the key to the success of my book. First, I realized from Giordano's *Die Bertinis* that people didn't know anything about "mixed marriages." So I started to write my book only for myself and my family without any order. I can describe my state as writing and living in a trance for four months. Later a friend, Heinz Knobloch, a lecturer in Freiburg, who formerly worked for Hoffmann and Campe, a Hamburg publishing house, read the book and said he'd talk to this publisher about publishing my book. I felt lucky and thankful that they would have it, as they had edited all of Heinrich Heine's books. Although I had been writing for Herder [another publisher] in Freiburg, and they would have published my book immediately, I wanted to be published by Hoffman and Campe. Before the book was published, in 1983, the publicist, Wolf Brümmel, wanted me to come to Hamburg to do a presentation and attend a large festival and prepublication party. There was unending press coverage. Shortly after my marriage in 1948, around 1951, I started to suffer from a phobia that kept me housebound for over thirty years. I couldn't travel more than thirty kilometers without having a panic attack. I didn't go far on the street. I didn't know at the time what caused the phobia. So I was actually unable to go to Hamburg. I told them I couldn't do a presentation. But a friend, Margot, a physical therapist, invited me to ride in her van, a VW bus furnished like a little apartment. She reassured me: "We'll cover the windows with curtains, and if there is a traffic jam, we can make tea." On February 14, 1984, I left my shelter after thirty-three years. My legs shook all the way to Hamburg. My grandchildren came from Berlin for the prepublication party. Before this, they had only known me as their grandmother enclosed in her apartment.

I wrote in the first chapter of my second book about how every night on the radio I listened to old seafarers' songs about homesickness, and I thought, "I *have* to go to Hamburg once again in my lifetime." So I went. I had seven weeks before this presentation when I said I'd do it. I'd had fears of going out for thirty years. In the first chapter of my second book I wrote how the psychiatrists later found out that the writing process of this first book resulted in my mental recovery. I was given a second life through writing the book. And the more I gave presentations, the stronger I became. From then on I have been able to go outside in the company of friends. Nowadays I am often invited to "psychiatry grand rounds" [*Visite*] to talk about my case. These are held in the medical community and at universities.

In the first year after publication, the first English translation was edited and my book received the go-ahead to be published in paperback. The second year after publication my work won the Anne-Frank Recognition Award Amsterdam.[25] To accept that award, many friends also accompanied me in order to deal with my former phobia. I traveled in the same bus, and Frau Hutton came from Hamburg.

$\backsim$ $\backsim$ $\backsim$

My feelings about being an outsider in the Third Reich are mixed. I didn't feel like an outsider because I had so many friends. The Nazis wanted to exclude Jewish people from society and wanted them to be minorities, outsiders. It was *their* language, not *ours*. But because I was accepted in my circle of friends, I didn't consider myself an outsider. My brother had substantially bigger problems. He was excluded from the Hamburg sports club, where he had played soccer. He was fourteen years old. This was extremely troublesome for him because he wanted to play soccer and to hang out with his sports friends. He had many friends in the Christian community. Also in school he had problems since only two "mixed" children attended his class. He was later forced to move to a Jewish school, which only increased his feelings as an outsider *as we weren't Jewish.* I was a member of the German-Jewish hiking group, and my brother was a member of the "non-Aryan" Christian Community.

An example of an outsider was if there were two Jewish students who have been isolated from the other students or excluded from activities, first they sat on different benches and then they were forced out of the school. The star characterized Jewish isolation, although I didn't wear a star *and wasn't called Cohn* [She says this with a slight lilt in voice]. I mention these cases of isolation in my second book. The Nazis made me an outsider but I wasn't with my friends. I didn't feel like an outsider. The Nazis tried to make me one.

You told me your father was beaten everyday by his Nazi teacher. I ask if he was hit because he was a Jew? Or just because his name was Cohn? I know a student could be beaten for a Jewish-sounding name especially if the teacher was a Nazi. That's also stated in *The Bertinis.* Have you read *The Bertinis?* Ralph Giordano was in *Johanneum*[26] [boys' school] and was handled badly but not hit. That didn't happen in a *Gymnasium* [college prep school]. I can't imagine where your father was in school. Do you know where? Was that a *Volksschule* [elementary school]? If so, at that time, they hit students anyway; it was common. But in a *Gymnasium* students were not hit. Ralph Giordano encountered similar debacles—but from words—when he attended *Johanneum.* The teacher stood over his shoulder. Ralph was so nervous he couldn't write essays or solve math problems. That didn't happen to

me. The torment was subtle. In my school, there were many Jewish
students.

I wrote about religion in my book. Now, I am not religious at all. In
1938 a Protestant pastor baptized me and Inge Hutton so that I did not
have to wear the Jewish star. For this reason, I thank the Protestant
church and would never leave the church. But I am not religious, neither
Christian nor Jewish. Since 1946, *Woche der Brüderlichkeit* [Brotherhood
Week] has been celebrated in Hamburg, and in March 1995 I was asked
to become an "honorary member" of the Christian-Jewish community
because I concern myself with the dialogue between Christians and Jews.
I am very happy about this honor. But I am not religious.

I have no trouble with the Jewish or Christian communities. My
relations are just human, not religious. I have written a requiem for three
voices to be performed for the annual meeting, the ninth of November,
in memory of a fire that burned Freiburg's synagogue. They read the
names of those who perished in the fire. The writer Lotte Paepcke, who
also lived in Freiburg but now resides in a retirement home in Karlsruhe,
is also involved. On March 6 she's invited to speak. Lotte Paepcke has
written a book about her Jewish father who owned a leather shop.[27] Lotte
and I have differing perceptions. Lotte Paepcke's opinion is: "Nothing
can become good again." I disagree. I can't be that sad all of the time,
and it's not good for the schoolchildren in particular. Of course these
times were horrible, but we can't alter it anymore. We have to talk about
it—that's important. As long as we witnesses of that time are alive, we
are happy to be invited to the schools.

When I visit schools, I give a kind of "cross-section" of my entire
life so that the students will know more about my life.[28] I cover from
1933 until the time it was clear my father wouldn't come back. I talk for
forty-five minutes. Afterward, I am very pleased to answer their questions. Furthermore, I tell the students this is not only *my* life but also the
life of many Jewish and "mixed" children during that time; many

children had similar experiences. Our children now have no clue about the time of the Third Reich. Americans also, but that's not so important. Even their [German] parents didn't have history lessons about the period 1933 to1945. The schools only taught up to Bismarck's empire. Sometimes the lessons dealt with the Weimar Republic, but usually the whole twentieth century was excluded, unless students were personally interested in this time. In the second book, I've included my talks to children.

It is very important for students today to get to know their history and to know arguments against the neofascism that is developing. It's not that they're guilty but they need to know what happened. I am a witness of this time and try to give perceptions and facts to the students. Many of them read my book and other literature. For inquiring students, the *Landeszentrale für politische Bildung* [main office for political education] provides all kinds of literature about concentration camps, *Mischlinge,* and immigration. This historical data has been published only for ten years. In 1979 many young people watched the documentary-type movie *Holocaust.*[29] This movie caused an "awakening" for young people; they wanted to know what was going on. They went home and asked, "What happened in the Third Reich?" This started a wave of curiosity. Often the grandparents had difficulties answering the questions, or they didn't want to discuss this topic at all. We mustn't hide our history; we have to talk about it. It is not necessary to bring up many statistics, *six million or so*; destinies of single individuals are crucial. That's why I have visited the same schools for many years, in order to tell class after class my history. Many of the school classes willingly travel to Auschwitz.

I have been invited to America, but my phobia doesn't cease for flying. I can go outside but can't walk long. I can go by car and train, but not by plane. In Freiburg I go alone by taxi everywhere in the town. I feel insecure because of my physical problems; before that it was just mental. I have many friends, who watch over me, although I have problems with my legs now as well. Soon I'll have to have a back operation.

≈   ≈   ≈

I didn't set out to be a writer. When I was a child I wanted to become a lawyer like my father. That's what all kids do, right? Later I chose the profession of a journalist, but the *Hamburger Fremdenblatt*, Hamburg's daily newspaper, couldn't hire me because of my "half-Jewish" origin. After 1945 I started to write. I haven't studied anything at all. I never had any higher education, did not go to college, and then I was sick. I have absolutely never been a student. All of my books are on one shelf. There are lots of histories of places, *Ortsgeschichte*. I never acquired a profession as I was not allowed to attend a college, and after the war I started suffering from this mental disease. Although I have been ill, I have written many books; for instance, stories of villages. Since 1965 the mayors of the villages have been visiting me in order to convince me to write chronicles.

The father of my daughter Barbara, Hans, and I did not get a license to get married because I had no *Ariernachweis,* proof of being "Aryan." My fiancé wanted to marry me but he was sent to the Russian front instead and had to suffer so much for my sake. Also, because of the way the war on that front was fought, he wrote to me that he would rather not come back from the war at all. He saw Barbara once on a visit to Hamburg. He died during battle at Lepel on the Russian front, June 29, 1944. To have an illegitimate child at that time was quite unthinkable in bourgeois circles. Because of my pregnancy I didn't go to China but stayed in Germany, and that was—for my mother's sake—still better than the shame to be an unwed mother. I got to know my husband, Hanns Studniczka, in 1947 and married in 1948. My husband had read Hitler's *Mein Kampf* before1933 and was able to speak many languages. He worked as a young diplomat at Amt für Auswärtige Angelegenheiten [Foreign Ministry].[30] The German government ordered him to go to Italy as an ambassador. He didn't want to work for the Nazis so he went to see a doctor and finagled his retirement "due to health reasons." He definitely was not a Nazi sympathizer. His role was a public prosecutor. My husband lived with me bravely for thirty years even though I was very ill and he had thought, because he was thirty years older, he would have married a young, healthy woman. He had to care for me, rather than vice versa. He wrote his book about Italy, and Herr Bahlsen immediately published it.

It's not possible to have favorite stories in my book. Everything is important from a to z. Especially the pictures of Barbara, my daughter, and my father. This picture shows Barbara and another shows my father shortly before he was deported. With the other publishing house we didn't have photographs. It is a specialty of *this* publishing house to include old family photos. What I've written about my father I didn't know in the past. My father was Jewish. I couldn't write about my father because he couldn't see my child; he wasn't allowed to see my mother either. Although they were divorced and did not remarry, it did happen that they remained close. The most important things I've written were about my father. Do you remember reading that? Because my father couldn't see my mother, he also couldn't see Barbara, who was living with my mother.

What the students ask me in the schools is interesting to me. Often they ask private things. For example, "What happened to Barbara?" Unfortunately, Barbara died in 1977 within forty-eight hours due to an aneurysm. This has been *das I-Tüpfelchen* [the one negative spot][31] of my destiny. They always ask about Barbara. Other questions refer to my relationship to Germans and Nazis, whereas I distinguish between Germans and Nazis. *The Germans and the Nazis were not synonyms for me.* You have to be predisposed to hate. Although I always keep in mind the murder of my father, I cannot hate people because I don't know who exactly did it. So, I will always be in despair and ask how this could have become possible. Among the people of my generation there will always exist a feeling of *lähmender Schrecken* [paralyzed terror]. Do I need to translate?

I know a woman who survived Auschwitz; her name is Esther Bejarano. It is obvious why she might hate! [Esther had mentioned she thinks that it wasn't as terrible for *Mischlinge* as for "full Jews."] The cruelty was "a German thing." Naturally, when one is in a camp as she was, I agree. She is Jewish, not a *Mischling*. That is something else. Understandably she must hate, but she can't hate the young Germans. The Nazis, naturally. She also speaks at schools. I got to know her personally three years ago when the Wannsee Museum was opened in Berlin. Esther is also a little on the left—more alternative in her politics. She was in a camp; she can't do anything else *but* hate. She saw such horrible things, no? She belonged to the girl's orchestra in Auschwitz. Crazy! I did not experience the camps. I cannot judge her right to hate. I never wore her shoes. I simply choose not to hate.

It was fortunate that I didn't have to go into a concentration camp. It was by chance that I wasn't in one. It's been fifty years ago, 1995, on February 8, that there was an air raid on my village, Staufen. At that time, I was staying in the hospital in order to undergo a serious operation. I came back to Staufen on the tenth. They had let me go earlier because of the air raid, and there wasn't enough room in the hospital because of so many sick and wounded. I couldn't walk. Two days after I was discharged from the hospital, we heard boots on the stairs. My mother was there with Barbara and leaned against the wall in fear, remembering her time in the prison. A man from the Lörrach's Gestapo came and wanted to take me to a poison gas factory in Kassel [for mandatory forced labor]. He saw my condition and said he would be back. I told him I was "half Aryan," from a privileged mixed marriage. He gave me an unforgettable look and said, "Half Jewish you mean, and that's as good as Jewish. Jews and Negroes, they're all the same to me."[32] Fortunately, the Gestapo offices had no desire to take anybody who couldn't stand upright. They were also probably busy destroying their files. Thank God! For this reason, I stayed at home and should have gone to the Gestapo three weeks later, as the Gestapo officer had ordered, but after three weeks the French army had already marched into this area. This was a big *Zufall*—how do you translate *Zufall?*— "coincidence"—and spectacular luck.

Cynthia. How are things between you and your father? Do you have a father? Do you like your father? Imagine then you find out your father has been killed by gas in Auschwitz. Can you imagine this always in your dreams? You can't formulate, let alone explain, the desperation, but it's always there. I have always had the vision of my father having to suffocate like a rat just because very primitive people ordered it. This horrible picture appears night and day. Because of the popularity of my book, editors asked me to review books of similar subject matter. Despite the psychological ramifications, I wanted to do this. Once an elderly lady handed me her memoir after one of my readings. It was about her survival in Auschwitz, and I had terrible nightmares. I began to hope that my father never actually had to see the extermination camp, that the SS physician Mengele[33] had not directed him to the gas chambers when he got off the train. Associations haunt me.

A weird thing happened this morning. I was watching an American movie from 1935 that showed a race between two ships on the Mississippi River. It was a bit funny. The film is called *Full Steam Ahead.* One ship had been loaded with items that were supposed to become part of a museum. After a while the people on this paddle steamer started to burn everything—these museum pieces like human-size dolls—in order to lighten the ship and to win. I immediately had this vision of the murders in the Second World War. I switched off the TV and thought, They wouldn't have produced a movie like that ten years later. These associations happen all the time, even if I see goods wagons. I remember these wagons when my father was deported to Theresienstadt. My brother, Wolfgang, had hoped that his father would get off the bus returning from Theresienstadt. He never did. No, we don't know for sure what happened to my father. My family doesn't know exactly. What's definite is that he never arrived in the camps because he was older. He was registered on a train from Theresienstadt to Auschwitz. In Jerusalem there is an institution where I was able to identify him. It was unbelievable—the Germans had written it all down from the moment the victims stood on the platforms.

Yesterday I got an invitation from a radio station in Stuttgart because they want to perform a radio play for the first time on which I had done some preliminary work. On Ash Wednesday they wanted to perform it. This radio play is called *Die Rampe* [the platform], and they want to perform it in a little theater, which is also called The Platform because it is an old train station. I called this group and said, "Is it necessary to give it this name?" The leader answered, "Well, the young generation

does not know how horrible the word *Rampe* is for the older generation."
It's a train station with an old platform [but signifies the ramps where
Jews stood to board the train for extermination].

We have these associations all the time. I criticize young people who
say without thinking. "*Ich habe heute gearbeitet bis zur Vergasung*" [today
I have worked to the point of exhaustion].[34] That's a figure of speech.
This saying is even used by amiable people. I did a radio show about this
saying called *Gedanken zur Gedankenlosigkeit* [thoughts about thought-
lessness]. This word *Vergasung* and its horrible meaning, referring to the
Jews who were gassed in the gas chambers, is not imprinted in the
consciousness of all generations. I said to them, Please don't say it ever
again in my presence, or better yet don't say it ever again—period.
Everyday these associations appear in very polite talk.

I realize some people think words such as *vergasen* and *Vergasung*
just haven't been used for so long that the words are now picked up again,
meaning something different. Words that Hitler created have never been
used after 1945. Sometimes I argue with my Jewish friends about
"Reichskristallnacht." Jewish people want to use "Pogromnacht." I use
"Kristallnacht" because it's a nightmare term for us. These words with
Reichs as a prefix were also made up by Nazi opponents in order to make
fun of the Nazis because they used *Reichs* in front of every word. For
example, Veit Harlan, film director, made horrible movies such as *Jud
Süß*, a terrible film with his super-super-super "Aryan" Swedish blond
wife, Kristina Söderbaum, and in every movie she had to go into the
water.[35] That's why Jewish people called her *Reichswasserleiche* [national
water corpse] in an ironic way, although some Jews think that it was
cynical. Hitler twisted the German language quite a bit. For example, a
term like *Vaterland* [fatherland] was a great word, but we can't say it
anymore because it's associated with Hitler and the visions he had for a
New World.

Not all of the Germans were Nazis but a lot of Germans were Nazi.
I am German, of course. The Nazis were cowards, but I have to confess
that I didn't do anything about it [take action]. Anxiety is legal but I
didn't participate in the *Weiße Rose* movement against the Nazis.[36] Many
Germans were easily deluded. They got confused by Hitler's ideas

because they hadn't had any political education, except a few, like Esther Bejarano, who I mentioned earlier. She lived in a Social Democratic family. The origins of anti-Semitism are older than 1933. I believe that at least lawyers and priests could have done something against Hitler's power in 1933. But they had a very high respect for authority; they thought that the people had elected Hitler so that's fine. Many Protestants or Catholic people supported Hitler, although some of them were killed as well. They followed "Gott, Kaiser und Vaterland" [God, emperor, and fatherland]. These priests were religious, but they thought they had to support whoever was the leader. Priests made pacts with Hitler without knowing what he would do later.

Ralph Giordano has previously published a book, *Wenn Hitler den Krieg gewonnen hätte* [if Hitler had won the war], with all the documents about Hitler's plans: He wanted to destroy religion, wanted to get rid of priests and any other people of high position other than the government, and wanted to expand German territory even more. All other nations in the East would become slaves of Germany. These documents exist that state Hitler will make Eastern Europeans the slaves of Germany.

Some say Hitler became like a god to the Germans. But the term "God" isn't appropriate in this sense. I am surprised how many people neglect or deny their past. If you were listening to Hitler's speeches or reading the newspapers, you must have realized what kind of jerk he was. Nowadays people say they didn't know anything about the politics and didn't read the newspapers for lack of time. Trying not to see, to repress, is terrible.

Hitler had charisma and the power of suggestion, but now our children are raised with political education, and although there are always some right-wing people who promise everything, there would be enough opponents today. For forty years now we've been living in a perfect democracy. In the time of Hitler, the system had been cruel and degrading. Then the left-wing approach didn't work with people, either.

The Communist system had ideals but they didn't work in many socialist countries, like the former DDR [German Democratic Republic] or East Germany. People like Esther want "the third way." I criticize comparisons with Hitler and Stalin because many people compare their cruelty. I say to those people that I am talking about Germany, about a country with history like Goethe, Schiller, and Beethoven, not about Stalin and Russia. I think people want to be relieved of their history this way. That is no exoneration.

I had no role as a woman years ago, only today. My social role started with the publication of my book. My role now is *fabelhaft,* fantastic, and I have been awarded the Verdienstmedaille des Landes Baden-Württemberg (a merit medal) from Minister President Teufel in Schloss Ludwigsburg because I support the dialogue between young and old people. I got letters from former president Richard v. Weizsäcker in response to my books, and I am very happy to visit schools and to write books.

I didn't have any problems as a young woman because I immediately got the custody of Barbara. Because Barbara's father died while fighting for Germany, I got financial support from the *Deutsche Wehrmacht* [the German army]. There are many examples of Jewish women who had children with "Aryan" fathers who were killed in the war. These Jewish women lost their children to the dead father's family. I had lots of luck. Women have been intellectually discriminated against because two-income families were not allowed. Men had to go to work and women had to stay home. But when the men had to fight, the women had to earn money. I worked in an office as secretary first and then I painted tiles. The topic of emancipation has never been interesting to me because even after 1945 I didn't have problems with my illegitimate daughter in the Catholic village Staufen.

I never did think about emigrating to the United States because I love my homeland and would have become homesick very fast. I have written about the problems of emigration. On one hand, people saved their lives; on the other hand, they had to leave friends and property. In Germany these people had been businessmen, and in America, they were nobodies. *Furchtbar!* [Dreadful!]

I am not an artist. I am a bit of a historian, but an amateur. I have a large library of historical books to look up important dates and events, but I never learned anything and don't have a high school degree. When I am writing books, I talk to historical experts. For example, in my chapter about Shanghai emigration, I discussed it with the former ambassador in Shanghai. I learned writing from my husband who was a truly humanistic, super writer. He taught me how to edit. It is especially important to describe a fact briefly without negatively influencing the contents. I don't feel like an artist because I cannot come up with new stories. I am able to describe stories I know very well. I can do documentation. I couldn't write a novel. I don't write with my eyes but my ears. I just describe things I know—from talks with people. I think that I am not capable enough to describe beautiful things like trees in an avenue. The literary critic's opinion about my work is: It is not literature. But Americans would think what I'm doing is literature. It is a very good documentation. For this reason, I have not been listed in the book *German Literature—History from Past to Present* because my work is not considered literature in Germany. [Poetry is considered literature in Germany.] I called and asked, Why am I not included? They said, If you realize other writers are missing as well, give us a call. They included a lot of political writers. Alfred Andersch's *Sansibar oder der letzte Grund*,[37] a novel that I saw as a play and an opera is literature. I couldn't write like that.

I have described my parents' divorce in my book. Their divorce didn't result from political concerns. They separated as friends because they realized that they didn't get along with each other as a married couple. My mother protected him in our apartment because she found out that the Nazis wanted him in the concentration camp. Later they moved into a smaller flat and got separated. Even when my parents were divorced they kept in touch. When my father lost his practice, they tried everything to get enough money to live. My mother cared not only for us children but also for my friends, like Inge Hutton, because she was able to listen to anybody's problems. On the other hand, she was a horrible housewife. Later she became mentally ill due to three weeks' imprisonment, but she relaxed and recovered while working as a doctor's aide in Badenweiler. All the old people remember her as a very trustful and trustworthy person.

It is very painful for me to talk about my father because I think that I am guilty in a way because we didn't help him enough or didn't do enough to protect him or to save his life. I don't like to talk a lot about this.

CHAPTER TWO

INGRID WECKER

*"I was a wanderer between the waves,
belonging to no one"*

~

On my birthday, June 2, 1995, K. Ernst Dohnke, writer
and friend, drove me in an old muffler-dragging Opel to
Marne, a provincial town comparable to such "close your
eyes and you'll miss it" towns in the Midwest, an hour away
from Hamburg. The streets and buildings were somewhat
run down. It was the type of place I pictured most often —
probably enhanced by descriptions of German hinterland in
Anna Segher's novel, *The Seventh Cross* — when thinking
about pernicious Nazis and where they dwelled. I doubted
anyone of Jewish descent could have survived in a town this
size during the Third Reich. Indeed, many Jews fled the
village for the city, where they believed anonymity was

possible, a notion quickly dispelled by the Gestapo's seemingly omniscient thoroughness. In fact, the Gestapo was not
thorough at all. They had very few people actually working
for them. Denunciations by neighbors and work
colleagues—in other words, the collaboration of ordinary
Germans—was what made the Gestapo's work easier and
made them appear more organized.

We had trouble locating Ingrid's apartment, counting off
nonsequential numbers among a maze of buildings within this
adult-living complex. Finally, Ingrid Wecker, in baggy, mucky
gray shirt and gray pants, greeted us heartily. She was not
interested in the pretense of "making herself up." She wore
silver glasses that blended with her white, baby-fine, blunt-cut
hair. Her only extravagances were small silver earrings, an
antique silver necklace, and three plain circle rings. Her
simplicity contrasted to her bold artistic endeavors.

Her living area was cramped—a tight living room and
kitchen—where we spent our time together. She had a small
backyard with a distinguished bird feeder. A handmade oak
letter opener with "Shalom" and a bird etched at the top lay
on the table next to me. Her Hamburg friend, Ursula
Behrens-Gottbrath, who had sent me Ingrid's address with
permission to contact her, had given this delicate gift to
Ingrid. Ingrid often disappeared behind a curtain into her
bedroom from which she brought out an assemblage of her
pen-and-ink sketches that depicted mainly deportations but
also ghettos, concentration camps, victims, survivors, the SS,
and the Gestapo. One was a sketch of Jews in the Lodz
ghetto. The Nazis have black faces, colored-in features like
those in Ernst Ludwig Kirchner's painting "Street, Dresden"
(1907)—their mouths are open like the figure in Edvard
Munch's painting "The Scream" (1893). Ingrid, whose father
was "euthanized" by the Nazis, found solace for her father's
murder through her art. From an early age, her father had
encouraged her artistic zeal. Since our initial meeting, her

artwork has continued to frame our dialogue. In 1995 she had copies made for me of her sketches, and at Christmas 1996 I received one of her original handcrafted and painted Christmas cards, her signature freshly inked in the corner. Many of the women I interviewed connected their lives to me through some symbolic or real cultural dissemination. All had books that pertained directly to their Third Reich experiences; a few books overlapped in their respective collections. They referred, pointed to, or read from these books as "proof" of what they had undergone. They held the words of these scholars, novelists, and poets in high regard, as if their own stories could not be believed without the anterior accounts of "authorities"—if these writers had not spoken and been published, where would the women have gained the courage to speak? Some of the women stressed the illustriousness of German culture pre-Hitler, when such icons as Goethe, Schiller, and Rilke made the Germans proud. By reconnecting to this preeminent artistic past, these women found a way to talk about Germany that helped to assuage their mixed feelings toward their country. As psychologist Louise Kaplan has stated, "Our cultural attainments, the sentences we utter or sign, our poems, dances, monuments, paintings, symphonies, songs, are all a way of refinding and restoring lost dialogues."[1]

Ingrid read a great deal from a large scrap book she had on her lap that contained files of family history and also general facts about the Third Reich. As she talked, Ingrid read through specific laws that had been pertinent to her life. I was familiar with the over 400 pieces of anti-Jewish legislation (beginning in 1933), which included particular injunctions for "half Jews." Ingrid adamantly continued to read and refer back to them. Because of their importance to her (and, by extension, to all the interviewees), I have listed some of them here. We can see more clearly, through this selection, how noxious and, at the same time, how absurd these laws were. Ingrid

explained, "Here are some selective historical dates of importance *to me* that I have researched in the archives:"

MAY 9, 1933:   All civil servants of Hamburg are ordered not to
                         buy in Jewish shops and to cancel present accounts
                         in these shops.

MAY 17, 1933:   Drugs that are products from Jewish brands are not
                         permitted to be prescribed except if there are no
                         other drugs from "Aryan" brands available.

JUNE 30, 1933:   Nazis are not allowed to go to restaurants or cafés
                         in which Jews appear, the exception being hotels.

AUGUST 17, 1934:   Jewish hiking groups are allowed, but they are not
                         permitted to participate in cross-country sport.

APRIL 4, 1934:   Jews are not allowed admission to universities or
                         higher educational schools. If schools admit non-
                         Aryan people, then they have to prefer students
                         who have some "Aryan" blood and can bring the
                         evidence for that. Children of "Aryan" origin
                         must not have any disadvantage; they have to be
                         preferred.

MARCH 13, 1935:   Children of "non-Aryan" origin have to be sepa-
                         rated from other students in the *Volksschule* [ele-
                         mentary school]. Jewish schools have to be built.
                         The directors of the schools have to get statistics in
                         place about the racial origins of their students in
                         order to separate the races.

JUNE 11, 1935:   Signs that read "Jews not allowed" are to be put
                         away, made inconspicuous on the main streets
                         because of the Olympic Games 1936. [People from
                         all over the world visited Germany and the Nazis
                         wanted to hide their anti-Semitism. Ironically,
                         there were Jewish members of the German Olym-
                         pic team.]

AUGUST 31, 1935:   Jewish students are not allowed to receive any
                         awards.

Ingrid commented, "I was also concerned because I got many semester awards but my teacher said, 'Ms. Riemann, I'm sorry, but you know why you don't get any.' One award was DM 200-300, and I needed this money badly."

SEPTEMBER 15, 1935:	Law for the protection of German blood and German honor.
I.	Marriages between "Aryan" and Jewish people are not permitted and present marriages are no longer valid.
II.	Extramarital intercourse between Jews and nationals of German stock is prohibited.
III.	Jews are not allowed to give jobs in their households to women under the age of forty-five. Old maid servants could remain.
JULY 13, 1936:	Non-Aryan people are not allowed to get any discount for calls. [Actual law: Concessionary telephone calls for war-blinded veterans will not be granted to non-Aryans.]
MARCH 24, 1938:	Jews are not allowed to go into archives, except if they want to know something about their family or to explore Jewish folklore. Within these exceptions, the archive workers have to pay attention that the Jews use only those books that are indispensable to these purposes.

Ingrid said, "This seemed harmless. Then the Jewish lawyers were not permitted to work anymore."

AUGUST 17, 1938:	Jews who do not have appropriate Jewish first names listed in the circular dated August 18, 1938, must secure additional names: "Israel" for all males, and "Sara" for all females.
NOVEMBER 10, 1938:	The concentration camps Dachau, Buchenwald, and Oranienburg admit 10,000 new prisoners in

each case. Jews who own guns have to be taken into protective custody for twenty years.

Ingrid said, "My mother had some honor swords from my father, but she gave them away because of her fear."

NOVEMBER 12, 1938:   Jews are not allowed to go to the theaters, movies, or exhibitions, or to use public transportation.

Ingrid said, "As I mentioned, my mother was not allowed to go to the movies."

Furthermore, the Jews have to pay the money for restoration of their institutions themselves [after Reichskristallnacht, the "night of broken glass"].

DECEMBER 12, 1938.   All safeguarded prisoners over the age of fifty have to be released.

Ingrid said, "Some of my relatives like my uncle came back from Dachau but with shaven heads. This was horrible for me to see."

FEBRUARY 24, 1939:   Jews are bound by law to give away their jewels, and people who get these jewels made of precious metal or pearls are not allowed to deny taking them.[2]

SEPTEMBER 1, 1939:   [The war had just begun.] Jews are not allowed to leave their homes after 8:00 P.M., and in summer after 9:00 P.M.

SEPTEMBER 20, 1939:   Jews are not allowed to own radios. This prohibition is also valid for "Aryan" people who live in Jewish houses and half-caste people.

Ingrid said, "One of my friends threw his new radio out of the window although his friends said, 'Moritz, don't do it.' Later on he was picked up and taken to a concentration camp."

OCTOBER 17, 1939:	If Jews and "Aryan" people live together in one apartment complex, Jews are not allowed to take part in *Luftschutzübungen* (air raid drills). Reason: They would take spaces in the air raid shelter and probably not all "Aryan" people would have the chance to get in. [Her interpretation of this law may not be entirely accurate.]
SEPTEMBER 1, 1941:	From September 15, 1941, it is prohibited for Jews over the age of six to go out without *Judenstern* [the yellow star of David affixed to their clothing]. They are not allowed to leave their living community without police permission or to wear medals or any other decoration. This is not valid for "privileged mixed marriages."

Ingrid noted, "If the Aryan part of these 'mixed marriages' died, the Jewish part could be deported. My mother was afraid of this fact because her husband was already dead. My mother didn't wear the *Judenstern* but my grandmother did. They had stars for everybody and I had to sew press-studs on the jackets so that they could clip these stars on their coats. These stars were crudely made."

After going through the laws, Ingrid told me, "I realized everything. We no longer had a radio. All big factories had been taken away from Jews, part of *Zwangsarisierung,* forced Aryanization [stepped-up after Kristallnacht]." Ingrid explained, "Many Jewish families didn't know anything about these laws. Newspapers published only a few of them. We had almost no contact with 'Aryan' people after we knew of these laws, since we didn't know with what kinds of people we had to deal, just like having the wrong friends."

Ingrid was interested in facts,[3] but also was a proficient storyteller, emotionally involved in her past, whose delicate, almost imperceptible voice nearly lulled me to sleep. She tapered off when we started to eat and shifted her efforts to being a gracious hostess. She laid out a spread of food—a variety of fish, breads, cheeses, salad, and coffee. As it neared the time we had to leave, about 2:00 P.M., Ingrid geared up and began talking about her mother's "deathbed scene." Her mother started to hallucinate and had delusions that apparently came from her Third Reich experiences. She relived specific events as she neared her death. I had to turn the tape recorder back on. Ingrid then started to talk about her two husbands. The first one, with whom she had children, died. Her first son was born in 1947. She divorced the second husband, an alcoholic. Finally, she lived with a third man. They had a house together, but after he died it was too much upkeep. She spoke briefly about her wealthy great-grandparents. They had lived in the United States, made money in drugstores, and then returned to Germany to invest in real estate. She described all of their finery. She still possessed the yellow star worn by her grandmother and a menorah.

Ingrid was classified as Jewish because of her Jewish mother, who, through legal routes, managed to shroud her Jewish identity. But Ingrid talked primarily about her "Aryan" father and his supposed "craziness." As she spoke of her father she looked at a vacant space as if he were standing right there. A sense of admiration and love filled her face, but it lasted only a brief moment. Then she looked away from the ghost that occupied the space in the middle of the room. The center of her story is her father's demise, and she recognized the importance of passing on this history. Much of our conversation continued off tape. Ingrid mentioned her brother as one who "gets by" or is "less affected" by disturbing events. When she asked him his recollections of their shared past, he said cynically, "*Warum? Schreibst du ein Buch?*" (Why? Are you writing a book?).

On her seventieth birthday she went to Friedrickskoog, a summer resort on the coast of the North Sea, alone. She said to herself, *"Du bist siebzig"* (you are seventy). She was surprised by suddenly being this age because her mother had believed that all the women in her family died at seventy. Because she lost so much, especially after the war when jobs were scarce, Ingrid said she "wishes for beauty."

~ ~ ~

I was born on August 2, 1924. My father was a lieutenant for the security police in Hamburg. My mother was seventeen years old when they married in 1923, the twenty-second of May, when there was high inflation. When my mother was almost nineteen, I was born. Life in Hamburg was not without troubles, yet it was very nice. We lived in a grand six-and-one-half-room flat that belonged to my grandmother in the Grindelallee, which was the border for the Jewish part called Klein Jerusalem. I had an "Aryan" father, to repeat this horrible word, but surprisingly was raised in this big Jewish family.

On my mother's side, my great-grandfather was German American and my great-grandmother, British. They immigrated to America and bought a number of drugstores, which had not developed into very good businesses, in New York, and they worked in these drugstores. Two of their children have the nationality of the ship on which they were born. They improved the business of these drugstores and sold them for a profit. Afterward they went back to Germany and bought large apartment complexes on Schmuckstraße. Chinese people with laundromats often lived in the basements of these houses. At that time, it was a very good area where salespeople and doctors lived.

Before the First World War, my great-grandparents were very rich, and every son got $1,000 for a trousseau. Most of them went back to America. The daughters got a huge red salon, a red dining room with a table for twenty-four persons, specially handmade by a joiner. The daughters had to attend a private school at Paulinenplatz and learned French. They obviously didn't take English because they spoke it at home in a horrible way. They learned how to play the piano and how to embroider. After this private school, they went to a marriage bureau in order to get a husband. The family owned lots of silver from England and valuable pianos. Everyone had the same silver and piano. Unfortunately, they lost all the houses in Germany's inflation and a tinsmith bought all six "Hirsch houses" *für einen Apfel und ein Ei* [for an apple and an egg]. Incredibly cheap. Hirsch was my great-grandparents' name, my grandmother's parents. My great-grandfather was a bit stingy, but not my great-grandmother. He didn't want to spend a lot of money for jewels for his daughters. My great-grandmother was tricky. Every time her husband counted gold coins on the table, the money for rent at the first of the month, she came in with her funny English accent and said, "Oh, Father, please. We must take away the tablecloth—such a good tablecloth and such dirty money." Of course, a few pieces of gold always got stuck on it, but he didn't notice it. With this money, she bought her daughters a shawl made of ostrich feathers for going to a ball or dance. My great-grandmother wanted to support street vendors; she bought their old and dirty stuff and put it under her bed so that the smell below her bed was really strange, like rotten apples. She wore a lace hat and black clothes (over the age of thirty you were considered old and had to wear black), and she looked outside of the entrance door to see who rang the doorbell with the help of a window-mirror in the shape of a butterfly. They were a really funny family.

We, however, didn't have much money. When my father got his police income he ran to the office to check the current value of his salary. My parents wanted to buy a bedroom suite at an auction, but instead got a pair of crystal vases and some tins of green peas and beans, and lentils, and bags. That's all they got for their money. Many women had to work in this time, too. My great-uncle from New York came to Hamburg before my mother's wedding and gave her ten dollars as a gift. With this money she could buy her bridal dress, shoes, and the meal for all the wedding guests. This Uncle Adolf—he was the oldest—came again when I was three years old. He wore a vest and pocket watch. I remember the smell of a cigar, which he used to smoke all the time, and one day, when he took me on his lap in order to give me a child's ring

Don't lie. Although sometimes we had to lie in order to survive with the Nazis. *Don't lose your honor.* A typical officer saying. *Be helpful to people in danger.* Always be prepared to speak for those in danger. These three things I received from my father, and I try to live them. These characteristics are still a part of me. I could never hate people. I try to teach this to my sons and grandchildren. I have an open ear for everyone in the same way I learned it in my parent's house. People may drop in without calling first, as is sometimes the case here. My children, my two sons, and grandchildren call me from Meldorf, and then they are here.

From talks with my father I realized very early that something happened to frighten the family. My father was a member of an officer corps and told the family stories and made comments a child shouldn't hear. I eavesdropped. Some days he said, "If Hitler comes to power we hope that God would have mercy on us" *(Gnade uns Gott!).* This stuck in my ears. "If he comes to power there's really nothing we can do about it, except pray." He said this again when Hitler was elected chancellor of the Third Empire. When Hindenburg said, "Adolf Hitler is our new president" my father talked again about God supporting us. This time the men in the officer corps shut out my father. He was *drangsaliert* [horribly tormented], because in this corps there were many anti-Semitic National Socialists. He was really pushed out of this corps, but he had to state that he would voluntarily leave. I knew my father as a vitally healthy sportsman, an athletic man, and a tall man. The official reason for his leaving was illness. We would say today what they did to him was a kind of "mobbing;" everyone improved his position except for my father, after which he lost his self-confidence. Everybody else was getting into higher positions, but nothing happened with my father. He could stay in the police corps if he divorced his Jewish wife, and this was before 1933. He said, "I haven't thought about that. I would never leave my wife and two children." At this time, 1928, my brother was born, four years younger than I. In 1930 my father left the police. Other men followed his example—not because of any racial persecution they endured but because they were politically discontent. My family ran into them later; they had become businessmen, such as insurance agents or customer service reps, who carried funny briefcases through the streets.

[She laughs.] Nevertheless, they were good fellows, good to talk to. They left the police after 1933 because they were Social Democrats. My family's political direction was also left—SPD—Social Democratic Party of Germany. A historical book for Hamburg's civil servants was published that reflects exactly my father's experiences with the National Socialists.[4]

My father had a very small pension. He was actually a forester by profession and was born in Bielefeld. We bought a house in the Lüneburger Heide, which was isolated. My father found a job—one can't call it a position—through friends as a private forester for a large hunting area. This land belonged to the family Luehmann from Harburg. This family was known for publishing *Der Harburger Anzeiger,* which is comparable to the current Axel Springer family's right-wing publishing company. My father got a job in a hunting area and whenever people wanted to go hunting, my mother invited them for dinner or to stay overnight—our house was a kind of restaurant/hotel. This was the source of the family's survival. We started to cultivate plants and vegetables in a garden and preserve game, wild meat, in order to sell it to get some money. I now hate the sight of wild animal meat.

After 1933 life changed. For example, when I walked the one and a half hours to school, I noticed that people in our village cultivated *Hitlereichen* ["Hitler oaks"], and at the village square they built a flagpole with a golden *Hakenkreuz* [swastika], the sign of National Socialism. My father was bothered by this display and couldn't avoid critical words. He was not loved in the village, especially among the farmers, because he was fighting against poaching in the forest. One day my father asked the farmers: "Why do you have a swastika on your flagpole in addition to that on the flag?" They said, "If there is no wind, nobody could see the swastika on the flag, so people may believe we are Communists." [Because it would have been just a red flag, politically opposed to the swastika flag.] My father had a flagpole on his property as well, so he mocked the village people and every Sunday hoisted his black-white-red flag, a conservative, German national flag.[5] Because our family's house was located on a little hill, people could see this flag very clearly. My father did this even after 1933, and the village people were angry about it.

A "false friend" tried to meddle in the relationship between my mother and father with the help of the "friend's" wife. My father's name was Karl Riemann, but the "friend" called him Karlos, and said, "Karlos, you don't deserve this. Get divorced from your wife. *Schick Sie in den Wind* [Kick her out] and you can work as a policeman again. You are a faultless civil servant." In this way my father got into conflicts; he started arguing with his wife because he was mentally tormented or influenced by these people. My father had a vast array of weapons and guns. I think that my father wanted to kill his own family. He said, "There is no way out." Finally my mother decided to return to Hamburg to my grand-mother's big apartment, and she took us with her. My father stayed alone in this huge house in the Lüneburger Heide.

His "false friend" had no real profession, just a big property, and his wife sublet rooms to summer guests. Suddenly this man got the idea to leave the village because he wanted to become a nonmedical practitioner in Hamburg; apparently he had problems with his wife. And, indeed, he opened his practice. So this "friend" was begging and imploring my father to move into his house, which my father finally did. My father stayed alone in this friend's house and neglected himself more and more until he wanted to commit suicide. The mailman realized one day that my father's bicycle was missing. He had told the mailman previously, "I can't live without my family. I want to commit suicide." So the mailman ran into the village and asked the farmers to look for my father. For this reason, many members of the SA [party security force] started searching the forest, but they couldn't find my father. So, the village sheriff, a big Nazi, gave information to Hamburg's police, and the following message: "There is a man, a former police officer, who is armed with various weapons and wants to go to Hamburg to kill his wife and his children!" My mother got this information from the Hamburg police, and police-men picked us children up from the school. That happened in 1935. My mother wanted the police to leave. She said, "I know my husband very well. I can deal with him." My father had suffered from malaria since World War I and got "malaria seizures" all the time.

The police left my mother's house and eventually my father did arrive. He was exhausted. My mother made him dinner and suggested he go into a hospital for a physical exam because he didn't feel well. He agreed, but suddenly the doorbell was ringing. Police! They said, "Mr. Riemann, we have to take you into protective custody." But my mother made a fuss, complained about it, so that the police decided to take my father into a hospital for mental illness, to the "famous" psychiatrist Bürger-Prinz in the Hamburg-Eppendorf Hospital.[6] From then on he was "officially" mentally ill. He was incarcerated between 1935 and March 1941 in mental homes like Friedrichsberg, Ochsenzoll, and, afterward, he was moved to Lüneburg without any information given to the family.

Because we had to pay for my father's treatment, the family's financial situation was wretched. My mother got only RM 35 per month and an additional support of 1.75 Mark per child per month. My mother was not allowed to work. My grandmother could rent the rooms of the apartment only to Jewish people. It was obvious that we were impoverished, to the point that my teacher said, "Ingrid needs a new winter coat." It is absolutely absurd, but I got a new winter coat from the Winterhilfe, a group consisting of National Socialists who supported only "Nazi kids."

My mother and I visited my father every weekend in the hospital. Of course, he wanted to escape. Each time he tried to flee, or when he became loud—he had an officer's voice, which is very loud—they moved him to a new building with more observation. Finally they brought him into a house which had only one pathway in the shape of a snail shell. It was like a prison with just one little spot to look out. My father became afraid of "white coats," and he said to his wife: "Wilma, please go into the administration building and say to the people there: I want to take my husband with me. He is not crazy. I will take care of him." I was ten to twelve years old and it broke my heart to see my father "losing his mind," because he was really tormented. My mother still believed that my father was not ill, and I will never forget one day when a heavy doctor—he needed a special chair because he was so overweight—said to my mother: "Get divorced from this sick guy. You deserve a better life." Even later, members of the Gestapo tried to convince my mother to do the same. [It was not certain if this was just a ruse.]

My father was moved to Lüneburg. From this time on, I couldn't see him very often. He began to speak in a strange manner, but he still wrote letters to his family. These letters were censored; some parts were marked out. I remember one letter in which he swears about Hitler: *"Wenn ich den Kerl zu fassen kriege, ich drehe ihn das Genick um"* [If I can catch this guy Hitler, I will wring his neck]. It was horrible inside this hospital. When my mother and I visited, the guests had to be in a big hall, and this was a *Schlammgrube,* muddy patch, because only severely mentally handicapped persons were running around and bothering the guests. One day my father had red boils above his ears. He said, "I have to cover my ears because they are always talking insistently to me!" He had white hair at this time and was only forty-five years old. Furthermore, he said to me, "Ingrid, promise, you will never tell anybody about the following." "Yes, Papa, I promise." "I want to set up a new state. In this state only people with white eyes are allowed to live there, and you, Ingrid, you have white eyes, you are permitted to live in my state." I will never forget this last talk with my father. He always covered his ears and said something about *Todesstrahlen* [death rays]. My mother gave him a sweater with a zipper but he completely damaged this zipper and said: "Don't give this to me anymore. This zipper attracts death rays." By this time, he was "out of this world."

The next time my mother and I wanted to visit him, he had disappeared. So my mother talked to the director. She only talked to directors, never to persons below this position, and I too have done this my whole life. She asked him about my father: "Has he died? Where is he?" The director answered: "He has been moved out with two other people to an unknown destination." A fortnight later my mother got a letter from Burg Sonnenstein[7] in Pirna near Dresden stating that my father had suddenly died from a brain swelling, which was infectious. For this reason [the infection], they had to do the cremation immediately; the family could have the urn if they wanted it. But the urn was never sent to my mother and me. I called this "sanitarium" in Burg Sonnenstein. I did almost everything for my mother because her name was Jewish: Wilma "Sara"; the Sara added to identify her as Jewish. A woman on the phone was upset about my calling. Some days later we got a parcel with the urn and a 0.42 Mark fee. My father is buried at the

Ohlsdorf Cemetery in Hamburg. None of our relations appeared and only one aunt wrote a letter of condolence.

A police officer from the place where my father used to work visited us. I asked him if my father should get special "honor words" on his gravestone because of good work for the police. The officer answered: "No way, Miss Riemann, because of your Jewish mother." I said [laughing], "Oh, I'm sorry. I almost forgot!" At the funeral which my mother, my brother, a Jewish couple who were friends, and I attended, a cemetery worker came with the urn and said, "Mrs. Riemann, would you please confirm that it must be your husband in the urn." It was so ridiculous! My mother had a laughing fit until she started crying. Basically, my father died because of this "Euthanasia Program," which killed many Jewish and non-Jewish people in March 1941. [8]

One of my uncles, Leonhard Blumenthal, my mother's brother, was invited on a world trip. A friend from high school days, now a lawyer in Hamburg, pushed him to go on the luxury liner *Lloyd Triestino,* to travel from Geneva Italy to Shanghai in 1939. [Shanghai was a German settlement for political persecutees.] When another cousin of his wanted to go on board this ship in Geneva, World War II began. My aunt, Herta Rodemund, living in a "mixed marriage" with her "Aryan" husband, Felix Rodemund, was a leader of a ballet group, first in Königsberg, then for a short period in the Hamburg state opera house, and then back to Königsberg. Later her husband was pushed out of the Reichskulturkammer [Reichs Cultural Chamber].[9] I have a letter of my aunt's and the paper stating this. He decided to set up his own young girls' ballet group and his wife took care of the girls. At one performance each girl said "Heil Hitler!" as they left the stage. My aunt told the girls later: "It is enough if one of you says 'Heil Hitler.'" One girl finally ran to the Gestapo and betrayed my aunt. That morning my aunt was picked up by the Gestapo and the same day she was punished by a Sondergericht [special court] to eight months' imprisonment in Hamburg Fuhlsbüttel prison. My uncle had to finish the ballet group work and from then on was a coffee seller for Café Specht in Hamburg. Later he had a bad accident; he rode his bicycle into a streetcar and had to stay in the hospital. My mother had to visit her aunt in the prison. This happened in 1938, a brief time before Reichskristallnacht.

In these days the government decided on a political amnesty for people who were imprisoned up to one year for political reasons. In this decision my aunt was also involved, but she had to sign a paper that she'd make every effort to emigrate. Both my aunt and uncle had good luck. They knew a family from Uruguay whose two daughters were educated as dancers in Hamburg. This family wanted to have their daughters back in Uruguay, so they paid, in addition to their daughter's, for my aunt's and uncle's passage as coaches to Uruguay. This is how my uncle and aunt immigrated to Montevideo with ten Marks in their pocket, and no Spanish, and they had to work on a farm collecting eggs. I can understand how my uncle, a fantastic dancer, went crazy after two or three years and later died in a mental hospital. My aunt came back to Germany in 1953, when she had collected enough money for the flight. Even the Jewish community didn't support her immigration back to Germany. It was easier to get my uncle Leonhard back from Shanghai in the year 1948, although my mother had to argue with Hamburg's mayor in order to get the immigration permission for him. As I mentioned earlier, my mother only talked to high-positioned people.

In 1942 my mother won a *wahnwitziger Prozess* [a crazy court case]—a lawsuit that was simply crazy—with the result that my mother was considered "half Jewish." My grandma died in November 1940. She was buried in the Israelische Friedhof, the Jewish cemetery in Hamburg. After my grandmother died, my mother was rather unprotected because when a *Mischling* lost the "Aryan" parent, he was considered Jewish and could be deported. In her last days, my grandma had the idea that my mother should claim she was the illegitimate child of an "Aryan," Christian father. In reality, her father was Jewish. After my grandpa died early, my grandmother had to rent rooms. One of the renters was a sailor, Captain Fuchs, who became friends with the family. With the help of "witnesses" such as neighbors and friends who gave false oaths, my mother could convince the judge that she was the daughter of Captain Fuchs, although in reality she was about seven years old when Fuchs first rented a room. My mother and I then had to go to Kiel, where our bodies and skulls were examined for "Aryan" features, and because we looked "Aryan," the judge decided that we were half and quarter *Mischlinge* respectively. A remark he made during the process revealed that he did this knowing we were not. My brother and I were "quarter Jewish" because of our "Aryan" father. That's why the family was not transported to the concentration camp, Theresienstadt, where many Jewish people died. In March 1945 a superior judge from Leipzig questioned this decision. To win time, my mother's lawyer, a "half Jew" himself, said that all paperwork was destroyed during the Hamburg bombing raids and it would take time to get new papers. Two months later everything [the Third Reich] was over.

≈ ≈ ≈

Many of my family's friends emigrated from Germany before 1933, and I couldn't understand that because they lost all their property. Later I understood why. These Jewish people were anticipating the danger and left. Furthermore, after 1933, it was much more expensive to emigrate because of the high taxes. Before the outbreak of the war, my family wanted to emigrate, but at the office we got only a waiting number. My mother wanted to go to England to work as a helper-nurse since English people only gave permission if you had a profession. For her children, she applied to go to Sweden, but it was a mass of papers that they had to fill out. Besides this, you had to pay a tax *[Reichsfluchtsteuer]* if you wanted to emigrate. In case you wanted to take something with you, then you had to pay at least the new price of the item as tax. Vice versa when the Nazis took away Jewish property; the Jews got only a small amount of money or nothing. My mother sold all our furniture in order to survive. She had to bring evidence [photos] that this furniture belonged to their apartment. Finally, she got RM 200, almost nothing, for everything. She sold the golden rings to a jeweler. The rings also contained diamonds, but the jeweler destroyed the rings and said, "We'll only pay you for the gold!" Many fathers went ahead with emigration to set up an existence for the family. In many cases, I know of three, the fathers already lived in the foreign country, and their families stayed in Germany and were transported to concentration camps.

During the last days of World War II my mother protected refugees, AWOL, fleeing soldiers, French and American, in our house and considered these soldiers her sons. She said, "These are my sons!" Anything could have happened to her. The English came to us and asked, "Please." They were all in civil camps, deathly ill in beds, and needed help. My mother had her yellow star and said, "I'm Jewish. I'm Jewish." My brother committed himself to working for prisoners of war and foreign workers. He always stole and smuggled bread to them. In our apartment in Hamburg we were hiding many factory workers from foreign countries, for example, Polish Jews. They had come in the fall of 1938. The Gestapo continually searched our apartment; they were almost "at home" there. We had Polish people renting below us. The Gestapo took them away at 4:00 A.M. in a so-called *Blitzaktion* [round up]. Many other Poles were caught as well. Even today I am more than happy to help somebody in misery, although I close my entrance door tightly because I don't trust the people in my neighborhood. I am not confident of them. Only women of my age live here, and I am uncertain about what they did during the Nazi years. I know now quite a bit about some present neighbors and their Nazi activities. However, if someone here is sick or in need, I am there immediately.

I loved my father a lot. Even after the war I had to defend him because everybody, even my own cousin, was saying: "Your father was *meschugge* [Yiddish term for crazy]." The Nazis stamped him with "schizophrenia," which was considered an inheritable disease, and my mother was always anticipating the day when my brother and I would be sterilized for this reason. Fortunately, it didn't happen. My father had enormous authority during his police days, which makes it even more tragic. Almost all the Hamburg Gestapo members had been taught and trained by my father. I was a volunteer helper in the Jewish community for the entire deportation in Hamburg. I did not wear a star, but I could help in ways a full-Jewish person could not. Sometimes I made remarks to the Gestapo, not very harsh, but pointed. If they grumbled at me and said, "What are you doing here? What's your name?" I answered, "Ingrid Riemann." And they said, "Riemann? Riemann?" "Yes," I said, "My father was with the police and trained you." They responded, "Oh. Never mind. Continue on." Then I could continue with my sad job. One day I complained about the fact that a young SS man was beating old Jewish women. Their bodies were shaking with fear all the time. First I spoke to the women and said, "Please don't shake, don't cry, try." Fear, this horrible fear that did not come quickly or leave quickly. Instead for years people, as Jews, sunk deeper and deeper until they reached the level of an animal. This fear was caused by harassment, which had been going on for years. Jews were not allowed to buy anything in the shops, so the men couldn't get shaving soap. People developed prejudices and stereotypes, such as Jews are dirty, don't shave, or don't clean their bodies.

$$\approx \quad \approx \quad \approx$$

I couldn't risk writing a diary before 1945 because the Gestapo, who were often in our house, could have found it. After the war, I wrote everything down but not with dates because I'm not sure of them. I'm very particular about that. I remembered in the form of stories. I'd rather say I don't remember any more. Then I can say I'm sorry, I made a mistake. Some years ago, my partner in life and some journalists were shooting a film about the time before 1945. This was a good opportunity to speak the truth about my father. "He was not insane. The Nazis drove him crazy. It was *ein Teufelskreis* [a vicious circle]." In addition, I mentioned you could never get out of a mental hospital then and also that the Russians used this method of "silent/cruel mental murder" in order to kill political persecutees.

My mother loved my father very much and knew that he was not crazy. After the war she sank into bitterness and was angry with people.

When she applied for the political rehabilitation of her husband, these responsible, competent people said: "First you have to bring in the evidence that it was not *you* who made your husband crazy." Isn't that cruel? This was the most horrible experience for my mother after 1945. For this reason, my mother became more shy and unsociable. She died in 1982. When she died she was the oldest of her siblings—her sister died at seventy; my uncle died at fifty. He suffered from a tropical disease caused by his work as a medical assistant in a hospital for immigrants in Shanghai. Later he had to stay several months in special hospitals for tropical diseases in Hamburg and died from pneumonia. My aunt died from cancer; many people who had survived the concentration camps died from cancer some years later.

I talked frequently with my mother about this time so that I am able to continue the family archives. Later, in many other families, denial pervaded, and they declined to speak about the Third Reich. German families didn't used to talk very much, if at all, about that time. Today there are more talks and documentaries about this time because of the fiftieth anniversary of World War II's end. The older generation didn't talk at all before, and now they want to tell everything to the point that people don't want to listen to them anymore. Talking to children about this topic is another concern. I don't think anyone should force his children to eat with the argument "Eat now and think about how we had to starve in time of war when we were kids." War was an exceptional condition and today's children can't understand that; they take eating everyday for granted. I admire young people like you for trying to transfer your minds a little bit back into the time of World War II and to work up Germany's history. I was born and pushed into this time, but the youth nowadays know nothing about it

Out of my family's entire circle of friends, many had to go to concentration camps. There was a very intense bond between these friends. We held together in the Diaspora. My mother, fortunately, didn't have to go to Theresienstadt. I mentioned to my teacher some-times: "I'm afraid of losing my mother. I expect her to not be at home anymore when I return from school." The only comment the teacher made: "Don't worry. We will provide you with a room to live here." Of course, all teachers were National Socialists. They wanted everybody like us to go to Theresienstadt. In school I was the best student, but my transcripts were torn apart. I got worse grades than other students did because I was "mixed"—half German, half Jewish. The teacher said, "Especially you, Ingrid, you have to make a stronger effort in school," although I was the best.

I remember one teacher, Fraulein Schulze—little, heavy, handicraft teacher—who had long hairs that she brought together in a knot on top of her head and wore a big hat. All the students wanted to play a trick on her. I usually didn't participate in student tricks because I was afraid of the consequences for my mother and me. The students manipulated the teacher's hat, put it back on the desk, and stuffed it with a couple of potatoes. They asked me, because I could draw very well, to draw a cartoon on the blackboard of this teacher putting on her hat while all the potatoes fell out. I did it. National Socialism obsessed another teacher, a 180 percent Nazi, which means more than normal. He wanted me to come into his office after that incident. First he just was swearing. Later he slapped me once in the face, and asked me, "You must have put the potatoes in the hat too, right?" "No," I said. Then he answered, "This is one example where you can tell the lying of your Jewish people!" I wanted to apologize for this drawing and gave him my hand. He refused it and said, "I don't shake the hand of a *Judenschwein* [Jewish pig]." This teacher excluded me from physical education as a punishment, so I had to sit in class alone when the other students were playing sports.

I was not a member of BDM [league of German girls], although my teacher mentioned, "It's a pity that you are not 'Aryan.' You are excellent in social studies. You could be a wonderful leader in the Bund Deutscher Mädchen."[10] Many "mixed" children did not go into the Jewish community, and even some of them were big Nazis. For the Nazis it was very easy to get rid of somebody; they could claim the slightest infraction, and nobody could bring evidence that it was not true. [The "onus of proof" was always on the Jews.] One teacher, Frau Gottbrath-Behrens, left the school together with me. She was Catholic. My teacher had this class very much under control. Many Nazis' daughters attended this class. It was a part of *Oberbau* [middle school]. At this time I had to attend first, *Grundschule/Volksschule*,[11] secondly, *Oberbau* (until *Mittlere Reife*, an exam), and thirdly, *Lyzeum* for girls or *Gymnasium* for boys [similar to American sequence: elementary, junior, and senior high]. I attended this class three years before I was kicked out, so that my degree was just a *Volksschulabschluss*, the first step of education. This *Oberbau* school was located next to Eppendorf Hospital. My class teacher had a typical Jewish name, Rosenbaum, but he always denied being of Jewish origin. He told people all his relatives had been "Aryan," that one of his relatives three generations before owned a big farm with many *Rosenbäumen* [rose trees]. That's where this name allegedly comes from. My mother met this class teacher. My mother said, *"Aus dem kannst du drei Juden machen"* [He looks so Jewish you can make three Jews out of him]. I describe him as having a Stürmer-Ponem [face of a little ugly figure].[12] These "big Nazis" really suffered from their Jewish appearance. This teacher wore a woolhair cap, and he was very anti-Semitic.

My family celebrated the Jewish New Year and Christmas. My uncle was very religious. He took all the children to the synagogue, for example, the Laubhüttenfest, in Yiddish; Zimpristaure [Ecclesiastic Feast of the Tabernacles] because the children got candies and this was the only opportunity for getting them. When I was twelve years old, I had to sit upstairs. In Jewish synagogue the women have to sit upstairs. It was Laubhüttenfest as well. We conducted *Lulev schütteln*, to shake lulev. *Lulev* is a sacred bundle of twigs from a citrus fruit, a pomegranate tree or bush, a palm branch and a bay leaf that are bound together, and you shake it in front of your body and then swing it across the right, then across the left shoulder, while you say a prayer. But it was the first time I had to deal with this Lulev, so I felt fearful when I saw it arrive in my row because I didn't know what to do. This Lulev was passed from woman to woman and when it was three women before me suddenly the divine service finished so that I didn't get this Lulev. Luckily. I was sweating but happy.

I am more connected to the Jewish faith. I can't feel like a Christian. I don't believe in Jesus Christ. But I know a lot about religion because I deliberately participated in religion lectures. I made my class teacher, Rosenbaum, very embarrassed when I said, "Jesus Christ is a Jew as well because he's circumcised." I told him the date of Jesus' circumcision, and my teacher was quite upset about that and threatened to exclude me from the lessons if I interfered in this manner again. I told this story at home and my family was amused. I am a Jew according to the Israelische Gesetz [Israel Law] because I was born from a Jewish mother. I have never been a member of the Jewish community because if you were registered anywhere in connection to Jews you were considered Jewish, and the Gestapo used, or rather abused, this for their own purposes. I gave birth to my second son in Hamburg's Jewish hospital and the physician asked me, "Do you want your son to be circumcised?" I said, "No way." The doctor was angry about that and asked me, "Why do you come here in order to give birth to your son, if you are not following Jewish rules?"

I now go to a very nice general practitioner, Dr. Lafi, who is Palestinian. When I arrive at his practice, we talk about *Gott und die Welt* [God and the world], everything except illness. Dr. Lafi told me that his wife encounters many problems here in Germany because she wears a headscarf, usual attire for Muslims. When I told my neighbor, an older woman, this story, she said, "Why is she wearing a headscarf? She should adapt to wearing a German outfit if she wants to live here." In my family, which was very religious, almost all women wore wigs since they didn't want to show any of their headskin. I learned about Jewish culture and Christian culture, but actually I am a heathen, not religious, not baptized. When I want to talk to "my God," I go to the dike [the dam, which is typical in North Germany] or walk along the mud flats, the *Wattenmeer* [shoals], on the North Sea. God is in nature.

I can tell you a story of my father's family. They wrote him a letter and asked, "When will your daughter be baptized?" My father's answer, "I don't care. My daughter is being baptized everyday in the bathtub." My parents did not want to force any religion on me. I could decide later to what religion I wanted to belong. We have never tried to solve our problems in a religious way. Many Jews came back from concentration camps and said, "We have no God anymore."

≈   ≈   ≈

I was friends with a family, Spiegel,[13] who were cruelly murdered. The father had been a member, a pilot, of Die Rote Staffel des Barons von Richthofen [Red Squadron of Baron v. Richthofen] together with the "famous" Hermann Goering, later the official speaker for Adolf Hitler. So the family believed the Nazis, because of their father's former position, would not maltreat them in any way. Unfortunately, they were wrong. The whole family was killed in 1942 or 1943 after he was brutally tortured. The mother was hanged, the father also, although he had been only a skeleton anyway, and the two daughters, thirteen and fourteen, were beaten to death with guns. [She is reading from a book.] Mr. Spiegel was working for HAPAG shipping company in Hamburg and dealt with the Jews who wanted to emigrate. He helped them considerably. When they could not take their money with them—the Nazis allowed only a small amount to be taken on the trip—he took the money and gave it to Jews in need. He paid for my *Meisterschule* [art school]. In Minsk he was elected *Lagerältester,* spokesman for the ghetto. The father's family was Jewish. He smashed all his awards and medals from former times when the Nazis informed him to leave the country. More evidence of the Nazi brutality was the fact that they even, and particularly, killed disabled people, old, without legs, blind. People were picked up from Altenheim Seelandstraße [old people's home in a neighboring street of Grindelallee in Hamburg's Jewish community] and were taken into concentration camps. The Nazis never respected other people's human rights.

My social life was lonely. To the Jewish people I was considered a *Spitzel,* an informer, of the Gestapo, because I looked very "Aryan," and to the "Aryan" people I was not even considered a human being. That is why I always drew incessantly, and that is what I am doing these days as well. Sometimes I didn't feel like a German at all. I have been lonely. I was a *Wanderer zwischen den Wellen* [wanderer between the waves], belonging to no one. I was lucky to be admitted into the art school for clothes design shortly before this admission procedure was closed to Jews. Sometimes my teacher said, "Ms. Riemann, please avoid your Jewish colors," when I started drawing in multicolors, since the students wanted to draw in gray, typical for war. My studies were paid for by the family I mentioned previously who were brutally murdered. Later I was secretly engaged to an Austrian man who described himself as a "boot of the German," served in the German army, and died in Russia. He also paid for my studies.

$$\approx \quad \approx \quad \approx$$

I am content living in Germany. I have had opportunities to leave because my relatives are all over the world. But I married early and my sons were born in 1947 and 1948, and the main reason was my mother, who didn't want to go anywhere else. My mother raised my children as well because my first husband died very early. One of my sons, Claus Wecker, works independently in stage work and design for the TV channel NDR in Hamburg. I was married twice. My first husband died early. He suffered from juvenile diabetes that he got while buried alive as a fourteen-year-old boy. [Statistics show that many children suffered from shock diabetes after this experience.] I have always looked for men who could talk to me about everything. My second husband worked as a captain on a big ship and had known many countries and different cultures. He was *weltgewandt,* worldly. But after forty years of being a seaman he didn't want to do it any more. He had started at age fifteen on the ship *Pamir* [a highland in Russia], and in Marseilles he had to go ashore because of an accident. He started drinking. One day, when he was boozing, he called me and said, *"Du Judenschwein"* [you Jewish pig]. I immediately wanted a divorce. I didn't have to stand for that! He married again, at Helgoland because nobody would know about it, and he owns a nice shop in Hamburg. He almost killed his second wife while boozing. For this reason, I changed my last name again. I didn't want any connection to this man anymore. Later I got to know my partner in life. I had twenty-one wonderful years with him. I've never been married for that long.

The man I lived with was a Kronprinzenköger.[14] He sustained severe war injuries and died two years ago from pancreatic cancer. He was a very understanding man who had lived in and known about war. He put into every child's hand a book for them to read that informed them about different religions in order to make them develop tolerance. I told every man with whom I used to "hang out" about my history, but the most accepting man was the man I lived with most of my life. Two people must have acquired similar experiences in life; otherwise, they don't get along with each other. That's my philosophy. My partner had been a member of a party different from mine after the war but that didn't matter. Our common hobbies were fishing and cultivating a garden; our favorite color was green, which means environmental protection.

I left Hamburg after my retirement and after my mother died, since I never would have left my mother alone. Basically, I and my mother were together up to the end of her life, so I could follow how my mother developed bitterness about all these things that happened to her after the war. For example, the fight for a little pension for her dead husband, DM 400. This pension almost never increased, and it was a hard struggle to get his "rehabilitation." My mother said, "I will tell you, Ingrid, if your father would have hanged himself and have written a farewell letter with the words: 'I committed suicide because the Nazis forced me to do it,' we would get a pension immediately, but this way nobody believes that he was killed by the Nazis, and the old Nazi lawyers have maintained their positions in the courts even after the war."

My mother never received more than DM 500 until the 1970s when a new law was set up that all former civil servants that had to leave because of political or racial reasons would get a new pension. Then my mother received DM 1,000, which she couldn't believe. Actually, even DM 1,000 was just a little amount of money compared to other pensions. For example, my brother's mother-in-law gets DM 3,000, a combination of her own pension, her dead husband's pension from being a teacher in East Prussia, and the pension for the death of her husband while fighting for Hitler's army. This woman was annoying my mother and me very much because she always said, "I don't understand. You get so much money, you could buy a house or whatever you want!" My mother was upset about that and answered, "I'm sorry, but my husband wasn't a Nazi."

Even today people think "the Jews will make me poor" because they believe Jews received an abundance of reparation money. Only a few people got reparation money. My relatives in California who owned houses in Berlin have never seen any money for those. Also, the house in the Lüneburger Heide was gone and given to a "big Nazi," and our family didn't get any money for it. [She smiles.] If my mother would have caught an American officer after the war and gone to this house with a jeep, probably this Nazi would have given us back the house [simply taking him by surprise], but she never did it. When my father died, the Nazis said, "Now this house is Jewish property and we can take it." So my mother had to give up the key to this house. The Nazis made the deal in the best way for themselves. Unfortunately, the reparation committee "twisted" the case in their favor. The committee said my mother didn't need to register this house under her name. But obviously, her husband had died so she owned the house. My mother never dated or married again because, from her point of view, people had disappointed her so much she would never trust anybody again. This is probably due to this whole struggle for the "rehabilitation" of her husband.

I'll tell you the story of my pension application. Usually those four years at the School of Art would be counted for my pension. But the public authority denied it, unless I could show transcripts with a degree. I answered that I was not allowed to stay in the degree program because I had a Jewish mother. Now the public authority wrote back and said: "Bring the evidence that your mother is Jewish." Was I upset! I never thought there would ever be a day that I would have to show evidence of my Jewish mother because I had to prove all the time that I was of "Aryan" origin. This is horrible! The pension authority never wrote me back and counted these four years for my pension. Basically, people think the same, just with other symptoms.

The students in my gymnastics class, with whom I chatted, asked me, "Are you afraid that this could happen again?" It was a time in Germany when acts of violence against foreigners were high. Yes, I said, I have this fear that Germany will come under the same conditions as after World War I and that the politics will fail again. I would like you to search for the reasons why Hitler could establish himself in Germany and come to power. If you realize and understand these reasons, then you will know why I'm afraid of it. But my hope is you. You are young, honest, open-minded, and critical students. If everybody would be like you, having her own political opinion and not being influenced by one single person, this is my hope. The development in Germany lies in your hands. If something were to happen, believe me, it would also affect you. There are many "Aryans" who were Catholic or Communists and they say, "After the Jews, the Nazis would have killed us, simply because we didn't fit into their image of a good German." I like to talk to young people. I have spoken on many occasions. Some journalists and I went to *Kleine Jerusalem* in Hamburg and they asked me questions. And a group of schoolchildren at a *Gymnasium* advertised for a person who had lived through the Third Reich to come speak to the class after they had read *The Diary of Anne Frank*. Nobody volunteered. I decided to go.

When Ignaz Bubis, head of the Jewish community in Germany, had been invited to a discussion in Hamburg, I thought, "Poor Mr. Bubis, if you only knew what 'brown soup' you will come across here!" [Brown is a Nazi color.] After Bubis's speech I went to him wearing my Jewish star and said, "Hello, Mr. Bubis, very nice you could make it, nice to have you here." Bubis was really perplexed and bewildered; he couldn't say anything. On my way out I asked some young people the reasons why they came to this discussion. One young man, a science student in Göttingen, answered, "I wanted to see how a real Jew looks." He mentioned that in his studies he never had any contact with historical data or events, so that he had never had the chance to learn anything about Jewish families, how they live, etc. [Although it was a vapid answer to Ingrid's question, it was a response related to the one-directional education at the university.] I said, "You are in luck, young man. Mr. Bubis is a male Jew and I am the female pendant [accessory] to him." I gave the right answer. The student apologized because it was embarrassing for him.

There are many culturally valuable works from Jewish, Catholic, or Communist artists, painters and writers, which have been destroyed or thrown away just because the Nazis didn't like the characteristics of these people. I think the Jews have made mistakes. For example, their worship services have always been *Geheimnis krämerei* [mystery mongering]. Nobody, especially among the fanatic Jews, was allowed to speak about the services. If only they would be more open to other people, then nobody would assume that the Jewish religion is a sect like the Ku Klux Klan. The Jewish "missionaries" always want to convince; they are not very open to other opinions.[15]

At age fifteen, my brother had to serve for *Heimatflak*[16] since he was a "half-caste of the second degree." My mother said, "If anything happens to my son, I will commit suicide. In order to rescue my own life, I risk the life of my son." My mother was stigmatized physically and mentally from this war—it was a vicious circle. Here is a picture of my ballet group, my dogs, the girls' shirts, and cabarets and plays we performed in Königsberg. My aunt got a higher amount of reparations because she saved all the bills from the performances. After the war, I worked as a painter, an artist, for the Crusader Club in Hamburg for English soldiers. Once they wanted to perform a play about a king called Richard in their own theater. I don't recall what number this Richard was. They owned all the materials and clothes, silk and velvet, confiscated from the Rheinland, and they wanted me to help design the dresses for the actors. When we worked together I smoked my first cigarette—very strong—and I was sick. This was August 1945, a time of great hunger. I drank my first strong beer without eating anything beforehand. Talk about high!

We knew many theater people. I knew Ida Ehre [a famous actress in Hamburg] because she was a friend of my cousin's mother, and Mrs.

Ehre had been at my family's home quite often. Also Henny Porten, an actress, was a friend of this family. Henny lived in a "half and half" marriage as well. My uncle worked as an engineer for Draeger-Werke Hamburg and invented the gas mask in World War I. My aunt became Deutschnational [a party on the extreme right], which was horrible. She got baptized and said continuously to my mother, "Nothing can happen to me!" My mother answered, "You are almost anti-Semitic, that's why you will always keep being a Jew!" Later my aunt converted her religion again and went to the Jewish community, at which time my mother said, "You are a care parcel Jew!" My aunt has not been the only "wrong" Jew in the Jewish community. When I wanted to register my mother again, the Jewish community was somehow offended because she hadn't been a member during the war. After the war, my mother got the designation Jew of the first degree. The Jewish community and my mother had tremendous trouble with each other. I possess many old prayer books from my uncle. I would like to confer them into faithful hands. But I miss the heart in the present Jewish community, and the old rabbi, Dr. Carlebach, who had been very nice.

Now I live in Marne, and nobody knows where this city is situated. People think it is in France. Often they can associate Brunsbüttel with Marne because a nuclear power station is nearby. Whoever lives in Marne lives a little bit outside of this world. In addition to this, because of my profession, I have always been an outsider, and I have always said what I thought. Here in Marne people, especially women, talk considerably about others. They meet for coffee and cake, twelve women and fifteen cakes, and I am in no mood to go there and join them. That's why they talk about me as well. It's a *Klatsch.*

I don't go to church. Many people of my generation or older are dying, so that they have a bunch of funerals every week in Marne. Mostly the buried people are women who survived World War II, but their husbands had not. The women who died were eighty to ninety years old. The people in Marne didn't have numerous sorrows because only one bomb was dropped here. This was not as tragic as the many bombs dropped on Hamburg. I show the book *Firestorm over Hamburg* to all inhabitants of Marne who say, "Oh my God! We didn't know you had bomb alerts in Hamburg even when the war began." From my perspective, the people of Marne don't know anything about the war because they were not directly affected. When the people in Hamburg had to go into the shelter while bombs were being dropped, my mother and I and other people were intrigued when a bomb hit the earth just because we didn't realize that we could be killed ourselves. We viewed them more like fireworks. My mother got a little *Weltempfänger* [short-wave radio]. This radio was hidden in a wardrobe. My mother got it from a neighbor woman who was very friendly with Jews. We called it *Goebbelssäge* because it sounded like a saw. My brother drilled some holes in the wood and installed a little receiver. Mainly, we listened to BBC England, but my mother also checked the French news and invited French war prisoners who worked in the neighbor's house as joiners to listen to their news. My mother always waved a kitchen towel to give them a sign. We realized the danger but we made any effort to help others. My mother got increasingly excited about the war ending, but she was afraid to go into the air raid shelter. One day a Nazi woman said, "What business do you have here?" when my mother wanted to protect herself in the shelter. For this reason, she wanted to walk toward the English army, but I held her back and said, "Stay here. Everybody is throwing bombs and the English low-level planes can't recognize you as a Jew." I said around the end of the war, *"Am liebsten hätte ich jeden Engländer geknuddelt"* [I would have liked to have hugged every Englishman].

When my mother died, I didn't grasp it. I could never imagine her death because there was only an eighteen-year age difference between us. A brief time before she died, the Jewish hospital wanted her to sign up to go into an old folks' home in Oberaltenallee Finkenau and I visited her everyday there. She started to live her life in reverse. Her mental faculties restricted more and more. First, she talked about the air raid shelter and said, "See, Ingrid, there, the Gestapo is observing me." From her room in the home she could see the former shelter. Later she got a new room and yelled, "Shut the door, the gas is coming!" One day she saw a shadow in her room and said, "See, there in the corner is Hubert [Ingrid's brother]. The Gestapo has hung him in front of my eyes." I said, "No, Mom, this is a shadow. You are dreaming." "No," my mother said, "this is him and I am guilty that they killed him." Later she fantasized about her time in school, and one day before she died, she said to me with the voice of a child, "I am sick. I have got diphtheria." It was suspected my mother had diphtheria when she was a little girl.

My mother was born in the Bornstraße, and attended the *Israelitische Töchterschule* [Israeli daughters' school]. I have kept books from my mother's school time. I enjoyed it when my mother talked about school and displayed her transcripts. She did poorly in Hebrew, a five.[17] But they had swimming, cooking, French, and English in school. The director of this school at that time, Mr. Alberto Jonas, was deported to Auschwitz. I remember the time when the Nazis wanted to take thousands of Jews to concentration camps. First they deported the men, bolted all apartments tightly, and the women were sitting on the streets. Many women stayed in the gym of the Israelitische Töchterschule or at relatives or friends' homes. Many women were pregnant. Two or three months later the women were transported, and people believe on the way to the concentration camps the Nazis killed all the children. Nobody would believe men and women were separately transported, but there is evidence in accordance with death books. I worked in a market research company for five years as a graphic artist and had to deal with statistics. I checked all dead people and compared their names and dates of birth, which was important evidence to prove these separate transports. The children had almost all been only four weeks old and were killed. [Perhaps four *months* old?]

After the war, I attained a new life as a gift. I had to learn to lose my shyness. Even now, when I have to go to the financial administration office, or a policeman talks to me, my knees shake because I was used to not speaking my own opinion in wartime. The sky opened up for me when the English army came to Hamburg and finished the war. Later I got an offer from a magazine called *Burda* to work as an artist, but I was too shy to take this offer. I always had to think about what I would be allowed to say and it was not easy to change this quirk. This lasted until I was forty-one years old.

I am fighting against the forgetting. I would like to write about my experiences, but there's already so much written. I have read different books, for example, Dr. Starke's *Der Führer schenkt den Juden eine Stadt* [The Führer gives the Jews a city].[18] I knew Dr. Starke's husband personally. He had a beautiful daughter who was gassed by the Nazis. Dr. Starke's husband was transported from Theresienstadt to Auschwitz together with an actor, Fritz Bänscher. Fritz rented the apartment below ours in my grandmother's house and was very amusing. He had a type of "gallows" humor. That's why many cabaret artists, such as cabaret star Günther Hagen met at our, the Blumenthals', home.[19] Mr. Starke, who survived Auschwitz, told me more stories about Fritz Bänscher later. During one festive evening when they had to perform in Theresienstadt, he said, "My dear people, if you ever go over the Jungfernstieg Mountains in Switzerland, don't forget to take your spoons out of your buttonholes." They had a habit of carrying valuable objects. Mr. Starke was with Bänscher after Auschwitz and finally came to us after the war. Those who survived trusted us and told their stories. I experienced all of this firsthand. From these survivor stories, which I believe, and with my ability to imagine the conditions in the concentration camps because I am an artist, I have nightmares about it quite often. It was almost always winter when the Jews were transported. I can tell many gruesome tales that happened in Hamburg, such as in the Logenhaus.[20]

Suddenly, the people there were denied water because the toilets were stopped up. I worked as a coffee maker in the community's home. Fritz Bänscher and I, in our social group, made coffee for them. Somewhere we received a present of coffee in Thermos bottles. And he said, "That's enough. Stop. No more brewing. They aren't allowed to drink any more." And that's the worse thing you can do to a person— not give them anything to drink. Then after two days, without heat, horribly cold weather came. This happened in winters 1941-42 and 1942-43. Fritz came to our door and said, "I need a few of those large soup spoons." There was a large restaurant kitchen downstairs. Fritz whispered, "I need them to open the toilets so they can go to the bathroom, give them a chance to get rid of their excrement." After Fritz Bänscher survived Auschwitz, he never came back to Germany. He said,

CHAPTER THREE

RUTH YOST

"I was born completely poisoned"

≈

Ruth Yost was my first interview of a *Mischling*. She remains, even though she took her life, a woman who was very much alive and whose enthusiasm I will never forget. In contrast to the other women, Ruth was highly emotional, sometimes extreme in her passion, alternately venomous and tame. The splits in Ruth's psyche (namely between a Jewish and a German identity) were highly pronounced and explain, in part, an ongoing battle to maintain her mental health. She cried numerous times when with me, which was painful to sit through, but she defied the German stereotype of being dispassionate and matter-of-fact. She said that after she and her father reunited, they cried for fifteen hours. Her hypersensitivity to intrusion and her mistrust of others was evident when her doorbell buzzed in the midst of the interview. She excused herself and went to her intercom. When no one answered, she shouted, panicked, over and over, into the intercom *Wer ist da? Wer ist da?* (Who's there?) It took some time for her to calm down.

Ruth often used third person to look back at herself as "the child," at what happened to this child, an object, in the past. In some ways she displayed a simple view of the world and beheld all Jews as exactly like her father, whom she deeply loved. Ruth insinuated that her mother "appropriated" the Jewish faith when she married her father, whereas Ruth came by it "naturally" through a devout bond with her father, so that her mother, perhaps out of jealousy, was against the "Jewish part" of her daughter.

Ruth was a champion of the underdog; she consistently aligned herself with whoever was not in power. As Ruth described her political activities and government denouncements, the energy level in the room rocketed. All of that dynamism became exhausting to me and eventually, after four hours, to her. This was the first time Ruth had been asked to talk about her past. The interview gave her the opportunity to voice her stories and, in some small way, cleanse her mind and free herself.

When Inga, a German student who assisted me, and I arrived at Ruth's building in Winterhude, Ruth was pleased to see me but was puzzled by Inga's presence. When she realized Inga was German, she became visibly uneasy and asked her if she was a Nazi. After we reassured Ruth of Inga's interest and unsullied intentions, she relaxed.

Ruth had an uncluttered appearance. She wore plain dark pants and a blouse. Her hair—black and gray, wild and kinky—mirrored her fissured and turbulent personality. Throughout the interview, Ruth rapidly shifted between emotions. Often she raised her voice, her sable eyes squinting with vexation underneath her thin-rimmed, bifocal glasses, and squished her lips. She was a magnanimous hostess who stuffed us with a variety of cakes she had spread out on a small, cramped table.

Ruth called me a few days after her interview to tell me that a *Mischling* friend of hers had consented to talk with me. Although Ruth knew about my Christian paternal family and that I was not Jewish, she seemed to have fixed in her mind for purposes of identification that I was. In her statement to me before we said good-bye, the splits in Ruth's heritage were again evident. Simultaneously, as a German, she clung to Jewish stereotypes, but as a Jew, she repulsed them. Ruth exclaimed, "*Ja. Du hast die schönsten, großen jüdischen Augen!*" (Yes. You have the most beautiful, big, *Jewish* eyes).

Her Jewish father raised Ruth almost single-handedly; her "Aryan" mother was young and had no interest in motherhood. Ruth, unlike most of the interviewees, attended synagogue. She told how her mother tried to "educate out of her" all that was Jewish. She forced Ruth to join and attend a Protestant church, which for Ruth was too "metaphysical." Her father escaped to Belgium in 1938 but was captured by the Nazis. After the British liberated him, he went to England. Twenty years passed before Ruth saw him again. In some ways Ruth epitomizes Sylvia Plath's words in her poem "Daddy": I must "get back back back to you." "Daddy, daddy, you bastard, I'm through." Ruth was "abandoned" by her father at age eight, from which she never recovered. She wrote to him and eventually visited. He refused to speak German or return to Germany. Thus they were physically as well as linguistically separated. Ruth stuck to the German land and language, both of which her father had had to reject in order to live. In the meantime, before her mother remarried, they nearly starved. An accumulation of events led to Ruth's eventual collapse. Although she tried to live with her memories, she had no one to talk to about them. Ruth attributed her resultant fears and repressed emotions to the crippling of her body: She was stooped, shrunken from having to hide in cramped quarters (bomb shelters, basement, and attic), and claimed her nipples were inverted from trauma. Both her physical and psychical "bodies" were violated. At liberation, Russian soldiers raped her at gunpoint. Her trauma was exacerbated by the death of her life partner, whom she did not name. All the years of repressing her anger, shame, and grief led to an attempted suicide, for which she was institutionalized in a state psychiatric hospital. At various stages in her life, Ruth attempted to "purge" her past through action. She adopted two boys, visited her father, listened to his stories, and fought against any zealous ideologues. She continually denounced any extremist factions that appeared to employ Nazi tactics. Philosopher Susan Neiman spoke about people in Germany like Ruth who "agree that *Vergangenheits-verarbeitung* ["working through the past"] means maintaining vigilance toward everything in the present which shows signs of repeating the past."[1] Ruth was against "organized communities" for good reason. She saw only mayhem in groups — from the political right and left. She didn't survive in a vacuum (her mother was with her), but all of her escapes and hidings were solitary. Although Ruth seemed to have a renewed faith in her fellow Germans, at the time I left Germany she was suffering again from depression. While Ingeborg Hecht's unbearable memories of innumerable losses, including her father's presumed murder in Auschwitz, did not break her, Yost's memories of abandonment, brutalization, and anguish did. For Ruth, the search for expression and securing an identity ended with her suicide in December 1996.

I usually don't talk about these horrible events. To whom would you talk? People are so preoccupied with themselves. My parents met in Berlin. My Jewish father from Poland was born in 1900 and my mother, let me look it up, 1909. [She gets out her journal and reads a poem]: "In 1929, Berlin was as free as Danzig and was the first time I saw light. But later, my life was so cloudy that it turned out to be the only light I saw."[2] I was born on December 11, 1929. My mother came to Berlin in 1926. My father's parents had an eight-room apartment in Grenadierstraße. I will talk about these extraordinary grandparents later." [Stops reading.] My father's family came to Berlin in 1904. They were Jewish Poles from Bieko near Lodz. My grandparents owned a chicken butcher shop in Berlin that was kosher. My father owned a fur shop. They were strictly kosher and Orthodox. My grandmother's hair was parted "like so," called a *Scheitel*—she cut her hair for her husband and wore a hood. I was *Mischling ersten Grades*. My daddy was called Brenner, and my mom, Yost. I attended a Jewish school and went under the name of Brenner, but afterward switched to Yost. My mom wanted me to survive so she changed it to Yost. My mother died in 1987 at age seventy-eight.

My mom was nineteen when I was born. She came from the country Glindow near Berlin and had learned to clean and sell furs. She worked with my father in his fur shop. She had *learned*, however, beforehand. During her pregnancy, she ate coffee beans everyday. It wasn't good. She bought quarter-pound coffee bags and just snacked all day. She did it out of greediness. Pregnant women, back then, were greedy. She hid this. Pregnant women even ate the edge of newspapers. They waited for the paper—not to read—but to eat. Today you can't imagine but back then it was true. Greediness came with pregnancy—pickles, fish, something sweet—always out of greediness. For my mom, it was coffee beans. I looked brown when I was born and the doctors thought my mom wanted to abort me [because of her eating the beans]. But my mom was just young and didn't know. She was from the country. She didn't know she was killing me. The doctor said if she'd continued a few more days, I'd have been born dead. I was born completely poisoned.

My father came to visit me. The babies were all behind a glass window because back then the men couldn't be with the women. There were eight babies and my dad walked by me and said, "Oh, there's an *Afrikaner* [from Africa]!" He asked the nurse which one was his. She kept

saying "No. No," each time he passed by one and asked. She told him it
was the *Afrikaner.* And he said, "What? That's mine? " There was a big
fight. I was triggering a marriage tragedy. [She laughs.] My dad yelled,
"You terrible mom! You wanted to kill the child?" But she didn't know
she was poisoning me with caffeine. The struggle didn't last. My dad
took me home, a little bundle under his arm, and never took me back
again! My baby color wasn't pink like the other babies, but lilac. My
father was promptly convinced my mother was too young to take
responsibility for me—she didn't know enough—so he bathed me, fed
me, changed diapers, carried me, sang songs like "Armer Gigolo. Schöner
Gigolo." In the evenings, he tied my cradle to his wrist and the moment
I made a sound he rocked the cradle. My mom, you know, he didn't let
around. When he went away he said, "Don't let the child cry." But she
had heard that children should cry to strengthen their lungs. So he left
but stood behind the door listening. My mom hit me when she thought
my dad was gone, so I'd be strong. Dad came in yelling, "You
Rabenmutter [raven mother]!" My mom told me this story later; she
thought it was a funny family story. She thought it strange that her
husband was the way he was—pushing the baby buggy back in 1929.
No man would push a buggy, but my dad took me out and pushed me.
I had an intimate relationship with my father. He never yelled, was
continuously loving. He always explained everything calmly and factually. He treated me like a young lady.

In this way, I grew up very bonded to my father. He had to be at
work all the time. He was the *Kürschner Meister* [master furrier]. We had
a fur shop and we had several employees. I was able to speak at ten months
old and walk at one. Before I could walk, he used to drag me around
hanging onto the bottom of his legs. I was always in the fur shop with
him and we had a great relationship. [She laughs.] His slogan was "the
most beautiful and the best is almost good enough for my daughter." He
used to kiss my hand. Finally, at one year and two months, I got up and
took my first steps. My parents were happy. Later on I was allowed to
brush my dad's hair. They had a huge birdcage in the house with five
types of birds. In the morning, we awakened to the singing of these birds.
We didn't need an alarm clock. To the hired people, I always had to be

friendly and courteous. I didn't need to be told to behave as everyone was of the opinion that I was a well-behaved and understanding child. My mom sewed me beautiful dresses of silk and velvet with handwork around the cuffs. My father sewed me a coat from horse skin with fancy lining. I dressed so richly that I was barely able to move. When the sun shone, my dad put the buggy in front of the door and gave me a piece of fur to play with. On these occasions, I practiced patience.

My earliest memory reaches back into my second year. My mother went shopping with me. She left me sitting in the buggy outside of the store. Two boys came up to the buggy and wanted to have my silver ring. I took off the ring and gave it to the biggest guy. I thought he would give it back to me. But I, being too young to know better, was wrong. The boy disappeared with the ring and I was left upset. My mom returned with her shopping items and I anxiously told her about this incident. My mother yelled at me for allowing people to steal my possessions. I started crying and fell asleep out of sorrow. Two horrible things happened: not only was I robbed but my mom yelled at me for it. [She laughs.]

My mother, father, and I—together—got along, but mother and daughter, no. My mother thought, "This daughter receives so much love that she needs discipline." My mother had a very strict father, a quality that she carried on. I was a sensitive and obedient child. It was unnecessary to treat me strictly—love and caring would have been just fine. I grew up with terrible fear—first of the Nazis, then of my mother. As a result of this "angst," the nipples on my breasts, rather than growing outward, are inverted. When a child grows up with so much anxiety and fear, it's terrible. My mother never hit me, but she directed me with her blue eyes. If I got a dirty look from her, that was enough. My mother always believed in God and prayed. She often sewed beautiful clothes, and she'd say, "God has given me these hands. Good things come from God. Bad things result from human sinfulness." My mother referred to Hitler as a mass murderer, like Stalin, but with differences.

In 1938 my father left Germany. When an eight-year-old has a broken relationship with a loved one, it fractures the child's soul. I used to hide under my covers at night and cry and pray for my father because I knew he was in a camp. We had gotten a letter from the Swiss Red

Cross with twelve words in it. That's how many words he was allowed to write. In 1938 he escaped to Belgium and stayed in a "feeding camp." He knew a smuggler who left him in No-Man's Land between the borders. They hid him with a "mixed-marriage" household. The second time he accomplished crossing over the borders, he came into the feeding camps. Germans invaded and asked them, nicely, to come out, to give up. But it was a trap. This was near the French/Spanish border right by the water. They were SS men and treated the hideaways in the most undignified manner, completely subhuman. The SS put them like animals into the ship's bottom storage rooms with the rats and shit; the ship was sailing to North Africa. In the work camp, my father had to dig *Schutzwälle* [protective walls]. He was under Erwin Rommel in Morocco, Tunisia, and Algeria. He was always in camps and got almost nothing to eat. The Spanish people caught rats, which they gladly ate. My father lost weight to his skin and bones. My father was liberated shortly before the war ended when Montgomery had victory over Rommel in Tunisia. The British liberated them after four years.

My father never stepped on German soil again because Jewish blood was used to fertilize the soil that gave us German bread, and he would never eat the bread.[3] He could never hear the German language again. He said they only screamed, like those in the army, no? My father had always spoken in a mannerly and calm way *because we weren't deaf.* He spoke at an appropriate level of pitch. Because the Nazis had screamed and shouted—done all of that—he didn't want to hear the language. The dates I haven't put together yet but that doesn't mean you have to doubt my word. I am glad that I wasn't in a camp; I was able to escape and live in hiding. As a child my only wish was to stand upright, to be unafraid of exposure. At the end of the war, I thought the Russians were my liberators, but the way they liberated me I could have done without, as you can imagine. I was raped. That happened to me. It was a shock. I even wanted to commit suicide when I was older. Although I did try, it was good that I didn't succeed because my father is still alive. He survived. He's ninety-four.

My father was very proper. He played soccer. He was a great man. I knew only good Jews, none who were nasty. There are some Jews who aren't good, I realize, but only a small percentage. Some of the Jews were *Kapos*[4] in the concentration camps. They were promised that if they'd take this job, they'd live. They mistreated other Jewish people, their own blood brothers, even shoveled them into ovens to burn. That is a very bad chapter in history. If you plant badness, then badness comes out—evil nurtured and promoted brought out the worst in the Jews as well. I have a great respect for those I knew who were in camps and survived. They've lived through torture and martyrdom that one can't imagine. In comparison to that, my fate is not so severe. You must always do what's right by people while alive because once you're dead you can't do anything. We must do good. [She repeats three times]. One has an obligation to do good. That's my opinion.

My father loves England. He speaks only English. Nevertheless, he writes letters in German to me. I speak only a little English. I stay in Germany because I speak German. I used to speak Oxford English. I'm back at zero. You forget a language after a while when working and living. I visited my father twice. He remarried to a Bavarian Jew and had a son. My half-brother, Stuart Brenner, is a professor of literature. He is in his thirties and lives in London, near Wimbledon. Both live in my father's house. My father has, unfortunately, an unhappy marriage. He says that his wife is Adolf Hitler. I can't see that. It's sad that he hasn't had harmony in his marriage. My father cried over the camps. If my father speaks about the camps, he cries. It's incapacitating if one doesn't get it out. I'd like to have spared him from the need to cry at this age. The world should be such that no one needs to cry. Mentally he's unclouded, but slower at ninety-four. He writes perfectly clearly.

At the time I went to visit my father in London, 1957, his second wife said to me, "I'm Clara. I'm not your aunt. I'm not your mother. Just Clara." That was very decent of her. I was twenty-eight years old. I hadn't seen my father in twenty years. He was so much shorter than I, which I couldn't understand at all. I had only childhood memories, and at that moment couldn't grasp why he was so short. I couldn't deal with it, but I said nothing. We had written to each other always. He wrote that he'd been remarried. But he didn't inform me that he had a two-year-old son—this when I was twenty-eight. A sign in the living room said: "Happy Birthday.

Two Years Old." And I thought, what is this? Then Clara comes out with a boy on her arm. She said, "This is Shamala, after my grandfather who's called Shama." He was called Shamala at the time. It means "poet." She called him Shamala but he took an English name, Stuart, and henceforth was Stuart. Shamala came forward with blue eyes and blond curls, and I didn't understand the world anymore. [She laughs.] "Why didn't you write to me about this, Papa?" He said, "I wanted to surprise you." And I said, "Well, you succeeded." That was that.

In 1989 I went to see my father again. I insisted on seeing him again, but he didn't want to have me because it was too crowded in the house. His wife was living on the top floor, and he on the bottom floor, and the rooms were arranged so that Stuart was upstairs in another room. I was booked in a hotel, not in the house. I stayed three days. But I wanted to see him again. He looked rundown. It's true. Naturally, he's terribly upset that they [Germans] killed his parents, and his brothers were killed. But he was glad one brother, Jakob, was in America. But then Jakob died. And it got to him. It was hard. My father had raised his son in London. He sold fur in London because the dealers still knew him. He got merchandise to sell on commission. And then came Greenpeace and you weren't allowed to sell animals like before because back then there were more animals than people. You didn't pay attention to tearing apart animal families. [She smiles.] Today you pay attention to that. But in business, not really. He wasn't able to sell minks anymore. So he sold shirts and jewelry. He always sold goods on commission. When a Jewish person was in a crisis, he tightened his belt and didn't eat. That's how it was. No one talked about it. You didn't cheat or swindle, as the Nazis claimed we did. If someone came to bargain for a fur my dad said, "You think because I'm a Jew you can bargain. I have fixed prices. I'll raise the prices and you come back in and we'll bargain to the regular price." He had to pay taxes and other expenses like everyone else.

My head went crazy and my nerves were shattered without my father—a child's nerves go *kaput*. [She alludes to a psychiatrist who seemingly told her that a child would be destroyed without a parent.] I don't want to complain at all because I didn't have to go to a camp—I should be humble—I escaped when I was fourteen.

My mother, forced to expose herself to the Gestapo, was mistreated, beaten up, and called "Jewish whore," and was asked where her husband, "the Jewish rascal," went. My mom couldn't withstand the pressure any more by herself, you understand? So she married to get the pressure off. She met a Communist and later married him and he became my stepdad, who was a good man. But still I always missed my dad because I'd worshipped him. My mother probably remarried around 1940. The first marriage was considered annulled. A Jewish marriage wasn't legally recognized. Because of that, I was considered an illegitimate child. Sometimes we hid German Communists in our house and sometimes Jews. We always were in danger because of that, that's clear. Once my stepdad and I were together in the backyard and we promised with a shake of the hand that we would shoot each other if we got crippled [from the bombings]. We didn't think about the fact that one of us could have been hanged if the other survived. It was a clear agreement between my stepfather and me. He was a Communist, a good Communist, which I separate from the other Communists.

At the time [before her mother remarried], we lived with Jewish people, as the Nazis had taken everything we owned. So my mother ran with me through the streets. She said, "Little Ruth, you haven't had anything to eat yet? Why didn't you say anything?" I said, "Oh, Mom, you have so many concerns, why should I come to you with my stupid worries and my hunger?" *That* I said as a child. They took the fur shop, housing, and furniture away so we were on the street. We didn't know where to go so we found a place with a Jewish couple on Koloniestraße 85. We obtained a room and my mom asked her parents for a sewing machine so she could make a living. We were very poor—we didn't even have a mannequin—so I had to try on all the clothes.

When I was in the Jewish school, I had a Jewish Pole teacher named Herr Berg. He was picked up in the school room by the Gestapo, and all the children had to line up against the wall. As we left the school,

Nazis threw rocks at us. I always ran with my school bag in front of me. I told you already that I must be grateful that I wasn't in a concentration camp. But I did have suffering and worries. These events don't leave a child without traces. After all, I was sensitive and intelligent, not dumb. I was also empathetic. It was horrible for me that my cousins, male and female, were in camps. I heard from my cousin Leo that he was with his father and his entire family in Sachsenhausen [a "work" camp]. He had to carry his own father to the gas chambers. The son had to carry his father into the gas chambers! The Nazis had thought of purely bestial actions against humans— undignified and mentally torturing. They had done such horrible things that I, of course, had a fear of being taken [to a camp].

My mom decided to transfer me to an Aryan school. When I went to the German school, I never felt bullied. No one bullied me. My mother was of the opinion that I was. However, *I* was *not* of that opinion. I was unhappy, no? Because my father was not there. I did not feel compelled to say "Heil Hitler." I had to say it because I didn't want to go to the camps where others were. I had to say the German *Gruss* [Nazi salute], which was horrible for me. But what could I do? I didn't want to go to a concentration camp so I said the *Gruss*. I always felt like a bad person when I did this, so I found a way to reinterpret the greeting with my hands so that it looked as if I was unlocking a door.

Once, in school, there was a reptile exhibition. They always said that Jews were cowards so I had to prove to myself, and to make the point to others, that I was not, so I agreed to have a snake wrapped around my neck. I was surprised that the snake wasn't warm and wet but was cold and dry. As a kid I always heard about these horrible things [done to the Jews]—that they had to stand in water in the basement with rats, and I heard what the Nazis had done to them, pulling their skin off to use for lampshades and misusing them for medical experiments; the most horrible for me was the experiments they did on twins.[5]

And when a child voiced a wish, he was killed. When I heard about this I was so unhappy, as I loved the Jewish people. I had only loving, caring people around me when I grew up, but now they were all in camps. My grandparents were back in Poland, picked up in 1938, and killed.

[She is looking at pictures.] This is my father's fur shop. That is Uncle Isaac who was killed in the gas chambers, and Uncle Bernhard who was killed. Jakob was in the ghetto in Poland and had a relationship with a woman there. They had a baby who had to grow up in a *Stückensack* [a sack]; otherwise the SS would have killed him. That is a four-cornered world to grow up in. Horrible. There were four brothers who each had a car, and that is my dad's car. That is my father and Uncle Jakob who came out of the ghetto with his child and wife to go to London. My father was shocked when he saw the child. Uncle Bernhard. Uncle Isaac. You see. They drove to the place that distributed the furs. They were all furriers. These four brothers. There were six kids. Uncle Oskar, on the right side, and his wife with his daughter and son immigrated to Buenos Aires in time. They were the only ones who were saved; they had left already in 1934.

I found out about the camps because, you know, in the Jewish community, everything goes from mouth to mouth. People spoke about a Jewish person being here or there. We transmitted any information we could get, as we had the same fate. The Communists were engaged [with Nazis] in street fights. Communists were the first to be eliminated. The Nazis weren't against just the Jews but also the Gypsies, the homeless, and infirm. They stuffed them together in camps. A real factory of killing; a machinery of murder. There had never been anything like it before. In Bosnia and Serbia, we see horrible similarities. But that is *war*. Only the Nazis have thought of machinery in order to kill people. For example, in a regular war, unlike the war against the Jews, the next morning an officer will sit down and write "150 dead." Death is not that systematic in war. But in order to kill 6 million people you need time; it can't be done at once. That's how the Nazis did it, by a system.

The fact that I was close to the Jewish people is clear because as a young child I learned Hebrew but forgot it because when you don't use a language, it falls asleep. The only thing I have left is a family Aggadah that I got after the war.[6] I can speak Yiddish. [She says a few words.] I had to learn German in school as a foreign language because my mother spoke Yiddish at home. My mother learned all the rituals that belonged to the Jewish religion and kept a strictly kosher household. My mother was Lutheran, then became Jewish. She had to learn everything—the codes of Jewish law, *Shulchan Aruch*, and the rites for directing a Jewish household, to keep milk and meat separate, and *Lichten Bentchen* [candle lighting]. It's like a test. The rabbi oversees it. I grew up with biblical teachings, strictly Orthodox. I prayed for my dad, even in church, but never let my mother know. We never talked about it. I was silent. This strictly religious aspect is still a part of me, even though I'm atheist.

When Hitler came to power in 1933, I was four years old and went to synagogue. They screamed after us: "Jews! Jews! Jews!" I don't have the type of voice to shout like that. I asked my dad, frightened, "Are we something like that?" and I leaned against him. "Yes, little Ruth, we are Jews." And then I *knew* we were Jews. This is how we went to the synagogue, very quiet and thoughtful inside. In the synagogue I was allowed to stand with the men. In the Talmud Torah there is one spot in which the entire community has to turn around. Excuse me, while I cry. [She does, briefly.] I had to turn around with my back to God. I stood by my daddy. He said, "Little Ruth. You have to turn around because in the Talmud Torah room, there is God." So we all turned around. I was a little child and I was curious, so I secretly turned back around to see God. And as we went out, I whispered to my dad, "Papa, I wasn't able to see God. He wasn't there." He said, "But, little Ruth, I told you not to turn around and you turned around anyway, so you were disobedient. And if one is disobedient, one can't see God." From then on, my dad was not only the dearest but also the greatest of all to me.

I became Lutheran because my mother wanted me to survive. I was fourteen years old when I was confirmed. I was in the Church of Zion and received religious instruction. Then I was torn apart—suddenly I had two faiths—you can't even imagine it. I'd understood the Orthodox Jewish faith, but not the Protestant faith because it's metaphysical. So I had to have metaphysics explained to me. I had to adopt another faith to stay alive but being in two faiths gave me more responsibilities. I was caught between what I had learned as a youngster and as a teenager. I was here and there.

Sometime during the war, I couldn't get point and food cards.[7] My mom and stepdad shared their bread, but they only got small portions. The worst thing is that I was growing and they could have asked me day and night if I was hungry and I'd have said, "Yes!" Back then, the beauty ideal wasn't Twiggy like today. Everybody was skinny then—everyone had limited calories. A twist from how it is today. A person was supposed to have 1,800 calories but no one had it. At night I stole bread from my mother who caught me and yelled, "You're lying. You're stealing." I got up at night and cut off pieces from my parents' bread. I didn't have the courage to say I'd done it. So then, I guess I lie, I steal, I'm a very bad person. I felt guilty but the fact that I did it out of hunger, no one explained was okay.

My mom made it possible for me to escape in 1944. At the time, I was an apprentice with an engineer and a blacksmith. The blacksmith told me not to come back. He said, "We had another half Jew here, Herr Petts, *Mischling ersten Grades,* and you shouldn't come back because you will be picked up at my office." Of course, I was to be put into a concentration camp, that was clear. In the second to last year of the war, the civilians couldn't travel any more. We learned there was a person who would allow us to travel to Tirol, Austria, which was part of the Reich then, but seemed a place where my identity could be hidden. I packed my bags. When I left my mother I wondered if I would ever see her again because of the bombs. I experienced all of the bombs out in the open, not in the bunkers. Every bomb attack. I wasn't allowed to go into a bomb shelter. Later on it was impossible for me to ever watch fireworks. It was the same as an air raid. Because the Americans always had their area marked with light rockets you knew where the next bomb would fall. Splinters were all around me.

With my meager belongings, I went to Tirol and when I saw the Alps for the first time, my mouth stood open. I had to be careful everywhere. I didn't have any food stamps with me. My mother had given me travel stamps. That was, at the time, very difficult. In any case, I was there for fourteen days or three weeks, I don't know for sure. I think it was three weeks. Then I got a note that I had to come to Kitzbühel [in the Western Alps] for a heart examination. I got an appointment and rode out there. I had the habit of always getting round-trip tickets. Again, I had unbelievable luck. The doctor examined me, then sent the assistant out and said, "Listen. There are two men who want to pick you up. I will send you up to the back door and you will say, 'I need to go to the bathroom.' If anybody asks you, say you have to go to the bathroom." He was supposed to examine my heart but he didn't; he warned me. He had courage, civil courage, I call that. I went out and ran through Kitzbühel—at fourteen you can run quickly, no? The two *Hässlers* [thugs][8] came after me. Of course they couldn't run as fast as I could. At the ticket office at the train station they were punching the tickets. I went up to the guy, punched my ticket, ran into the car, and the doors closed. I had incredible luck. I arrived back in Fieberbrunn and of course no one knew I was *Mischling* there. So I packed my bags and rode back to Berlin. There was an air raid in Munich. Back then the trains were packed and had no windows. After twelve hours you start to collapse from fatigue, but you can't fall because there are so many people crammed together. I had to go to the South Station, then to the North Station with heavy baggage. I asked a troop leader whether I could check the bag through because I couldn't carry it any more. This bag was all I had, and I knew that I couldn't go out and buy anything to replace it, as things weren't available. I had no "point cards" left for buying merchandise. I couldn't check it through, but the bag went through every man's hand in the company and was passed on through the North Station. When I arrived in Berlin there was a preliminary air raid alarm and everybody was already back in the basement. This was my luck because they couldn't see me arrive. When I reached home in East Berlin my mother screamed, "Oh no, what now?" I said, "Don't worry. I'll hide." I couldn't stand it any more—they were persecuting me in Austria as well. They were organized through and through—one thing they were capable of—you can't take that away from them. Today they're still not worth anything, excuse me. We had a weekend house in Mahlsdorf Süd [part of Berlin that was in East Germany/the Soviet Occupation Zone] that belonged to my stepfather. He built a basement hole where there were shelves to store food, as back in those days you would can food—we had a garden from which we got fruit. And there I was sitting on the ladder; I couldn't

straighten up. Mom put the carpet again over the trapdoor and put a
chair over that—there were no windows, only a little trapdoor to bring
in air. I lived there until the Russians marched in, May 8, 1945. I waited
for them as my liberators. But you can't imagine how disappointed I was.

My mother wanted me to study. As a "half-breed first degree" I
wasn't allowed to study. It wasn't an option. I couldn't go to *Gymnasium*
[college prep school]. I was an apprentice for a technical draftsman. Then
I had to escape. When the Russians came, my mom sent me to Humboldt
University. I was so stupid that I didn't know the German Democratic
Republic [DDR] was building their communism on Herder's philosophy. I didn't know back then, otherwise, I would have chosen Herder as
my topic. I chose Gottlieb Klopstock, the man with the odes.[9] That was
completely off base so they didn't accept me in the university. My paper
was off the party lines. My mother was shocked. The one thing they
could say about me: I carried no traces of a National Socialist because I
had been persecuted.

The population was starving after the war; we had a lot of hunger. I
was employed by the magistrate and earned Allied money. [Her Communist stepfather probably was able to prove that she and her family were
innocent, not only anti-Nazis but even of the correct political persuasion.]
I was only fifteen. The mayor, Assmus, came out of a camp. He was a
Communist. One of the cows died in the summer and we didn't have
cooling houses. So Assmus wanted to share the cow with the population
so everyone had something to eat. The commander was always drunk on
vodka. I don't remember his name, unfortunately. One should always write
down life events. The commander said, "*Nyet. Nyet*" concerning the cow.
Assmus divided the cow. The commander found out and put Assmus in
solitary confinement for fourteen days and took away his office and honors.
[She is disillusioned by the way the Russian commander treated the
German Communist mayor.] I was a young person; I had high ideals and
didn't understand that. It was a time of chasing down Nazis. All the Nazis
were liquidated by the Russians, which I could understand though I never
betrayed anyone. I didn't want anything to do with it. It would have been
below my human dignity to betray other people. The ones who wanted
names were Russians, but I was still German. I was born in Berlin and I

never would have given a Nazi away to a Russian. When they found one, I had nothing to do with it. And then the question arose: What will we do with the NS [Nazi] children? Well, you know, those were women forty years old who wanted to kill them too, and there I was the youngest and I said, No, make FDJ people out of them.[10] You have done so much to them already, you took away their father and mother, let them become FDJ people. And they listened to me and did that. It was Berlin, Mahlsdorf—the east sector in Berlin was bad. The following situation happened. They wanted to give me the Communist party book so that I could become Communist. I rejected it. I was so young back then that they didn't do anything to me. As an older person I wouldn't have gotten away with it. But I told them, I'm so young. I don't want to decide yet. That was my excuse. My job with the magistrate ended. My mother yelled. I was the one bringing home the money.

When I was nineteen years old in 1948 I made an attempt to escape from East Berlin. My parents stayed in what was to become the DDR in 1949. On the American side, little death flags indicated minefields. On the Russian side, there were no markers. The Russians were celebrating at the border. I heard screaming and kept running. I didn't know where I was. I ran through a potato field that looked mole-ridden. The Russians wanted people to be blown up. I would have gone up in the air as well if I hadn't been lucky. I got through to the American side, leaned against a tree, and looked back. I thought, "My God. You just went through a minefield."

My mom was still in Mahlsdorf Süd. I worked as a social worker on a farm. I took retirement applications and when the refugees came, I often gave out bread. It was nasty—lots of lice. Russians came and there I met a woman, a translator, and learned Russian. I didn't trust the official translator; he had that kind of face one couldn't give a loaf of bread to. I rejected the Communist party. I don't believe in clubs and parties. I'm not interested. A person needs to realize himself as an individual, to get his head in motion, his spirit ruling over all, and to not conceive of himself as part of the masses, just accepting everything. If you don't think on your own, you become stupid. There's a cultural cliché: A German who's not involved in politics poses no trouble for the state. They are part of the problem. They are the reason I have a repulsion for the masses. The masses fall easily into mass hysteria, into this or that, allow themselves to be directed. They need a leader. Each person is an individual. Each person should develop his own character and get his faculties and guiding spirit *[spiritus rector]* going, put them into action, and critically view everything presented to him, not get a sense of self through *Vermassung,* from becoming one with the masses. That is something detrimental. Everyone should develop the ability to express himself in words in order to intervene, in order to influence events. So when you have the chance to make an impact, you can. I had bad luck; I was not able to develop myself. I would have liked to learn languages— I had the talent—but I had to work and earn money.

I am not against communism, just organization. There are good Communists, who want positive things, and there's communism that makes the masses daft, and I consider that dangerous. You need to protect yourself. At fifteen and a half, I saw what the Russians did to their own and to Germans, an admirable Communist like Assmus. You can choose to be nasty, base, and oppressive, but you don't have to be. The war made people so awful. And the population was starving, but the commander wouldn't give up the cow. He celebrated his victory with vodka. He said, *"Nyet!"* That was pure nastiness. Why? People are just people—whether you're a doctor or whatever, you're still a person. But when you don't prove yourself as a human, then to me you're an idiot. There are those who are highly educated who are idiots. You have to watch out. Through all I've lived through I've become careful. Basically, I've become an *Eigenbrötler* [a loner or eccentric].

Later on, I had a partner for ten years. We did not marry. He died here in my lap. It doesn't have anything to do with the persecution, but these events can still affect people. He had a brain tumor, surgery, and for eight hours, I supervised the machines. When he was thirsty, I gave him something to drink. He learned how to walk by my side. We weren't married and you don't need a piece of paper to be a harmonious pair. My dad is legally married and it's not a happy union.

But my partner died in my lap and I was so in shock that I wanted to commit suicide. There was no one left who loved me anymore. Naturally, my father loved me. That's clear. But receiving mail two to three times in a year and with 365 days, there's just not enough contact. I felt alone and by myself. My partner died August 8, 1989. I lay for thirty-six days and did not eat, but I was stupid and drank water. Maybe it was meant to be that way so that my father, who had survived everything, wouldn't get a notice that I'd killed myself. A friend of mine saved me. They put me in the state psychiatric hospital. For an intelligent person, that was so humiliating. But it was my fault. Why would I want to kill myself? During this time, everything becomes a mess—the dates and events. *It is always good that one doesn't remember events so exactly, so horrible things can't be remembered.*

I wanted to write a book about my experiences. But then I decided there was even much suffering after the Second World War. There were fifty-four wars in the world after the second war. People had absolutely not learned anything from the destruction. People are neither noble nor humanitarian. They are nothing. It is possible to tempt humans to use any weapon. It is possible to convince them to abuse others while performing the worst deeds. And what's the use of that? When I was a young girl, I thought, If I had a child now—I could have had children because I was healthy and always loved children as I still do today—could I protect it from war and persecution? [She makes a connection to her mother as the cause of *her* persecution, when, in fact, she was persecuted because of her father.] I forbade myself to have a child. Because if you can't protect it from the world, you have no right to put it into the world. You have to assure a child a decent life, and if you can't take responsibility for that then you must not have a child. For these reasons, I didn't allow myself to have biological children. I asked myself, "Can you have kids? Can you protect them from war and persecution?" "No," I answered. I'm not going to expose my children to the filth of the world. Only someone who's been through terror would think that. In a normal family, they'd just want to continue the genetic line, to have children. I didn't act without first reflecting. Instead, I took twins out of a shelter because I always wanted to have children. I had to take them forcibly like a lion.

My double obligation is my twins. They are lovely kids. They're one-quarter Indonesian. This was the Nazi way to describe people, and I admit I fall into using this jargon. I received these children when they were seven. I met them when they were four. I saved them from the filth and feces. The mother was Sylvia, half Indonesian from her mother, half Dutch from her father. In Hamburg, she was exotic. The boys tugged on their mother's skirt when they wanted something. I taught them to speak. [Apparently, Sylvia cleaned in the apartment building and left the boys to play with Ruth.] Sylvia was taken away by a young, blue-eyed guy. Her husband was an alcoholic. He started drinking in Chad [Africa]. There was reason to believe he hit her, or at least, it wasn't a happy marriage. Her husband had an inn and had to keep it open twenty-four hours. It was renovated in 1961. One day he took the kids to the orphanage. I said, "Why not give them to me?" He didn't give the kids to me because he knew that Sylvia knew me. I thought, What would have happened if they'd learned to speak in an orphanage? I wasn't a foster mother but a genuine parent. I took over custody of the kids. I gave up my job to care for them. I had to rent a bigger apartment. I had to work with them because of problems they'd had with their violent father who had beaten them. If someone had not stepped in, I don't know what would have happened. I took them out of the home and put them into a special school for retarded children. They were *Milieu geschädigt,* damaged by their surroundings. I had to take them to school. They used to beat their heads on the wooden headboards before they slept, so I spent nights by their side. But I succeeded. I gave them tea to quiet them in the evenings.

I am not religious today. I'm atheist. I was at a meeting organized by the Catholic church where they discussed categorization and its problems. Each religion—Catholic, Jewish, Protestant, and Muslim—sees itself as the right one. We must reenvision, resee, abandon categories so there's less conflict. Warfare results from thinking "My way is the only way." Use of religion in politics is a pretext, a way to start wars, create division. It's a scheme.

There was unemployment before Hitler. Jews were the scapegoats. I wrote that in my childhood memory book. Hitler was looking for "guilty ones," so he used the minority in his country as scapegoats. Jewish people were blamed for everything. This is from my childhood memory book; it's not a diary. I wrote, "National Socialists gained power in 1933. They're looking for scapegoats for their bad situation. They found that the minority of their country had caused unemployment and poverty. They invented the *Übermenschen* and *Untermenschen*.[11] These Germans were all failures. They found support in this party. They mistreated Jews wherever they could."

Hitler wanted to conquer the whole world. In school I had to learn a poem that said, "I'm born to feel German," totally geared toward German thinking. "First comes my people then all the many others. First comes my homeland and then the world." That is an attitude, can you believe it? I still feel sorry today for those who learned and internalized that. Those who have attached their identity to this attitude, "I'm great because I'm German," are boastful.

Do you know that Germans have learned absolutely nothing? There are still anti-Semites as before. The youth are, in part, open-minded and informed about what happened. But the majority is easily tempted toward National Socialism. One can see it with the neo-Nazis. I know that the Americans gave the Nazis Persil certificates.[12] I don't know if it was 1954 or 1956. Because they were "pardoned" through the Persil certificates, Nazis sit in the critical position as bastions, as protection against Bolshevism. The SS people put their fortunes in the factories and stabilized the economy, and they had the say in West Germany. Now we have the reunification, and in our government the former "Bolshevikies" [Communists] have their say, and the National Socialists have theirs. We have the extremes together. Not all of them fit the stereotypes of their group. There are exceptions. You can't generalize and put them all in one basket. I wouldn't ever do that. If someone tells me so and so is a certain age I won't assume he's a nationalist. If I know the type of household from which he came, I'd know if he were morally educated. God bless, I think you, Cynthia, would be one of the educated. I would never attack them or anything. Ever since I was young I always said not to live with hate. It's impossible to function with hate.

Unfortunately, I never felt anything good about my mother. I always thought she might be a stepmother. I was left alone with her. I grew up scared of her. I never had an intimate relationship with her. Never. She was very strict with me. [She yells this sentence.] Only when I was thirty did I forgive her. Before that, I was unable. Then the relationship changed. I sent her parcels from the West because in East Germany there was nothing to eat. I had to support my parents. My mother had always taken care of me, and I had never forgotten that, so I always sent packages. It was clear I would do this because we had shared money and ration cards. She took care of me and made it possible for me to flee. She was responsible and industrious, but my misguided upbringing was horrid. She seemed to enjoy inflicting punishment. But she was too young; she couldn't free herself from naiveté. With my twins, I took the right path, brought them up differently. Even when things went wrong, I was positive. Even when they spilled milk. When we went Easter egg hunting, I'd show them the eggs. The kids are self-confident. That's wonderful. One is a healthcare practitioner. The other runs a press agency. I put all of my efforts into raising them. I was here; I didn't want them raised by TV.

Everything that was Jewish my mother tried to educate out of me, but you can't educate that out of me. That word "Jude" was a *Schimpfwort,* an insult, no? Among the Jews, you say *Juredisch,* not *Judisch,* which is an insult, a disparaging word. These were words ingrained in people's minds at that time. Anti-Semites say, *"Ach, die Juden, die Juden."* Fifty-four wars have occurred after World War II. Suffering from natural catastrophes has occurred. We can't forget. When anti-Semitism is brought up, the Germans wonder why, as so much has happened since, and the Germans too suffered from the war. They say, That's been some time ago, why talk about it now? I came into this world of suffering and now nobody wants to know about it. The focus today is Bosnia, which is understandable. But somehow that doesn't make the sufferings of Jews smaller.

≈ ≈ ≈

How I feel as a woman in Germany I relate to the emancipation. [She comments on the outdated use of the words *Frau* and *Fraulein*.] In the 1960s, people asked me if I was married and they'd say, no, then, you're *Fraulein* Yost. I could never become *Frau* Yost. I had to get married to graduate to *Frau*. Silly. I never married at all. I had a strict upbringing: Orthodox, Jewish, Lutheran, and I suffered from rape. You can imagine how I felt at the time. My mother said, after I was raped at age fifteen, "The best thing has been taken away from you." Can you imagine? The attitudes from when I grew up and those of today are so different. I can speak with you today; it's a freer sexual atmosphere. Then I was very inhibited and I didn't know anything. At twenty-one, I saw a naked man and was horrified. When I was raped, they had pistols. I couldn't see anything. They pointed pistols right at me. It was awful. Before the war, I was in the basement, and after the war, in the attic hiding from the Russians. The women were defenseless. But afterward, nobody talked about it. About rape. It was a taboo. Several women were with me in the attic—there was not enough room to stand up straight. This was a problem in my childhood—not being able to stand up straight or sit upright. My only wish in life was to stand up straight. The Russians were drunk and rousting in the house and we had to be quiet. The door looked like part of the wall. We opened it and saw khaki uniforms outside and closed the door.[13] All the women who were raped had to come to terms with it. There was no psychotherapy. It was silly what my mother said— that the most beautiful thing was taken away from me. Is that supposed to be some consolation? I wasn't able to absorb what she meant. I'm sorry to talk so much. [She laughs.]

I don't associate the Americans with liberation, as the Russians liberated us and whom, ironically, I had to fear. We always asked ourselves, Why didn't they [Americans] bomb the camps, or at least the train tracks, to stop the suffering more quickly? Why destroy the civilian population in the streets? The horror came from the undignified manner of the deaths in the camps. The people in there had experienced such misery that one can't even imagine it. A quick death would have been something humane. Then one asks over and over again, "Why don't they bomb the camps?" They were never bombed. That was also a question.

That *is* a question. It's an ethically difficult standpoint to take. One with horror, horror without end. Of course, some have lived, thank God. But for their entire lives they'll suffer. My father, for example. He still cries today at ninety-four years old. Why does the poor man still have to cry? Why? He didn't do any crime. He wasn't an inmate. They put him in prison just because he was Jewish. Well, that's an argument. I quit writing down my childhood experiences as I told myself my family were *becovete Leute* [honorable people]. They were principled humans but would anybody believe me? What if some *Leberwurst* [jerk] comes and says, "I am *Heil Leberwurst* [self-important]" and says to me about my writings, "You're lying," then I'm in the same stupid position as always. So, why take the risk? As I say, my family were honorable people.[14] They were honest citizens. Even if you're in a lower class you can be honorable if you go to church. Retired people, like myself, are not appreciated; they don't have a good image. I am an outsider again.

An outsider is always in opposition. In Hamburg they're called *Quiddje*.[15] If you're not born in Hamburg, if you came in by train, you're a *Quiddje*. So the Hamburgers say. Outsiders are always in conflict with themselves. With other people, I have always tried to get along. I mean, I have not lived in conflict with other people; at work I adjusted and always worked in jobs as a salesperson. You know I come from a private business household. I always learned my jobs within fourteen days and studied during my working hours and on evenings at home. That is also stress. In this way I was hired to sell clothes, jewelry, and German health insurance that I sold independently. I have never spoken about myself. I've never said, "I'm half Jewish and was persecuted." That is no one else's business—that is my intimate life. I wouldn't know how that would be taken because I didn't know who at work was a Nazi or wasn't. One couldn't have known, and I never asked. I just did my job. Today there are still many Nazis. That's why anti-Semitism is so powerful. No one passed down values or ideals to the young neo-Nazis. Frequently as kids they were beaten. They were hit in their parents' home. They come from "uncivilized" households. That is an assumption on my part. Parents didn't set any ideals or values. The kids were put on the wrong track. In gangs, they have a community and with their beer-drinking colleagues they feel comfortable. They have a community where they're accepted and where they're wanted for their own personalities. That's the problem. Because you see I have taken care that the children of Nazis have not been killed. For that I took care. I didn't want their children killed. I don't approve of killing children. The kids of the Nazis are not the neo-Nazis. This generation is not the neo-Nazis, which would be an easier explanation. Then they have kids. This way, I may have even enabled the Nazis to develop again by saving Nazis without intending that. I was intelligent as a young person, and I always thought that peace was essential, but for that to happen, one has to keep peace. But in those households, peace wasn't kept. I experienced that here three years ago in the Goldbek Markt [a market area in Hamburg]. I experienced those big guys, like the SS men, always really big, and they talked about the financial assets of the Jewish people in America. You know what I did? I jumped in front of those three guys and I spit and said, "You don't know what you're talking about. Don't talk like that. They, the Nazis, are the ones who stole the Jewish money." I can yell very loudly, projecting my voice from my stomach like an actor on stage, so loud that the whole marketplace could hear. The guys just left.

I don't think anti-Semitism was strong before 1933 in Germany or that there was always a hidden feeling about this in society. Among the German National Socialists, yes, but not in the general population. There, no. Because they liked buying from Jews. They loved Jews. The Jewish businessmen were popular as bosses. Employees liked working for my father. Why? They were treated like family. When somebody worked for him, he didn't suppress him but treated him like a human being. All Jews did that, and that's why the population basically liked them, but not by the German Nationalists, not by them.

The mood that turned people against the Jews was, for one, the *Hetzpropaganda* [inflammatory propaganda]. [She repeats this phrase five times.] This was horrible. The *Völkischer Beobachter* [people's observer][16] showed the Jews with such a nose and sitting on the top of a bag of money and with such a stomach and so on. [She displays with gestures.] And today—three years ago—they were standing again in the marketplace, such tall guys. Those weren't neo-Nazis; they were National Socialists, do you understand? I am stronger within myself because I do believe in God, although I say I'm atheist and keep a distance from everywhere, do you understand? I am very strong inside because I tell myself that God is with me, and then I am definitely strong, you see, because they all said, "My goodness, do you have courage!"

You know the Zingi[17] were also killed in the camps and have not been reimbursed for any money they lost, or just a little bit. One time I spoke up for the Gypsies in the marketplace. Some people were standing up for the dead Kurds and I stood up for the dead Armenians, Zingis, and Jews—and they all said, "Well, Ruth. Why do you do all that?" Yes, I was screaming loudly and the Zingis drove their cars before my door with their families—children and women—and were happy that a woman had spoken for the Zingis [she sort of laughs], because whoever does speak for a Gypsy? Nobody anymore. Yes, Sinti and Roma they call themselves.[18] They were *Sternenvolk,* people of the stars. They went with their carts through the world and maybe they stole a few apples once. What's the big deal? But they begged! Oh well, so? They were a traveling people. They are not comfortable because they don't adjust, don't send their children to school, so they are not accepted. They speak their own language and nobody else speaks the Zingi language. Although the Gypsies did a lot of crap—criminal stuff—that has nothing to do with it. They are humans also. [She laughs.] I feel connected to them because they too were in the concentration camps, and because they too went through such horrible things. Whoever made it through so much suffering because of Hitler, to him I feel bound. Three years ago [1991] I was very political. Then, the *Grünen,* a political party, said to me, be more careful, yes? I took my money out of the bank once and said, "My entire money in silver so that the Nazis, who are sitting on the top, won't eat themselves fat."[19] Because the Nazis still sit today in the banks and everywhere, and the SS people have factories and so on here in West Germany. They are *Bollwerke,* fortification against Bolshevism. I was only political to a degree, that is only in this year, otherwise not, but only with the provocation that the Nazis were again blowing out the same slogans as in 1933. They too should have learned; otherwise it would have remained quiet in Germany. Do you understand how I mean that? I felt challenged, provoked, because I told myself I was always quiet, I never said anything. But to revert to fascism again? No, not again.

People were apolitical. They went to the election and did not know what they were voting for. This is no excuse. I always went to elections and have always thought about which party I will vote for here in the German Federal Republic [BRD]; now that we are a reunified Germany. This is all different, and they have already become more brazen. You can see that in the press. They are unified again. They are already more arrogant in the press. [She says this twice.]

≈ ≈ ≈

I still owe you an answer about what I thought about the Americans. You know, for me, America was something quite big. I had a German American friend and she got a care parcel. I was allowed to eat some of the chocolate. But I didn't know that we had been sent laxative chocolate and [laughing] the bathroom was busy all night and for me America was somehow something really huge, if you ask me, yes, something overwhelming. What does one hear about America today? I mean about the teenage criminality, about the slums and so on.

For me, it was the most wonderful thing that so many groups live together in the United States. When I was sitting in the East, I always thought, "How can I get into the American sector?" Do you understand? I first drove to the American sector in Berlin. It was a city divided into four sectors. America was for me something very large. [She repeats this.] But also promising. It was the land of unlimited opportunities.[20] Yes, just like you always heard, but now I know there are dark sides as well, naturally. That will always be the case in a large country. That's how it is in Russia now. They are falling completely apart. And they are falling apart within and are certainly trying to force through their dictatorship again and start a war because of that. When I was young, for me, America was something gargantuan. How can I say?

I had not thought about emigration. I was young. I didn't think about it. I also did not say about Americans "you're always so bad to blacks." Other people have said this. I did not think that as a young person. We read *Uncle Tom's Cabin* later on. I educated and informed myself about each country through literature. That was a given for me. This way I also raised my boys to be international, but not going toward the Communist train of thought [She laughs], that too is international. And the neo-Nazis call themselves international as well although they curse the Turkish people. You see everybody calls himself international and I do that too. [She laughs.] But I really think this way: For me a human is a human. If he really proves himself to be a decent person, he is human. That's that.

Emigration was not an issue because I could not leave my parents, and I didn't know what there could have been for me in a foreign country.[21] What would confront me there? I had to take care of my parents, had to send parcels, and I had my small income and living, so I lived here. And then, before 1956, in April 1949, I came here to Hamburg?—the Persil certificate had not been issued yet and then the Nazis had diminished. Then everything was completely different. The Nazis only became stubborn and firm again when they were really challenged. Because here they had nuclear rockets standing, you know, aiming at Russia, everybody knows that, and the Nazis got always cheekier and cheekier. At first, when I came here it was not like that. Then I had to struggle with other difficulties. I arrived here and had nothing. I had *Igelit* purse and *Igelit* sandals, that is not leather, it is some plastic, and one pair of sheer tights and one outfit and a few furs[22]—that was all, and a toothbrush and a Bible, and I still have the Bible. [She gets the Bible.] I had it during my escape. This is my Bible, and that is something I will not give away. One toothbrush, the Bible, the *Igelit* purse and the *Igelit* sandals—those were my only belongings.

The German people had to be given a chance to establish themselves out of the ruins after the war. This had to be. One felt bound to the West and especially to the Americans who were rebuilding Germany. With American money we were built again and it was a humane act, I want to say, and the best thing is that peace was maintained all these years. That is very good politics, very good politics. And *Hohlköpfe* [empty heads] are everywhere, aren't they? They have become so strong again with their Nazi and SS ideas. It was contained in them; a thing that was passed on or inherited and it will stay that way. The people themselves have learned; the people have become more open-minded. I'm talking about simple folk. They have become more open-minded and more easily accessible, and those in the higher positions, they feel strengthened in their spirit and they see their spirit come back again. The bulk of the people act more responsibly than one may think. But the politics. Adenauer had no other choice than to make politics with the West and with the money of America. West Germany has been rebuilt, and one shouldn't forget this. But most people are directly anti-American because of TV. Now they haven't just heard about it but have also seen it. The people are manipulated through TV. Everything that is reported, the people believe because it is manipulated, made believable; so they all believe. They don't glean their knowledge from literature or from true insights into life.

Out of the ruins, Adenauer had no other choice than to behave like he did and he couldn't engage in any other [type of] politics; he also went to Russia and made sure that the German prisoners were freed, thanks be to God, and one cannot blame Adenauer for bad politics. Because in Austria, a Nazi was sitting in first position again, at once. You know, Nazis won't die out because there was an entire force of them. They escaped to South America and they probably also live in North America and everywhere else. They are everywhere in the world. Nazis had to hide and cover their bad deeds. They hid everywhere and infected the people, no matter where they were. Anti-Semitism is in the whole world, especially in Russia and Poland. Everywhere. Not just in Germany. The murder done in "factories" and the fact that it was programmed was only here. And that with Goethe! But as I said in my political diatribe, one spirit alone is not sufficient for the entire people.

CHAPTER FOUR

RUTH WILMSCHEN

*"In the Nazi years,
I acquired an elephant skin and could
handle any kind of treatment"*

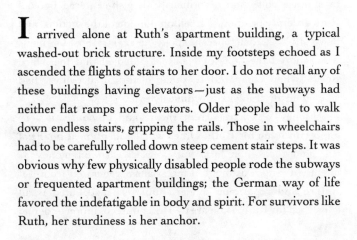

I arrived alone at Ruth's apartment building, a typical washed-out brick structure. Inside my footsteps echoed as I ascended the flights of stairs to her door. I do not recall any of these buildings having elevators—just as the subways had neither flat ramps nor elevators. Older people had to walk down endless stairs, gripping the rails. Those in wheelchairs had to be carefully rolled down steep cement stair steps. It was obvious why few physically disabled people rode the subways or frequented apartment buildings; the German way of life favored the indefatigable in body and spirit. For survivors like Ruth, her sturdiness is her anchor.

Ruth, a former schoolteacher, was a friend of Ruth Yost. Her apartment was compressed and compactly furnished. She wore an orange wool jacket and matching skirt. An antique circle pin lay over her heart. Her thick, curly, reddish-brown hair stuck out all over her head like a helmet. Her mannerisms were jerky—she took her glasses off and on and thrust her hands through her hair. During the interview, she clacked her dentures through every sentence, often making her rambling stories even harder to follow. Ruth sat at her kitchen table with copious notes in hand, from which she read her history chronologically. She was insistent upon visual representation to accompany her narrative. She had carefully placed her pictures into numerous photo albums divided between Jewish and non-Jewish grandparents, which, along with her wall hanging, served to augment her identity split. The looming tapestry of an apple tree, gray on one side and white on the other with various sized leaves and fruits, divided a wall. She flipped through pictures of grandchildren and her two daughters and many pictures of her pesky poodle who interrupted us with whines, licks, and his paws scratching our legs. Ruth predictably stopped midthought to converse with the dog, accommodating his behavior as if he were the prodigal son.

I noticed a menorah centered on a bookshelf, surrounded by quite a collection of primarily Jewish-centered books.[1] Ruth ardently positions herself on the side of the victims, and like Ruth Yost, for a time, she spoke out against those Germans who ignored the facts of Nazism or denied that the Third Reich, when compared to other historical atrocities, had assembled anything extraordinarily evil.

Money was a recurrent theme and obviously a very important issue for Ruth. Other women mentioned financial ruin and reparation loss, but none dwelled on money as intently as she. Postmodern materialism generated from TV culture and reparation money "unfairly" distributed is all enmeshed for Ruth. Both are tied to a nonrecognition or denial of the past, which has led to a troublesome relationship with her immediate family. Outsiders might see Ruth's atypical behavior toward her granddaughter and son-in-law as intolerant; after all, her granddaughter was only thirteen years old, and her son-in-law had a new wife. Ruth has tiptoed uncomfortably around their lives, whereas she would like to secure their understanding of her history, to dent their consciousness, to make an impact on their lives. Instead, she yells, gets confused, and despairs.

Ruth survived the deaths of her entire family; only a granddaughter remains. A seemingly common task, the taking care of her dog, has helped her to cope with excessive tragedy. Ruth had written notes on a small legal pad in order to follow her life in as orderly a fashion as possible; yet her conversation was the longest and most scattered of all the women. By the time I found the core of Ruth's experiences during the Third Reich gleaned from so much excessive, almost child-like talk, I wondered if she had unconsciously tried to muddle the narration of her life. It seemed the more she tried to make sense of what she was saying, the more digressive and unpredictable she became in her conversation. Her notes, which were marked off with dates, were meant to ground her to the facts, but she did not follow them. Now and then she picked up the sheets and tried to locate herself again at some point in the past. The anger toward her father, former husband, and son-in-law, each who tried to control her, contrasted sharply with her intense love for her mother, who survived Theresienstadt (a work camp) but later died in a freak accident, and her two daughters, one who died as a child and the other in childbirth. The tyrannical elements of Hitler's patriarchal machine were evident in the men in Ruth's life: She never shook off their power despite her own success as an independent woman. Ruth had to get married because she was pregnant and later, she discovered her husband had been in the SS.

Ruth's responsibility to her mother kept her in Germany. She nursed her sick mother after her return from Theresienstadt. As long as her mother needed her, Ruth felt compelled to remain at her side, even though she had the urge to flee. After her mother's death, Ruth, despite her opposition to it, became caretaker for her father. She became extremely angry toward her son-in-law after the death of her daughter, his wife, Helga. Ruth did not have a close relationship with her granddaughter, which she blames on her son-in-law, as he never allowed her to fully explain their origins to her granddaughter. She remembers that her mother and her daughter Helga had a wonderful relationship, and Ruth simply wanted the same bond between herself and her granddaughter. Ruth suffers great difficulty trusting and understanding the behavior of others. The Third Reich symbolized for Ruth an acute helplessness; the chaos it rammed into her world had far-reaching, long-term effects—she would never live the life of her choosing.

≈ ≈ ≈

I am so happy that you asked me what is hanging here in the middle of the wall. You are the first visitor to ask me about this. This is a *Mischlingsbaum,* a tree for half-breed children. A dark side. A bright side. Gray as well as orange. This is a *Masurischer Apfelbaum* [Masuren apple tree].[2] You have to think about something and put it in this tree—all the things that happened in your life. I didn't have many good and important life events. I added to it, as you can see. I embroidered extra pieces that weren't originally there in these empty spaces. Now I can see when this happened, *that* time as a kid, or *that* was a miscarriage. Frau Yost laughed about it. Frau Yost asked, "Which is the Jewish side, the dark or the light?" She doesn't have any sense for it. But this is my life tree.

I was born in 1925, Ruth Ogrusch. My father had already been a teacher for two years in the elementary school, and my mother married him at eighteen. However, I came sometime later. My mother didn't really have a job. She wanted to become a pharmacist at one time, but because of her early marriage she did absolutely nothing. It was also not planned that I should come so quickly, however, you see I came, no? The beginning of my childhood was very good. My father's parents were workers in Wuppertal. My mother was born of Jewish parents in Wuppertal-Süd, a much richer area. Both grandparents were not happy about my parents' decision to get married because of their difference in origin, but later my grandparents often were together.

I was not baptized when I was born. I remain, in theory, unbaptized. My parents were, as one says, "without confession." My father came from a very religious Protestant family, but at seventeen my father went to war on his own volition and at nineteen had fully lost his belief in the loving God. He then had vast difficulties with his mother, my grandmother, who was religious. My father believed in nothing. My mother and her parents were not religious Jews. So we were neutral, one could say. When I was five, a good acquaintance came and said to my father, "Werner, let your daughter be baptized." "Why?" my father said. "Well, it's better." It turned out later that it *was* better if you had some Christian sacrament because perhaps you were handled differently by the Nazis. So at five years old I was baptized. At the time, I didn't understand it at all. I stood there as water was poured over my head, and suddenly I was Protestant, no? My non-Jewish grandmother was naturally very agreeable. She dragged me every Sunday to the church. I was confused and because of that I became more involved in the Protestant religion later. I thought it was related to a special purpose, although it was only something someone else had suggested.

I can say that I had four loving grandparents. These are the two grandpas. [She shows their picture.] That is Opa David and that the other. This one [presumably David] was a merchant and had a cigar shop, an affiliate of the famous Tabakbär in Mannheim. He led the Wuppertal division. The other grandpa was a civil servant. This grandpa also had done a variety of things with his one son, the 200 percent Nazi, and my father. I never grasped the pro-Nazism at the time. I knew nothing. There were only civil servants in my father's family. I had two pairs of loving grandparents: one, so-called non-Jewish and the other, Jewish. They eventually got along very well; every week they went walking together. My favorite grandpa was David, my mother's father—a unique and totally fantastic man. It's unbelievable how many thousands of stories he made up. Grandpa David, whom I loved so much, died in 1934. God be praised! For a while we couldn't make sense of why he died—afterward we could. It was the best thing that could have happened. He wouldn't have been able to stand what followed. In 1934 there was the first Goering[3] speech and Goering was yelling and started using words like *Judenschweine* [Jewish pigs] and so on. My grandfather listened carefully. My father came into the room and said, "David, don't pay attention. He won't remain in power for a long time." My father had always thought Hitler wouldn't last long. Yes, I apologize for my father because later he could have acted against the deportation of my mother. I have to say it again and again. He thought too well of this Hitler.

Grandpa David's widow, Grandma Olga, moved to a single-room apartment near ours. She was very healthy. She would have been a hundred had she not been deported and killed. She had some fear and always said: "I am called for Eternity. We all have our time." And then my father began to scold, "Olga, don't talk that way. It's not so bad." I heard *that* my entire childhood. Oma Olga already had conflicts with her fellow lodgers. Most of them were, unfortunately, Nazis. One must be lucky to be left in peace and quiet. Good Germans existed. There were also Germans who judged people solely by appearance (from pictures in *Der Stürmer*). My grandmother didn't look especially Jewish. I have a photo. Here are the Jewish grandparents. There are the non-Jewish grandparents. I still have all of these. This grandpa was twelve years older than this grandma. There I am with my father. There I am as a small child with my mother. And these are my parents. That was after the cottage, the Nazis destroyed their weekend house. Without reason, I know now, but I don't know the details. They took out the chimney and the oven collapsed, and the whole thing burned.

[Ruth shows pictures drawn by her father.] My father's family has a famous ancestor, the painter Adolph Menzel.[4] All my other ancestors have been either goldsmiths or painting teachers. But I didn't inherit this ability. Here's a picture of my father. He was a young teacher in Wuppertal. One of his students came to school in black clothes. Once my father asked him the reason why he wore black. He said, "My father died from pneumonia in a concentration camp." Then my father said, "The fat Goering is the father of the concentration camps." For this sentence he had to go into prison in August 1934. After four days he came back. From that time on, my father developed anxieties.

The school where my father taught was in a working-class district—KPD [Communist Party of Germany], SPD [Social Democratic Party of Germany] and so on—and at that time there was nothing in the air about hatred of Jews. [Ruth looks at her notes.] In the first year we noticed absolutely nothing. Not at all. And then I started school. I didn't attend the school where my father was. They had fears I'd not be educated properly. They believed a child should go to a school other than where his parents taught. Later on, when I had been in the *Volksschule* [elementary school] for four years, I couldn't, unfortunately, go on to *Gymnasium* [college prep school] because at that time the Nuremberg Laws already had been instated. "Half-breeds of the first degree" couldn't go to the higher class. In 1935, when they enrolled me in the middle school, called *Realschule* today, a few difficult times began. The schoolmaster who was a definite Nazi came into the class. [Mimics in deep voice]: "Who here is still not in the BDM [Nazi youth organization]?" I always stood up. Otherwise, everyone was in the BDM. That was that. Afterward the teacher said to the principal, "We know now that nothing has changed. Must you ask again and again?" My class teacher was pleasant, but the principal, Knut von Horfe, was a Nazi. He insulted everyone named Eva, Ruth, or Esther. [Mimics principal in deep voice]: "How can a German girl be called that?" That was really awful.

This Nazi headmaster made my life difficult as I was the only one who wasn't a member of the BDM, and so children also began to tease me, which they did if somebody like me demonstrated in class they were an achiever. Later on, I wrote extra bad essays because I knew that high marks would make someone jealous. In this class, there were also three Jewish girls. One of them was Hella Altgenug, who later appeared on Höfer's *Mittagsrunde* as Hella Pick.[5] She emigrated early and the other two, along with their families, were exterminated. I wrote to Werner Höfer to get Hella Pick's address. I saw her in this Breakfast Circle with Werner Höfer. Do you know what this means? Werner Höfer was suddenly unmasked as a Nazi and over decades he hosted this *Presseclub* that was broadcast on various German channels. There were many speakers—Inga Deutschkron was always with Werner Höfer, at least twenty times.[6] We thought about Werner, *that* is someone who remained good to the Jews. Suddenly, after many years, it turned out Werner is an old Nazi and had published his pro-Nazi writings. Naturally, you become mistrustful. Also this Hella Altgenug went right away to London although her parents owned houses. I mean, one could, if one had money, escape from everything. You had to have money in order to flee and also have as many relatives as possible because you had to have guarantors abroad. We couldn't think about that at all.

In October 1937 my father received a letter saying that he should separate from his non-Aryan wife. Otherwise, he would be forced to retire. It sounded mild; everybody thought he'd retire and go into another profession. My father said, "Divorce is out of the question. As an old soldier, I should be able to keep my wife."

My parents never had conflicts and my father would have never left my mother. My father immediately complained about his upcoming forced retirement and wrote a letter in protest. My father never would have said anything against Nazis in his lectures. He would have been careful not to do it. He was on his guard. He had always been very proper. My father reminded them that for four years he had given his bones for the Germans in the world war as a first class and second class soldier. And he didn't do that out of enthusiasm. Probably when he volunteered he was enthusiastic, but he was scarcely seventeen. I still have the official letter sent to my father from the second-in-command to the Führer. Here is the paper. It says at the top NSDAP.[7] It was by decree. He [Hitler] had not signed it himself. It says, "In your letter of October 5, 1937, you want me to reverse our decision concerning retirement. According to the Law of the Reconstitution, going back to work as a civil servant is disallowed." This law was established to remove people from the civil service who were living in "mixed marriages." That's why nobody who had a Jewish wife was allowed in pedagogy. This law was established. I have it written down and I'll read it to you: "I want to make the point that we have to follow necessary steps according to paragraph 5 and 6 of this law in order to maintain the interests of the civil services. We decided to retire you but this decision does not reflect any defamation." [Ruth thinks these words are just *Wortklauberei,* quibbling.]

To put the letter in simple terms: All teachers who had Jewish wives had to leave the school. And now the "highlight" of the letter: "Because of basic considerations [meaning Jewish people are humans of lesser value], I have to refrain from influencing the decision of the administrative office in these cases. That's why I regret that I can't do anything for you under these circumstances."

It's an accident that I still have the document. Here it states that "in the name of the government, I am replying in accordance with paragraph 6 of the laws that govern the reinstatement of the job and civil duties of the *Volksschule* teacher, Weiner Ogrusch, that he remain in retirement." I only want to say, some people from our circle of acquaintances, a master clockmaker and shopkeeper, who were on the Board of Directors of a factory, divorced their "non-Aryan" wives for appearance sake. [Ruth implies they did not legally divorce.] How it later turned out for all of them—whether they were deported or not—I don't know at all. We had parted ways. It worked out for one of the couples; they came back together. But civil servants couldn't do that. Because they got their money from the state, they had to register everywhere. Therefore, they couldn't easily say "Now I'm divorced" whether they actually were or not. There were too many records. It wasn't possible.

We were acquainted with so many families who divorced, for example, but they weren't families of civil servants. Married people get different raises than unmarried people as civil servants; they are, for better or worse, dependent on the state. I have had a difference of opinion over this with Frau Yost. She said, "Be happy that you were born into a family of civil servants." I ask, "How so?" We had a great deal fewer, how should I say, possibilities of doing anything against the Third Reich. And as I said, to my shame, I must admit, many of us thought (and some verbalized), "Ah, that is temporary. Hitler won't last too long." To add to that, my father's brother was a die-hard National Socialist. The break went through the family. That was terrible for my non-Jewish grandmother, very sad. One son spouted "Heil Hitler" and the other spouted nasty phrases against Hitler. My grandmother didn't know what was wrong. She escaped within her Protestant church. She had been through a lot. I grasped that only afterward; only later did I understand. Speaking of the non-Jewish part of my family, and my father's brother, once Adolf Hitler visited Wuppertal and the whole family went to listen to him speak. My uncle, Hans, came back seemingly in a trance because he stood very close to Hitler and saw himself in Hitler's eyes. My grandma said, "Hitler must be a great person when even Hans is enthusiastic about him." I want to make the point that the Nazis had very easily influenced this part of the family. My grandma said, "Oh, Ruth. You'll never be allowed to marry!" She was certain that the *Rassengezetze* [race laws] would endure. Uncle Hans responded, "Oh, sure, she can marry another 'half-bred' Jew."

After my father received this "wonderful" letter that blew him out of the school profession, we had to evacuate the apartment because it was a civil service apartment. These few months were not at all fine. My mother said to my father, *"Ich bin ein Klotz an deinem Bein. Hätten wir uns scheiden lassen"* [I am a millstone around your neck. We should have divorced]. It was dreadful.

Then someone in Düsseldorf at the steelworks union, a good German, who continued to be so during the Nazi time, took care of my father. He gave him a position as factory educator. My father had no clue about how a factory operated, but his position was a teaching one, so he could work with young people. Unfortunately, I don't know who the man was anymore. If only he had come forward and wanted a *Gutachten* [favorable report] as so many did in 1945, I would have assisted him with my best kick and given him a report that stated he had not abetted the Nazis. My father then "went aboard," was well paid, and the state minister of education granted us a half retirement. I can't say much about finances—at that time, we had great losses that were not financial—*that* came with the Gestapo.

Ruin really began before the so-called Kristallnacht in 1939. We still had a Düsseldorfer aunt, one of the many who later was deported never to be seen again, who had us take care of an apartment in Düsseldorf. When we had to move out, I went to another school and again there was a Nazi principal. It was a tough break. The kids were talking about Jews being unworthy of life, but you cannot think of the kids as evil because their parents spoke this way at home. They influenced the kids. They didn't use the word *vergaßt* [gassed], as it wasn't popular then. I held myself back. Nothing else happened. I was told afterward, however, that my father had been somewhat craftier. He went to the headmaster and had me registered as "mixed breed of the second degree." This was the so-called "quarter Jew." I asked him ironically in later years, "Why weren't you afraid? How did you do it?" He said, "Don't ask. I did it." Yes, he said that. The headmaster knew that earlier my father had been in the teaching profession and that he, by "race arguments," as they were called at that time, had been discharged. And then the headmaster said [she speaks in a low, mimicking voice], "We already have three half-Jewish children in our middle school." My father said, "Under another class of Jew, however?" My father said that. Yes, one shouldn't, but that had been only a formulaic lie. People like the principal who dealt badly with you could be lied to. [Ruth apologized for the lie.] I was then "half-breed of the second degree."

Then trouble began again with BDM. Unfortunately, I had bad luck. I didn't have a teacher who was friendly to the Jews, but rather an enemy. I had a woman teacher who was conceited, affected. She was 150 percent Nazi, and naturally that was unpleasant. My grades suffered. It didn't matter to me. I listened only to my father's conversation: "Ah, later when you are in a profession, you will be a teacher." I said, "How should I become a teacher? Where should I learn? I still can't attend high school." He said, "Wait for it, wait for it." He was right in the end. Yes, and now it became horrible in Düsseldorf. Perhaps it would have been better if we'd stayed in Wuppertal.

That horrible November 9, Kristallnacht arrived. On that day, we had to deal with all three apartments of our Jewish relatives. All three. At 5:00 P.M. I was at one of them and still nothing happened. They sent me in again and said, "Is everything still in one piece?" "Yes," I said, "everything is there." "Oh, you all are lucky. They have forgotten you."

I will never forget Fürstenwald 236. I arrived there about 5:30 P.M. It was still dusk. Everything was on the street, everything. I went up into the apartment and nothing was there but a telephone in this wonderful, beautiful apartment.

My great-uncle Salli, the brother of my grandpa David, who, thank God, had died earlier, had his violin hurled out the window in the Schadow Street in Düsseldorf. He went crazy and jumped out the window. They didn't push him, as it was reported afterward in the newspaper. I can absolutely not think about that. When I get too much— if I think about these days—I always have to pinch myself in the arm. They smashed not only musical instruments—grand pianos and regular pianos—but everything! It was horrific. That was November ninth. My uncle Salli couldn't cope with it. Not only in regard to his violin, but this entire violation. He was dead after a few weeks. We had sent away our aunt to Litzmannstadt. She didn't arrive at all. It was the middle of winter and we didn't know. My father's brother was in the railway station service in Litzmannstadt just at the time when the Jewish transport was there. Isn't that terrible? He was a Nazi who changed his mind. The Nazis gave him a revolver. Officially, he died doing his service for the German army and was shot by the partisans. However, that's not true at all. He shot himself. There were people like him, perhaps, who couldn't look at it. Auschwitz wagons continuously drove in full and came back empty. He went through that for many years.

A decade later the Nazi headmaster, whom I mentioned, asked me to be his witness for the defense. Imagine—*me!* He was thrown out of his profession because he was a Nazi. So he approached me to be the witness and said, "Look here! You still know, Ruth, what I said to all of you in school: 'Go home peacefully and don't look at the burning synagogue. Don't join the riot. Go home quietly. It's been ordered that there will be no more lessons today.'" And I said, "I don't recall anymore if you said that." That was such, such a tribunal. And he shouted, "Please. Here is my diary. I can prove it throughout." Indeed, the words stood there in his handwriting, "The 9th of November," blah blah. And then I said, "Oh, but you are capable of clairvoyance. Everything happened on the morning of the 10th and you want me to say the 9th." He turned red. By this I discovered that he had falsified his diary with information that would have been viewed as a Jewish-friendly entry. At this time, he had already been fired. He still had to wait a few years for his retirement. So it goes. Sometimes you are on the top, and sometimes you are on the bottom.

To come back to the actual time of Kristallnacht. We had to hide two aunts with us in the apartment. We had to send them away because they did not grasp what was wrong and that was a little dangerous for us because the tenants in the house picked up on what was happening. They were not all Nazis. One of the renters even listened with us to enemy transmitters. For us that was very dangerous. At the time, my mother also cracked up. She said, "If only we had separated then everything would be different." It was horrible. We hid them [aunts] four days, and four days was too long.

I don't know what my aunts did afterward. I do know they all lived in basement apartments in Germany. I know my aunt wanted to immigrate to Lisbon. She had lots of relatives abroad. She had papers prepared and started to leave on a winter transport to Lisbon but never arrived there. The Gestapo in Düsseldorf was known to be very cruel and we had bad luck. If only we'd stayed in Wuppertal, maybe it wouldn't have been so bad. The Gestapo didn't have a special uniform. They were dressed fashionably. My mother had to go to St. Prinz Straße, I think it's called, to the Düsseldorf Gestapo's main headquarters, just so she could show she still existed. They feared we would "dive under the Earth." I cannot tell more about it. I don't know more. When the ration cards entered into the picture one could imagine escaping, since this was a reason to. When my mother was deported, she didn't get any cards that month. But when she had to visit the Düsseldorf Gestapo it was 1938, not even wartime. People who are trying to excuse Nazi behavior always say that everything happened only during the war, as if nothing happened earlier. When my mother reported to the Gestapo, we were not at war. *It was 1938,* I could say again and again. The ration cards didn't exist yet. German people always said later, "Ah, that happened in the war." What I'm talking about now is 1938. In 1939, you will be surprised, my father was drafted because he had been a soldier in World War I. See, now it's happened! His wife must report to the Gestapo and he's drafted!

It was a local defense unit, mainly older people, who went to France and so on. He was a noncommissioned officer and later became a sergeant. What do you say now?

My childhood was really good until they drafted my dad behind the Westwall.[8] He didn't have to participate in the war even though he was in the army. I want to think about the year it happened. Shortly after, my grandmother and mother were deported. My father was a soldier for Hitler and then his wife was deported! The Germans were all completely unpolitical. I had been at the military base in Aachen often. I was allowed to visit. The men were really not Nazi, rather, old common soldiers. Later the major had to tell my father, "You are dishonorably discharged from the military." It was not possible any more for someone with a Jewish wife to remain in the military. When my father was drafted, he sent small packages. They were in occupied France and my mother was at home checking in with the raincoated Gestapo. It was a muddled time. My non-Jewish grandparents died a year before. My Jewish Oma still lived in a small apartment in Wuppertal and had to wear a star. That was a problem. People said to me then, "Young lady, be happy that your grandmother lives in Wuppertal." Nobody could say any more that I should be happy. I drove specifically to Wuppertal. I deliberately went walking with my grandmother with the Jewish yellow star attached to her clothes. We experienced things then. There was a public lavatory, a toilet that was in the neighborhood of the cemetery where my grandfather was buried. Every time we went back to visit, my grandmother had to go; she had a weak bladder. She could not use the public toilet this time. A guy walked by and said, "Star-wearers can't piss here." Dreadful! She couldn't go to the bathroom! When I was in my grandmother's house once, the Gestapo came in and wanted to take all the appliances [radio, iron]. Then they saw my grandfather's medals. They only took the soap and left behind the appliances they had originally wanted.

When I continued to visit my grandmother, my father said, "Don't go to Wuppertal!" I said, "Why? I am going there on purpose. We should be lucky that she's still alive." I don't want to blame it on my dad, but he had to explain it to me in another way other than "no." My mother was very sensitive. She cried all the time. She was happy that I visited my grandma quite often. That was basically the way it was with Jews. My mother didn't wear a star because she was in a "mixed marriage." If she had, it would have made the situation even worse. The husband [Ruth's father] was a soldier in the West and the wife [Ruth's mother] had to wear a star? Inconceivable.

It was also the case that we were not informed. Grandma said she didn't want to be a burden to us. She absolutely feared visiting us in Düsseldorf. Sometimes we finagled to hide the star so it wasn't seen. She was taken to an old folks' home where old Jews, sick people, and even those blinded in war resided. Just imagine. First the blind person's dog is missing, and then the person himself is missing, and, in fact, dispatched in the same cattle car—freight car—in which my grandmother was also dispatched. Between July and September 1942, she was deported after a half-year together with the people in the old folks' home. Was she really one of them? We absolutely had no idea. They were gone when we came to Wuppertal.

Later my mother reproached us: We should have made inquiries from the beginning. We couldn't have stayed at the train station. We wouldn't have survived it. There's a large memorial stone there now. My son-in-law took a picture of my grandchild standing next to it. "That was your great-grandmother. She was taken away." The child found it very interesting but she didn't remark upon it further. Also, all the old people were deported to Theresienstadt, and my grandmother could not work there as a seamstress. When my mother was in Theresienstadt she discovered that her mother was only in Theresienstadt for one month and immediately was deported somewhere else in 1942. My grandmother was moved. For that we had to give evidence later. We still could not put factual information on the gravestone. "When did your mother really die?" we were asked. Then: "How do you know what the state of your mother's health was?" They asked my mother! Namely, my mother wanted another reparation payment, but at no time did she receive it. She filed an application for an explanation of her mother's death in order to engrave something on the stone. Until that time, we could engrave "In September 1942 in Theresienstadt" and write under that "Missing."

We didn't know at all what happened. No idea. Not one person returned from that old people's transport.

I just wanted to add, they called my father away to work at the Westwall, otherwise he would have been around in summer 1944 when my mother suddenly didn't get ration cards any more in Düsseldorf. These cards were distributed; otherwise we could not live. But she didn't get any. We had to go to the Gestapo. This Nazi says to my mother, "It is just for your security, you have to leave and go to central Germany." I hear his voice in my ear right now. I was there at the office. "Take the tickets for your furniture with you, as evidence of being bombed out." A few days later Jews were sent to Leuna to work. By the way, many people later got reparation money who lived in central Germany at that time, although nothing happened there in the Magdeburg district, Schönebeck, southwest of Berlin. [People who had stayed in less exposed areas did get compensation.] The Nazis started to uncover "mixed marriages" from the West to send systematically to the Mid-East. If the war had not ended who knows, maybe they would have gone further.

I was allowed to go with my mother from Wuppertal to Hagen when she was deported. One blond-haired girl who looked quite "Aryan" flirted with an SS officer, maybe because she had thoughts of fleeing. In Hagen people had to change the trains and this young girl and another woman, a gardener, tried to flee but were caught. From then on the entire group was vilely treated with shootings and worse. First they were transported to Leuna. When they arrived in Leuna, they didn't have their clothes any more but *Drillichanzuege* [canvas uniforms]. Every week these dresses had to be deloused, although they didn't have any lice. My mother always had deep, red stripes down her bare back because the SS soldiers had fun mocking the prisoners by throwing the hot iron hanger with "clean" clothes onto the backs of the nude women. From this transport, my mother gathered twenty-seven "Jew stars" and money because as she said, "There will come a time when nobody will believe what happened. So, let's keep this as evidence."

My dad was released from the army because he wasn't worthy. We were bombed out when the English army came.[9] In Düsseldorf we were bombed out again and again. Everything was screwed up. From my point of view, we should have grabbed an opportunity to fake passports so that maybe my mother would not have had to go. This was in 1943. She almost didn't come back. Nazis put drugs in the women's food so my mother got an infection. Maybe she contracted it because they forced stuff on her that caused menstruation cessation. Her group was not immediately deported to Theresienstadt. They went to Halle-Angersdorf [in central East Germany, a suburb of Halle] and worked. Three people died there and nobody knew from what. My dad sent me to Dessau where we had relatives from the non-Jewish side so that I was closer to my mother in Halle. I could visit and talk to her but I was observed by *Flintenweiber*[10] [large women with guns] who spoke with a Saxon accent. It was the first time I had to eat a sausage made of fox meat. I always thought, Now it will be over pretty soon. Soon it will be over. This happened right before Auschwitz was liberated. Then I thought, So now it will be over soon.

Then my mother worked in an important war factory located in Halle-Leuna.[11] Women had to work on milling machines without scarves for head protection, so that sometimes their hair got caught in the machines and was yanked out. They worked there for two months and then they went to Theresienstadt in the beginning of January 1945, before the end of the war, can you imagine? That late! I didn't expect that at all. Had it been otherwise my mother wouldn't have survived. Then I got a call in Dessau from a medical assistant: "Yes. Your mother is being deported but we don't believe she'll arrive alive." A Nazi told me that. My mother had high fever and maybe mononucleosis, a bacterial infection. Another deportee, a female physician from Prague University in Czechoslovakia, made the right diagnosis and gave my mother an injection against mono [probably antibiotics] in a hut in Theresienstadt. Maybe she would have died in Halle had this physician not saved her life. I believe in and stick by the last hope—and my mother survived. We got this message in June [the war ended in May 1945] because somebody wrote a letter home that we had to go to Theresienstadt. In Auschwitz they no longer had a camp since the Russians were already there.[12] My mother was kept in Theresienstadt until June. A typhus epidemic attacked Theresienstadt. She couldn't come back, but we knew she was alive. That was the main thing. My mother enjoyed being with the Russian soldiers because they didn't rape these Jewish women. These Russians gave her food. After the liberation, my mother had to sit for five weeks on the fortress wall at Theresienstadt. She came back looking like a dried-out lemon.

Because we failed to obtain fake passports, I had trouble with my dad. I blamed him; maybe I offended him as well, because we should have come up with some better ideas to act against my mother's deportation. Eventually, I couldn't locate my passport—everything was bombed out. Perhaps we could have rescued my mother and other relatives with fake passports. My family scolds me for implying they are guilty. But why should I worry what I say now that Hitler is not in power? At least I can say what I feel. Most of the families were happy that it was over: "The bums are out, fine!" I think about what Frau Yost went through, going alone over the borders. My mother came back totally exhausted and irritated. But she said, "Now forget everything quickly." That's what she always said. Old Nazis came by later on and wanted reports from my father—Nazis who had made our life so bad earlier in the war. That's why I scolded my father and said, "Why did you allow them to enter the door?" I couldn't understand. My mother said, "We don't want to count an eye for an eye." My mother was awfully sensitive, and how can I say, she never did anything against the Nazis. I tell you, I was more upset and excited than my mother, although I was not deported. I don't know why. No clue.

I also don't know why I stay in Germany, but where should I go when the entire family is gone? How and where should I go abroad? I cannot easily rebuild an existence. Many people asked my parents to leave the country. But there was a mental border too. My father was a civil servant. Every year these people got an increase in their salaries, and Germans don't often want to take risks and go outside of the country. For my father it was safer to stay in Germany. Some of my grandfather's seven brothers immigrated to Amsterdam, which was a bad choice. They had to go in a concentration camp. One of them immigrated to America in 1935, and I regret that I have no contact with this part of my family overseas. Why have they never looked us up? They went to Chicago in

1935. No idea where they are now. America is too big for me to make any inquiries. I have always thought about the Jewish relatives abroad who haven't come forward. The others all went to Holland and were put in the camps before my grandmother. The ones in Holland were taken away in 1941, and my grandmother in 1942. The others had already gone. And then I was too old. If only I had still been young. I can't say I'm happy in Germany. Many people asked me why I didn't emigrate. My life was too far along, so I couldn't emigrate any more. But I never felt fine in Germany.

When my mother came out of Theresienstadt, she was sick and I nursed her for four years. At that time, I couldn't leave. And then I made a mistake. Yes, I made a mistake. I married a German. That happened as well. We'll not talk about that. He was not Jewish. Not at all. The opposite, unfortunately. He came from a family who really had liked Hitler. It caused a separation in the family. I married, and after ten years he died. Even *then* I couldn't go abroad. How should I do it? I don't have that much initiative any more.

Later on we got to know people who received tremendous amounts of reparation money. I was really excited about that. They should pay those people who had really suffered. [She means *her* family.] My dad didn't take one single penny. But my father secured a good position as a school principal, which he always wanted during Hitler's reign. Then he said, "Now I don't want a penny." He didn't take anything or demand any money. Frau Yost doesn't believe this. She said, "He must have had tons of money to deny an offer!" No. She doesn't believe me. Then he was principal. Then he moved to Moers, where fox and bunny say good night to each other [which means it is a remote village], and I cared for my mother. It took many years until she recovered from her deportation and camp experiences.

My father had a social democratic way of thinking. For this reason, he has been called *der rote Schulrat* [red superintendent]. This area of Moers was mainly Catholic, and his political attitude was an exception. The great work he did as superintendent was bringing together all village schools so that everybody, no matter his or her religion, could attend all schools. Before that, separation ruled. In one school, which was divided into Catholic and Protestant parts, Catholics and Protestants had to use the same bathrooms. Whenever the toilets were plugged up, students quarreled about whose paper—Catholic or Protestant—had plugged the toilets. Even these little problems my father had to solve. He was proud to gather the schools together and he was awarded with a Bundesverdienstkreuz [Federal Service Cross], but he made fun of it. It had no value for him, and he always felt sympathy for blue-collar workers in Wuppertal.

In Hitler's time I was under the illusion that I could be a famous singer because people told me I had a very good voice. That is why I took singing lessons in Krefeld and Düsseldorf. I lived in Moers and took care of my mother in order to make my dream come true after Hitler was gone. But then I made a big mistake and married. Oh, my God. Nobody believes me about this. My father was seventeen when he started fighting in the first war without permission from his parents. Similarly, my husband was sixteen and wanted to be involved in the war events, so he faked his mother's signature and had to fight for the Waffen-SS, the weapons division. Even in the last days of war he believed in a German victory. He was overenthusiastic, was caught by the Red Army and locked up for eleven years in a Russian prisoner-of-war camp. I didn't know anything about this when I met him for the first time.

My father had been the boss, the school director, of my husband's elder brother, Willy, and they arranged the first meeting. Later I got pregnant, and because my father was a principal, I had to get married. I wouldn't have gotten married, but my father wanted me to because it was not easy to live with an illegitimate child. Since he was a principal, the relationships in the family had to be in order too, right? That was 1951. We didn't have the Pill then. I can't forgive my poor dad because he was always involved in my destiny. Parents are destiny, aren't they? An illegitimate child would have ruined my father's reputation as a principal; otherwise, I would not have married. My father said, "It doesn't matter who you marry."

My husband, Bernd Wilmschen, was a *Spätheimkehrer* [returned very late from the war]. Later on I found out what horrific circumstances my husband had survived in imprisonment. They were locked in steel cupboards for days. Once I recognized a tattoo on his body, under his arm, while at the swimming pool. It was the sign of the Waffen-SS. I did not know that my husband had been a member of the SS when I married him. We had been very intimate after two or three months, but I didn't know. Most men had been killed in the war. I was too young to think about it. I thought, "What my mother likes, or at least doesn't hate, is good enough for me." Now I think it would have been better to have taken my child and said good-bye to him. I am not happy about my conscious decision to marry this man. It was a shock when I saw the sign of the Waffen-SS on his arm. He wanted to tell me something, like could I imagine how he could have killed civilians? But I didn't think about it and he didn't show me the sign.

I didn't have a cordial relationship with my husband's family, not because I had been half Jewish but because I "took away their son," who had just returned after eleven years. His family once invited my mother over and got along with her very well. So his family said, "If she is like her mother, then we give permission for marriage." My mother had the qualities necessary to reconcile all people. [Probably that's why her mother hid the fact that Ruth's boyfriend and later husband had been a Waffen-SS member.]

I had two children. This illegitimate child died at age four from an electric shock in my parents' apartment. In my parents' apartment! *Zack!* [Just like that!] We were celebrating my husband's new job. My father promoted him. Everybody said, "Now you got your bad luck. Now you have only one daughter." This daughter, Helga, I adored. Then my husband and mother died. Guess how my mother died? Traffic accident. There is no justice, is there? A soldier in the *Bundeswehr* [German Federal Armed Forces] had leased a Cadillac and he wasn't familiar with the car yet and even on a normal street he hit my mother. She took walks in this area. That's unbelievable. That beats everything! She had survived everything. For my father it was horrible when she got hit by a car. He didn't even visit her in the hospital. I went to the hospital everyday. It was hard because my mother had a fractured skull and it was difficult for her to breathe. My father didn't want to see his wife's misery, which was astonishing to me—a man who has survived two world wars and is not able to accompany his dying wife.

At the moment of death, I was there. I couldn't take my daughter to her grandmother when she was in the hospital. Later, when my mother was dead, my daughter took offense because she wanted to see her grandmother again. My mother and daughter, Helga, had a wonderful relationship. It's the evil irony of history, isn't it? But in those days when my mother's father died, we said, "Oh, the poor guy, why did he have to die?" He would not have survived the Nazi horror. They both should have had more years to live. They died in the prosperity of their lives.

Before my mother died, my father told me, as he had during the Third Reich, "Now you're going to become a teacher." "How?" I responded. "With my middle-school education?" Adenauer gave me DM 5,000 as a gift for the fact that I was not allowed to study. Can you imagine only DM 5,000! I was hampered in my professional education and got only 5,000 for that. I spent this money for two vacations on the Spanish island Teneriffe.

Examinations began for especially talented people. You had to work very hard to pass these exams. It was not like this: You are the daughter of the principal, so you automatically are admitted. In my second attempt I got admitted, although it was no replacement for the *Abitur*.[13] Today nobody talks about that anymore. I didn't want to become a teacher that badly. I didn't know *what* I wanted to be. I lost a bit of my mental strength due to the war events. Actually, I was quite old at the time of these special examinations. I was twenty-nine when I was told to start a college education.

I studied in Kettwig and one of my teachers kept saying "We have to learn from the past so that the future will never be like the past." He hammered this in twelve times a day—it was more than clear. I had to undergo a *Begabten-Sonderprüfung*[14] in Dortmund in order to become a teacher. This was a special exam for talented people because in this time nobody had any grades from high school or college. The examinees were given a story or a book on which to write a little essay. The book's title was *Saisonbeginn* [Start of the Season] by Elisabeth Langässer. This book was just right for me because it dealt with Jewish history. Other examinees complained about the choice. One episode in this book was a big obstacle for most examinees, but not for me. It was about a little village that had a crucifix at its entrance. In 1937 there was a big crowd of workers gathered around this crucifix doing construction and no one knew what was happening. The next day there was a big sign next to the crucifix: *Juden unerwünscht* [Jews not welcome]. The other fifty-five examinees felt unable to write much about this story, but the professors wanted them to write down their personal opinions about it. I didn't have any problems with this subject matter.

The next examination day I did well on a passage from Goethe. I only had trouble in the geography part of the exam, which I almost failed. In history I did a good job. I knew a good deal about the Weimar Republic. Finally I got admitted and studied education with many very young people. At first I didn't have much fun. Later I could take classes like philosophy. I was very enthusiastic about it because it was a fairly new subject for me.

I started to study in Kettwig upon Ruhr without permission. I got permission when I was in the third semester. Usually we had to study six months, but after the fifth semester we were told, "Because of the lack of teachers, whoever has enough self-confidence and courage can start teaching now." *Zack Zack!* I was a teacher.

The first class I taught was in 1958. I always had a double-sized class, which was a big mess. My father complained a bit that I spent an exorbitant amount of time preparing for classes and taking care of the children. At this time my father had retired and was with me because my mother had been killed.

First, I had to work very hard. I grasped that because I was raised in a teacher's family, teaching must be something "innate." I could deal with the little kids in elementary school very well. I was happy there for a few years. I felt a sensation in my life—that this was a positive change.

Then when my daughter was older she fell in love with a guy who was raised in an old Nazi family. That was a bad omen. It runs through our family—the past. My daughter and her husband gave birth to a planned child. Everything was planned exactly. My son-in-law was still a student and my daughter had worked for a long time in a rehabilitation center for disabled people in Düsseldorf. My daughter got her husband a job in this center as well, although he didn't like disabled people that much. He is excessively intellectual. My daughter was pregnant for the first time. Four days before the birth she went to the hospital in Düsseldorf-Gerresheim, known as the hospital for Cesarean sections. I didn't know anything was wrong beforehand.

Four days before birth she called me and said, "The baby is in the correct position, but I want to go to Gerresheim since there is 'rooming-in,'" the babies are next to their mothers. Then they did the C-section and, the physicians can't explain this, she got septic shock. The child was thirty-six hours old and my daughter had to go into the intensive care unit. She had to stay one week like a living corpse. Everyday I visited and watched her hair become grayer and grayer. Horrible. I couldn't go any more. On the last day a vessel burst and they transported her from Gerresheim to the university hospital [in neurology] in the city of Düsseldorf, Friedricksstraße. Later a Vietnamese doctor told me that on the way everything burst. She had bandages everywhere when she was in the university hospital and even my son-in-law couldn't see her. He just told the doctors: "Do me a favor, don't open her again. Don't do an operation if there is something wrong." At 2:00 P.M. the doctor said, "Until tonight we'll keep the tube there to the heart circulation machine." My daughter *was* a machine. After this last visit we went to a café and thought about the cemetery where we wanted my daughter buried. Punctually at 8:00 P.M. the doctor called and said, "Cardiac arrest." Horrible. For us relatives, horrible. Then we got a detailed report about the medical diagnosis that was called "professional blunder." Four years later Peter Beauvais produced the movie, *Der Kunstfehler* [professional blunder], in which he changed my daughter's character a fraction. The woman who died in the movie already had kids and the setting was a different hospital, but he got his data from my daughter's case.

That was my fate. I gave birth to two daughters. Both are dead. My mother had a strange death after having endured the concentration camps. Is there any purpose in my life? At best were the times I was a grade-school teacher. I was a teacher with my heart and my soul. My favorite grades were first and second. I think I actually accomplished something in those years. But, since then, I've totally degenerated into poor mental shape. They gave me this dog after my daughter died. I asked, "What should I do with this dog?" "Here, read," they said, "this is the dog's birth certificate—12th of May"—which was, coincidentally, my daughter's birthday as well. I said, "Okay. Give the dog to me." I was still a teacher, but I applied immediately for early retirement. This application was accepted after six weeks. I could have worked four more years. That's why I don't get my full pension now.

My son-in-law got married again to a terrible woman with whom I never got along. That's why I moved to Hamburg. I could not remain any longer in Düsseldorf. I don't know many people in Hamburg, but I think that Hamburg is much more *Weltoffen* [cosmopolitan], so that people do not develop prejudices against other people very quickly. I can compare it to the little town of Wuppertal, which has many narrow-minded people who said: "Our ancestors hated the Jews, the Jews have always been our enemies, and Hitler is just doing what *everybody* wants."

Before I moved to Hamburg, when I was still a teacher, I used to go shopping in a little market. The children in grade school next to this shop knew that I had a granddaughter. Once I met my son-in-law's wife and my granddaughter sitting in her shopping cart. The shop owner said, "Oh, you are here, Frau Wilmschen." My grade-school kids were screaming "Frau Wilmschen, look, your granddaughter." As soon as the *new* mother heard that, she ran away although she was not finished with shopping. I couldn't deal with that in my current condition. After all, I took care of my granddaughter three quarters of a year before this new mother appeared. My son-in-law and I shared the daily care of my grandchild. And I love kids. When they turn ten, eleven, or twelve, this love for kids decreases, I would say. I couldn't visit my granddaughter for two years and five months. This also happened. And suddenly everything was fine again, and right now they want money from me to rebuild their new house. I responded, "I want to be selfish just one time," and "I have found in my old days a nice old man who has a grandchild as well." From this letter on, there was no contact. Out! But I am not that desperate about it. My granddaughter writes me letters. I don't want to meddle in the child-parent relationship. That's not good for her. But her handwriting is exactly like my daughter's. She writes, "I will have my confirmation soon. How much do I get?" Money. This kind of stuff I get in her letters. She receives nothing else from her parents. Money, only money. But she is like that all the time. When she visited my flat, she said, "But *this* picture I will hang somewhere else." I responded, "What exactly are you talking about?" Imagine. She is thirteen years old and thinks about how my furniture might be rearranged when she lives in this apartment, assuming I'm going to die soon. My daughter was totally different. She was sensitive. Whenever she opened her mouth to say something, she thought about it beforehand. She thought, "How might this be taken by the other person? Am I too rude?" She didn't inherit this characteristic from me, I have to confess. My daughter was absolutely loved in the home for disabled people. Two hundred sixty-two people came to her funeral. They all couldn't believe her death and had not expected it. I tried for a few years to find my daughter in my granddaughter. Here is a picture. Sometimes she looks like my daughter here together with her two stepbrothers. She looks like my daughter [shows her picture], but she inherited her father's character; otherwise, she wouldn't act as badly as she does. Her *new* mother talks about money morning until night. Of all the friends who visited the family when my daughter was still alive, a quarter of them still come. They couldn't manage her death. They think like I do. They think always, It's rubbish. If she is not alive any more, she is not alive. I have so many photos.

My granddaughter was taken away from me when my daughter died. I never understood that because I had bought children's furniture for my granddaughter and only sometimes from Friday to Monday was I allowed taking care of her. My son-in-law said to me, "It is just the little piece of Helga (my dead daughter) that you want." I am confident that no other woman took such good care of my granddaughter. The pediatrician asked my son-in-law, "Do you want me to prescribe a mother for your daughter?" Finally my son-in-law married this woman about whom I'm not happy. I think he is very smart and had contact with many beautiful and smart girls but *so eine* [such a one]! From my point of view these other girls were smart enough not to marry my son-in-law. His new wife is simply horrible—she can not even get along with her own parents.

It is terrible for me that I am not loved as a grandmother. I think this is because my son-in-law has never had a lovely grandmother. Once I said to him: "What kind of a man are you?" Fortunately, Helga is no longer alive and doesn't have to handle this husband.

When my granddaughter was five years old, she drew a pancake on a sheet of paper, separated it into four parts and later into eight, and asked me, "What am I? One-eighths or one-quarter?" Somebody must have told her about her Jewish origin, and she didn't know what one-sixteenth was. Her father listened to this conversation and said *"Quatsch* [That's rubbish]!" I was angry about his indifference, and my grand-daughter never asked me again about her origins.

The times I mentioned were between 1961 and 1971. These ten years were especially rough. I lived a lonely life in these years. Although it sounds stupid, I realized that my problems and experiences didn't attract other people that much. And when I said something, they responded, "Your current problems are enough. Don't focus on old ones." Then my daughter died and I thought, *Jetzt, gehst du ganz vor die Hunde* [Now I'm going to the dogs]. I myself wondered about it. I met tons of people who either had to cover up something as far as the past is concerned or did not care at all about history. A few times I started to join different clubs, but whenever they talked negatively about Jews I could not just sit there and listen to the scolding about Jews. I always had bad luck with these clubs. At least five or six times. This bad luck, I know for sure, followed me; it was always around, sticking to me. Later acquaintances said, "Aah, you are not involved in anything, you live so lonely." I was happy to be in my school.

Unfortunately, after my mother died, my father was helpless so I had to take care of him. I lived with my dad for six and a half years. Sometimes, under these conditions, the relationship between my little daughter and me suffered. She was sensitive. Often I have a guilty conscience because, from my point of view, I didn't pay enough attention to her. It is not easy handling an old father and having him at home. I had no choice since my father wouldn't have survived in a retirement home. He always wished for a fast death, which he got. He died from a heart attack. In my family, nobody has ever been ill for a very long time. Either they died from being killed in concentration camps or from car accidents or heart attacks. My relationship with my father became more difficult when he got older. My father was jealous even of my dog. He said, "For your dog you go to the doctor, but for me you never pick up medicine." The older people are, the more attention they want you to pay them. I got to know some Italians who lived in my house for quite a while. These friends were born in Iscia and had no clue about politics but were very nice. They realized that my father was complicated and demanded too much from me, so they called him *el commandante!* I always had a better relationship with my mom, who always said, "It's good to have you around, but I will never live in your apartment. Let's have separate apartments and meet as often as we can."

I could compare my relationship to my daughter Helga with my mother's relationship to me. I think both relationships had been sincere and tender. I think I was more energetic than my mother. I was very consequence-oriented in educating my daughter. When she didn't clean her room, I put all her stuff from the desk and shelves onto the floor so that the room was a mess and she had to clean it. My mother had a good friend to whom she talked openly and honestly. When she died I met this friend at the funeral. He cried buckets and said to me, "Your mom loved you more than anything else and she thought you often act stronger than you actually are." Maybe the fact that I was a single parent and also a teacher made me stronger. Sometimes I think I was despotic but my daughter never blamed me for that. Wilmschen people are more gentle and soft rather than strong. Even my SS husband had been gentle. My first daughter had a quirky violent temper. Although I was, in general, a pleasant child, sometimes I was even boring for my mom. Later, in school, I became a little too brazen. My daughter inherited my mother's good nature.

I could come to my mother with every problem, although my mother thought I had inherited being choleric from my father. But because I don't like people yelling at me, I didn't yell in school when I worked as a teacher. With my mother I had a wonderful relationship.

With my father, I don't know. Maybe we are too similar. Only once did I have trouble with my mother, but she never beat me. My grandson is still beaten by *his* father because *his* father was beaten in his childhood. I further believe that my daughter would have avoided having her children hit, but the new mother doesn't care. Ruth Klüger writes in her book about her mother being neurotic.[15] I agree. Many people developed mental illnesses as a result of the deportation and the Nazi cruelty. The anti-Semitism and propaganda made life within the Jewish family even worse because nobody foresaw what could possibly happen to them.

I would like to talk about *Mischlinge.* I wonder about people's interest in your book because Americans are usually just interested in their history. I am curious about the shape, contents, and context of your book about *Mischling* history. Will it be a mixture of novel and documentary? Or more superficial storytelling piece like the work of Johannes Mario Simmel.[16] I don't think it's a good idea to put history into a novel because people wouldn't believe it. Ralph Giordano's novel *Die Bertinis* has been very surprising and maybe risky because nothing had dealt with Jewish history before, but Giordano also included *Phantasie mit Schneegestöber* (fictional accounts). Besides this, people are complaining about Giordano's political attitude, that it was similar to that of the Communist party before 1946, but he denied this later. Since 1961 Giordano has made efforts to clarify events and inform the public about Jewish history. I can't say there was a distinction made if a man or woman was Jewish. I don't know people I could compare because among my acquaintances only the women have been Jewish. I don't think Jewish men have been more resolute than women in terms of action and emigration. All Jewish men I know—my mother's uncles—have been very soft. Of all the people I know, the women have been dominant over their Jewish men. In my family, my father happened to be dominant. Sometimes my mother exerted a strong will like when this new short hairstyle *[Bubikopf]* became modern and she went to the hairdresser without asking her husband.

As far as *Mischlinge,* my friend Frau Yost is slightly disturbed. She is scattered. Frau Yost always acts unbalanced after she has talked to other people about the past. I said, "Don't do it. Don't go crazy because we have to know that the past happened." Well, without her knowledge I called Dr. Loeffler although I shouldn't have. I don't want to meddle, but Frau Yost always screams "Hallo" in her phone, "I can't hear you." Nothing was actually wrong. I called the office for intervention. Then I went to her house, rang the bell, and she didn't realize anything. Dr. Loeffler didn't say that I called him. I don't know him very well. I said to him, "It's your patient. I just wanted to tell you." The day before yesterday he went to her, that's what she told me on the phone. I was afraid. I have to visit again. She always says: "I admire you. You're a strong personality, that you can live alone with all your memories." I always make jokes. What should I say—"I've got a dog, I talk to him." That's a bit strange, but I don't know what I will do when he dies. I think I'll travel everywhere. I have to take my mind off things. Ruth has a nice old man who always scolds when she talks about the Jewish past, although he had a Jewish grandmother. I feel guilty that she became sick again. She couldn't talk to anybody about her life all these years, not even with her life companion. She really suppressed her thoughts. But I didn't know that. When I told her about me, she started to talk. Dr. Loeffler prescribed this therapy: to write down her life. She didn't take that very well. She endured many predicaments. Russians raped her—horrors like that. My experiences are minor compared to hers. Yes, this type of therapy takes time: She told me she's going to quit. A day before yesterday. She'll quit it and I shouldn't give her any books to read. I told her about Hecht's book, but she won't read it. It is not necessary for her. She lived her own similar experiences. I responded, "Don't I know better than anybody else that you had these experiences?" That's why now I only bring her funny books. If you have to describe these experiences precisely, and you have to remember them, it is very hard. That happened to me in 1988 as well. I went to a play in the University Theater. I thought I could get rid of all my bad memories by watching this play. Suddenly I became sick. My skin was enervated; it was so numb that I would not have reacted to a pinch. I don't know how it happened. Actually I did not repress anything. I always opened my mouth and said what I thought.

I know about another *Mischling*, Ingeborg Hecht. A few years ago she came to a bookstore to read in Bad Bevensen, a spa near here. Only four people, including myself, showed up. Four people! The rabbi was very disappointed. We thought there'd be a crowd. A bookstore owner asked her to come on behalf of school classes, from middle to high school, and there was not a single class. I said, There's no interest here. No interest. If the Germans say they are interested. . . . I read the book. I lent it to someone for half a year and haven't gotten it back. But I have it in my head. My son-in-law read [Hecht's] book and immediately complained about it. For him, the main point was that Ingeborg's parents had marriage trouble before Hitler, not just later because of political reasons. That is why they got divorced and her father was deported later.

I got to know another woman who had been half Jewish and wanted to be friends with me. I trusted her a lot and told her stories from that time. I was also wondering why this lady had trouble with all her siblings although everybody was still alive until one brother visited and said, "She was the only Nazi in our family." That was very disappointing to me, and another reason why I live in seclusion, why my social life is restricted. This "friend" who said she had a hard time being half Jewish told me that she had to live in East Germany with a false passport in order to remain unknown. She talked to me in a restaurant and I told her my experiences honestly, maybe a bit too loudly, as my friend said, "Be quiet. Don't talk too loudly." I answered, "Why? Does it happen again that we are not allowed to say anything?" I met with her until her brother told the truth about her. That was horrible for me. I was ashamed of all "mixed" people because of this one bad example. Another Jewish friend of mine told me about the Jewish community and how people in it did not help her when she had financial difficulties. They had said, "If your persecution would have taken place in the Western part of Germany, you would have gotten *Wiedergutmachung* [reparations], but since you came here when you were sixteen years old after the war, we can't help you." She said, "I don't like the Jewish community's perception. Just because I didn't want to be a believer, the Jewish community denied aid to me." This friend also told me, "I don't want to know anything more about that time." I wanted to borrow a book for her, *Briefe an meine Töchter* [letters to my daughters] about a mother who expected her deportation and wrote her experiences down. My friend said, "I don't want to read this. I lived in that time." I am interested in communicating with other half-Jewish women with whom you have talked. Half-Jewish people are getting very old—friends of mine, Evelyn Kurnecke, Inge Meysel, Annagrette Schropsdorf. My "false friend," Frau Hellmann, said, "That is because we have two kinds of blood." I responded, "Hey, listen, do you want to confirm Hitler's theory of races? Shut up!"

My son-in-law said, "Why don't you write down all your stories?" I ask, "For whom? For one granddaughter who maybe wants to read it someday?" No. My granddaughter is too superficial. Maybe she isn't ready to think about this difficult history. On the other hand, to write down experiences makes you free. I don't expect my granddaughter to be introspective. She is very materialistic. Once they visited me and we didn't have anything to talk about until my granddaughter switched on the TV. Her mother said, "This is the preadolescent phase, don't worry." But I'm particular about this. I decided to separate from my family a bit. My son-in-law sends me newspaper clippings about World War II. Sometimes he is only pretending to be interested in my history. I doubt he's interested in me, otherwise they would write me more letters, for example, now that people talk about Auschwitz. My grandchildren are materialists. I have a friend in Wuppertal with two well-loved sons—one is more intelligent than the other. The intelligent son, Udo, had a girlfriend fifteen years ago called Gabi who was a nurse. When my daughter died, this Gabi started dating Markus, my son-in-law. My friend told me that Gabi has only two aims in life: a husband with a big pension and her own house. Maybe that is why I have prejudices.

In 1989 I went to a seminar at the university, and I gave a speech. What I experienced was horribly difficult for me. I had tears in my eyes when I saw how the young people had a genuine interest in what I was saying—really genuine. I wasn't used to that. I told stories about my experiences and felt close to the youth. It was completely fantastic. In the middle of my lecture, I was affected deeply by the response. This good feeling didn't last long. A few weeks later I was sick. Suddenly the entire seminar was temporarily cancelled because the Gypsies, the Sinti and Roma, were here. They felt cheated. They didn't want to talk about my problems any more but theirs. We couldn't do the seminar where we wanted to do it, but where the Gypsies wanted to, in the school in the Karolina suburb. They didn't want to make any distinctions between Jewish people and Sinti and Roma.[17] They thought their situation was still awful in the present. Many attendees were unhappy that the Sinti and Roma threw everyone into one pot. This controversy over the seminar overwhelmed me. I was mentally distraught. One guy there wrote a doctoral thesis about Jews, especially the Harburger Jews. He even owned lampshades that had been made out of Jewish skin. I don't know where he got them. He was married to a half-Jewish woman, and his parents gave him a book from a priest when he was ten years old. This priest saved many Jewish children. This is one guy educated in tolerance, especially as he had read this book at such a young age. The professor wrote the book about the lampshades. There was uproar against it. "How can you write this?" The professor himself couldn't get a job in the West because he was collaborating with the Communist party in the East. He was blacklisted professionally. I told them in my speech about my dad and the loss of his job, and this professor said, "Yes. You can compare my case to his." One woman stood up—I don't know her name: "I must leave this seminar. How can you compare these two cases? A work prohibition because of Communist attachments and the Nazi policies cannot be compared." By the time I left, this seminar had burst at the seams. It was good I participated, but from then on I didn't attend anything else related to this topic. I stayed to myself. My contribution to political purposes ended. What is the point if even your own granddaughter says it's nonsense?

My son-in-law wanted to reprimand her for the negative words she said to me, but he didn't. In order to teach his children about the Nazi time, they went to the train station frequently. It didn't make sense to me. The people in Wuppertal built a huge monument at this train station. My son-in-law took his four-year-old son to this station, took pictures, and told him about the trains to Theresienstadt. His kids didn't grasp the whole picture. Every time the little boy sees a train now he says, "Oh. Are there Jews inside?" You can't tell a four-year-old child such stories with complicated subtexts. He told my real granddaughter something incorrect, otherwise she wouldn't say, "Go away with your *Spastics* [craziness] and stories about your paranoid people, the Jews." I was totally crushed. After that, her godmother took her to see *Schindler's List*. Obviously, there are people who still think about the Nazi time, but her own parents would never have taken her to the movie. She wrote a letter to me and said, "Go to this movie and take a bed sheet with you." I complain about my granddaughter who told me I have to take a blanket to *Schindler's List*. Why? To wipe away the tears, or because I'll fall asleep? A thirteen-year-old girl has to be able to think about things before she actually says them. She doesn't think about how we ourselves went through all of what she watched. She called and I said, "Kerstin, why should I go? What I experienced for myself, I don't need to see on film." She kept asking her godmother "Is it really true?" And since then, things are a little different. She's thirteen and I don't know if she's for or against communication between Jews and Christians. But she's as superficial as her stepmother is. They think, "It's a long time ago, so don't whine about it all the time. In the meantime, other horrible things have happened." You hear that all the time.

There's a Jewish synagogue that was recently built by the Jewish community in my city. I am not happy because the visitors find the acoustics inside much more important than the history of the synagogue. My grandmother lived here fifty years ago when the Nazis kicked her out of her apartment. People say, "We want to go there and talk to Jewish people." I answer, "If you want to talk to Jewish people, talk to me. In the synagogue you won't find anybody who could tell you about Jewish history anymore."

The Germans have no interest. That's the German mentality. That was the case before the First World War and before the Second World War. It's always been that way. This can only be explained very badly to an American. I also can't explain it to a Swiss or an Italian, who says, "What are you talking about?" I don't speak about hate, I speak about indifference. I speak from Ralph Giordano's work. Do you know him? He wrote *Die Zweite Schuld der Deutschen* [The Second Guilt of the Germans].[18] I operate around the second guilt of the Germans. The big indifference of the Germans. In the classroom, when I was a teacher, I wanted to tell stories about my experiences during Hitler's regime, but my boss says, "Ah, that's not so important. You can't give history lessons. You are too emotionally invested. You can only teach German and arithmetic." I wasn't even permitted to teach history and politics. I was not allowed to relate to the children what my family and I and eleven murdered relatives endured. He said [imitates man in low, authoritative voice], "No, that, that is no longer interesting." Today you hear *"Das ist Schnee von gestern"* [that's old stuff]. Why? Today there's interest in Yugoslavia and, above all, in those who were banished—evicted from East Prussia and Poland. That's of interest—the other is not anymore. So I said nothing more to my school children.

I had another experience while in a subway train with my granddaughter. A young man told a friend about going to a speech with the topic "Never Forget Auschwitz." Another old lady listened to them and said, "Again and again the same topic. It's all just exaggerated." I was very upset about the woman's twisted perception and yelled at her that it's true people were killed by gas in Auschwitz. The lady yelled back and the young man, who was the reason for this yelling match, asked me, "Oh my God, did you have a similar experience?" The other lady couldn't calm down and other people supported her more than I. That is why I am very aggravated over people's indifference to these problems. My granddaughter tried to hold me back and told her parents at home, "Grandma is hysterical." Once I got together with Frau Yost and took my granddaughter along. She seemed very bored with the meeting. I think she seems indifferent to my history. For this reason, I don't care to write anything down.

I am very concerned about today's youth, which basically think these historical episodes are just old stories and no one wants to know about them. I frequent cafés where little plays are performed. If anybody says something about or against Jews, I react very hyperactively and yell at them, so much so that a Czechoslovakian woman told me that I wouldn't have a positive impact on other people if I couldn't be more tolerant. I talk more often to younger people in their forties because I am not willing to talk with older people about that time. They are more likely to mix up historical data or to distort it. When older people realized that I talked often to young men, they said, "Oh, she is looking for a young lover!"

I feel like an outsider. I have the right to be an outsider because I have been disappointed so often. My son-in-law accused me twenty years ago of never going out, and basically I had withdrawn into a snail shell. Finally he convinced my daughter that he was right. I like to be alone. Even when I was a little kid, my mom recognized: "You play best when you are alone. If your friend is here it's not so much fun."

Do I feel excluded? [Thinks for a while.] Yes, I do. But this is a "mixed children" thing. Frau Yost feels similarly. But God gave me the power to survive even though I'm an outsider. Perhaps I am lonely because I was an only child, never went to kindergarten, and all familial adults—my parents, aunts, and uncles—spoiled me very much. In the Nazi years, I acquired an elephant skin and could deal with any kind of treatment.

I do think about the past, but not everyday. In 1989 when people remembered Reichskristallnacht, all the horrible images came back to my mind. Usually I don't think about it, except if somebody is talking about it in a disparaging manner. Then it is like "lightning in my brain" and I start to complain. If anybody talks about this time with indifference, it hurts me. My head heats up and the ache spreads throughout my body. I often think about the eleven people who were killed in my family. Whatever happens in childhood, you never forget.

CHAPTER FIVE

URSULA RANDT

"One had, at the time, enough possibilities to die"

~

Ursula Randt lives in a quaint, cozy house on a quiet residential street in Klein Flotbek. All afternoon she had escorted a group of former Hamburg citizens through Karolinenstraße in conjunction with the Senatskanzlei program. This program, run by various city governments in Germany, invites formerly persecuted Germans, primarily Jewish, who have never been back to their former "homes" to return at the city's expense. Their airfare, hotel, cultural events, and tours are paid for. My father could have been part of such a group. He chose not to, and when the Senatskanzlei kept pressing him, he insisted with sincerity that he *is not* and *was not* ever Jewish. He did accept their invitation to visit apart from this group, primarily because I was living in Hamburg. Ursula told

me that my father would have been fine in this group atmosphere as she was surprised how many people in the group
were *not* Jewish (rather, were "mixed," as she and my father
had been labeled) and had been baptized. Some clearly felt out
of place. K. Dohnke, a journalist with whom I worked, told
me that when he was interviewing members of this group, he
noticed that Ursula, one of the leaders, did not mention her
Jewish background to the former Hamburgers. Why not?

Ursula was clearly tired and was sleeping when I arrived.
She had forgotten about our meeting. Her living room was
incredibly sunny. You could hear the birds singing in the
background. She wore a brown and blue suit with white blouse
underneath, a simple string of pearls, and a square, silver watch.
I remember most her beautiful smile, which covered her entire
face, her white, wavy hair, and dark eyes. She talked with her
hands. She had an impressive, overpowering library with a large
stereo in the corner. A melange of flowers was arranged on the
windowsills. An array of pictures that Ursula talked about were
displayed on her walls: Jewish women about whom Ursula had
written, including Mary Marcus, the director of a Jewish girls'
school, and a picture of her mother that hung alone.

Ursula had trouble talking about her past and said, as a
preface, that only recently has she been able to discuss it. She
said her sister absolutely will not speak of it. She also displayed
much embarrassment at being singled out as something
"other." I noticed this occurred with the other women as well.
In part, they do not want to talk about being "different" or be
seen as "dirty" or "tainted" with some "unclean" blood. Ursula,
I think, does not want to face this separation from her
Germanness. She wants to believe in the fairy tale of the
unblemished German folk, but does not. Although Ursula was
trained as a speech therapist, she became a Jewish historian
of sorts and wrote a book about a Hamburg Jewish girls'
school.[1] Her honorary doctorate, given for her work, is
displayed.

Ursula had been a special education instructor in this school for six years when in 1972 they were forced to move to a modern building, and an elderly woman told her the old school had once been for Jewish girls. Ursula then decided to write the history, which is some sign of her need to be recognized as an intellect in Germany, but the topic she chose helped her to embrace her own past in a secret, roundabout way. According to her recollections, she had experienced only one negative incident, for which she felt very lucky. In reality, she experienced many negative times: deportations, her sister's suffering, her own unfulfilled desires of continuing school, separation from her father, her parents' divorce, and innumerable bombing attacks. On the other hand, as a *Mischling*, she was still, unbelievably, able to be German in many ways. She was protected by her mother's "Aryan" family and was even a member of Hitler's youth group for girls, BDM. I think many of the *Mischlinge* scamper to be alongside the "good Germans," even though many of those Germans turned against them and were ardent Nazis. They do not want to be associated with those "bad Nazis" who just dropped from the heavens—either by agreeing with them politically or by being persecuted by them. They want neither one in their history.

Although Ursula feels uncomfortable being viewed as "different" from her fellow Germans, it was clear she feels an affinity to her Jewish heritage. She became sick in the fall of 1941. She felt certain it was related to the deportations and to seeing family friends wearing a Jewish star. These events, she said, "had such a creepy, threatening, and atrocious dimension that I simply could not endure it." Ursula recovered enough to leave Hamburg and live in Giessen with her mother's sister; however, at the end of the war the "split" in her identity once again was pronounced. Her aunt was unhappy the Germans had lost the war, but Ursula was ecstatic that she was unshackled from persecution. As a German, she had to worry now that the Americans and British might harm her—a terrible irony—as during the war she had been considered primarily a Jew.

For such a private and cautious person, Ursula has become very public. Why did she begin working with the Hamburg Senate in its mission to bring back formerly persecuted citizens? Why does she conduct tours for returning persecuted Jews when she herself had skirted her past? Since our meeting, Ursula seemingly has transformed. A mutual friend wrote to me, May 7, 1998,

> I was surprised myself when I met Ursula Randt. When we talked about her meetings with visitors who participate in the Hamburg program, she told me about several misunderstandings she experienced—how these "refugees" are hypersensitive to certain terms. Ursula mentioned "Arisch" [Aryan], and then—almost with a wink of her eye— "Halbjude" [half Jew]. I'm very sure that she talked about herself, and wanted to show me that this doesn't have to be a secret to me any longer. During one of her introductions into the history of the Jewish Girls School at Karolinen- straße, she briefly mentioned her own background, and I have the strong feeling that she now tends to accept her own history.

Today she appears to have conciliated her fractured identity—as long as she continues to speak and to lead community tours for former persecuted Germans.

My name is Ursula Randt, born Klebe in Hamburg on May 25, 1929. My father was a doctor in Hamburg, Dr. Egon Klebe, born 1887 in Eisenach, hence, in Thüringen, and my mother was Johanna Klebe, born Krumm. She was born and grew up in Giessen, in Hessen. She was a bookseller. My father was Jewish. He came from a truly traditional household. I didn't know about that then but I was told; for example, they had eaten kosher at home. He had attended, naturally, a non-Jewish school. In Eisenach there was not a single Jewish school. He graduated, then studied medicine at various universities, and in World War I he was a volunteer front-line fighter for four years. He had one single half-brother who was younger than he. His mother died at a young age. His father had married again. His half-brother studied law and in 1917, as a volunteer in Galizeen [Galicia], was killed in action.

My father received medals and badges of honor. He had the Iron Cross and the Distinguished Service Medal, and I don't know what all else. He was through and through a German. He came back to Hamburg after the war and did specialist training in Altona. He had pursued his education in dermatology, to be a dermatologist. He met my mother, who came to Hamburg and worked as a bookseller in a large bookstore. They married in 1922, and my sister, Eva, was born in 1926. In 1929, I came into the world. When I was born, my parents were, what one calls, well situated. My first memories go back to an apartment in Winterhude, a very large, well-proportioned, well-furnished, very beautifully located apartment and servants who came every day but did not live with us as my father didn't like that. We lived very well. My father's practice meanwhile had begun to flourish—he had opened his own in the 1920s. His father died in 1927 and his stepmother shortly thereafter. He was the sole heir. His parents were wealthy and so my parents came into a considerable fortune. I was very little when the Nazis came into power. I was still not four years old, so I have no memory of it. I didn't grow up Jewish. My parents had agreed that we should be raised neutrally, without religion, and when we grew up we should make our own decision between Jewish and Christian. I had no idea what Jewish was, and I had also not known at all for many years that I had a Jewish father. However, I detected that we were in a special situation—*that* I picked up very quickly. Everything that had to do with the Nazis, uniforms and flags and marching troops, alarmed me enormously very early on. That must have come from my parents' reactions, although they had tried not to let anything show. Besides, I knew that my parents were "against *it*"—at that time one was either for or against *it*—and I knew that one mustn't say "against."

I sometimes heard conversations at the table that definitely were not for me to hear. They said, "Mind the child," and my parents grew silent. Sometimes I overheard conversations when my parents had visitors. I know now that the visitors were mainly Jewish colleagues of my father's and that the conversation always revolved around the theme "Emigrate or stay." If I walked in, they said, "Mind the child," and it was quiet again. I knew something or other wasn't right. But sometimes I caught words and then I would be reprimanded: "You must not say or repeat that anywhere."[2] You probably know that it was inordinately dangerous to be against the government, against Hitler. Even if our situation was self-evident, I mustn't say anything under any circumstance. I believe there are still forebodings that haunt me today; the fear that somehow saying something wrong or saying too much could have terrible consequences. I also feared that I could bring my parents to a catastrophe, that I would somehow betray them. I believe a child who grew up in a free world, in a free country, couldn't conceive this. That is something I notice again and again, even with my own children. What is absolutely inconceivable: these commands to silence, to experience or say only what's permitted, and everything beyond that can be deadly. I don't know whether I knew that it was deadly, but it was by all means terribly dangerous. I have said to begin with I didn't know that my father was Jewish—my parents didn't say—they wanted to go easy on me. They wanted me to stay unbiased, as unbiased as possible, and then they had allowed my sister and me to be baptized with my father's consent in 1938, an event I remember well. I was eight. This baptism took place at home. We were no longer in that big apartment. My parents had already lost a large part of their inheritance. My father, of course, had hardly an income because his salary had been taken and many patients didn't dare go to a Jewish doctor any more. And so in 1935 we had to move to a cheaper apartment. I don't want to tell now how it came about that my parents lost their entire fortune that year. In reality, they so utterly lost their fortune that nothing remained as a result of the persecution except for debts. I don't know whether I should tell you this. Naturally I learned everything later. I noticed only the effects, of course. I went to a girls' school, a typical public school, in 1935. I was unbelievably lucky to have a fantastic teacher. Because your origin had to be declared at registration, it was nearly impossible to cheat and [for students and teachers] to act as if it were nothing. I had a wonderful teacher, and I actually had four very nice school years.

In fall, October 1, 1938, all the Jewish doctors had their licenses revoked.[3] My father lost his license and had to give up his practice. It was no longer possible to keep my father's Jewishness a secret from me. My mother had to tell me. It was a shock. You can't imagine today what kind of a shock that was because I knew that Jews were being persecuted. One saw caricatures everywhere in town, in the *Stürmer* cartoons [nearly pornographic], on the front page of newspapers. One heard inflammatory speeches. As a child, you learned that the most horrible enemy of the Germans were the Jews and they must disappear. Suddenly we were apprised that we belonged to this group. This was a blow I probably have never completely overcome. And along with that came the expectation to emigrate. My mother said, "We will emigrate. We're just waiting for an affidavit, a guarantee from America. As soon as possible we have to get out of Germany." As you will see, it didn't turn out that way.

I can still remember much about this time, for example, the so-called Kristallnacht ["night of broken glass"] on November 9 and 10, 1938. At the time I was with my mother; we went into the city and I beheld innumerable pieces of broken glass. Do you know the Kleine Alster [lake] and the Alsterarkaden? Window display mannequins floated there from a plundered business called Robinson and from other ravaged stores. There were several large, Jewish-owned department stores that had been destroyed and the mannequins swam, floated in the water like dismembered people. That greatly affected me. I also feared for my father, who had remained home. He wasn't imprisoned then, probably because he was in a "mixed marriage," protected by my "Aryan" mother.

I also remember a house search. I came home from school and found two men busy searching in the cabinets. We had a large hallway in which there were many closets. The two men busily cleaned out the closets. I was nine years old and didn't realize this was a house search. I believed my parents had employed these men to clean the house. I sat down and started to chat with them, to the horror of my parents, who were sitting in the living room and naturally were terribly afraid that these men would somehow or other get information out of me. Perhaps I would unwittingly tell them something, which was inordinately dangerous. The entire event was harmless conversation. They asked me questions about schoolwork and school, and they were also friendly to my parents. They excused themselves, took leave, and so it seemed like it was no big deal [as if they were just polite cleaners].

In 1939 my father had to give up his valuables, and at the time I already understood what it meant. Most of the things he could give to my mother. By doing that, they would be in "Aryan" possession. For example, he had a gold watch his father gave him in 1914 when he'd volunteered. He had to give it up. That was incredibly painful for him because it was his father's souvenir. One day I came home from school and my father carried an airmail letter with colorful edges in his hand and waved it saying again and again "I have an affidavit. I have an affidavit." I didn't really believe my father would go away. At the time he was joyous. Later, he couldn't use this affidavit. His passport was cancelled. It was a very nerve-wracking time. How my parents succeeded in having us notice relatively little is still a mystery. In our presence they kept to themselves and tried to keep as much as possible from us.

In spring 1939 I completed fourth grade, the last grade of primary school, and then passed the exam for the next level, but my parents wanted me to get away from Hamburg because my father was about to emigrate and they didn't want me to take part in all the frenzy. My mother managed to have me suspended from school for an entire year. Not going to school at all for a year was not necessarily a positive move for me. I was, of course, bored. They sent me to my mother's relatives in Gießen. My mother's father and two sisters were there and one sister had a family, a husband and three children. I spent months in Gießen and heard about my father's emigration through a letter from my mother at the end of June 1939. I had seen him for the last time before I rode to Gießen. I spent the beginning of the war in Gießen, which I remember very well. I lived at my grandfather's and his unmarried daughter's.

Together, they managed a large wholesale operation for groceries and other things, which were then sold in the village stores in Hessen. One evening my grandfather brought a woman with a small child into the house. They had been evacuated from the Left Bank of the Rhine. In 1939 some women and children had been evacuated as a precaution and brought into the interior of the country. My grandfather had just taken them in. I had to give up my bedroom to the mother and daughter and move to my grandfather's bedroom to sleep for one or two nights. When I awoke in the morning, my grandfather had already gotten up and gone to his office. The housekeeper, a middle-aged woman, came in, opened the curtains and said, "There's war. They've been shooting since six A.M." I will never forget that. Soon the first alarms began in Gießen. We went down to the basement. We had ration tickets and you couldn't buy everything you wanted. And there was a general tension. I also saw something that I absolutely won't forget: the somber atmosphere of the very first days of the war. In no way did the people celebrate, quite the contrary. We lived not far from the train station. The street led to the train station where I'd stand in the evenings and watch endless columns of soldiers with horses heading for the station and moving forward. Many people stood on the edge of the street, and, as I said, the atmosphere was depressing—quite a contrast to the First World War. My mother had told me how people had celebrated and gone crazy. That was not at all the case now.

In October 1939 I returned to Hamburg. I was quite bored, I must say, because I wasn't going to school. On Easter 1940 it started. My mother registered me in a Hamburg girls' school. There I had my first and only really horrifying experience with a fanatical anti-Semite. It was pleasant in the school. I soon had friends. I felt good there. Perhaps one week after the first school day we had an assembly in the large hall and the school director spoke to us. He was, at the same time, our English teacher. I noticed after a short time I wasn't listening well. Who's interested? A ten-year-old is not interested in such speeches. Then I *did* listen. I soon noticed he was a fanatical Nazi, a traveling speaker of the Nazi party, and he told us about his struggle for the National Socialists before 1933. I had never before met a Nazi, or hadn't known I'd met a

Nazi. They were always somewhere in the distance; they were marching around in other places but you didn't have direct dealings with them. That was the first time someone stood eye to eye, opposed to me, across from me, on whom I was dependent. He began to speak about the enemies who threatened Germany in 1940 from all sides and about Germany's struggle for its existence. The worst enemies, he said, were, however, not outside Germany's borders. No, the worst enemies were inside the country—the most dangerous, the most devious enemies— and those were the Jews. And that was a few months after my father had emigrated. He went further and said not only are there enemies in the country, but also here inside the school. He said, "Ah, you will ask yourselves who? Jews are not allowed to attend German schools. Thank God there's a law that forbids it." I tell you, I was ten and you perhaps believe that I no longer remember things exactly, but I know it in distinct detail because it burned itself into me, pressed itself into me unforgetta- bly—I am not making something up. He said, "Jews certainly no longer go to our school, that's forbidden, thank God. But there are still half Jews, and unfortunately these half Jews are still at our school because it is not possible yet to remove them." And then he reported a few incidents in the school, all possible disagreeable occurrences. I know about only one. He said a valuable piano in the auditorium was scratched up. Investigations had revealed that "Aryan" children had scratched it up. But, he said, we researched further and found the instigators had been "half Jews." This speech ended with an urgent warning about "half Jews": Beware of them. My fellow pupils knew nothing about me, but I went home half numb. There I began to cry and told my mother everything. She was absolutely beside herself. My mother, a very courageous woman, said, "You no longer go there. Don't go into that school, not a single step will you make into that school."[4] One must imagine the situation: The school year had begun and now to take a child out of school and register somewhere else? With what reasoning? To say "I can't let my child into the school. There's a terrible Nazi and anti-Semite" wouldn't have worked in 1940. But for my mother it was definite. She wouldn't send me there. I had a wonderful former grade-school teacher whom she called and asked for help. He came over immediately and reflected. He knew no school director whom he trusted except one to whom he could speak openly. He simply called up this person and told him the story. That was a courageous deed at the time. I don't know if anyone who didn't live then can conceive this. He explained the situation and this other school principal said right away I could come to his school. Nothing would happen to me there. He gave his word and would stand by it. He even called the Nazi colleague and told him I had switched schools and why. I tell you this now to show you there *were* courageous people. I find this completely tremendous, inordinately courageous. As an American, you probably can't make sense of it, what it meant. This school was the Heilwigschule. It still exists today. It was also a girls' school. My teacher and school principal was Dr. Luethje. The Nazi teacher had a similar name, Dr. Lueth. So, I came into the Heilwigschule and felt good from the first moment on. I was accepted lovingly and in a friendly manner, and had the good fortune that it remained that way for four years. I didn't have a single unpleasant experience with a teacher. They treated me the same as they treated others. I don't know whether my fellow pupils knew about my Jewish father. With regard to some of them I *knew* they knew, of course. For instance, my best friend. I only told others, "My parents live separately." I was taught to say that. Not to say, whenever I was asked, "My father doesn't live in Germany; my parents live apart." I revealed nothing, but of course everyone had to know what I was because I didn't go to the Jungmädel [pre-BDM], a young woman's Nazi group. At age ten, one went to the Jungmädel, and later, at fourteen, the BDM, and I wasn't allowed to participate in that either. That was also naturally conspicuous. Of course everyone knew, but I didn't have any unpleasant times. Quite the contrary. I always had friends, was invited to birthday parties, was in the midst of activities. In this respect, everything was fine.

My father could write only as long as America wasn't in the war. We were supposed to follow him as soon as he had established himself, but that didn't work out because my father had to pass exams once again. He was already over fifty and it was rough for him. He spoke no English at all and my mother had large debts that my father left behind. First of all, my parents had lost their entire fortune, then my parents had to go to court. My mother still had debts to the attorney and so we were completely impoverished. There was absolutely no possibility to travel to America. Ah, my mother! How did we live at the time? We had four rooms. My mother rented two rooms to two young ladies and worked at home. She typed letters for an office in order to earn money. She was no longer a bookseller. First, there was a war, and second, she didn't want to leave us alone. She always had the feeling she must be at home so my sister and I wouldn't be left to our own devices.

I knew of no other children from "mixed marriages" in my class. In other classes, there were some. In mine, no. In a class a year ahead of me, I knew for sure there was the daughter of the *Reichsstatthalter* [similar to state representative], [Karl] Kaufmann. No, she was in the class behind me. This was a school in Harvestehude where some prominent Nazis lived. I have no memories at all of any sort of difficulties for me. Maybe it would have been difficult if I had flunked a grade and ended up in the same class with the Kaufmann daughter. I actually have only good memories. No unpleasant memories. I enjoyed going. I felt secure. I was almost a favorite student, one could say. A teacher with whom I met and spoke after the war told me that someone had informed the *Kollegium* [school board] of what had happened to me in my other school. In response, this school board had resolved unanimously to stand by me. I think that's important to know.

Perhaps another reason for my lack of bad memories was my mother. My mother was very popular. She was an extraordinary human being and could get along beautifully with others and impressed people very much through her style. She was very clever, full of humor, quick-witted, smart, and beloved by others. That of course helped me as well. My mother provided me with strong support. I know my mother did much for others too. She was admired by many.

My mother was of medium height. How should I describe her? Medium height, not extremely thin but not fat. She had a good figure, very graceful, and earlier had been very athletic. She had unbelievably lively eyes and a very lively, beautiful, clever, and kindly face. My mother was very popular with my friends in school, and she had a sense for silly things. Loved to laugh. She played with us, read, told stories, and was always full of ideas. In spite of the whole depressing situation, she was always there for us. There were children who when something went wrong were afraid of their parents. I would never have thought of being afraid of my parents. Quite the contrary. At home, you could inform them, tell them. My mother listened attentively to stories, even like the terrible one with the anti-Semite. I could depend on my mother and her protection. I always had the feeling she could cope with anything, even with Hitler himself. As a child, that's the way I always felt and thought.

My mother came from a Social Democratic household. My grandfather in Gießen was a Social Democrat from its beginnings. He was one in the previous century when there were the socialist laws, and the party was banned. In Gießen he was one of the founders of the Social Democratic party [SPD]—a council member up until the First World War. He played a large political role in Hessen. In 1910 he was also a candidate for the parliament. I say that now, but I know that only because of what my mother told me. I have tried with the help of the Friedrich Ebert Foundation in Bonn to learn more about the development of Social Democracy in Gießen and they wrote to me, "Everything is destroyed. In part in the war and in part after the Nazi seizure of power." Everything that in some way could have been dangerous for former members of the Social Democratic party was destroyed in 1933. Whatever I know about my grandfather is through my mother's stories. As a young girl, she was passionately interested in politics. She was a pacifist. She was also greatly interested and involved in the women's movement. She was an ardent socialist. That's the way she was and that's the way she stayed. I believe her cosmopolitanism, that she married my father and was always swimming against the current, didn't upset her at all. My mother was really suave, liberal, and involved herself very much with society.

She put energy into Social Democratic and women's associations during and after World War I, but I don't know for sure if she was a member. I know only for instance that she read *Lilli Braun: Erinnerungen einer Sozialistin* [Lilli Braun: Memories of a Socialist Woman]. I have that here on the shelf. I bought it again. She spoke with enthusiasm about it. I just found a book in an antique store and read it with great interest, a book that today nobody knows about but about which my mother talked. It must have made an impression on her as a young girl: *Die Katrin wird Soldat.* [Katrin Becomes a Soldier].[5] It is a pacifist, no, not pacifist really, but an outspoken antiwar book. It deals with a young girl, should I tell you? It strongly influenced my mother, and us indirectly, as well. I just read it for the first time. It's about a young girl born in 1897 just like my mother, in Lorraine, Left Bank of the Rhine in Metz. She was a Jew but that plays no role in the book; it's only mentioned now and again. [At this time, the doorbell rings.] Who's there? [She whispers.] It's probably my second cousin who's mentally slow. When I don't answer the door, he goes away. [She does not answer.]

I have to admit, I don't know if my mother ever campaigned for a woman's right to vote. She was a supporter of the women's movement. In 1918, I believe, the right to vote was introduced in Germany. She was twenty-one and committed herself to that as a young girl. I know, for example, she was a very good but uncomfortable student in school. She was an unwilling student because she always thought very independently and came from a very Social Democratic family. In bourgeois society that was a provocation. She had, for example, a 3 in conduct at graduation, not very good. Conduct is how one behaves toward *adults,* and behavior was measured that way. How one got along with fellow students or how willing one was to help or cooperate wasn't measured.

My mother didn't take part in certain home economics classes[6] because my grandfather used her near sightedness as an excuse. Home economics was taught in such a mentally stunting manner. Instead, my mother could go for a walk and read what was made available to her during that class time. But the needle-work teachers took offense. One time someone in the street recognized her and she didn't greet her because she was nearsighted, so she was viewed as arrogant and mean-intentioned. And she received a 3 in conduct. That wasn't easy to have on a diploma, because it's detrimental. It showed on applications at that time. But that simply was my mother who always swam against the tide. My mother died in 1969 at seventy-two, scarcely seventy-two, unfortunately. But I have inherited very little of my mother's fighting spirit. I was always anxious, timid, and accommodating. I shared her thoughts and feelings very strongly and always wished I could be like her but I must say, I'm not. She acted very bravely.

My mother was actually dominant in her marriage. My father was rather dependent and always a bit *Gedankenabwesend* [absent-minded]. He was immersed in thoughts somewhere or other ruminating over subjects. "Spacey" might be the accurate English term. He was always in thought, not entirely in this world. My father was not someone who stood with both feet firmly on the ground; rather, he was often captivated by some idea. Often he needed someone to relieve him of practical duties. My mother did that. Before my father emigrated my mother made all the trips to the consulate and to the German offices and so on. She relieved him of everything because my father was so helpless in everyday life and he was also in danger then. My mother was the only one who performed wonderfully, so we always expected that she would do everything. And when we were long since grown up, my sister and I, we still expected my mother to manage each situation. My mother said once, shortly before her death, "I would gladly have been the weaker." I still think about that. "Yes, I would gladly one time in my life have been the weaker." She told me the following: After my sister's birth she was seriously sick. She had a sepsis, a kind of childbed [postnatal] fever. She was suspended between life and death. My father came to visit her, everyday, hours long, and sat on her bed and cried. My mother, who was deathly ill, consoled him. I believe that was significant somehow or other. He always said he had lost his own mother so early. It sounds so funny now when I tell it. He said, "I can get another woman but I can't get a suitable mother for my child." And my mother had to comfort him and say it would be okay and she would be healthy again. So that is the relationship between my parents. My father was the weaker one and in need of consolation and my mother would have gladly, just once, been the weaker. We always saddled her with everything because she was really the one who managed.

Yes, I think my mother felt weak at times, certainly, but she never revealed it. She was a person of unbelievable self-control. But, ultimately, that was something she overtaxed. Then she was also indescribably weighed down from the entire Nazi situation, and added to that we overburdened her. And I think sometimes, my poor mother, it was all so inhumanely unreasonable. We lived under the conditions of war and the Nazis.

My father couldn't send money in wartime. After the war he helped us greatly. During the war that wasn't possible. My mother was left entirely to her own resources. The time came when my sister had to leave school and go into her *Pflichtjahr* [mandatory year of service].[7] The girls, having left school, had to work a year in a large household that had many children. As far as that goes, she lucked out and lived with nice people in the country. During my sister's duty year I was alone with my mother in Hamburg. In 1941 my father's relatives were deported. I caught on to that. I still have the deportations horribly housed in memory. I knew nothing exactly, saw nothing precisely, but I know my mother, even at that time, had tried desperately to prevent the deportation of my father's relatives. And ineffectually. They were deported to Riga [Latvia][8] and killed. The entire situation, beginning with the introduction of the Jewish stars, made me sick.[9] It was a dreadful shock for me when suddenly people in the street ran around with these stars attached to them, and I was mortally terrified that I also must wear one. Friends and relatives and acquaintances here were suddenly wearing these stars. And then they disappeared. I knew they had been deported. I was very sick in fall 1941. I am absolutely certain it had to do with these events. They had such a creepy, threatening, and atrocious dimension that I simply did not easily endure. I didn't go to school for months. I don't know how long. Until spring 1942 I lay in the hospital a long time. Nobody knew what was wrong. Depressed, mental problems, yes. I suppose it was more. I was absolutely no longer in the position to do anything, and I could eat nothing. I untiringly vomited everything. I had terrible stomach pains. My appendix was held responsible for it. I was operated on. It turned out that it wasn't the appendix at all. I contracted pneumonia after this appendix operation, and truly, I just survived. I recovered very very slowly. I think this condition into which I'd gotten was, without question, related to this persecution. And with the shock over my relatives and what happened to them and what occurred around me.

My mother talked about it sometimes. I know that. Meanwhile we really knew everything. Once when my mother was out, she saw signs of the deportations. And she came home—and I can only faintly remember, I never asked her questions about that, strangely enough—she was perfectly colorless in the face, she vomited and talked about what was so terrible. She had seen how the Jewish people had been rounded up. And she was regularly in a state of shock. Unfortunately, it happens everywhere. No nation is safeguarded against it.

My sister and I got along fairly well with each other, even though she always did better in school. School basically played a minor role for us. My mother certainly was interested in our report cards and our work, but even with that she had a totally different attitude than other mothers. My mother was completely novel in many respects. For example, if we had bad grades, which almost never occurred with my sister but several times with me, my mother said, "We must now compensate for that somehow. We must celebrate." Then we went to an ice cream parlor or confectionary and my mother said, "If anything at all unpleasant happens, then you must equalize it with something good." We stopped anywhere we felt like it, ate an ice cream or took a walk—anything beautiful I was allowed to seek out for myself. This happened a few times. That's how my mother functioned, no? My father, as long as he was still there, wasn't interested in our school reports. He had entirely different worries. I could hold whatever I wanted under his nose. If it was nothing but poor grades, he said, "great, great," because he didn't look in to see at all. To him it was regarded as trivial. He was busy with more important things, and it wasn't so serious to him.

In 1942 my sister had to leave school. She was a brilliant student in contrast to me. I was not so awfully good in school. My sister gladly attended, was an unbelievably good pupil, and had to leave in 1942. They knew perhaps about this *Rusterlass*,[10] which was directed at the *Mischling ersten Grades*. Entering into the secondary school was forbidden for us, and if you were already there, you had to finish as if you had genuinely completed, had achieved a certain level. My sister finished the tenth grade and immediately had to leave the school. I had been advanced to the seventh grade and was allowed to remain according to this *Rusterlass* until the end of the eighth school year. I could stay two years and then I must get out. That was a new shock for my mother. You must imagine our financial situation. We had really nothing at all. We had unimaginably little money. What we had, my mother earned from renting rooms and typewriting work. It didn't suffice.

My sister was horrified to be thrown off track through the Nazi years. My sister would have studied in the university, and I believe she would have been a splendid lawyer. Perhaps a doctor, I don't know for sure, but I think really she would have been a good lawyer. She had to get out and didn't finish the diploma. She had to earn money at first after the war. It would have been good for her self-worth if she had gotten a diploma then, but she didn't see the necessity right away. On the contrary, first she earned a little money, which was fundamentally important at the time for us. We had nothing. In the last year before the end of the war, April 1944-1945, she was an untrained office aide. She wasn't allowed at all to study. Occupational training was forbidden [because of her Jewish parent]. Her job was recognized later as a business apprenticeship. After [the war], she worked her way to a decent position. She was business director in the Hamburg Journalist's Association, a very respected position. Then she worked her way into insurance law and to this day she's consulted as an expert in this field even though she didn't go to school. Today she's often asked, for example, in the former East Germany, to give speeches about insurance law for journalists. She's still needed very much. But what she gladly would have done, and what she would have done extremely well, she didn't do, and for many years she had to work her way through the world.

In 1943, you probably know there were heavy bomb attacks on Hamburg, Operation Gomorrah by the Royal Air Force. Summer 1943 [July 24, 1943], we were bombed out. It was catastrophic for my mother. For everybody. But especially hard for us, because the apartment was our source of income. The house burned out; the apartment was gone and we had saved nothing at all. My mother lived in Gießen for a while and there the political climate was horrible, not by our relatives, but in such a small city one couldn't put up with it. She wanted to return to Hamburg although Hamburg had been almost completely destroyed and one could go back to Hamburg only if one proved he had a job there. Booksellers were no longer sought after. There also were no more books, none to

buy. My mother applied for a job as a house employee. She really loved
Hamburg. She wanted to go back, above all, for political reasons. In small
cities and the countryside the people observed each other more closely
and the Nazis in Gießen were highly fanatical—completely horrible
Nazis. Not my relatives. I have to make an exception for them. My
mother succeeded in getting a job as a housekeeper and returned to
Hamburg in Fall 1943. She got one small room. When my sister returned
from her *Pflichtjahr* in the summer of 1944 she lived with my mother in
this room and, after the war, I joined them. We sometimes had to move,
but we always lived in one small room altogether until 1953 when I
married. You can't imagine how primitively we lived at that time.

After the bombing in 1943 there were no lessons held in Hamburg.
The schools remained closed. I had no more schooling. In January 1944
my school was transferred to a small town, Wittstock, in Mecklenburg,
situated between the Baltic and Berlin. It was mainly rural country. It
was called *Kinderlandverschickung* [sending the children to the country-
side].[11] I don't know if you've encountered that term. The children from
areas likely to be bombed were—at the time it was voluntary—sent into
the countryside in order to be educated. In the cities, under the
circumstances, it was no longer possible. Probably there were other
reasons for sending children to the countryside—that is, it could have
been so the Hitler Youth, the NSDAP [the Nazi party], the Nazis, and
the BDM [League of German Girls] and so on could have a more
intensified effect on the children. That was also the intention. At the
time, although I was a person of "mixed race of the first degree," I traveled
in January 1944; I took part in the "sending the kids to the country."
Most children lived in large camps but the girls at our school were housed
in private quarters, and so was I. My foster-mother was a seventy-year-
old widow. I was fortunate because she was not a Nazi at all but had been
a Communist. In this way we trusted and understood each other. That
was the most important thing of all there. I did not experience bullying.
In this regard, I was always very lucky. It was difficult in a small city to
not be in the BDM. Almost the entire school was nothing but girls and
we had our own camp leader, a BDM leader, just for our school. She
visited me in my private room shortly after I arrived, and she said, "In

such a small city it is highly conspicuous if you aren't in service, and I want to ask whether you want to come into service?" I said, "Yes, I am not allowed, you can guess for which reasons. I also have no uniform." One said "Kluft." I said, "I don't have a 'Kluft.'" She said, "Ah, that doesn't matter. Certainly you have a blue skirt and a white blouse and a jacket and bobby socks? Simply put these on and make do and you don't need to worry, it won't be noticeable. Some of the others were bombed out, so they also don't have everything according to regulations."

In order not to be conspicuous in a small town, I joined the BDM on excursions. I still have a letter in which I describe a Nazi assembly with grown up leaders of the Hitler Youth and more Nazis who had to instruct us politically, and I made fun of it. I was very improvident in my letters. I have these letters, and now I must say again that nothing terrible happened to me. It was my school and they were all dear to me. I belonged there absolutely and I was in the choir. I sang madly. We performed theater pieces, not Nazi pieces, but normal fairy tales and operettas. Perhaps you think it seems strange. I was elated then in the children's evacuation and it was worse to think about being away from home. When I think of that time, I think it was *always* really sad because I was afraid of the war. I was afraid because of my father. I was afraid because I didn't know what had happened to my mother and sister in Hamburg—we always heard bombs were dropped on Hamburg again and again and again so I didn't know what had happened to them. And I didn't know what would happen to me. It was a gloomy time.

But, in spite of all this, life with my teacher and all of these girls, who were very kind, was somewhat good. The old woman I lived with was my substitute mother. She was not so old, but I thought she was very old. She was seventy then and I was fourteen. For me she was very very old. But she was not a Nazi and there were no Nazis in the house. It was a good feeling for me to have no Nazis there. Everybody was kind. In spite of all this, it was awfully gloomy. You had the feeling that you couldn't survive. I didn't think that I would survive. I thought, These are the last months of my life. I thought this way until after the war.

I remained in Wittstock until the summer of 1944. Then I had to leave. I still have the complete correspondence. My mother had tried to reach the school agencies so that I'd be able to stay. It was rejected. She made many requests and always was turned down. I was to leave summer 1944, after completing the eighth grade. I wasn't allowed to stay in Mecklenburg. I wasn't allowed to perform the *Pflichtjahr* nor learn an occupation, nor attend a different school. I was sought out for compulsory labor. The work agency wanted to direct me to forced labor. I still have many documents pertaining to that. Once again I had tremendous good fortune. I was still very small and looked twelve and had the strength of a twelve-year-old. In Hamburg, I was exempted from this labor and was allowed to go to relatives in Gießen. My mother couldn't provide lodging for me and wanted to get me out of the bombing areas. I have an appalling fear of bomb attacks that started after I was in them a few times and had barely escaped. You can't imagine how horrifying it is— you can't imagine it—to fall victim to a bombing attack is unimaginably ghastly. I had immense fear. My mother thought I'd be safe from Nazis and bombs in Gießen. I lived at my mother's oldest sister's house. You know where Gießen is, in Hessen? This older sister was married with three grown children. Her oldest son, a soldier, had already died in battle in Russia, 1942. The younger son was in France and missing. The daughter was in Gießen but had been called up for work as an aide to the Air Force. While living there, I tried to behave as inconspicuously as possible so nobody would notice anything about me. I couldn't do much—only help with a few odds and ends in the house. I hoped the war would end. I liked my aunt. She was close to me. And my cousin. My aunt's husband was difficult—he could hardly put up with me. Both of his sons were soldiers and one died in battle. He knew what I was thinking and hoping even though I didn't speak. He knew on which side I stood. And I did nothing, sat around. In a certain way, I was a spoiled child. I had never helped out in the house and there were difficulties between my relatives. I didn't grasp it then, but later it was clear.

We also heard stories about the camps. Nothing exact. I knew that my relatives were taken away. I knew that the Jews were gone from Hamburg. Deportations. I didn't see deportations myself, but I knew they had happened. I knew from my mother also, and it occurred sometimes that news trickled through, for example, from soldiers who were on leave.

Above all, from the Russian front; they had almost all experienced a great deal of mass executions and so forth. My mother had a cousin, older than she, who was called up to be a staff doctor. He was a general staff doctor in a high position. He was sent to Russia to a military hospital in Minsk. I know that while he was in Minsk he had happened upon the Jewish exterminations in close proximity and had told my mother about it during leave. My mother was completely beside herself. My uncle wasn't a Nazi but had grasped what was wrong there. I know myself that he said once that an SS man was taken in by them, off and on; he had gone crazy from the executions. He had a mental breakdown. Hence, we knew a heap. I think the majority knew, more or less, but had, in part, not believed it. No one could be cognizant of specific expressions like "Auschwitz." They did know "concentration camp." They knew about that for a while. One *knew* there were mass killings. One *knew* the Jews had disappeared, that is, those who hadn't emigrated. The *Sternträger* [Jews wearing stars] had disappeared and one surmised what had happened to them. This and that was said or whispered. One must know that the theme was suppressed, was naturally awful. One wasn't permitted to listen to the English broadcasting system. It was a capital offense. I know in Gießen, before we were bombed out, there was a death warrant against a married couple we knew who had listened to the English broadcast and had spoken about it. They were sentenced to death. I know this for sure because I knew them. The BBC broadcast German news. We listened to it always.

In December 1944 it was Gießen's turn for heavy bombing attacks. We were all bombed out. Likewise, my grandfather with his single daughter. They lived ten minutes from us. Their private house and business were destroyed. My grandfather, my mother's father, died shortly after he got out of the bombs as a result of this attack and smoke inhalation.

I was separated from my relatives. I don't know why. I came into a small village in the Marburg area quite some distance from my relatives where two young women lived—one unmarried and the other widowed. Her husband had died in battle. There were hardly any men around—young men were a rarity. In this entire village there were only women, children, and old men. These women took me into their home. I don't know if they knew what was going on with me, or what my situation was. In any event, I lived there. I was the niece of Mrs. Fuhr, she was my mother's sister, and they knew that. So I remained at their place. I had, of course, fewer possibilities to do anything. We had two puny little rooms that we lived in. One of these two women had a four-year-old son, and we four slept in two beds. One can't imagine the primitiveness. I no longer had anything except for a small little suitcase with a few cheap articles of clothing. I received no more clothing—there wasn't any. I got ration coupons but no clothes. I still had a pair of shoes and in them I had run out of the burning city of Gießen. They were worn out, taped together. I had nothing more than that. These shoes were too tight and the winter was cold so my feet were terribly frozen. Then I just sat and hoped that the war would end. I couldn't do anything else. I was busy with the small boy.

In March 1945 the Americans were already close, and the younger sister of my mother, who directed my grandfather's business, came to pick me up. She arrived with the company truck one early morning. There was no more gasoline. The truck ran on charcoal. There were large charcoal containers to the left and right of the cooling system, which were then turned into gas. My aunt wanted to take me to her place. We traveled the entire day because, at the time, American low-flying aircraft were out and shot at everything that moved. I have to say it seems like a miracle to me that I'm sitting here. I think of people who were trying to do me in—not just the Nazis but also the British and Americans. My aunt didn't sit in the driver's cab but stood outside the door clinging to the door handle to see if low-flying American planes would appear. I sat beside the driver. If there were some planes, she'd hit on the windshield and we'd stop, jump out, and roll into the ditch next to the road. Most of the time they roared by us. A few times they did shoot at us, but we always got out. Today a survivor told me that his relatives had stayed in Germany and endured the war, Nazi Germany, and a time in hiding—they withstood the war until a few days before the war's end when they were killed in a bombing attack. One had, at the time, enough possibilities to die.

After the war started, contact from America was also broken. Until then my father had continued to write and we had been able to write back. It took an eternity for the mail to arrive. Later on you could still write a few words by means of the Red Cross, but that was practically nothing compared to earlier. I knew nothing at all about my father, and as I sat around in Hessen I knew nothing about my mother. But now and then we still got letters through to Hamburg and from Hamburg. I could show some to you, but I believe then we would sit here until midnight. For example, we got postcards. I couldn't write any more letters because there wasn't any paper. One can't imagine the scarcity. The postcards all had an imprint that said—if you want, I can show them to you— *"Der Führer kennt nur Kampf, Arbeit und Sorge. Wir wollen ihm den Teil davon abnehmen, den wir ihm abnehmen können."* [The Führer knows only war, work and worry. We want to ease his burdens by taking up a part of his work]. I still have one.

After the war, I knew I *had* survived. I think with the air raids in the summer of 1943. They were so awful, I can't describe. After the first air raid in Hamburg, the night between July 24 and 25—it had been a heavy air raid but we weren't bombed out—our house was all right but we saw the sky and it was red from fire. In the morning when we awakened it was dark because of the smoke. And it was dark all day. It was a wonderful day—clear and sunny—but in Hamburg all the day was dawn, yes? Not quite dark, but dawn. You couldn't see anything because there was smoke everywhere in the sky. You had a feeling of *Weltuntergang* [the world is going to end]. I didn't think that Hamburg would survive. Yes, later it was rebuilt. I thought it is the end of Hamburg, and it will be the end of us. That day, after the first air raid, friends of ours who were bombed out came to us and I can see their faces—horrified, gray faces—with the expression of, oh, I can't say it, *äußerster Entsetzen und Schrecken* [extreme terror and fright]. And from that moment on the Nazis were on one side and these air raids on the other. You couldn't think. I only thought, these will be the last months of my life. From all sides, men in uniform tried to kill me. [She raises her voice.] Today when I see policemen in uniforms it doesn't really bother me. Soldiers, yes. I can't stand to watch them march.

I can talk about how the Americans came—should I talk about it? My aunt took me into the village. Should I speak in English? I can try.

[She switches to English.] She took me to Grossen Linden, where she lived. The driver of that car had saved her and my grandfather during the night when Gießen was destroyed and he had come and helped them escape. But my grandfather, as I told you, died some days later. He was injured. My aunt, the younger sister of my mother, stayed with this driver's family in that village in Hessen. She took me with her. She had a very, very small room in that house, an old house. It was too small for one person, and yet two of us slept together. We knew the Americans were very near to us. We could hear shooting and so on. People began to show white towels. We had one towel together—my aunt and I. [Laughs.] And we put our towel out of the window. It was forbidden. There were SS soldiers who came to the village and they said we were not allowed to show white. [In German.] Oh, they wanted to fight. [In English.] They wanted to fight to the last shot! [In German.] It continued here and there: white flags out, white flags in. We saw the remains of the German army marching through our village. They were ragged and starving and their feet were partly wrapped up; they no longer had shoes. They had bloody bandages. They dragged themselves through the village. They still wanted to fight! No, they didn't actually, but there were still SS people there and *they* wanted to fight and they came with bazookas. Do you know what bazookas are? They were huge. I still can see them. These were used to shoot at tanks. SS people waved their bazookas around and suddenly were in the village and wanted to fight until the last shell.

One morning in March, early 1945, we heard a loud machine noise in the air and I thought, Airplanes, and went out to look at the sky. None in sight. I looked over the fields from my village to the neighboring village and saw the tanks coming forward. [In English]: Tanks. Jeeps. I knew they were Americans and it was the happiest moment of my life. Perhaps they could have shot, but they didn't, luckily. It was a wonderful feeling I can't describe. [In German]: I observed everything: how several men walked out of our village with white flags in order to hand over the village without a struggle. Then the American tanks came into the village. It became louder and louder. We lived on a hill on the main street and they came uphill and had to change gears—an indescribable noise! I was standing upstairs in my room at the window and was not allowed to show how happy I was because I was only among Germans who didn't think favorably of these events. I was the only one. I couldn't share my feelings with anyone. Not with my aunt because now that the Americans came it was not what they wanted—it's difficult to describe how people felt at the time. But I looked at the Americans and they looked at me. [In English]: They looked like people of another star because they were healthy and they had clean uniforms and they were really fat. No, I must say, fat is not the right word; they were *stämmig* [brawny], strong, and we were all so [in German] run down and ragged, badly nourished and looked pretty pathetic. The Americans looked like completely different people.[12] They were in sharp uniforms and neat, and they had an enormous quantity of weapons and materials. For three days and three nights they were always riding through the village. Nothing happened. On the third evening a troop had gotten drunk. They'd found some schnapps. Supposedly there were assaults. I didn't notice anything, I have to say. The idea never occurred to me that one could fear the Americans. For me, they're exactly what I'd hoped for. They stood in the streets and played baseball. We saw for the first time these large baseball gloves. The children stood around and watched. The Americans passed out chocolate and anything else available to the children. From the very beginning, they were friendly. I'd experienced unpleasant events but never anything horrible. We heard American music. Next door to us was a guest house/tavern where many Americans were quartered. Everything had been forbidden. We heard jazz for the first time. All of that had been previously prohibited and all of a sudden we had a feel for [says in English] the American way of life. [In German]: It was nice. Everything loosened up. The Americans were so relaxed in their behavior. I was very happy then.

I was still in Hessen and had to go back to Hamburg. There were no trains and no cars. In June my mother succeeded in coming from Hamburg to Grossen Linden in order to pick me up. She needed three days and three nights to get there. Today one arrives in five hours with the train. We drove back to Hamburg. What an adventure! Three days and three nights we were on the road. First we were taken by company trucks in the direction of Hamburg. Then we were dropped off, and we stayed overnight in empty train compartments. The next day we traveled some distance by train to Hannover and couldn't continue. Then we sat around and saw a freight truck carrying coal. You weren't permitted to climb on to it. We jumped up and lay on top of the coal. Then these freight cars rode northward very slowly, and it rained and we lay up there in the rain on the coal up until Uelzen, not far from Hamburg. This was the end of the second day. In the evening we were in Uelzen, and suddenly British railroad police rounded up all the people who were riding on the truck. We were totally black, filthy, and wet. That didn't bother me at all, I have to say. It was no longer life-threatening. The war was over, so I was happy. Somewhere we spent the night in a school on straw. The next day a truck that had taken many refugees loaded us on. Then the third evening we were in Hamburg. I didn't go to school. There wasn't any yet. In summer 1945 courses were organized for us *Mischlinge,* all those who had been thrown out in the early 1940s.

I began to go to school in August 1945 and in October or November 1945, I returned to my old class and my old school. School in Hamburg began again. Because, now, why not? I graduated even though I'd scarcely gone to school for over two years. I received my high school diploma in 1949, and I began to study. Then I married, had two children, gave up my occupation, then took it up again and began again to study [in English] special education. [In German] I am a teacher of special education for the deaf and for children with speech disabilities. I began to write books about Jewish schools and so on. I was already sixty when Hamburg University gave me the doctorate for my books about Jewish history. I'm not connected to a political party, but I'm still influenced by my mother. I've always been more left-wing. That runs in our family.

After the war, my father and I saw each other again, but he did not come back per se. He visited us again. I would prefer not to talk about it on tape because it is very personal. After the war I asked my mother, "Can we go be with my father now?" She said it was not possible; they were divorced. I was heartbroken. My father got to know a woman in America, and he asked my mother for a divorce because he could never be alone. My mother consented, and they were divorced in wartime: my father in America, my mother here. But my father allowed my mother to control his entire compensation matters from Hamburg after the war. My parents, after all, had a close relationship, the same as before. My father visited us in Hamburg in 1953 for a quarter year. Without his wife. He wanted to come back to Germany for good. He didn't accomplish it. My father died soon after his visit. So ultimately he never came back. He supported us generously after the war. We were among the first to get packages from him. He provided us with everything: groceries, clothes, and genuine objects of which we no longer ventured to dream. It was hard for my mother because my father had remarried in the middle of the war. That must have been 1943. He asked her for a divorce by letter. My mother remained alone. I never spoke with her about it. I can, therefore, only speak poorly. I'm not in the position to talk about it. I think that my parents' marriage wouldn't have broken up without the intervening circumstances, for my parents had an unheard-of understanding. I believe it was still an exceptionally satisfactory marriage. I never met his new wife. My father was in New York and later in Delaware. He got support at first. Later on he worked as a doctor, but he didn't succeed in becoming a recognized doctor again. He worked in a large health center. I must look it up. I still have the address somewhere.

Later on he succeeded in learning English, but only with many attempts, not right away. And he didn't really rise in the profession as he initially had. Rather, he worked always more or less in subordinate positions. He never again achieved self-employment as he had in Germany. My father lived until 1957. I reflect on my parents now, but then I reflected mainly on my own problems.

Looking back, it's difficult to say if I saw myself as an outsider. I always had friends and was well liked in my class. But I always had the feeling that I didn't belong. I was never allowed, for example, to talk about how we behaved. That didn't have anything to do with the ways of behaving but had to do with the situation in Nazi Germany. I knew I belonged to a group of people who were held in contempt, persecuted, who had fewer rights, actually no rights at all, who at all times figured there had to be arbitrary use of force by the State. And nowhere was I allowed to talk about myself and my situation. I always had to try to keep silent and inconspicuous. When I was treated with kindness and had friends, I was still somehow in an extreme outsider situation. I also had the feeling that I always had to behave exceptionally well because I was really only tolerated. I was not allowed to render even the smallest impropriety. I had the feeling I could be called away at any moment, that somebody could throw me out or fire me at any time because I was tolerated only out of grace and mercy.

I would like to define "outsider" but I can no longer define this evening. I'm too tired, I must admit. An outsider is someone who stands outside the social group either voluntarily because he has completely different convictions or because other people don't want to tolerate him in their group. That wasn't the case for me at all—certainly not in class. In spite of that, I was in a different situation from others. The others had brothers and fathers who fought as soldiers and fell in battle. Some of the others were Nazis. I always had to keep quiet about many things that were very important to me. I was only allowed to talk about them among close family members. I always had to be terribly careful.

I told you about my life, and I think you see. At the time, I was in a special situation, and I've never completely come out of it. You can't live a normal life in Germany if you've had this past. My friends today are all older than I, and they were, more or less, Nazis. Germans were like that at the time—maybe up to 90 percent were Nazis. There are many topics that we never discuss with each other, about which we talked at some time or another but about which we no longer want to speak. There are topics on which I, of course, keep silent because for others it would be embarrassing or unpleasant. In that way I don't lead a normal life in Germany. I feel free only when I'm in America, Israel, or England. In spite of that, I am, however, here. Somehow I belong. Back then I felt I belonged, yet I actually didn't. Somehow that kind of feeling remains. When one has been Jewish, one can't live a normal life in Germany. My sister makes certain that she absolutely is never put in the position to talk about this topic. I never talk about it with my sister. For her it's an absolute taboo. Otherwise, she couldn't live in this country. I'd talk about it again—I'd do that—but somehow it's always hard. Among my very dear older friends there are subjects on which we hardly touch. None of them were evil Nazis. They weren't active. They simply believed that Hitler was the great savior of Germany. After the lost war, from 1914 to 1918, Germany was very humbled. I think you can say that the people felt unjustly treated. I don't want to apologize for it, but the people were just as crazy, and then we had success. Suddenly everything was fine again. The people didn't like what came before 1933. There were endless street fights between Nazis and Communists. Suddenly there weren't any more, because naturally the Communists had been confined. But for the people, once again, harmony and order prevailed. That was everything. Again, life went upward. People felt they were respected and they had work. Germany was rebuilt. Yes, there is this ideology. Some historians have said that Hitler just spoke about what people wouldn't speak about. That he grabbed onto what many Germans wanted. That they really felt the Jews had taken their jobs. There are so many theories. Germans deified Hitler. They were crazed. They knew the images of those fanatic eyes. Horrible. Certainly, there were already roots of this anti-Semitism that he played on, which made it easier for him to be elected. He built himself up on propaganda. Hitler built his propaganda on this anti-Semitism. It was not only anti-Semitism but rather a hatred of foreigners—and that existed before Hitler. Also, the notion of the "Aryan" or German race as superior to everything else. The inferiors had the task only to esteem the master race. The Germans, the master race, must rule over all others and everything that didn't fit in, that was not healthy or normal, according to the Nazi norm. Also, art and culture were wiped out. The primary enemy were the Jews. Many Jews were in finance, doctors, academics. When they killed the Jews, they killed the core of the culture.

I can't really say that I have fear now, although I have occupied myself lately with this subject of the Third Reich, and my name is also mentioned in connection with this subject, and sometimes somewhere or other my name has been published, and everyone knows that I do this work. In spite of that I have no fear, no, I can't say I have fear. It *is* the case that I don't live a normal life here. I am not spiritually free. I also notice when I am together with friends that they live in another world. One can say I have a different conscience. There is also perhaps a collective Jewish conscience. I think I have a part of that. That is a subject that changes with the circumstances—if I am together with friends. Everyone has a different end point, a limit. Not that someone doesn't understand and that there are not volumes about which someone can speak. I was never asked afterward in my circle of friends, "What are you doing now, how far are you with this work?" and so on. Very seldom. Really, I live in several worlds. Yes, I feel split. On one hand, I have many Jewish friends and also a small circle of acquaintances who concern themselves with this topic of the past, and on the other hand, I know people who have absolutely nothing to do with this topic and for whom this topic is entirely remote. I feel Jewish, even though I am not. I can never become Jewish because I don't have a Jewish mother. It would be very difficult, and I don't intend to do it. However, I feel Jewish, yes. Absolutely. This has been a stressful week. I'm sorry for being so tired.

Chapter Six

ILSE B

*"I was treated differently because I looked Aryan.
That helped me a great deal."*

~

Iset out for Ilse B.'s house in Grosse Borstel (western Hamburg) on a chilly Sunday in March. Our meeting was set for 10:00 A.M., but her home was far out and a friend and I got lost after departing from the train. After a few phone calls to Ilse, I figured out the location and arrived at 11:30. A well-preserved, beautiful, and smiling older woman opened the door. Ilse was tall and thin with fine white hair. She dressed as if ready for church: She wore an exquisite peach cashmere sweater, a wool brown-blue skirt, and carefully chosen jewelry. She was not bothered by the delay, but her nervousness was immediately discernible. It took some time to arrange ourselves in separate chairs. I was conscious of her jewelry the entire interview: the pearl circle pin, green-colored pearls, black onyx ring, green coral bracelet, and a large watch. Her house with its cherry furniture and four Oriental rugs, like herself, exuded expensive taste. Pictures of her two grandchildren, both with dark hair, and four colorful paintings and sketches, one of her daughter, dominated the room. She had numerous animal china pieces — a goose with a blue ribbon and a yellow egg candle, and two dogs — and a collection of thimbles and old books.

Before the interview, Ilse had spent time hunting for information and items that she had saved from the Third Reich to share with me, which was ironic considering her talk was one of the most difficult to get into and to sustain. Ilse had trouble with her memory, and also would center on certain phrases or terms, such as *"Stikum,"* which kept her off the deeper, more sensitive topic at hand. A part of her had definitely lost interest in her past and the Germany that was behind her. She wanted her life to be like a new house without the ghosts. She, like many of the other women, could not comment effectively on her parents' personalities. When I asked if she made any educated guesses about her mother's silence, she ignored me. Ilse was curious if I always did these interviews and said, "It's nice you are doing that." She wondered if people in the United States liked to read books about the Nazi time. I said yes, very much, and sometimes it seems we are better informed.

Ilse had called me after she saw a notice in the *Eppendorfer Weekly* and invited me to talk about her life as a *Mischling.* Her mother was Jewish and her father, "Aryan." But after the first hour, primarily of superficial conversation, I doubted she would talk about her past in depth. Indeed, she provided only vignettes of that critical part of her life and did not appear eager to fill in missing details, no matter how many times I asked her. She was dependent on questioning and, unlike the other women, did not offer up a subject on her own or answer any questions with long stories. She cut her replies short with deliberate intention. She managed to avoid or change the topic as often as possible, usually by offering me more food (meringues), drink (coffee and sherry), or slippers, and on numerous occasions she asked if the tape recorder was still running. Ilse played with her hands obsessively, and at one point teared up. In the middle of our talk, she took off her pearls, periodically picked them up, played with them, put them down, and later put them back around her neck. She not only played with all her jewelry but also her coffee cup and later her long-anticipated glass of sherry. Constant, restless body movements, nervous laughter, alternately whispering and raising her voice, heavy breathing in and out, and strange noises punctuated her conversation. She simultaneously displayed obvious discomfort and extreme self-composure, being careful to avoid labeling herself as a "half Jew" when she clearly felt *Deutschblutig,* pure German. She spoke in a middle-class dialect of Hamburg, what is called German *gutbürgerlich.*

Ilse placed me both close and removed from her. Because she addressed me with *Sie,* the formal form of "you," it would follow that she would address me as Ms. Crane, but she familiarly called me by my first name throughout the interview. According to German language rules, if she used my first name she would address me with *du,* the familiar form of "you." Ilse often talked about herself using inclusive generalities, such as "for a young girl," instead of "for me," not speaking of herself specifically, as if she were someone else. She says of her own mother, "It was hard for *a mother.*" A few of the other women, namely Ruth Yost, also displayed this understandable tendency to separate or distance themselves from their personal experiences.

Ilse was very interested in my family background, asking me questions about my grandfather, his life as a doctor, his emigration, my grandparent's religion, and my father throughout our talk. She was concerned about what other *Mischling* women had said and was particularly disturbed when I told her that there were differences. She wanted her stories to corroborate with those of the others, perhaps so that she would not question the validity of her own experience. She asked if the other *Mischling* women felt like outsiders and was surprised that they still did, even though she admits to feeling this way herself. She wanted to know if I was going to analyze all of this later, and contrary to many Germans' preference for scientific inquiry, Ilse was upset that I might be looking at the Third Reich scientifically, which she said was impossible to do. I assured her I was not. When the topic came up of taking her photograph, she asked why I needed photos, shied away from this idea, and said no. A year later she conceded.

We discussed how men talk about their lives, about the fact that we have many accounts by men who have told their stories, but not by women. The women who survived the Third Reich do not feel as important. They do not as readily tell their stories even though they probably have more to say because women were immersed in family situations and they talked with and supported each other. While men worked outside of the family and came home at night, women experienced the "everyday." Some theorists have even claimed that women, in part, caused the Third Reich. With my mention of the Third Reich, Ilse said, "The Third Reich—I haven't heard that in years."

Ilse did not know much about current events that harkened back to the Third Reich. I had a discussion with her about Altona-Ottensen, where a shopping center was built on a Jewish cemetery. It made the news in Germany as well as the United States. After some Rabbis checked into the religious laws and after some negotiation, the developer agreed not to build a basement or underground parking. The graves were moved elsewhere and in a conciliatory effort a memorial was constructed in the mall. Many people are upset and say that the graves were desecrated. A similar incident happened in Bavaria, where there is a lot of radicalism: Over ten years ago, a memorial inscribed with the names of Jews who were killed was desecrated, with the names obliterated. Ilse said she had not heard about this.

very sensitive. Embarrassed. You know what I mean, don't you? It didn't matter to me. At the beginning of the war, a pretty bad time, people said to my mother such things like "*Judenweib*" ["Jewish woman"—derogatory]. But later some of the neighbors' sons and some of the sons of people that lived in our house were killed. The young husband of the woman above us was killed. We heard her crying. She didn't say "Heil Hitler" any more. She spoke in a very kind manner to my mother even before the end of the war after she had lost her husband. The Nazi time was over for her. My mother was sorely afraid of the other neighbors. These Kräute [slang for "Germans"] had greeted my mother with "Judenweib," but that was the least of it. We were glad that we were able to get into our apartment with just a "Judenweib." They could have pushed her down the steps, and she wouldn't have been able to defend herself or to say "He pushed me down the steps." It happened to others but not to my mother. We knew a woman who was Jewish and her husband was "Aryan," and someone tripped her and she fell down the steps. She was about my mother's age. Her daughter was as old as I was. But she couldn't say "He tripped me and made me fall down the steps." Then he would have said, "You're lying!" No one could do anything. One could only stand by and close the door and be happy when one had peace. My mother only had to endure the name-calling. Luckily no one ever physically accosted her. She never went out at night, and whenever she had to go anywhere she never went on the bus or the streetcar. She just stayed at home all the time like a prisoner in her own house.

My grandfather, my mother's father, wore the yellow star. He had to give up his apartment. He had to go to a "home," of sorts. He lived on the Bundestrasse near the university in a little Jewish *Pension*. It really wasn't a *Pension*—he had a room there. We visited him and he told us that we shouldn't come. He didn't want anything to happen to us, but I visited him. I would walk him home some days. [Her voice becomes shaky.] The boys threw rocks at me and yelled, "Why are you walking with a Jew?" I was blonde when I was a child. My grandfather said, "Go home, my dear." I didn't want to. The boys did not attack me because I was a girl with blonde curls. It was very difficult for our father. And my brother too. Strange how the men seem to take hardship more seriously. Can that be?

We women are stronger. They gave all the responsibility to me. My mother always said, "Ilse can do it." Me. Ilse did everything. I was more courageous.

In school there were no problems, at first. The teachers were very respectable. There were four mixed (Jewish and "Aryan") children in our class. It was a girl's *Gymnasium*. Back then the boys and girls were separated. Three Jewish girls emigrated just in time. They were smart. In their case both parents were of Jewish descent. The rest of us stayed. [Makes a kissing noise.] Later it got harder for me. The teachers were not very cordial to us anymore. I graduated in 1936, so 1933 was when it began. Maybe even one or two years earlier. For a while it was okay; these people were really good teachers. When I was finished with school, nobody asked, "Well, what *are* you?" Nobody asked. Did you know I wasn't allowed to keep studying as a half-Jewish girl? My brother couldn't either. As a close second, I became an employee at a business firm. I earned a lot of money and didn't need to defend myself there. I was not so stupid after all. Nobody asked, "Are you?" It was later that they always asked what I was. Yes, for our family [breathes in slowly] at first it was not so bad. Are you recording this? And then bit by bit it changed. In the [breathes out] company where I was, nobody ever asked. Nobody. They didn't even speculate because I was blonde. But I believe that they wouldn't have asked anyway. They asked when the boys had to go to the front and came back wounded. Then it was the Jews' fault, right?

Once the doorbell rang and three SS officers were standing outside. With those horrible boots. Both my uncles were officers in the First World War. They had received the Iron Cross. Young people hardly ever got the Iron Cross, but they were very good, engaged officers. Good soldiers. The SS men tore apart my mother's closets, threw everything out. They were looking for information about her brothers. At that time there was no bank, and our mother had saved a little money, which lay underneath a pile of bedsheets. They took everything. My family couldn't say a word. They were happy when the men left, happy that the SS men didn't take anyone with them.

It got worse when our relatives were taken away. There were five girls and three boys in my mother's family. My Jewish uncles were in Neuengamme concentration camp. My mother and I were able to get two of them out. We scratched together all the money we had, and my mother went all over the place with me to try to convince the officials that one uncle was planning to leave Germany within three days. He made it too. He [breathes in through nose] immigrated to America. The second one did too. The third one was beaten to death in a concentration camp. My mother was supposed to get him out too. I was young. I was blonde. And men like young people. So I talked to the officials.[1] My mother sat next to me. But we weren't able to get all three released.

My mother had to get her brother out of Neuengamme by going to the Rathaus [city hall], or maybe it was some army post. I don't know anymore what these organizations were called. I just know that she went there trembling and returned trembling. She closed the door to her room. Perhaps she thought she was going to be taken away.

One of my uncles came home from Neuengamme. He was there at least six years [this seems a long time]. He was not married, or not any more. Our mother had very little money and she bought twenty or so pieces of cake on the day my uncle was supposed to return. Before we kids, our mother, our father, our uncle, and an aunt started to drink our coffee, the cakes were all gone. He ate them very quickly. He looked unbelievable. He scared us children to death. He had such a skinny throat and a small head. It was horrible. He was starving! It was an image that my brother and I remembered for years.

My mother had fetched him with a taxi. She never saw anyone look like that. I was already working. I must have been about eighteen. It was a shock. For three days we tried to get him over the border; otherwise, he would have been dead. Most people didn't know he was there—he couldn't be seen. The few days before he went to America, he was with us, with my parents. We hid him. In any case, he didn't come out. No one came for him. My mother had papers for him that showed he was released; otherwise she couldn't have gotten him out. He was *freiwild* [fair game]. Whoever wanted to take him could have, but no one did, thank God. He went to America. Those who say that nothing ever happened at Neuengamme are crazy. They worked the prisoners to death. Some have said that Neuengamme was completely harmless, that it was only a work camp. My uncle was not allowed to say anything;

therefore, out of fear, he didn't. He had had a big business that had already been closed down. We packed his bags and took him to the train station, and, like many other Jewish people, he went over the Pyrenees to Spain. He went from there to America, where he married an American woman, and then after ten years he returned to Hamburg. He was so homesick. His sister was in Hamburg. Most of us thought that he was only in a work camp. No, no one saw a prisoner that looked as bad as my uncle did. But all my uncles had it hard over there in America. They didn't know the language; they had no money; they were in a foreign land; they had nothing but a suitcase. I don't know anymore where they went. Probably New York. Strangely enough, I heard from cousins twice or three times removed who got out. They took some of their clothing and furniture and cut off the leg of a chair or table and hid their jewelry and money in it, and that's how they got to America. They had a lot of money. The others didn't have anything. I had relatives too, the Simons, who had a large department store in Peine.[2] I visited them often when I was a child. Suddenly they arrived in Hamburg with all their earthly possessions. We had to rent them a room in Eimsbüttel. They were able to get out, thank God, before 1933. But they had to leave their whole house and everything behind. My aunt from Peine sewed on a sewing machine in order to survive after they emigrated. Freedom is important. But you had to work hard in America too. They wanted and had to get out of Germany. There was no peace here.

My mother didn't visit my uncle that was beaten to death. She tried to get him out like the other two uncles, who were already gone, I think. He was the youngest one and someone said that he would be released, and then my parents got a letter saying that he had tried to flee and was shot. But that's not true, because we heard from another prisoner in the camp who visited us after the war that Nazis had beaten him with a pitchfork or with a shovel. They beat him to death. The prisoners were weak and they had to work. They were all so thin and emaciated with thin necks and tiny heads like the other uncle I told you about. He probably couldn't work as hard as they were pressing him to. This was not in Neuengamme, but another camp, probably Ahrensburg.[3] It was near Hamburg. I don't remember anymore. It was not Theresienstadt—

my grandfather was killed there. My mother had to go get her brother's
things, his watch and his papers. *That* was never his watch or his clothes.
He had never worn anything like them. It couldn't be changed, nothing
could be said, and there was just no money. My mother repressed her
anguish and always helped. Yes, our family was really split up. And so
the family just kept getting smaller.

My one aunt got hauled away to Poland.[4] I visited her in Poland. She
lived in a ghetto. [Breathes in.] In any case, my mother called me at
the office in Poland where I worked. I was in Krakau for a while, in a
German film company. I didn't have anything to do with film; I just
did secretarial work. I had a pleasant office and worked with nice ladies
and gentlemen and no one knew that I was half Jewish. They might
have had an idea; at any rate, no one said anything. My mother called
me and said that my aunt and my cousin were taken from the house
and that they were at the train station in Altona (now a part of
Hamburg). She went to Altona and brought underwear for them. I
remembered that for years. My mother just went. That was my mother.
She was bold and brave. I'm like that too. At the train station, nobody
but Nazis were around, and they knocked off the Jews' hats. [Ilse makes
a sound effect that conveys this action.] She didn't say anything. That's
how my mother was. She simply said, "I was there, I saw Aunt Jenny
and Ruthchen. I brought them underwear." She did similar things for
all the brothers and sisters: The one uncle who went over the border;
the second uncle too; the third was killed.

My aunt and cousin, Ruth, who was two years younger than I, were
taken to Wolbrom[5] and Bergen-Belsen [a work camp] after Kristallnacht.
Later I visited them there. I will tell you this: Bergen-Belsen was called
the holding camp.[6] There were all these rules about German men and
Jewish girls—they were not allowed to be together. Well, Nazis raped
this girl and my aunt. It is unbelievable. Where could I have gotten that
information back then? The two of them were not allowed to disclose it.

They only told me. That's how it was. There were also field prostitutes back then—Jewish women. Also horrible. Even worse, they sealed up the apartment so that my uncle, who was away on a business trip, came home and wasn't able to get back into his own apartment. He couldn't get in. He was a Jew. He couldn't tell anyone. He came to us and then some other relatives. We, and he, were lucky. He had saved some money and was able to get away, to leave Germany. He had a bad time of it, but he did get away. *Stimmt, stimmt, stimmt, stimmt.* [That's right.]

My aunt and cousin would call me every once in a while on the telephone. I had a boyfriend in Krakow who was a Luftwaffe officer, a very nice young man; we liked each other very much. He wanted to get the two of them out—Ruth and my aunt. But as I said before, I had nowhere to put them. My mother had nowhere for them in Hamburg either. They couldn't get over the border. It was impossible. It was a terrible, terrible time.

≈ ≈ ≈

I must tell you this story: I went from Krakow to Wolbrom ghetto where my aunt and my cousin lived in order to have shoes and an outfit made for me because the Jewish tailors are good workers. This was my excuse for going. I had my little radio with me—well, it wasn't so little, it was about this big. [She indicates the size with her hands.] You could do that as a young person then. We unscrewed all the light bulbs and plugged in the radio—only Jews and I—and we hung up a blanket as a makeshift roof and we all sat under the blanket and listened to the radio. It was the BBC—dee dee dee deeeeeee, dee dee dee deeeeeeee [She sings the opening phrase of Beethoven's Fifth Symphony.] My heart beat nervously, frantically, but we were hearing the truth on the radio. We were listening to the British. It was very dangerous. But I was a German girl and fairly pretty to the men in those days, so I could hide stuff under my clothes and go undetected, or talk my way out of situations. I was alone, but friends in Krakow thought I was with a boyfriend. I never said where I was going, but I went to see my aunt and my cousin and the men who were there. We were a group. The German guards at the ghetto always wondered why I brought so many suitcases and bags with me. I told them I had my clothes with me, but it was actually groceries—bread and rice, and grocery cards too. They never looked through German girls' bags. I dared to do it. They could have hauled me off or killed me. I knew what I was doing was dangerous. I was already twenty-two or twenty-three, and I knew what I was doing. I survived. [She pauses.] We had hoped that someone would come and save us. The Americans or the British. But the Russians were closer—we were in the East. So the Russians came, and they were no saviors. They had raped many women. Young women were raped as far as Berlin. But by that time, I was already back in Hamburg. That didn't happen to us there, but it was terrible for those who stayed in the East. Just like today in Bosnia and places where there is war and murder. One day my aunt and cousin called me from the ghetto and said, "Ilse, they are taking us away!" They were gone. I never saw them again. My aunt and cousin did not survive Bergen-Belsen. They were killed. [Ilse whispers.] They didn't survive.

I had a very good childhood before this all began. During this time, because of all the excitement, my uncles being taken away, my aunt taken to Bergen-Belsen, and nobody knowing where they were, I lost all of my hair because of nervousness. Do you understand? Not all of my hair. I had a lot of hair, but now I only have a few left! At that time it was modern in Germany to wear turbans. You are young, but ask your mothers, they still remember. At that time, wool turbans were popular and I wore them. Big chunks of my hair fell out when the Gestapo [secret state police] came to get my aunts. It was a matter of nerves. And the worst thing was, I couldn't tell anyone why. No one knew why. My mother had a doctor, and he was very fond of my mother and my father. He knew that my mother was Jewish, and he knew why my hair was falling out. He gave me a tincture that I had to put on in the evenings and wash out in the mornings. But now I'm okay. [She laughs.] It came back. I didn't tear my hair out as some women do when their nerves are bad. It just fell out. All from nerves.

My mother wasn't taken away because she was protected; my father was "Aryan." I don't know if other women who had "Aryan" husbands were taken away or not. I do know that our mother was taken to a big mirrored room in the town hall.[7] They took lots of Jewish men and women there. They couldn't even move because they were constantly being observed. How she got out of there was always a mystery to us. This roundup must have had to do with some setback during the war—the Führer must have lost some big battle and he blamed the Jews. The Jews were guilty, of course, so the Jews were locked up in the *Spiegelsaal* [mirrored hall] and harassed. My mother never said anything about it. She was locked up for about two days. Although she was not actually assaulted or attacked, she was intimidated and cursed. It was not a census action, just pure harassment. The Jews were not counted. At the moment I can't think of any other similar situations. I wonder, though, as I'm talking with you about it, how my mother was able to get a grocery card as a Jew. That is astonishing! It just occurred to me. I found a clothing card for shoes with little punches, but there were no shoes, so the little punches didn't help anyway. It did not cause any problems that she had to shop separately from my father or have to go to certain places to shop. Some women who had grocery cards were only permitted to go to certain stores. She didn't need her ID in all the stores; she needed only the cards. My father got the cards and gave them to us—that could be how my mother got them.

∾ ∾ ∾

I was treated differently because I looked "Aryan." That helped me very much, a great deal. Although [rattles coffee cup], strangely, the relatives were all taken away. I was blonde; my brother had dark hair but he didn't look like a Jew. Gerd, my uncle who immigrated to Ohio, looked like a Jew. [Her voice gets quieter after I mention "looking Jewish" is a stereotype.] Of course, in Hitler's Jewish propaganda everyone had distinct Jewish facial features. Would you like some coffee? The time when all this happened is a long way back for me. [Ilse is visibly uncomfortable, gets up to get coffee items, and tries to change the subject.]

≈ ≈ ≈

I had a hard childhood, you understand? Look here: This is my dead mother's identification card. With the "J" on it. Yes, with a "J." My mother always had to carry it with her. We all had to carry IDs. We children didn't have a "J" on ours. Our father didn't either. When we sat in the train or the bus, we were checked. We couldn't, or rather Mother couldn't, travel. But sometimes you took the train, say to Bergedorf. Then the ticket checkers would come by. We had to show our IDs—our mother's with the "J" on hers and Paula "Sara" listed as her name. There were officers who closed the passes right away and gave them back to our mother. [Ilse demonstrates with her hands.] They didn't say anything. There were others who were really nasty about it to my mother. We survived it. I looked for the ID yesterday. I found it too. The name "Sara" was forced on her by the laws. Terrible! [Ilse says this loudly and high-pitched.] The Jewish men were given the name "Israel." "Sara" was practically, at that time, a curse word. Oddly enough, no one ever called her that. Only once in our house was our mother slandered. I was not because I was only fourteen or fifteen. But that could have easily happened. Today the young women are still naming their children Sara. I can't understand that. In the United States women are named Sara, and the name is not recognized as a Jewish name. Children are baptized Sara. Here in Germany too. Our grandfather was named Abraham. I have his identification card, but I don't know where. I couldn't find it yesterday. The name "Sara" was always an insult for our mother.

My mother had a friend, an "Aryan" woman, very nice, who died recently. [Breathes in.] When the SS came to our house she went out onto the balcony because she was so afraid they would see her, an "Aryan." They would have heckled her. Do you know what I mean? [Ilse imitates SS in deep voice]: "What are you doing here in a Jewish house?" That's the way it was. It is frightening to read about this time in Hamburg, but it is much worse to have lived here! Reading is not that hard; you are removed. But we lived in that time and that was terrible. You can't imagine it. But I have nice friends who still call today. The woman who just telephoned has been my friend since I was a teenager.

She never left me alone. Never! That is nice, isn't it? Maybe it happened that way because my brother and I did not look Jewish. I could imagine if I had a nose like that or black curly hair, if I looked outwardly Jewish, that they might have kept their distance from me. I don't know. We played tennis. We went to the cinema. We did everything. Our father was allowed to go to the theater with us, but our mother could not. She wasn't allowed. [Ilse's voice becomes high-pitched.] My father went with me if he wanted to see a movie, but that wasn't such an important thing in those days. Even as a "half Jew," you were allowed to go to the movies. I did not have an ID with a "J." But my life was over at seventeen. During the war you couldn't do anything. I couldn't play tennis; I couldn't have any parties or social gatherings. It was hard. The boys were all gone; they had all been drafted. No fun.

My brother was in the war at first. He came back after two years. What a stroke of luck that they couldn't use any Jews or "half Jews." He had to work here in the Hamburg prison—he had to watch prisoners— Jewish prisoners too—in Fuhlsbüttel. He had guard duty. That was hard [Ilse whispers] for my brother. He, as a "half Jew," had to guard Jews. They worked on the streets. That was part of the forced construction work. Many women had to do this as well, but I didn't.

In 1945 my brother, my mother, and I were in the moors [countryside]. That was a really bad time, shortly before the end of the war. My father told us, "Leave Hamburg—it will either be bombed or they will do something to the remaining Jews." My father had told people in Hamburg that we were vacationing. He said, "My wife is sick and she went to the country with the children." My brother and I no longer worked at that point. We left under the pretense that my mother was sick. We rented a little room in the country because there they didn't know what was going on, and we had a little vacation. Later we learned that the Nazis had supposedly taken away all the Jews, also the "half Jews" [in Hamburg]. We were protected because we were in the countryside for about a quarter of a year. [Long pause.] My brother rode his bike to Hamburg to visit my father. It was far but in those times that's how it was. We rode bikes. It was about 30 or 40 kilometers, but young people did that then. We lived privately, and we had a kitchen so that our mother could cook. My husband, Karl, whom I married in 1945, was shot in the war. In those times it was called a *Heimatschuss* [the injury he received qualified him to be sent home from the war]. He was shot in the arm and he had his arm in a sling and came to Buchholz[8] to the country. Then our father told us, "Go to the hospital. Karl is there and has the bread." In Berlin they always let the wounded through with their bread cards first. We always had to wait three hours in line for bread or vegetables, but my husband got through because he was wounded. So because of that it went well for us. Yes, when you look back, it was not too bad. When we returned to Hamburg—we had a big house, five rooms, I believe—we had to rent out the rooms. My father had to rent them out, and not for money. It was obligatory. He *had* to. We housed a married couple who later moved out and there was an old man who got the half room that used to be my brother's. We felt so sorry for him. My mother always gave him a little something—turnip soup or whatever was available because he was almost starving, the poor guy. He was all alone. We were five people. My husband came with us from the countryside. The renter was not Jewish, and he did not know that my mother was Jewish. He did not slander Jews; he was neutral.

This is what I wanted to tell you, Cynthia. I am afraid that people are talking too much. Not about "mixed" people in particular, but about our whole history in general. About the Holocaust. About the past. The past fifty years. I am afraid that it is creating a lot of hate. You've heard that we have young people with these boots again, haven't you? They are going after the Turks, the Jews, the Kurds, and anyone who lives and thinks differently than they do. I am afraid that we should be doing less, you know how I mean that? My brother called yesterday and said, "Tell the young ladies that there will soon be repercussions because of too much talking." So there should be less. In America it is probably a little different. The people there are a lot more interested. I think the papers presently are full of this "fifty years ago," and friends of mine are complaining about it. They say that it was the same thing in Vietnam too. And, well, what do I know? These things are happening everywhere, in Rwanda and all over the world. It didn't just happen in Germany with the Jewish people. It is happening in Bosnia. The Serbs are fighting the Croats, and killing and torturing and mistreating. Because of this we should, at least in Germany [whispers], be careful with this topic. It is probably different in America.

What do the other women from "mixed marriages" say? Do they say the same things as I do? Maybe it depends on whether the mother or father is Jewish. I had a friend whose mother was "Aryan" and the father Jewish. He was a teacher at the Wilhelm *Gymnasium* and had a doctorate in physics. A very gifted man. A Jewish man. He converted to Protestantism. His children were confirmed. Nothing helped. He died in Theresienstadt. He remained a Jew, even though he converted. The Nazis found every single one of them. They were that detailed with their files. It was terrible. In Germany the government still knows everything, at least about people's religious orientations. They still do. It is all written down.

In my opinion, I can tell you exactly why Hitler came to power. Germany had a bad time. Everyone was unemployed. [Ilse speaks in a storytelling tone of voice, with occasional laughter.] Nobody had anything to do. And the Jewish people all had a lot of money. They had brains and were intelligent. The Jewish people were also hard workers. The others weren't; they were dumb. The Germans are dumb; they still are. Jealousy was a factor. And that is how Hitler came to power. He was able to practically catch his people in a cage. They all screamed and yelled. When I think of the way the women adored their Führer, it was insane. Do you know what I mean? I can still hear Hitler yelling in the back of my head. We were always afraid. I always got chills down my spine. All because of fear. Do you understand? [I mention that the intelligentsia persecuted the Jews too.] A certain group of them did. But there were other groups that stood up for the Jews as well. Groups from the Wehrmacht. Officers. Some of them stood up for the Jews. They weren't supposed to. The mother of my friend called me after the war was over and said, "Ilse, is it true that the

Jews were gassed? Is it true that the Jews were taken away?" I said, "Of course!" They all didn't know. It was that secret. You couldn't get it out of anyone. The people were all afraid to say anything. They weren't allowed to say anything. Some people said they saw the trains and knew that the Jews were going somewhere, but very few. No one was allowed to pass this on. If they had spoken, they might have been taken away. It was an unfree environment. [We laugh because this statement seems to drastically simplify the situation.]

My mother was only a housewife, a good mother and housewife. My parents were not open, but closed. I can't tell you why, I don't know. Maybe the time she lived in left its impression on her. My father didn't say much either, before and during the war. My brother was also very closed. It is only now, after so many years, that he will say something now and then. Something that I never knew had affected him. My parents were hard workers, orderly and quiet, so that no one could do anything to them, say anything nasty about them. They were as anonymous as possible. That was the time period. It left a strong impression on the people. Puberty was difficult. We couldn't talk about things during that whole time period. I was very reserved. My friends from school were happy and free, could laugh, play sports, and learn a trade. I couldn't. For a young girl going through puberty that is hard. Our mother always said, "Don't say anything, be quiet, don't worry about it." What else could she say, right? She would console me and I would read. I still meet with my school friends sometimes, but it's been fifty or sixty years now. I couldn't talk to them in my youth. I didn't have a single friend I could talk to during my school days. You could talk about boys but not about the fact that you were Jewish. For a young girl, it was terrible. There were no more Jews in Hamburg, and if there were, then only "half Jews" like me. I could talk to them and do things together, but they didn't want to say much either. They were just as reserved. This topic was taboo, you understand?

I can't say anything about my mother. She was so *"Stikum"* [close-mouthed]. Do you know the expression? That's actually a Jewish expression. She said nothing. She was quiet. She never came out of herself, like a tortoise. When you can't ask any questions at all, it's like talking to a wall. She said nothing but "Leave me alone." Of course I wanted to know why she was so quiet, and I tried to find out. But she never wanted to talk about it. She always got so excited when I did. She said, "Leave me in peace." She lost practically all her brothers and sisters. It had to have been dreadful. But she said nothing. She simply kept it inside. She kept quiet. And my father didn't say much, probably because he didn't want to dishearten or burden us children.

I always had the feeling that my brother was ashamed. When my mother came in, he left. When we were downstairs by the front door and someone came on a bike, then he would leave. That is hard for a mother to deal with. He was ashamed of his mother. Oh God, I don't want to insinuate. . . . He loved his mother, but when he brought boys over, and they stood downstairs talking, he knew our mother was Jewish, and he was ashamed. What can you say about that? Boys are different than girls. I am a hard person. I can take more. You have to. [She laughs.] Our mother used to say, whenever there was something going on, even in the Nazi era, "Don't worry about that, my Ilse will do it." That was me. She never said, "My son will do it." It was just me. She knew she had more support from me than from my brother. Up until her death it was that way. My brother stuck closer to his family, but not with our mother. Yes, that's the way it was. I have a good relationship with my brother. [She speaks quickly and quietly.] But we hardly talked about those things when we were children and later we both got married. Then we didn't talk about it either. Now as we are getting older we have started to talk about it more. Now the time is coming. We didn't have time to discuss this topic twenty years ago. Our children were still small and we were working. Now we are both retired. The children are out of the house, married. There are grandchildren. We have more time and things are less hectic. Now the past is starting to come out.

I coped all those years because I was young. When the war was over in 1945, I got married. Of course, the situation with my uncle certainly left an impression on me. But how we coped with it I can't say. [She pauses.]

They had hoped that everything would pass. One always thought, "Either it will be this way until the end of the war or we will survive it and things will get better." My mother lived quite a long time; my father has been dead for thirty years already. He didn't live very long. She was almost ninety-three—my mother the Jew! She was immensely strong. He was only sixty. But that's how it was.

Leaving Germany was not even discussed. My mother's youngest sister immigrated to America. She died of sadness and homesickness. My mother's other sister was killed. Three remained. As I said, there were five girls in her family. One of them died the year before last. She was eighty-eight. Also a Jew. Both of them were married to "Aryans." They survived somehow. Our mothers were lucky that the men stood by them, that they didn't say, "I want to get divorced. I can't live with a Jew." They stayed with their wives, and that was a plus for our mothers, right? And that's why we never even thought of leaving.

My family did not celebrate Hanukkah, only Christmas and other holidays in the German tradition. But Jewish people celebrated German holidays. There are people who celebrate both. For us children it was probably a lot nicer that way, to celebrate Christmas instead of Hanukkah. Here is something strange: The church in the Ober Street, near Rothenbaumchaussee, used to be a synagogue. Norddeutsche Rundfunk (NDR), a radio station, now has offices there. Once I wanted to hear a Sunday broadcast at this building where I had not been since the war. I asked, "What is this?" And a man replied, "Why, that's the old synagogue." We sat inside the old synagogue. [She speaks very quietly.] That was strange for me because I had been there a few times before at weddings of my mother's Jewish friends. But I hadn't been there very often.

≈ ≈ ≈

My father never thought about divorcing my mother. Never! He was very good to her. Our entire Jewish family was very close and stuck together. My father's side, the "Aryan" side of the family, protested my parents getting married. I had uncles on my father's side—they never visited us. Mmm. It was very hard for my father. He then probably went to see them alone. They didn't visit us because my mother was Jewish. Surely that was the reason. I had one uncle who lived in Blankenese. He had a lot of money but he never even gave one Mark to help. But it doesn't matter. It's forgotten. For us children there were no differences between our relationships with our mother and father, none at all. We were lucky our father was very good to our mother. Many men who were "Aryan," or the women who were "Aryan," left their partners. We were lucky because our father didn't earn much money. Money was very tight, but we were able to make it. We didn't let anything get out into the open. Today people talk to their neighbors. We weren't allowed to say anything. Do you understand? We lived a more anonymous life. We closed the door to the apartment and hoped to be left alone. I first noticed that things were odd, and that our home life was different from other families when they found out that my mother was Jewish, and when they noticed that my father had given up his business. We began to have hard times with money. I was still going to school. I left school in 1936. That must have been 1931, 1932, 1933. I was about eleven or twelve years old then. I realized what it meant for me. My father lost his entire business. We didn't get any money back during the postwar compensations. My father had too much pride. He was too forgiving. He didn't write down any amount on the forms after the war. There are people who are like that. But my brother and I got a stipend to help with our vocational training. Looking back, my brother and I did get *that*. It wasn't a lot, but it was something. [She laughs.] My father remained a private entrepreneur, like he was before as a shopkeeper. It was not easy for an older man to do this. He was a salesman and traveled around with a carpetbag. He sold suit fabric out of his suitcase. That was his whole line of work. He wasn't a tailor; there were numerous tailors back then. He always sold fabric and similar items.

My father was a very practical man. He was a good German. Not a Nazi! Heavens, no. He was a good German who never went on the wrong side of the law. My brother and I are that way too! We are good Germans. We like our Germany, except for its history, of course. My father never would have done anything bad. [When asked to define a "good German," Ilse hesitates and stutters.] Yes, well, he didn't put down Germany, just Hitler and this whole behavior that came from Hitler. But he loved Germany. He loved his homeland. And his siblings. [Breathes in.] And Hamburg. Maybe I am saying too much, but my father was a straight, honest man who was too good for this world; a person who probably never would have been able to get himself heard. Because he was so good and honest, nobody ever messed with him. After he lost his business and wasn't able to go out with his suitcase selling things, the army drafted him. It was fine. He got his money and it worked. We were happy to have our peace and quiet. But now, Cynthia, today there aren't as many good Germans as there were before. They are not *"Deutschland über alles"* [She laughs.] No, they want to go to foreign countries, and they like to travel. Germany has done well in the last thirty years, and maybe things aren't going as well now. Because of this there are no more good Germans. That's what things are like today. People don't just simply remain in Germany and feel satisfied.

≈ ≈ ≈

I got to know my husband during the war. We got married in 1945. We would have had our fiftieth wedding anniversary this year. He's been dead for twelve years. We met in Krakow. He was an officer in the Wehrmacht. He was very good-natured. He would have liked to have helped me. He was on my side. But then he was sent out to the other side of the front to Banat where people fought recently near Russia. I came back to Hamburg. Now he is dead. He was sixteen years older. That's too much. He was good-spirited; he was funny. Later when he was seventy and got sick and grouchy, then sixteen years was a big difference. But we did love each other. Those older men get difficult. He was very "rrr-rrr." [She makes growling noise and laughs nervously.]

My husband wouldn't let me work. Back then women didn't work. "My wife doesn't need that." But when he got so old and sick, then I worked, from age fifty-one to sixty-one. That way I got retirement. I only had to work half days. At least I was out of the house for half the day. You could say that I had some peace and quiet in that half. It was nice. I had coworkers. I liked to work. I was in university administration at Von Melle Park in the education department for ten years. I retired in 1981 or 1982. My husband didn't want me to work, but I am happy I did because now I receive a pension, more of a pension than I would have gotten for not having worked for twenty-five years. I also worked when I was a young girl, so the years get counted together.

My husband and I had a fine relationship even though he was older. [Laughs.] I have one daughter. She was born in 1948. I already have such an old daughter! [Laughs again.] I am surprised that she didn't come today. She wanted to be here. My daughter is not so interested. My granddaughter, Nina, however, is. The young girls are. [Ilse shows pictures.] That's my daughter and her husband. And my grandchildren: Nina is eighteen and Nicolai is fifteen. Clever kids—both of them. My daughter is a teacher but she has taken two years' leave. She had a stomach operation and could not recover from it. One can take two years' leave from their job here in Germany. Can you do that in America too? She is a state employee, so she can. Naturally that means that the income will be smaller, but then the income gets smaller and smaller anyway. When the children were born, she took a leave then too. [Chuckles.] In Hamburg people who have money don't talk about it. I don't have any money and I don't talk about that either! [Laughs.] It's a different country. It's not so important in Germany—either you have it or you don't. I don't have a good memory. I'm sure I missed some things. But maybe that's because yesterday I was looking through my dead mother's things and I called my daughter on the telephone and told her that she should come and see them. She couldn't come this morning. She was in the hospital because something was wrong with her eyes. My daughter doesn't have much time for things like this perhaps. She said, "If I can, I will come." Well, she didn't come. [Laughs.] Nina ceaselessly asks me questions.[9] She wants to know about my mother and my grandmother and I told her that you were coming. But she has a boyfriend and then, of course, she has no time for anything else. Such young girls. She wants to know everything and I want to show her. Yesterday I looked for memorabilia and other objects, letters from my mother and such things, from the Nazi time and found them. Nina is interested in that. I'm not as interested as my granddaughter is. But you know, Cynthia, I am afraid when she gets involved in clubs and organizations that these right-wing radicals will come and give her a smack on the cheek. I'm afraid of that. We had to go through that, but you haven't [referring to all young people]. They may not be able to find out that she is part Jewish, and I think that if she would have to walk around with a yellow star then the right-wing radicals would find out. Sometimes groups just hang together and do not plan any mischief. I think sometimes you have to be really careful with groups of young men. Boys really are dumb and when they beat each other up I think that's pretty bad.

As far as the situation in Germany today, I think that the government's halt on the immigration of foreigners is good. I think we are getting too many foreigners in Germany. That is our [a common] opinion. If you follow the news the Kurds are vandalizing the Turkish stores and businesses—hair salons and so forth—and they are bringing much unrest, and now the Turks want more police protection from us. On the other hand, the Hamburg police, like all the police in the Bundesrepublik, don't have that much money. We older people are therefore not protected. Only the other people are protected now. [Makes distinction between old people and the Turkish.] Now they're trying to say there should be more police protection for the Turkish businesses. I don't hate the Turks as such, but I find it is enough. That is my opinion. The Turkish situation is a major issue. It's not so bad with the other minorities in Germany, but they don't cause such a fuss either. They don't protest as much. They don't riot. The accidents and violence that happen at night, where we old ladies get our purses taken from us or get pestered, happens almost solely by foreigners. It's unfortunate. Germans do it too, but mainly foreigners. It's not that I don't see any of the foreigners ever being part of Germany or really ever being able to be called "German." Of course I do. There are also the children who are born here. There are so many nice young Turkish people who are German—more German than Turkish. They are charming people, clever and intelligent, and they do their work. I don't have anything against them. I only have a problem with the fact that so much happens—places get broken into and burglarized and people are killed and often it is predominately foreigners who are doing it. Naturally you get angry after a while and you say to yourself that the foreigners should leave. It's just that our courts are burdened with it, our police are burdened with it, and our economic system is burdened with it. I think foreigners can get along fine here. [Ilse ignores question about how she would describe "being German."] I think there are Turkish families who have older children, say, twenty years old, who have attended school here and they feel German. My hairdresser is a Turkish woman. She says, "I am more German than Turkish. I visit Turkey, but I am German." Basically I think there is no major difference between the Germans and foreigners, only when it comes to the church. For example, with marriage and the young Turkish girls. That is hard. I believe there are many tears. Otherwise there is no difference. I see it in my granddaughter's class—there are foreign girls who learn the same, wear the same clothes, and talk the same way. There is no difference. It is only when the fathers are Turkish and they want to stay in Germany. Then they demand that their daughters do not marry German men, and that is a problem. It depends on the fathers. Solely! The mothers are forbearing. It's the fathers who dictate everything, and I think that is very hard for the girls. They have to decide. Whether it's a "mixed marriage" or not, they all can marry, can't they?

Of course I saw *myself* as an outsider. Oh, yes! That goes without saying. Not anymore, but back then, yes. These outsiders had a certain fear. For

example, I had a friend for many years and we would get together—she
came over to my place and I went to hers. When her son was drafted into
the war and she found out that I was half Jewish, then the relationship
was nasty. Then her son was killed and naturally it was the Nazis' fault
and then things were good between us again. But, yes, of course, you
were an outsider then. I can't say that I felt just like the others, but at
home it was always "say nothing, don't attract attention, don't do
anything." Our parents were scared. We were scared. I can't believe there
were many women who said that they were not outsiders, but to still feel
that way? I don't anymore. Directly after the war I had known it was
coming to an end. I have to say in all honesty that since I have lived in
this apartment I have had friends—the children got the house when their
father died twelve years ago—and none of them knows that I am half
Jewish. No one has asked and I have not said anything. So somehow you
still feel like an outsider. Nothing is ever mentioned of it. No one ever
asks. Who do I need to tell? Our mother was so tense about it when she
died in 1983. She said, "Don't tell anyone that I was Jewish." No one
needs to know that. She lived in a big apartment building on the Alster
and no one knew that she was Jewish. I never told anyone. Why should
I? But in fact, when my daughter was in school, she had an altercation
with a friend's mother. My daughter had probably been ill mannered,
and her friend's mother had given the cheeky response "typical Jewish
manner." It was like that long after the war. Then my daughter came
home really upset and said to me, "Mrs. So-and-so said that I told Doris
[referring to Ilse's daughter's friend] off." My daughter is also very
temperamental. "Typical Jewish manner." You see? And that's what we
had to deal with. But my mother always said, "Don't say anything or do
anything." I consoled my daughter. I said, "Let her say it." The old cow.
What should I say? She has to get over it.

We heard about resistance but didn't think about it ourselves. We heard
what was in the papers, after the war, not during, not through leaflets or

propaganda newspapers *[Flugblätter]*. Heavens, no! My father would not have allowed that! Impossible! Then people practically had their blinders on. No one wanted to hear or see anything—they just closed their door and ignored it. We saw demonstrations against the Nazis—for example, the Swing-Jugend,[10] the people who danced. They were also in danger. The Nazis were very strict with those who swing-danced.

$$\approx \quad \approx \quad \approx$$

I don't know why this Jewish thing stands out, why this particular time in history stands out. People are raped and murdered in other lands and in other wars. But historians and journalists are so interested in this particular time. [We discuss the specific systematic murdering that occurred.] I don't know. I can't give you an answer. No, you don't know either, naturally. You never lived it. I think that Germany could overcome these judgments, and its stigma, but then it always comes up again. Always. There's hardly any peace and then the newspaper comes and writes some article and then the conversation starts all over again. Earlier there was no radio, no telephone, no TV. These communications did not exist. One could not write as much about the atrocities during the Thirty-Years' War or the Seven-Years' War. They could report about it, but there were no electronic apparatuses then like we have now. Everything [referring to the information about the war] was lost. Today reporters actually participate in wars, and they photograph it and write about it and have interviews like you're doing now—there wasn't any of that in earlier times. Because of technology, the issue is always stirred up again. The young people like you who want to write about it start it up again as well. [Long pause.]

It would have been great if the United States had intervened earlier, bombed the concentration camps. But then they would have killed a lot of people doing it, and therefore they didn't. My aunt who died about ten years ago had a Jewish family just like my mother did and she helped a family that ended up in a concentration camp—Auschwitz, I think. The parents and everybody were killed, but a girl survived. She was bald and hungry. I saw the girl when she came back from Auschwitz. After the war in 1950 I was thirty. She was about my age. But she survived. She came to my aunt and what I knew about her I found out through my aunt. I had no relationship with this young person. I was not afraid of her, but it was a terrible picture when she returned from the concentration camp. It left me no peace day and night. My husband scolded me for having looked at her because I was so upset. That's not a big deal. One can look. It was worse for the girl, who had been through it. We gave her clothes from Hildesheim. There was nothing. We didn't have money, there was nothing to buy, but we made it. I still don't remember her name. She would be an old lady now too. She said that she had always hoped that someone would save them. But like you said, if they had bombed the concentration camps everyone would have been killed. I don't know what would have been a worse death, being gassed or being bombed. Everything was terrible. Bombs and gas cannot be equated. I mean, if they had bombed, then they would have killed everything, even their Jewish—*our* Jewish people. Anyway, she went alone to America and we never heard anything else about her.

Many people who were in the Nazi party stayed in the government even after the Nazis fell out of power—everyone knows that, for example, Adenauer's administration were in the Nazi party. It's typical to believe that the same attitudes that people had during World War II still remain in Germany. The people still carry these attitudes with them and haven't given them up yet. I always have this fear that with some people the feeling is still there.

One of my friends has said, "I don't know why everybody was so upset over Hitler." She hasn't said it directly to me, but she has to others. I don't hear this much anymore. She has stopped. But there are still a lot of people who talk like that. If I saw anything like this happening on the street, I believe I would say something. If there were a lot of people around I probably wouldn't say anything. My fear is that I need to be careful not to ignore things because then it starts all over again.

CHAPTER SEVEN

GRETEL LORENZEN

"God took my life into his hands and I'm forever grateful for that"

~

Gretel wrote to me on March 8, 1995: "I have read your article in the *Hamburger Abendblatt* [daily paper] and am ready to talk about my 'mixed marriage.' The precondition is—just as you wrote—a confidential and anonymous conversation. [Later she consented to use her name.] Today I am eighty-seven years old, live in a place for seniors, am a Hamburger, and left because of the bombing of Hamburg in July, 1943. After about ten years, the possibility arose to come back. I will wait for your call or written answer." Gretel signed with her married name and then with her birth name, Steinfeld. Two weeks later I arrived at the retirement community. I knew that Gretel was somewhat reluctant to talk and that she had been encouraged to do so by her daughter, Sigrid. I reported in with the receptionist and was given permission to go up to Gretel's apartment.

When Gretel opened the door, I had expected an older-looking face, but Gretel looked and moved like a much younger woman. She stood tall and erect, was attractive and thin, and wore a light-colored dress with a string of pearls. She had white, thick hair and a long, straight nose. Her eyes darted everywhere and were pronounced by dark circles and a fan of lines that moved out toward her ears. She had eight prominent deep lines in her forehead and two brown age spots on her cheek. Immediately she told me to sit down and that she did not have much time. In contrast to the typical German custom, she never offered me a drink or any food. I looked for a place to plug in my tape recorder in her nondescript apartment. She told me she preferred that I not use it. I spent at least thirty minutes trying to convince her that taping her was necessary, and that she would forget it was there. Begrudgingly, and with assurances extricated from me for anonymity, she agreed. I sat on a low couch with a large window behind me that faced the street. Gretel's living space was cramped, so I understood later why she always wanted to roam about the city.

Throughout the interview, Gretel answered questions tersely and quickly. Clearly, she wanted to put as little of her life as possible on display and move on with her day. She paused often when her memory failed her, and when she did not want to deal with a question, she reverted to religious platitudes. Gretel often said, "Excuse me. I must jog my memory," and "You're asking too much." Unlike most of the women, she did not mention that she had pondered over or studied the Third Reich; she held a detached stance. Twice — when she discussed her relationship to her aunt Frieda and to her daughter — she choked up but never cried. Her repressed anger surfaced frequently; often she raised her voice and beat her fists on the table in front of her. Her eyes were portentous and watchful but became bright and excited when she showed me a picture of her father and daughter. No books related to the period she lived through were evident in her apartment.

Gretel ended the interview abruptly. She was noticeably tired, and the conversation had been a trial for her. It was raining as I headed for the train station. I turned to look at the retirement community behind me and saw Gretel at the bus stop, umbrella in hand and rain hat on her head, and I watched her until she ascended the steps into her bus. I marveled at how swiftly she had gotten herself together and left the building. After I interviewed her daughter, Sigrid, I decided that it was the daughter who had been most affected by her mother's past and tight-lipped silence and that she was more than willing to speak for them both. The story begins first with Gretel and then follows with Sigrid.

I was born in Hamburg in Eppendorf on Eppendorfer Landstraße. I myself was born within a "mixed marriage" and my daughter, naturally, also. And in the so-called Third Reich there were first- and second-degree "mixed breeds." I was first degree. My parents were divorced and *not* because of the "mixed marriage," but because my father liked other women. He was unfaithful. At the insistence of my mother, the verdict was guilty. I married in 1931. At that time it was fine. Two years later this marriage would have been impossible. I was "mixed" and my husband was classified "pure Aryan." I had mentioned to him before we married that my father was Jewish and he said, No problem. We had a business. To have customers in your store, you needed to be a party member. We depended on the business to live so my husband joined the party. We saw the news headlines in the paper and one can't describe it. [She beats on the table.] We always were fearful something else was going to turn bad. *Words can't describe it.* I had a very good husband. Since childhood, he had a weak stomach. He had an operation and didn't come through. Harsh pressure was placed on him and it struck at the weakest organ. He died during the Third Reich. He wasn't able to cope with the full extent of events.

My daughter started school. When I went to pick up my child at the train station, I thought, How long will you have the child before they take her away? We were always under pressure. How could the entire German people follow this man, Hitler? It was so. They had at least left my child with me. We faced the music. My husband went to the local group to inquire if our "mixed marriage" was allowed. We didn't get an answer. Maybe they couldn't send an answer because in Munich there was a bombing. We still had customers. One of my brothers-in-law, one of two brothers, was completely National Socialist and made rude comments. I can tell you how awful this was—he wouldn't see me and he supported the Nazi government. He celebrated his golden wedding anniversary and didn't officially invite us but did so offhand. We went but didn't really want to. When we arrived I said, "Thanks for inviting me, but go ahead and party." We didn't go in. He had shown all his cards. For that he must answer before the living God. What should I talk about?

We never felt safe. Not at all. I had entirely lovable in-laws. They said it didn't interest them whether I was "half Aryan." They always stood by me. We were bombed out and traveled to my in-laws. My father-in-law was a *Studienrat*, simply called a *Lehrer* [teacher] today. He had been sent with his class to the largest island Fehmarn on the Baltic Sea. My in-laws told me later that on the island I had looked at the end of my nerves, under pressure. They sensed my loss as a widow and knew one of their sons looked upon me as dirt. I knew what plans Hitler had. I knew a family—the father was Jewish and the mother not. The exact situation as mine. This man had to work as a street sweeper. Otherwise nothing else happened to him. I know many such incidents. This is just one. But living with uncertainty and fear, what happens then? What will they do with me and my child?

Most of my acquaintances did not know I was half Jewish, and I kept my mouth shut. Other people didn't know the whole business. Jewishness played no role for me. None at all. My father wasn't a practicing Jew, and I didn't know my grandparents. As far as I know they weren't observant. They were just Jews. I had no Jewish friends and my parents divorced. My father was in a concentration camp. I found a list of people who had been gassed and burned and those who returned. And I saw he'd come back. I met him. He was very friendly and happy that I came to him and that I considered it valuable to spend time with him. Every four weeks I visited him, after my husband was dead.

My father's second wife was Jewish. He wasn't always faithful to her either. He was just that way. I'm also of the opinion, whether one is Jewish or not, that if someone has an obsession or passion, it's impossible to free oneself from it. Only Jesus who says "whom I make free is really free" can unbind someone. That's right. And so I visited my father every four weeks. One time I couldn't get away and he called me. He said I should come. I said no, I can't come. I have too much to do. He pushed me, and I went to his place and told him everything I thought about him. I made an effort to enforce morality. I said, "I couldn't say all that to you if you'd been a father to us. You never took care of us. Mother had to fend for herself. You needed your money for other women." He admitted it was all true, and I could say whatever I pleased. Afterward, I went every four weeks, and as far as I could tell, he was happy. I have a picture here of him. He lived together with another Jewish woman, but they didn't marry. [She unwraps layers of brown paper to reveal a photograph of her father.] Here's a picture of him and his live-in girlfriend. And here is a picture of Sigrid when she was young.

My father had a brother, Albert, who died of stomach cancer, a natural death. He had an unmarried sister, Aunt Frieda. She lived with Albert. I could visit her whenever I pleased as if I was one of her children. We took walks together and Freida told great fairy tales. She also was in a concentration camp where she starved to death, so my father reported. My father said, "Whatever happened here to us, for her you can be sure it was much worse." My father was in Theresienstadt—not an extermination camp. Every evening someone came and pointed out someone—this person, that person—and they'd be sent away and gassed. The women of two couples were called forth and had to say good-bye for good. And where did they go? I believe Auschwitz wasn't far—at any rate, an extermination camp wasn't far. And what did my father have to do? In Theresienstadt execution was done by shooting in the back of the head and the victim would fall into a grave. My father had to shovel gravel into a grave. He had to shovel gravel over them.[1] He managed to survive because the Russians came. They had seen many sights that no one should ever see—the ovens, the skeletons. Russians discovered camps in the East, and later, the English from the other side. It's over now. I heaved a sigh of relief, even though we had lost the war. One can't describe this feeling of relief. [She speaks very painfully.] The two brothers of my father's [second] wife were in Berlin and people had said, "Get out of here!" They said, "We've been here for generations. Nothing will happen to us." Both were gassed. They were great men. That's the way it was.

It was difficult to hide. Often the Nazis checked in official files to look up those who didn't register. They went so far as to take the files from the government offices. Often they checked birth records even if no one filled out a form. When you voted in a plebiscite you had to indicate race. My husband could write "Aryan" and I, nothing. We turned it in. Nothing came of it. I didn't dare write "Aryan" because to be caught in a lie would have been even worse.

I was still very young when my parents divorced. Had my father been faithful, my mother would have gone through thick and thin for him. He was always with other women and never cared for us. He admitted it all after he returned from Theresienstadt. A few years ago it stated in the newspaper that whoever suffered in the Nazi time should write to the paper in order to receive money. No amount of money can compensate the suffering. My daughter went in and I received DM 2,000. My marriage went bad for a different reason. Ah so! My husband was in the party with most of his activity in the Red Cross. As a party member, he couldn't remain because of me. If the "Führer" [said sarcastically] didn't have anything against it, my husband could stay in the Red Cross. If he had been allowed to remain in the party then the Red Cross would have allowed him to stay. We requested clemency from "the Führer." I was very happy that my husband didn't receive the answer. The request was denied, but he remained in the "work front" and I did also. I could show that I had no objection to the National Socialist party. It was fortunate that before his death, he didn't receive the answer. That would have been a blow to him.

I couldn't be for Hitler. The Rechtspartei [right-wing party] should, when it sees such developments, eliminate them early. I'm eighty-seven and God will soon call me into eternity. One has to look at that very seriously. Aunt Freida, I believe, was Communist. She was a good person. Father was more toward the right wing, before the so-called Third Reich. He was *bürgerlich* [middle class] one could say. At the time, politics concerned only men, but today because of TV, even without wanting to, people are involved in politics. Before, politics was discussed only among and around men, and less among women. My father, most of the time, had a job; he traveled from place to place. Usually he came home for Christmas. At the time, it was customary for the man to wear a wedding band and my mom would look at his hand. He didn't wear one.

One time my father had a position in Stettin—today it's in Poland, it doesn't belong to us anymore. He wanted to take his wife and daughter along, and we went. It was a wonderful memory—both of my parents together. We woke up early Sunday mornings and just drank coffee and hiked in the woods. There were two restaurants in the forest. It was really the only time I had both parents. It didn't last long. My father went to Stuttgart; Mother wouldn't go. She went to Hamburg. It cost much money to leave—I don't know how she made ends meet. My father had someone else in Pommern [Stettin]. For my mother it was very hard. It was like throwing the glass into the mill. My mom believed in Jesus and put everything in his hands. One can't describe this time—so much pressure placed on an individual.

Frieda was picked up, locked up, and transported with other Jews. My husband was already dead and I had my child. I had a painting book at Frieda's that she asked me to retrieve. I didn't go, out of fear. My friend, who's now dead, went in my place. Frieda was startled when my friend showed. She said, "Gretel didn't come?" I'm sorry, but my kid was so important to me. [Gretel apologizes.] Then I received a letter from my father from Theresienstadt. I stood out in front of our place, and the mailman gave it to me. My husband didn't see it. "We can receive packages," it said. I sent nothing back; I didn't want to do that. [She was afraid of being tracked.] My father never asked if we received the note; he probably thought Nazis had intercepted it. We had a business and my husband was a party member because of that. A businessman who didn't join the party had no customers. We depended on the drugstore to live. A *Drogerie* [drug store] doesn't exist as such anymore. [It's called an *Apotheke,* pharmacy.] He wasn't inclined toward party ideology but did it for business. He knew I was half Jewish. My husband had a friend who loaned him money to start the business, and he paid off the loans.

I was baptized and married by a clergyman who converted from Judaism to Christianity. In 1931 I married. We met in 1930. It was a short engagement. As strange as it sounds, I met my husband on the streets. I had a woman friend who was invited to a house for a large party when the parents were gone. They danced all night. I saw him the next day with her and he *looked* like he'd been dancing all night. We met again. I saw him come out of a store and he asked if he could walk with me. In 1939, at thirty-one, he died. It was hard. I couldn't have gotten a better man. I never married again. I knew that I had a good marriage, and I didn't know what I'd receive a second time. I never would simply live with someone as people do. Today I'm too old. Around 1955 my father died. Both my father and Aunt Frieda had gone with me to the Jewish cemetery in Hamburg. My father was buried there and the grave is marked with a stone. I was at my father's funeral. It rained terribly. Someone sent a cross, not a wreath! The Jews don't believe in the Messiah. They're waiting for him.

My parents met each other in a home that offered lodging to young Jewish boys. My mother was working there. My father really liked her and carried coal for her. It was obvious they liked each other and got engaged, which my mother was not permitted to do. It was clear he wasn't Christian. My mom thought, When we get married, it will be different. He didn't go to Jewish meetings. It didn't change, and he soon had another woman. My mother was Christian but at one time had to choose one way or another. Later I did the same.

My mother was simple. She came from Mecklenberg, and her marriage was not good. My father came from a Jewish family and was better educated. Jews are clever and often have high-positioned jobs. One time, on a Sunday, everything was closed when my husband had the stomach flu. We went walking and stopped at the only office that was open. A Jewish doctor fixed him up. My husband said, "How much do I owe you?" "Nothing," he said. "I helped you and that's enough."

I don't know what role my parents played for me when my father wasn't always around. I can't pinpoint their roles. Before the divorce, my mother sent my father and me shopping one summer. We went to buy fruit at an upscale store where you had to wait in line. Someone else was waited on before us and didn't care. I stepped up and said, "But no, it's my turn. I should be next." My father pulled me away and said, "How could you do that? Go apologize to the woman." The woman lived in our building. I knew very clearly that my father *kommt von selbst*—he dealt directly with things and life goes on. My mother sometimes went weeks without saying anything to me when I was up to no good. That was terrible. I had to apologize and then I'd wonder why I did.

I didn't spend much time with my father. He was never there. He fought in World War I, was slightly wounded, and convalesced in the hospital in Hamburg. When he got better he stayed with us. While he was there I didn't have a mother anymore! He provided for me. Once he gave me some cake and a friend tried to take it away. I said, "You! Look. That's my father. That's my father's cake. You can't take it away." This is a childhood memory.

After my father came out of the concentration camp, he was happy I visited. He didn't deny anything when I confronted him. I visited every four weeks. He was in Rahlstadt. He moved into his own apartment—he got his former one back. Between the divorce and transport to the camp, I don't believe I saw him much. He changed jobs here and there. He lived in different cities. Before Hitler's time, he was self-employed. When my parents divorced he had to take care of me financially. Every Friday I went to get money from him. It was awful. As far as I remember, I rarely saw him and never got anything from him, and he rented out a room to a family where he worked. The wife was sneaking around with my father. Her husband actually came to our house and told my mother that *his* wife had been sleeping with someone she knew. My mother said, "Yes, I know him, but I can't do anything." After his camp release, my father and I spent time talking when I made my visits.

My mother and I had a four-room apartment in Eppendorfer chausee. She had to take care of herself and rent out rooms. There was a time when it was slow to rent a room. Other times it rented quickly. I was engaged at that time and wanted to marry. Whatever money I earned I left with my mother. It was unusual. She had to pay the rent that was due. I always gave her money. If I had not helped financially, then we would have had to rent out my room.

My mother and father had no contact with each other. I picked up the money. It was arranged that she rented rooms and would do tailoring. She couldn't keep appointments. She could sew well, but she couldn't meet deadlines. The relationship to my father wasn't special just because I was his first child. He lived mainly in Berlin, and when in Hamburg he stayed with Frieda and Albert. Frieda came to us once and told me he was there. I'd show up and he'd say, "Oh. It's my child." I always went to him. On my birthday, he sent greetings and packages—materials for sewing when he was a display window decorator. Very nice. I always looked stylish. But good looks don't replace everything, no? My mother had a husband who wasn't faithful and didn't take care of her, but she never prevented me from visiting him. I wondered about that.

I attended the *Volksschule* [elementary school] because Uncle Albert had a good job and paid for it, and my father had an illegitimate child for whom he had to pay. I was there three years and continued further to a *Mittelreife* [middle-school degree]. I trained in business—confectionery and coffee sales. I was raised as an only child; I never saw my half sibling. I'd have liked to have had several children myself but it didn't turn out that way. But when I look back even if I'd had two children God would have looked out for me, although without a husband it would have been tough.

Around 1950, when I lost the business and was unemployed, I came back to Hamburg. Previously I was in Pomerania and Stuttgart. I took a job I hated—I was sitting on a powder keg and could be fired at any minute. I learned sales. I said, "Jesus, I put this in your hands. I can't do it anymore." I had to return to Fehmarn. By now it was the 1960's. A messenger came to me and said, "I guess you don't like to work here." "No, I don't," I said. "There's a job in the newspaper for an accounts manager at Edeka." "Yes, bookkeeper. I can do that," I said. So I applied and one day received a phone call. An apprentice said, "You're requested to come to the phone." I said, "Can you bring the phone to me?" I was irritated because I figured it was another worker. With that tone of voice I answered the phone. "Hello, this is Herr Kruger." I thought it was Kruger, an apprentice from the company, and so I didn't sound too thrilled. He said, "No. Dr. Kruger from Edeka." He had received my application but had just sent a letter to me saying he would not hire me. But on the phone he said, "There might still be a possibility. Or have you found something?" "No," I said. "Then come over and speak to us." I said, "I can come this afternoon." I talked with Dr. Kruger. They meant to hire someone else and hadn't heard back from him so they asked if I wanted the job. I was employed there for over ten years and I never had been so satisfied as I was with Edeka. At sixty-five you are forced to retire regardless of circumstances. So I unfortunately had to give it up. I got a small pension that I have to give to the retirement home. I receive pocket money one time per year. I get DM 600-650 *Sonderrente* [pension bonus]. God took my life into his hands and I'm forever grateful for that.

I see myself as a Christian in the New Testament sense. I believe in Jesus Christ and that He, for me, went to the cross. I bear part of the burden of guilt. Jews are still God's people, and on the Second Coming, God will appear on the mountain again where the Ascension took place. One doesn't know where Golgotha is, but now people might know. I don't remember the date I became Christian, but once when I was traveling I was afraid of dying and death. I said to Jesus, "I want to be yours," and expressed thanks that He died at Golgotha. At that time, this fear of death disappeared completely. When I meet new people who are *truly* Christian, I'm not restrained in talking with them. Just because they were baptized or married in the church doesn't mean they're Christian. I am cautious because there are people alive today who still think along the lines of National Socialism. The Jews are all God's creation, but maybe they are no longer God's children. The child was to be born and the rabbi goes up to heaven and Jesus says, "One must be born anew." You must lay aside your previous life completely and believe in Jesus. Then you're born anew. Then there's a growth process. I have seen people who were chronically angry become calm and mild-mannered. I know that the Jews are God's people, even today. I know it. And what does that mean? I know that God is infinitely faithful but also severe. Yet he keeps his promises to the Jewish people. In the Old Testament one can read how the Jews were led out of Israel and were in the desert for forty years. In the Old Testament the Jews often had been disobedient, making idols. God said, "I'll scatter them among the peoples." I ask you, is that so? Have the Jews been scattered all over? I ask you, is that so? If it weren't that way, there wouldn't have been a Holocaust. They didn't have their own country—everybody had Jews in their population. They didn't have a state until Herzog came up with the idea of Palestine. I've read Golda Meir and she was one of the first pioneers of the State of Israel in the 1940s. She was sent to America to raise money for Israel. She gave lectures and raised lots of money, which was used to build Israel. She is buried in Israel. I was in Israel twenty years ago. I traveled by ship and then two weeks by bus through Israel to holy sites—it's not that big. I saw the *Klagemauer* [Wailing Wall]. I heard the wailing and was startled. I would like to go back but it's not possible anymore.

During the Nazi time, I felt like an outsider. Whoever would have found out about me would have seen me as someone not to look at. But not to true Christians. To them it didn't matter. I remember no radio, no cinema. I remember at one time I was anemic and I had to get to the doctor. I needed to fill out forms for treatments that had blocks for "Aryan" and "non-Aryan." I didn't even get past the form. [She slaps her leg.] Being an outsider is awful, when someone knows he belongs to a certain people and when these people don't want to know anything about him. I was born into the German people but they didn't want to know me. It's hard to describe. It's normal to love your country and its people when it's your home. One time someone said, "You should have left." To leave Germany with a small child was impossible. I have never thought about leaving Germany. Where should I go? I never thought about it. After 1945 I had no reason to leave. I may have gone earlier if I had gotten some help. Certainly I have a bind to Germany. I don't take notice of it. When one is German one loves her country and stands up for it. That's always the case. When someone says something untrue or disagrees, you retort with something positive about your country. The German people are what changed. First, we had large unemployment. Hitler built the highways to take care of this. The government was unable to build up a trust with the people, so they created a PR scam. What was to come later, no one foresaw. A lot of people supported it. I don't know how it came to persecution. One lets the mask fall from the face. The old field marshal, Hindenburg, made Hitler the ruler and he didn't know the future. Many people thought as Hitler said—the Jews are our misfortune. Perhaps it was German nature. Now if you asked people if they'd like to go back to Nazi times they'd say no.

Maybe if Americans had arrived sooner it would have made a difference. But from what I heard, other countries didn't know what was going on. They couldn't do anything but what they did—attack and conquer Germany. I never listened to the BBC. *And if I had?* I need to leave now.

CHAPTER EIGHT

SIGRID LORENZEN

*"The Hitler ideology was
stronger than my life"*

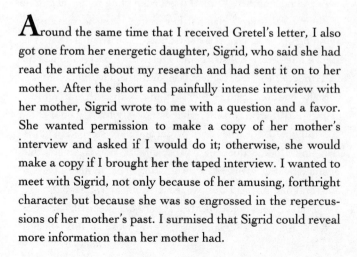

Around the same time that I received Gretel's letter, I also got one from her energetic daughter, Sigrid, who said she had read the article about my research and had sent it on to her mother. After the short and painfully intense interview with her mother, Sigrid wrote to me with a question and a favor. She wanted permission to make a copy of her mother's interview and asked if I would do it; otherwise, she would make a copy if I brought her the taped interview. I wanted to meet with Sigrid, not only because of her amusing, forthright character but because she was so engrossed in the repercussions of her mother's past. I surmised that Sigrid could reveal more information than her mother had.

Both mother and daughter, although continually in conflict, embraced their own religion to cope: Sigrid, progressive Christianity informed by Judaism, and Gretel, traditional Christianity. Both, although they professed Christian beliefs, hid from each other behind their respective discourses. Sigrid claims that my coming to Hamburg and talking with them brought them closer together; they have been discussing their painful, but shared, memories. Sigrid's father, an "Aryan" and nationalist, died when she was young. Out of anxiety and fear of exposure, Gretel, a *Mischling*, damaged the relationship with her daughter by overprotecting Sigrid as a child and then restricting her freedom through ironclad rules as an adult. It was apparent from these separate interviews that both women were divergently, intensely emotional: Sigrid displayed ebullient happiness with herself, frustration with her mother, and peace with Germany's past; Gretel displayed agitation with herself, pride in her daughter, and confusion about Germany's past—her voice choked and tears came to her eyes at points where she had to recall a particularly painful memory. She was not comfortable with crying. I realized after I left that Gretel avoided telling me certain stories so as not to lose her composure. Although Sigrid claims to be "more enlightened" and without crutches as compared to her mother, I found them both clinging to religion in distinct ways. Sigrid claimed her mother had no real understanding of Jews. Gretel is dogmatically Christian; perhaps this stance has been a shield against Germany's past—she has not had to confirm the persecution and the abandonment she actually endured. She merely says that with faith she can look at the past. Sigrid, on the other hand, is what I would call a "born-again" Jew. She is pro-Israel and very steeped in Christian and Judaic doctrines, especially at points where they commingle. Sigrid offered an evaluation of her mother's personality and life; through this, we learn about Sigrid herself.

I talked with Sigrid in April at her home near Blankenesee, a beautiful part of Hamburg. Sigrid wore a short-sleeved sweater, a long, clanking necklace, a multicolored scarf tied to hang in front, a silver watch, white hose, and a green silk skirt with green and black canvas shoes to match. Her gargantuan, silver-rimmed glasses complemented her oval, angular face and shocking silver hair. In her spacious apartment stood a large, wrought-iron menorah with white candles, eerily true-to-life porcupine figurines on the windowsill, and *The Jewish New Testament* and Russian matrioshkas (wooden dolls stacked inside each other) in clear view wherever one sat in the room. When I asked Sigrid if her porcupines symbolized something, she replied that she had received them as a present: "I don't know why they were given to me—if my personality resembles a porcupine!" She told me immediately that her mother felt like a hunted animal, and her conversation centered around befriending Jews.

Because of Sigrid's interest in Jews and survivors, we discussed the problem with wannabes. I had read a story set in Poland about a man who was too young to have survived the camps but said that he had. He would not have even been born yet. Because he wanted to be a part of history, he pretended to be a victim. Certainly there are some people who survived the war and then claimed falsely that they were in the camps. Why? Undoubtedly they had experienced other horrors. Because they wanted to make a bigger impression, to create an image, they said they survived the camps so that people could understand their behavior. Sigrid replied that their behavior was "masochistic." This is a difficult psychological problem. Everyone maintains the survivor/victim dichotomy that Sigrid said "doesn't work."

We talked about the appearance of Jesus. I told her about the Easter service where I heard a beautiful a cappella German chant that resonates in my head. I think the German language is most powerful, most spiritually stirring, in music. If I ever felt the presence of God or Jesus, it was in that dark church in Klosterstern. It is ironic how Wagner was played in the concentration camps and how the Nazis wanted classical music surrounding them. This music, this essence of what Germany was, became a perversion. Where was God in the Third Reich? So many lost their faith. I had heard stories about the appearances of Jesus in World War II, various accounts of seeing Jesus in bomb shelters and a stranger who appeared and told a soldier where to go in order to be safe. Sigrid said she had heard of people who have experienced a *Christus Erscheinung*, who believe they have seen Jesus.

Sigrid played some American gospel music. She smiled and clapped. She was overly-exuberant, religious, spiritual, and generous. Her joy was infectious, but why did I not trust it? Perhaps it was her insistence on "protecting" Jews? There are differences among Jews as well; not all are "holy" people, yet, if there is a Jew in her midst, she swarms. Perhaps this is her reaction to the hatred that poured forth from Germany.

After both Lorenzen interviews were complete, I received another letter from Sigrid with an analysis of the interviews. She heads her commentary of her mother's interview with "Supplement." She comments that Fehmarn used to be the largest island in the BRD (German Federal Republic) but now Ruegen is. Her mother had spoken incorrectly. Sigrid thought her mother had mixed up the time sequences, especially concerning what happened before and after Theresienstadt (a work camp), where her mother's father, with whom she had little connection, was imprisoned. Sigrid says, "One can gather what my mother means." Also, she claims, what her mother says about DM 2,000 is incorrect—the true story can be garnered from copies she enclosed that concern the *Wiedergutmachung* (reparations). Her demand for compensation was rejected, but she was given DM 2,000 unofficially. The following is the letter Sigrid wrote to the *Amt für Wiedergutmachung* [Office for reparation]:

Dear ladies and gentlemen,

I received your answer from the director, Mr. Draeger, of the *Reichsarbeitung*. The VDK was the first place I sought help because I didn't know to whom I should turn. It concerns the following: Because of differing family circumstances, my mother and I once again came to discuss the past; more concretely, my mother's past. She is a "half-breed of the first degree" as she was called in the Third Reich, and as such, she is still cloaked with fear, at times, intense, and feelings of worthlessness. The wounds refuse to heal. My parents' marriage bowed under massive tensions because my father was, as a young man, unable to withstand the pressure and wanted a divorce. It was requested of him to give up his present duties with the Red Cross, or to separate himself from his wife and child. There was an exchange of letters between my father and the *Reichsleiter,* Bormann, head of the NSDAP [the Nazi party] chancellery, who denied the request. I have the letter. My father died in November 1939. Concerning the question of my mother, whether she has at any time or anywhere received a small bit of compensation, she said no. I am pointing this out to you one more time in order to come to a resolution in this matter. My mother was born in 1907 and now has moved to a senior citizens home. She became a "social case" because her pension consists only of DM 1,000 monthly. She is not a war widow, and for reasons entirely psychological, she missed out on the recovery that followed the war. I know that the contents of the letters are late but not entirely too late, in order to somehow receive reparations. However, I am glad I have written this to you in the interest of my mother. I thank you for the effort of your response, and send friendly greetings.

Sigrid Lorenzen

She comments that her mother has no relationship with Judaism and that perhaps she is afraid of being linked to the appellation as well as the religious practice. Her mother has not been able to grasp what a great, positive significance Judaism has had perhaps because she still believes that her

father, Sigrid's grandfather, was not morally correct. She
hasn't accepted or come to terms with it, has repressed the
memories, and left his conduct to God. Sigrid believes her
mother does not have freedom within herself, and feels sorry
for her mother in this lack of freedom. Sigrid says that in
contrast to her mother, she contacts Jews wherever she can
and she likes doing it: "I am always happy when I see them
and if the situation allows it, I tell them I am happy to see them.
But I am twenty-seven years younger, and live in a different
time from that of my mother."

In another written summary of the interviews, Sigrid
writes: "I think my mother has an inferiority complex because
of her childhood [divorced parents] and because of her non-
Aryan race. I myself have always been spontaneous and
confident, at least on the outside, and that has made my mother
uncomfortable." Now Sigrid is trying to bridge the gulf on a
sentimental and psychological level — interior links — between
herself and her mother: "I am trying to love her at her age, and
accept and love her in her 'brokenness.'"

Sigrid is a follower of Israel. The books in her home
reflect her interest in Jewish and Israeli issues. She does
everything to display her solidarity. While in Stuttgart, she
wore a large Star of David on a silver chain. Arabs stared at
her. She got a reaction, as she wanted, and "sparks flew." She
mentioned the king of Denmark with the yellow star of David
and how it is too bad no one in Germany makes the same
overtures.[1] Sigrid is glad to live in her homeland, Germany,
to move about freely, because in Iran and other Arab
countries she could not have worn this chain, this sign of
Israel which, she said, is three inches in diameter. Her friends
conduct similar displays with variations — they place pro-
Israel stickers on their cars or bikes. Some of her friends take
every opportunity among general society or at specific events
to place reports of Messianic Jews (those Jews who believe
Christ is the Savoir), and cultural symbols, such as wine or

jewelry, onto a table in order to put Israel into the focus of attention. Sigrid writes:

> Among my friends, I feel completely accepted and bound with them because God put a very strong love for the people of Israel into the hearts of my closest friends. And they accept the guilt of Germany for themselves. We give money to Holocaust survivors, or, for example, we visit people in Israel who have little money, and give them money for dentures. Or in Hamburg, we try to get in touch with Jews who emigrated from Russia and want to find a new home here. This is a private initiative without government involvement.

I read your announcement in the *Hamburger Abendblatt.* I called my mother and she said, "Send it to me." So I sent the clipping to my mother. I told her that she could do whatever she wanted but to keep in mind that she is one of few survivors. "You can still tell people about this," I said. I tried to make it seem important to her. She's eighty-seven. My mother never psychically worked through the Nazi time. I've forgotten so much; it's left behind in my childhood. I had to work out negativity.

I don't know either Uncle Albert or Aunt Frieda, who my mother mentioned. I do know my grandfather came back from Theresienstadt. I was twenty-three or twenty-four when he brought up the subject, and I had absolutely no idea what he was talking about. My mother told me that my grandfather had been in Theresienstadt, but I didn't know that story, that history. My mother had said during the war, "If we're ever separated, then remain faithful to God." I didn't know what she meant. I figured out later that my mother was afraid we'd be torn apart, that she'd be arrested and stuck in a concentration camp. Ten years ago I asked my mother to write down her life story, a form of therapy, to free herself from the past. She did. I can't read it sometimes without weeping.

It is horrible. My mother wrote in her memoirs that she had a feeling of home *[Heimat Empfindung]* at Frieda's where her family received warmth. Something my mother's father could or would not give, she got freely from her uncle's family. My mother is incapable of bonding with people because of her parents' broken marriage. My mother abandoned Tante Frieda, although Frieda still accepted my mother.

My father was a Nazi. Did my mother say my father liked women? No. She gets a lot mixed up. Well, he was a handsome man, but it was my *grand*father who ran around. He had a small conscience. He was adulterous already at the time my mother was young. He was always gone, never home. *My* father was really not a "hero to women," the Casanova type. Not that I would know. But, he died so young, thirty-two years old. Certainly my mother told you that? She let out the entire report?

In his heart perhaps my father was not such a Nazi. He was in the Red Cross—this was a confirmation of and gave value to his life. Because of his "non-Aryan" marriage he was ordered to give up the Red Cross service. I have an official letter here from Bormann who was a *Reichshauptstellenleiter,* higher official, one of Hitler's aides. My father had made a plea for mercy, a call for clemency. The letter said, in summary, "As a result of your marriage to a 'non-Aryan' you are not allowed to serve in the Red Cross."

Here is the letter: *Reichskonzilei des Führers* [The Führer's Council]

> Your request has arrived and is being processed. [Sigrid notes they had crossed out sentences. She doesn't know why. Maybe as it went from office to office.] Your request to be readmitted into the Red Cross, despite your wife's not completely Aryan descent, has been subjected to close scrutiny and was carefully looked into. According to our calculations we have determined that your wife is *Mischling Ersten Grades,* and due to the substantial quantity of your wife's impure blood, you cannot be readmitted to the group. Acting as a subordinate of Hitler, I reject this request. You may remain an *einfaches Mitglied* [a low-ranking member] of the party. We're giving

you the opportunity to prove your desire to serve the movement and its goals.

Reichsleiter, Martin Bormann.

[Note: Supposedly Bormann was more focused on reinvigorating the nationalistic elements than persecuting the Jews.]

Oh, yeah! That *is* the Nazi *Sprache* [language]. At the time I was moving into this apartment and my mother into the retirement community, I asked my mother if she'd ever gotten compensation. I wondered because so many other refugees, especially from the East (we had many refugees from the East), had received money. My mother was so worn out by the Nazi experience that she had little energy; she didn't follow through. She let it go to sleep. I'll give you a copy. Keep asking me questions.

Today is beautiful. It's a joy to live, primarily because I am a conscientious Christian. God had something planned for the Jews. He had something planned for them at the time of the Third Reich and he still does. I can agree with that. God didn't abandon us; he didn't abandon the Jews. Somehow life continues. A female friend commented that I had Jewish ancestry for which she envied me. I was employed as a nurse in a hospital with a "half Jew" who had lost her wits and came into possession of lots of money and bought a mosaic desk. That was the first nice item she had owned. So I knew she shared my experiences, had been through a similar past. It was a painful thought. It made me uncomfortable. I was frightened of being laughed at, ridiculed, pushed off to the side. I thought about this for a while. I thought about the fears and anxieties my mother had passed on, the negative aspects. I felt intimidated and had a completely destroyed self-worth. My mother has a destroyed self-image. When one gets to know her more closely, goes deeper, knows her reactions, it can be unbearable. My mother can't say, "Ich bin ich" [I am who I am]. I am Gretel Lorenzin. My mother and I are Christian. I'm not of Jewish faith. I do embrace the Old Testament, the Torah. That is the basis of my life. The God of Israel is the God of

Christians—that is very clear to me. Their God is my God and my God is theirs. Jesus was Christian and a Jew. The line goes back to Old Testament times.

I don't feel like an outsider at all anymore. There was a long time of soul searching and ministry before I could accept my origins, to say "I belong here." Yet I'm in a group that's not accepted. I can only speak about the Germans now. I'm often confronted with the question, "If there's a crisis in Israel today—and I believe there will be war in the foreseeable future—would the Christians come to Israel's assistance? I would march with them if there was a demonstration in Hamburg. I have a large Israeli flag which I got in Jerusalem. I march on Jerusalem Day once each year. Yet it's an important question that I must ask. I accept harassment for myself. If people throw eggs and plums at me for marching for Israel, it's the price one pays.

I receive a monthly magazine from Israel. A journalist, a messianic Jew who immigrated to Israel, has done research and sees matters from a biblical view but sees other sides as well. He makes very clear how many lies are published by the Palestinian and Arab press. It has been proven that the money earned from sales of Arab oil has been used to control the media so that Palestinian and Arab opinions are pronounced and pushed, a "worldwide push": anti-Israel. In essence, the world media is paid off by Arabs to present a specific view.

I was in England more than twenty years ago—in a school where nine different countries were represented. I had English in school. If only I could find someone with whom I could speak. When I was in Israel, I also took Hebrew. I was in Israel in 1993 and I heard from someone about older people who had emigrated from Germany who had the urge to speak German, to read German, to hear Goethe and Schiller. It was true. I can hardly imagine it. All the good German writers are gone. [But there's Böll and Grass.] These Israelis have their roots in Germany and want to hear about the culture in which they were raised. There's an organization in Hanover to which I wrote a few months ago to mention that I'd like to travel to Israel and visit the people in homes. I haven't received an answer.

I worked out my problems with another person, a *Teilfach Frau*, who has training. She's *not* a therapist. I could ask her questions. But she knew my family too intimately. In the matters of caring for the soul there were two considerations: Where did my anxieties come from? Answer: I received my anxieties from my mother's breast, from home. And where did my mother get the anxieties? It all became clear. My mother was surrounded by this ongoing deadly power, this ostracizing, this telling someone "you're worth nothing—we'd prefer you get out of here." It was an ordeal for a young woman. It started from the time I was born and trickled into my parents' marriage. When my father decided he wanted to belong to the Red Cross and the party, he sacrificed his wife. That's hard. The Hitler ideology was stronger than the marriage—the consciousness that the ideology was stronger than my life. Grandfather said before he was sent to Theresienstadt he wanted to see his daughter. My mother couldn't go because of me. The main motivation of my mother was she didn't want the child, me, to be parentless. I imagine it was horrible.

After the war we were evacuated to Fehmarn on the Baltic Sea. My paternal grandfather was a schoolteacher who had been evacuated from Kiel with his school class, and we saw him there. I went to his school as a "Kiel kid." During the war, my mother went back and forth to Hamburg to the store. Even though it was bombed, there was stuff in the cellar. My mother first called a friend to ask if the air was clear. Is it safe to come? And she'd say yes, or no, they're waiting for half Jews. She would go back to the train and leave. My grandfather was supposedly in Auschwitz [an extermination camp]. Either I forgot it or my mother never told me or I had too much to take in at one time. I told my mom she never told me. Mother said, "Yes I did." He was ordered to leave Theresienstadt to bury corpses in Auschwitz and then came back to Theresienstadt. He was married to a Jew who starved to death in Theresienstadt. I read it here—in my mother's memoir.

I've never married. Two sides to why I didn't marry. One, I was a late bloomer, and, I believe, many men were killed in the war who were in my age group. Fourteen- and fifteen-year-old boys, called the *Werwolfe,* were sent to the front. And then there was a time I just decided I didn't want to marry. I'm not an easy person to get along with. I'd be divorced by now—at least once! At home I never had the chance to develop the character to get along with others, to learn the art of relationships. I reacted aggressively, which I learned from my mother, even though my mother finds any aggression an offensive affront. I discuss things with my mother and the conversation inevitably goes bad. My mother always ends up feeling offended. It's hard to find one's way. My father died early and so we were alone; there was no one there as a counterbalance. There was no correction until I was grown. The older generation didn't accept "back talk" from children. Mothers wouldn't allow daughters to express themselves. I didn't feel understood. I never felt understood. I had a terrible drive for freedom and my mother was terribly anxious. Those two separate traits didn't mix. The fact that it was the postwar time played a major role, and I grew up with the mother of my mother. Three women in the household.

I got to be too much for my mother. I remember a situation that my mother couldn't handle. We ran around the table, and she was spanking me, swatting at me. She was so furious and couldn't deal with me. She wanted a friendship. When I was older I said, more or less, "no" to a friendship. I said to my mother, "It's not going to work. You don't trust me at all." [Trusting others had to be hard for her mother after her life in the Nazi era.]

After the war, it wasn't possible to go anywhere alone. The way things were then is not at all how they are now. It was a struggle to survive. My mother was concerned with having food and clothing. We'd go to the fields of wealthy farmers and gather grain [wheat and barley] that was left on the field so we could eat. *Ja, vertrauen.* [She sighs.] Yes trust. I can't give you an example. I just know that a deep trust is not there. Later I came to the conclusion that my mother didn't mature; she stood still at one point and didn't have the strength or the opportunity to grow internally into an adult, to become conscious of reality. This is the impression I have sometimes. I think it's a result of the situation in which she lived—to put it into perspective.

Identification? Identity? Ah, *Identität!* Identity. Who am I actually? I had problems with that but not anymore. I worked on that and dealt with it. Who am I? I saw who I was and said "Yes! And now, Live!" I know I have this Jewish background that explains a lot to me. I see a great future in that. The biblical teachings. The basis of the Bible. It's tremendously important to me, and where the reason for such and such lies. Where does this positive attitude come from? I have no fear, no anxiety, even if a crisis would break out. I'm certain that there will be a violent outbreak against Jews. It's not finished with the Jews. The animosity toward the Jews can't be indefinitely suppressed. It's not a pleasant, conversational idea, but it's my opinion. And I simply know that God is there. He stands by and defends His people. Otherwise one can forget about everything and just cry about it.

In the Nazi time faith had disintegrated. I believe that the Jews, up until now, have survived in spite of the tremendous amount of persecution and destruction—bodily and mentally [body and spirit] simply because God is there and because God keeps His word. In the Old Testament it is written that the promise is made to Abraham and his children to support them until the end of time. It's God's spirit that calls the Jews to life from antiquity to a reawakening today. God has given back to the Jews the Promised Land in Israel. I believe that. Some say the Jews did not resist enough, that they walked into their deaths. I believe the Jews resisted. Unto death. But there was this overwhelming force and the cowardice of the Germans, also the cowardice of the Christians who didn't help. You know about this. When one looks at it more closely, one notices that the Jews resisted. Ninety percent of the Germans were fearful. It is still dangerous today. I don't go out into the street and say, "I believe this and that." It doesn't happen.

[As Sigrid recalls the following story, she turns animated.] I saw a young man on the S-Bahn train. He was very nervous, I could tell. He kept glancing over at my newspaper. So nervous! He said to me, "I have to speak to you. What kind of newspaper is that?" "It comes from Israel," I said. "Do you have something to do with that?" he asked. And I said, "Do *you* have something to do with that?" "Yes," he said, "I'm Jewish." "Fantastic!" I said. "I have something to do with it in that I had a Jewish grandfather. I receive news from Israel." The young man was so happy. He belongs to the synagogue in Hoheweide. A train connection flashed at the front, inside the car. He had to get off, change trains, go in another direction. I gave him my newspaper to take with him and told him he could pick up this newspaper for himself. I was very satisfied with that. This professing of one's identity is very important. It is so vital to give support.

But now it is Israel that has problems with race. In India there are 3 million people who say they are of Jewish ancestry and want to immigrate to Israel. People panicked in Israel. You must stipulate: (1) Jewish mother, (2) completely Jewish grandfather. When someone wants to come into Israel, there are considerations because it's so small. It's also a spiritual problem. If everyone claims roots in Israel, then Israel would have to open up to anyone who has anything to do with Christians, a vague relation. Not practical. Jews are the roots and Christians the fruits. The fruits from the roots.

I'm in a group and there's a circle of people there—old and young—who are interested in Israel. Probably more younger. It doesn't reflect a particular social class. I need to be cautious here; I don't want to be seen as taking up the Israeli cause. I don't want repercussions. Over Israel, my heart is moved. I'm convinced. My mother laid a certain foundation for my interest in religion, but I made the decision myself. That's clear to me. This I know. I said yes to God, yes to the life foundation that God gives us, yes to Jesus Christ, and in this respect it's my decision and according to it, I live. I was eighteen. I remember the scene exactly. I was in a vocational school and attended a Christmas celebration. One person in the class had to stand up and explain why we celebrate Christmas. No one stood up. Not even the teacher. I stood up when no one else would. [She laughs.] I don't know why. I said, "Personally, I celebrate Christmas because I believe Jesus Christ was born and came into the world as the Son of God." After I said this it went powerfully into my heart and I felt so convinced that I know this moment was the point at which God sealed it in my heart. In these few minutes there was a major change, an epiphany, for me. That's how I experienced it. It continues now. The profession of my faith was the opening of the portals.

Parts of Christianity are difficult. If God did not choose these ways that transcend Nature, he would be equal to us, and then we wouldn't need him. I'm not a theologian. I need someone—that's stated rather primitively—who is, from my view, *more* than I am. I am a creation. I was created out of His hands. I say that as a human being. I need a creator and a redeemer. During my life, I've noticed all of this. I need someone who frees me, liberates me, from all the manure I carry around with me. I find it very interesting that this—it's already been so long ago—Christian faith is interconnected with Jews, and that Jesus was a Jew, that he was sent by his father for the Jews. When the Jews didn't want him, he came for the Gentiles. For me, it's so fascinating, I cannot tell you. It lives in me like a new blossom everyday. I notice that the statements of God in the Old Testament, statements of prophecies—someone is coming, Jesus is born, people come to Bethlehem—is a continual process that's going on today. I find those stories alive, living.

I believe there are people who have seen Jesus, a *Christus Erscheinung.* I know that happened in the war. I believe wherever the enemy is so powerful and one cries out that God will appear in some form. He'll show a person the right path to the shelter and then disappear. It's no problem for God. That Jesus has risen and then appears to others is no problem for me. It's a personal thing when one confronts God and asks him, "Do you live or don't you? I have to know. I have to know it in my heart. I must experience your presence. Show yourself to me. Show me in whatever form you choose, whether you live or whether you don't." I think that anyone can do that.

I don't recall having difficulties with being of Jewish descent. Yes, sometimes Germans can be unfriendly and poisonous, such as saying Why do Americans talk so loudly? or Why do they treat black Americans badly? I don't want to descend to stereotypes but I must say, That's Germany. That still is and always and again Germany. You can try not to take it too seriously, or pack your bags and leave. I see myself as a human being approved by God, not condemned. [She laughs.] That's very important to me, and from that idea, I consciously live my life. I take my place with regard to my obligations in the community wherever I see that I'm needed and when I'm asked. It's now the case that I'm pensioned. I try to participate in the beautiful aspects of life. So, this is how I actually see my role, to not just live for myself, but for others, whatever name it has in the framework in which I operate. For example, I wouldn't go into the New Age movement and say, "I'll participate!" I

definitely wouldn't do that. That's how I see myself. My politics change.
I am sometimes Centrist, sometimes left: SPD [Social Democratic Party
of Germany], not KPD [Communist Party of Germany]. I also voted for
the CDU [Christian-Democratic Union]. Because of the massive *Abtra-
gungs* [dismantlings], I wouldn't vote for the SPD. I never was really an
active party member. I think what the Green Party does—raising
consciousness—is great. Up to now I haven't voted for them. I vote more
according to issues, which is very difficult because one issue agrees with
one party but then it's the opposite.

Having been involved in a strong female society, I had no trouble.
As a child, the things I went through with my mother were normal. It
was a normal instinct to want to get away from parents, to look at the
world, to go away wherever I could go. I had a desire to undertake new
things. I had to get out from under my mother's wings. I trained to be
a nurse in Eppendorf at the university clinic. In my time this business of
women's roles was not such a big theme. During the war I was concerned
with rebuilding, surviving, and finding an occupation. I was in nursing,
with which men didn't have much to do, or have a say in, anyway. At
that time there were lots of female nurses but not male nurses. It wasn't
seen as an occupation for men. I never became involved in these
thematics. I never had problems with women's issues. I never felt
disadvantaged as a woman. I led a colorful career. I was in Eppendorf
and then St. George Hospital. I spent a half year with wayward girls. I
was in St. Pauli [an entertainment district of Hamburg] for a year, which
was part of church work to help women who were prostitutes, to help
them get out of prostitution. It was part of the Christian social movement
undertaken by churches. Then I wanted to go to the United States. I got
as far as the consulate and no further. Then I was a nurse in Southern
Germany in a specialized clinic for persons sick from alcohol. When I
was a nurse in the clinic for alcohol sufferers [she doesn't call them
"alcoholics"], I had to participate in therapy. In the course of that, I
picked up information to help myself. Quite a lot. I received wisdom to
pass on. It was good. I myself didn't have an alcohol problem. Specialists
are sent to work with this—to find a way out of this addiction. To one
person, it's an addiction; to others, it's something else. Everyone sees

something in his life and wonders, "Now where did that come from? What is that?" I spent six years at a broadcasting station, Transworld Radio (TWR), an American broadcaster. It was a Christian broadcast. There's a German-speaking branch in Hessen. I worked in an occupation completely different from my earlier years.

In my work with prostitutes, every Friday I had to walk along certain streets in St. Pauli, and I would speak to the women who were either standing on the street offering their services or were on Herbertstraße, a closed-off street, where they sat in display windows. We had leaflets and tracts to pass out and gave them an address where they could go if they wanted to leave their profession—we offered that. Once a week I visited people who were in the hospital to administer penicillin to those who had been infected. About thirty years ago venereal diseases were common, and the prostitutes had to frequent the health agency and be examined. I also visited there and tried to get these women out of their occupation and into the "home" in which I worked, a shelter where there were beds and they could come and stay.

I don't know what the laws used to be in Hamburg about prostitution. It was thirty years ago. I think the laws are more intensive at present because of AIDS. Overall, I don't know how it is today. The women volunteered to come to our shelter. They had to go to the Board of Health first and then to the hospital, where I visited them. It was an offering from the church. If they wanted to climb out of their plight they could live in this home off the streets. They often didn't have an apartment—they could either go to the Reeperbahn [strip district] or the streets. Not many got out. Four or five. They were totally dependent. I don't have current experience—this was thirty years ago. I didn't really encounter the drug scene. At the most, it was at the beginning stages. It's worse today.

I can recall only a little bit about my father. I have a distant memory of his last fourteen days. He had been operated on and was in the hospital. I sat on his bed, a four- or five-year-old, and swayed back and forth. I was near his feet and he said to stop, as his wounds were fresh. That's all I remember. Everything else comes from my mother's accounts. He was very happy about his daughter. Whether my mother just wanted to reassure herself, or whether it was really that way, I don't know. He could have been a loving father, but what mother wouldn't say that when her husband's been dead for fifty years? One puts aside unpleasant memories. She glorified her husband—said positive things about him. He was proud of me, but other than that, I personally have no recollection. In the time after I'd been in therapy someone asked me, "Have you forgiven your father for leaving you so early, that he left you alone?" It unleashed the rage in me because I was alone. I could fight my way through it once. I had a few dreams but it wasn't reality. I think I missed my father. I know so. When I see people stroll along the streets with their fathers or when people marry and the fathers are there and they embrace their daughters at the altar, then I think, Man, that's fantastic. It would be great to have a father like these fathers; it brings tears to my eyes. Family is so important—men and women together. Marriage is so important. That's simply the basis. Certain feminists deceive themselves and are repressive. I feel sorry for those who are against traditional structure because of past experiences left unexamined. Our matriarchal household was not paradise at that time. Feminism wasn't on the table. We didn't think in feminist terms. We faced questions of survival. But I do see women as strong.

In this struggle to survive, my mother suppressed too much. Very much. Her emotional life is wrecked. I can tell you a story that's very fresh, a week old. It was my birthday and I invited a circle of friends over for the evening. I invited my mother for lunch the same day. The people from her age group I wanted to have over on Sunday. I called her and said, "Come here for lunch at noon," so she'd have an opportunity to see me. She showed up forty-five minutes too late. She said, "I came a little too late. Why are you making faces?" I said, "I had many good things planned for today and it was difficult rushing to get everything done near Easter time. I have to arrange other activities as well." She neither excused herself nor apologized. We sat at the table saying nothing, and my mother said, "I'll just leave now." She didn't congratulate me, just prepared to leave, wordless. It was horrible. Then I got the idea to ask, "Mother, do you still remember your birthdays?" She said, "A little." I asked, "How were they?" She said, "They were always terrible." "Why so?" I said. "My mother always came too late," she said. I could have cried out. My mother said, "She always came too late, was never ready, always found it a bother." My gosh. It was the same pattern. She can't get away from it, can't excuse herself for it. Everything is covered up. That evening I had a difficult time putting it out of my mind. Then my faith came back and I said to Jesus, "You were present and saw this. I put this on your cross. I can't live with it. It depresses me. It's sad for my mother that we're so speechless on my birthday. I want to be free of it. I put it on your cross." That's reality for me—that Jesus is present despite the feelings that don't come out. My mother can't embrace me. I never learned real expression either. I had great difficulties and in some ways I still have them today—to be close to other people, to take them in my arms, to be merciful, forgiving. I never learned or experienced that. I noticed this when I was younger and based on how others reacted, I knew something was wrong with me and, to an extent, still is today. I have to rearrange that. It's not the way I want it to be. It's still tough. Family life is vital and something I didn't have. There's no warm relationship, heartfelt emotions, nothing but covering up. There are severe problems in a family if no one can express feelings. If you restrain your emotions you become unhealthy. I experienced that with my mother. That's my mother's case. It's hard to separate the emotional down-stuffing from sickness. From my mother's writings, I noticed that she also came into this world without affection.

In Germany people can be uncommunicative. The post-war generation hasn't worked it out. An entire generation didn't face the past but kept it swept under. There's nothing in school to confront this issue. The generation over forty is problematic. One can argue they've pulled themselves out because life has gone so well for them—everything is good, too comfortable. [She refers to how quickly Germany was rebuilt, saying there wasn't time to reflect, only to forget and prosper.] They concentrated on their kids, having it better than the parents, and pushed everything away. They threw away [whistles] the crap—didn't deal with the issues—just put it all to the side. Didn't clean up. After the war people just wanted to stay alive. There is too much of the Third Reich on TV, but the good programs are on so late at night. The forthright, frank discussions, the Holocaust testimonies, such as four or five interviews with survivors who now have high-level jobs in Israel, are broadcast at 11:30 P.M. German people are sleeping. They should have it on at eight. We've become a superficial society. Broadcasters can say "Well, we had it on." I watched the films that came out ten to fifteen years ago. Often I was weeping in front of the TV alone. Simply from what happened to the people. Where was God? I forced myself to watch simply because I wanted to know it more intensely. Ask me more questions. It's not all that well organized from my end. I'm too fragmented.

I didn't realize in what kind of tension my mother lived. I was born in 1934 and war broke out in 1939. Six years of war. I was a child. I noticed only the tension but not from where it came. I didn't know about the Jewish background, didn't know what was going on. My mother held it back from me. And looking back that was certainly wise.

My mother wrote to me about the drugstore going under. After my father's death we got a letter from the Gestapo district leader in Berlin. He knew where the business was and he knew there was something about my mother, that she was not "Aryan." I don't know if this leader said "Don't buy from Jews. Don't buy from Lorenzens." When the business went under, I don't know if it was because of the Jewish ownership or because people didn't have money because of the economic downturn. Many people were unemployed; it was certainly both reasons. Mother noticed that Germans showed contempt toward her. I didn't notice. As a child, I didn't get it. The district leader could have easily arranged for my mother to be sent away. That's the reason she always thought, "I'll be taken away." Then also the child will be taken away.

I don't know much about Aunt Frieda, but I had asked my mother about her. I'll get the letter. [She reads from her mother's manuscript]:

> The brothers and sisters of my father had a household. Tante
> Frieda left Berlin for good, but I don't know why. She was
> engaged but somehow it was broken. She was a clever woman
> and could discuss all matters of cultural and intellectual life.
> Here in Hamburg, she was on the sidelines, not in the center

of activity. My second home was with my father's brothers and sisters. They were happy when I came. I visited whenever I wanted. They left the key in a staircase so I never encountered a locked door. In the neighborhood, I was known as if I was one of them. Often I came for lunch or sometimes for dinner. It was generally the case that I ate until I was satisfied. The apartment was only ten minutes away from mine. They also had a male cat everyone loved that often would be gone for days or weeks. It came back beaten up. I don't know where the animal is today but this memory is one I like to recall. For that reason, even if it doesn't mean much to you, I am writing this down. Those days we had nicer winters without snow. I'm thinking about such things. Every December 24th, I went with Aunt Frieda to church for a Christmas service and on the way back we'd see the trees with candles burning in the windows. It was a custom that Frieda was at our place on the 24th. Not Uncle Albert. We don't know why. He had his own interests. I loved both of them very much in my childlike way. Later, we became distant. The "guilt" was mine but I don't know why because this was long before the time of the Third Reich. When I loved them, they loved me in return. Maybe they wanted to replace something that I didn't have at home. Aunt Frieda was excellent at telling fairy tales. She had lots of time. And as I was often there we walked everyday—often in Marienthal and Wandsbecker Gehölz. Sometimes we took the horse-drawn carriage to Marienthal. She often used this time as a chance to tell stories. She had a wonderful imagination. Her stories always had new plots, new settings, and new characters. She magically created these elves, water maidens, kings and giants that I could imagine for myself before me. The tales always had the same ending: "So, if they haven't died yet, they're still alive today." If I was ever sick, she'd come in the afternoons. Of course she never came with empty hands. She made hearty chicken, grape soup, puddings, and

painful, but there was no other way, mainly because I could handle only one thing—my family.

Okay. That section is over. Then there's a family, Groette. She talked from there about a friend of hers who'd kept in contact with her father— Aunt Maria. That was the bind. In 1933 the Nazis had seized power and my mother feared for me. My grandfather was Jewish. Only my grandfather. Not my grandmother. My father was Christian. My grandmother told me that my grandfather was baptized, but I don't know the motivation. I know my grandmother married him for that reason— that he was baptized. I don't know about the pressure that my grandfather endured because of that. He certainly had it. Aunt Frieda, I believe, was in Theresienstadt and died. My mother writes,

> Aunt Maria, a friend of my mother, got to know my relatives. And she was also in touch with my father's family. During the Nazi era, she was in touch with everyone but me. She kept up with Aunt Frieda. She maintained ties with siblings of my father. In the beginning of the Third Reich, she went to Peking for a year with her sister. When she returned, the "Final Solution" was in the operational stage. She knew nothing. Initially she wanted to go back to Frieda's place. The two were estranged. They probably were afraid. Aunt Frieda didn't even want to go shopping because she had to wear the yellow star. Maria, being courageous, did the shopping for her. Albert and Frieda moved to a nicer place in Hamburg. Events became more harrowing. Uncle Albert died from stomach cancer. Before that he'd gone blind. He was engaged to a Jewish nurse who died shortly after him of the same illness. Directly after his death, Frieda gave shelter to several Jewish people. She also sent me things she had kept for me— with which I had played as a child—a big painter's book. She certainly would have liked to see me again. And she invited me. I didn't go. Aunt Maria went in my place even though it

could have been dangerous for her. In spite of that, there was
still a difference. It was an unhappy meeting. Frieda was
extremely disappointed that I had not come myself. She
couldn't understand it. She still had a doll she wanted to give
me but due to the circumstances she refused to give Maria
the doll. In spite of that, she spoke with an angel's tongue. I
never saw Aunt Frieda again. She was transported to Theresienstadt and, according, to my father's accounts, starved to
death.

[Sigrid cries.] It's awful. My God. [She searches the document.] One can't
imagine. I read this on vacation once—whew. I told my mother to write
what she could. She didn't really want to write it. She wanted to conceal.
I wondered if I'd demanded too much? I said, "Write what you know. And
what you don't want to write, don't." She was so startled that I still
confronted these issues, that I'd want to know. She still has fears. I told my
mother if you don't want to tell people who you are, then don't. I allowed
her complete freedom in this matter. I didn't want to put pressure on her
and I was simply happy when she wrote something down. [Reading]:

> One time your father said to me that he wanted to divorce
> because he saw no other possibility. He was of the opinion
> that for his people and his fatherland he had to make this
> sacrifice, even though it was difficult. I could only guess at
> how he reached this decision. I didn't know what he was
> thinking. Friends of his tried to talk him out of this. They
> said, *"Wilfried, das ist heller Wahnsinn"* [it's crazy]. You have
> a good marriage, a wife and daughter, why not forget about
> this Red Cross and party? You have a good existence—what
> more do you want?" But none of this affected him. He said,
> "A mistake made one time must be corrected." What all of
> this triggered emotionally in me I just don't want to describe.
> I couldn't do it anyway. It seemed to me as if I were beating
> my head against the wall and never hit on a hole. And I think
> this was the way it was. [Sigrid is crying.]

Then she wrote somewhere, after my father was dead, that she'd read suddenly in the newspaper that if women felt weak they could go get vitamin injections. So she went to the doctor's and waited. When she got there, a sign said it was only for "Aryan" women so she picked up her purse and left. Agh! You can imagine the effects when you are constantly bombarded with downgrading messages like "You're worthless. You belong to a race not worthy of living." Any messages like this. My father had two brothers, and one of them was a high-ranking Nazi official. After the war, at twenty-three, I went to England. My father's brother said, "What do you want in England? A German child doesn't go to England." [She continues to leaf through papers.] [Reads]:

> The tension your father had from waiting for an answer from
> the Red Cross caused a bleeding ulcer. He had to lie in bed.
> In his own eyes, he was very helpless because the loss of blood
> had weakened him. In this condition he said to me, "I know
> why I am lying here so helpless. Because I never showed you
> the letter." "What kind of letter?" I said. "I received a letter
> from Mother and Father that I held back from you." This is
> what I read: He had written to his parents indicating he
> wanted a divorce given the present circumstances. But first
> he wanted to wait for the results of the letter [a clemency
> request] from Bohrman. [Basically, he was asking to break
> the rules.] His parents both wrote, "Wilfried, under no
> circumstances must you do this, even if you have to support
> your family with a spade in your hand." This I must ascribe
> to them—they always supported me. Now everything was out
> in the open. What could I say about it?

My mother was too proud to take money but didn't have suitable training to earn money. She did a business apprenticeship. She often said she would have gladly become a teacher. Under better circumstances she could have finished the *Gymnasium* [college prep school] and done well. She could have somehow gained self-confidence. It's important to finish at the *Gymnasium* in order to attend a university and to have a decent profession. Also for internal knowledge, for mental development. My mother thought, "I can't become anything because my parents don't have money; my mother doesn't have any money." Everything she earned while she was engaged she had to give up to others.

I get the impression that this time in the old people's home—and she has also mentioned—is the best time of her life. She has no concerns. She receives a pension from the state. She lives well, does what she wants, and has no obligations. She's doing fine. She doesn't travel anymore. She used to travel a little bit but not too far. She gets out and walks around Hamburg. Her need to travel also has to do with internal turmoil. She can't stand being alone even though she's alone. She has to go out looking for company. I interpret her roaming as her always searching. She wants to move sometimes—a phenomenon of having missed out on something. One notices it much in older people—it's a common occurrence—that they missed out.

It's not so wrong if there's something missing in my story. It's okay as it is. It's finished.

CHAPTER NINE

MARGOT WETZEL

*"There was no part of life
where you weren't asked whether or not
you were Jewish"*

~

Margot was a tough, no-nonsense woman. She was very liberal in her conversation and manner. She was the only woman who said immediately, "You can smoke or drink if you want to" without knowing whether or not I did. Initially she impressed me as opinionated, pushy, and unfeeling, but, as I got to know her, I saw that she was still inwardly confused about the Nazi years; for instance, she claimed she was not an outsider in school, but said later maybe she was. She said her family was very affected by the laws but then later said she was lucky not to have been affected. She also talked about how people are not tolerant but then she exposed her own intolerance. Margot was very proud of her accomplishments and of having achieved financial success. Margot wore a rose-color top and skirt that looked like a dress, and a diamond and sterling necklace. She also wore a gold watch and gold ring bracelets. She had beautiful blue and white china everywhere and green and white Holland Delft porcelain. Her entire apartment on Hagenau Street displayed wealth. She did not grow up with it, however. Margot was in sales and did well in business. She rose in the ranks of a company. She was married for a few years, but her husband did not like her ambition. She felt oppressed by no one. Margot also pointed out that her family was not intellectual and that her husband had bored her.

Her mother was illegitimate, a "full Jew," and was deported to and remained in Theresienstadt (a work camp) for four months. Margot talked about this event nonchalantly. She showed me the gold star with "Jude" crudely written on it that her mother had to wear, and an armband that bore a number and the name of the camp. Her mother had not been tattooed but had to wear this band. It was chilling to look at, to touch, and to hold. I knew I was in contact with something dirty and unspeakable. It made my skin crawl. This was the first time I had ever seen materially, in my face and hands, the star and armband. Margot guarded these items but did not appear the least bit uneasy displaying them on the table. She mentioned that her mother really had not suffered that much in the camps, and, comparatively speaking, she had not been in the camp as long as others had. Margot's aunts and cousins were gassed, she assumes.

Her father was "Aryan." He broke down when her mother was taken away but "couldn't do anything." Because Margot's family had "kein Geld in die Tasche" [no money], they could not immigrate. They also didn't know what they would do for a profession elsewhere. Also, according to Margot, going overseas was not possible because they didn't know English.

Her father did not, however, divorce her mother. Had he done so, she would have been doomed. As discussed previously, some "Aryan" spouses did divorce their Jewish spouses, which I always thought was the height of cruelty.

At times, Margot emanated shallow attitudes; however, this could have been an attempt to protect herself. She often focused on physical appearances. She was curious if my grandmother was slim or not because she was connected to the Bahlsen cookie company, [yes, she is] and she complimented me on having a "perfect physique." She talked about her intelligent and formerly good-looking father, who allowed himself to turn into a balloon.

Margot talked about Orthodox Jews and their rituals; she seemed to think they were silly. She did not identify with being Jewish. She was appalled that neither the Americans nor the British bombed the camps or the train tracks. She said they had "information enough." We discussed the importance of telling her story and how sad it will be when the survivors are all dead. Margot agreed with this in the end, even though she was not terribly forthcoming about her past.

My talks with Margot were uncharacteristically short. Indicative of her personality, she was an efficient storyteller and did not waste words. This made our conversations run smoothly, and I was not so emotionally depleted. Margot controlled what she wanted to say and did not want to reveal too much, even though she had contacted me with enthusiasm in answer to an announcement I had placed in the weekly Eppendorf paper. She said that ordinarily she never talks about being half Jewish or what happened to her family. She does not feel comfortable doing so.

≈ ≈ ≈

My mother was born in 1896, an illegitimate child of a Jewish woman. My grandfather was unknown. My grandmother never told me who he was, but she said he was Jewish. So my mother was a full-blooded Jew. My grandmother never acknowledged her daughter [Margot's mother], and so, for a time, I never knew exactly who my grandmother was. It was a scandal in those times to have an illegitimate child. My mother went to foster parents. She was born a Danziger. My grandmother had three sisters and one brother. The family stuck together and cared for my mother even though she was given up for adoption, and my mother grew up in several different foster homes and really had a bad childhood. She was pushed around from one family to another, and that's not good for small children. When she was still fairly young, ten or eleven, she had to take care of things at home and be responsible. She delivered newspapers—because in those days everyone was very poor—*very poor*. My mother's family still took care of my mother, and she was with her family a lot. My grandmother and aunts all worked. They were simple honorable Jewish people.

My mother married my father in 1924. He was "Aryan" and came from a simple family as well. The relatives were not so happy [about the marriage], neither on his side nor hers. His relatives said, "You're marrying a Jew," and her relatives said, "You're marrying an Aryan." They didn't approve. My aunt said, "We absolutely do not agree with it." They always said, *"Goy! Goy!"* [not Jewish]. It was scandalous in those times. According to the family, my mother was not a devout Jew, but you could somehow sense the connection she had to her roots. My parents got married anyway and my father was eventually accepted into the family.

My father was a bookkeeper and my mother was a sales clerk. She stopped working at some point and I was born in 1926, a more or less quiet time. It was after the first war and things were bad everywhere. There was poverty; there were so many unemployed people in Germany that not even young Germans today can understand. I think from the few Germans that were left there were 10 million Germans unemployed. And with the little government support, you could neither live nor die. You can't compare this time period with today at all. In 1928 my parents got their own apartment—that was really not normal [that they were able to get an apartment], and until 1933 my mother's and father's family, for the most part, lived in peace and quiet.

In 1933 I went to school and Hitler came into the government. I know that in my mother's family, my aunts and their husbands were all Jewish. I was only six years old, but I knew that they knew a bad time was starting. This was all in Hamburg. I went to Ahrensburgerstraße school, then called a *Volksschule* [elementary school] in Hamburg. Today it is called Krausestraße and is a *Gymnasium* [college prep school]. We lived on Baumweg near this school. During the first years everything went okay. My father had a job and nothing negative happened to him. My father worked for a newspaper, the *Hamburger Fremdenblatt,* then a conservative newspaper, which was taken over by the *Hamburger Anzeiger.* Then in 1937 my father lost his job because it was somehow known—don't ask me how—that Daddy was married to a Jew. So my father became unemployed. He couldn't find work with a newspaper, so he went into the private economy sector as a bookkeeper again. We got by then. It came to the point where the question was raised, "Is Margot going to the *Gymnasium* or is she staying in the *Volksschule?*" [Parents, not the children, made these decisions.] My teachers in the *Volksschule,* who knew about everything that was going on, were very nurturing and considerate in their treatment of me. They told my parents, "Leave your daughter here with us. Nothing will happen to her here. We don't know about the *Gymnasium.* We don't know what kind of teachers are there, whether or not they will harass her or she will be able to stay there." So I stayed in the *Volksschule.* I have to say that I was not sad or upset about it because I was a lazy student. I would have had to produce more in the *Gymnasium.* I liked to go to school, but not to do too much work. I admit that. [We laughed.]

Then we lost our apartment in 1939 because we lived in an apartment that belonged to the city of Hamburg. We received the news because my mother was Jewish. We couldn't find another apartment. I don't remember anymore when we were looking for an apartment if we had to say my mother was Jewish, or Mother said she was Jewish out of pure fear. The landlords did not want to have us, and since we had to leave the apartment and had practically no prospects for an apartment, Mother finally decided—my mother was really courageous and my father was the softer one—now I will no longer say that I am Jewish. So we found a new

apartment because she ceased telling anyone that she was Jewish. Then my
mother was drafted into so-called work duty in Hamburg. It was not
voluntary. She had to work. My mother had not worked after she had quit
her job as a sales clerk. She worked in a chemical factory where rat poison
or something like that was manufactured. She had to work in packaging.
In 1939 we got the new apartment in Eilbek on Eilbeker Weg.[1] My father
lost his job once or twice more for the same reason as before—my mother
was Jewish—but always found another one.

In the beginning of the 1940s my father was drafted into forced labor.
He had to work in the garbage, along with relatives who had to do the
same thing. My father had to work in the rubble piles because my father
was the least robust of us all. At that time in 1941, I thought my mother's
mother, whom I did not know at that time was my grandmother, was one
of our aunts, her sister. I have to say that our relatives, my mother's relatives,
were pure Jewish. They were unmarried. They lived on Isestrasse, an area
where very many Jews lived. Then they got grocery cards. We all got them
in 1939 when the war began, maybe even a little earlier, I don't know
exactly anymore. They could only shop in certain stores. My mother got
grocery cards with a "J" on them, so all the stores where we shopped knew
that Mother was Jewish. For the most part people were okay. They didn't
treat my mother any better or worse than anybody else. Many people were
not in agreement with anti-Jewish actions. While they did not do anything
against the policies, they did not do anything against the Jewish people.
No, they simply left them in peace.

I began to study in 1941. I wanted to be a teacher, but that didn't
happen. I couldn't find a teaching apprenticeship. People said, "We will
not take you." But then there were courageous people—I found a few
companies who said "du" to me immediately. All of this transpired in
Hamburg. In 1941 all of our relatives were taken away. My mother's
mother was deported, but her sister did not have to go. It was very clearly
defined by levels. People who were over sixty-five did not have to go, but
my great-aunt said, "I'm not leaving my sister." So they went together.
We were not so rich that we could do without some of our jewelry.
Naturally some things we would liked to have had with us as remem-
brances. In letters that my Jewish relatives received in January of 1941

they were told that everything had to be left in the apartment. They were so intimidated they didn't even take a ring with them. Don't ask me what they thought—if they would be coming back or if they thought that things would go better for them, I can't tell you. They left just as they were, and apparently were deported to Riga and probably never arrived. All were purportedly gassed on the way. My mother's cousin—naturally he was Jewish—he's somewhere in this picture here—he left also about this time. I don't remember if it was before or after—he went to Minsk. He probably did not arrive. My grandmother's brother and wife immigrated to South Africa in 1935. The children, also Jewish, went before them, and they followed. I must add that they never really gained a foothold in South Africa. They survived, but they lost all roots. My great-uncle had two shoe shops here in Hamburg. Of course, the Nazis took those away immediately. All the people who owned businesses lost them. We didn't have very much, so they couldn't take anything from us, but the two shoe shops that my great-uncle had were immediately confiscated, and the money he received for them was nil—I don't know how much anymore—I was just too young. Nevertheless, it was enough to make it possible for him to get out because his children were sent to South Africa in 1935. My great-aunt died in Africa; my great-uncle came back [to Germany] after 1945. The daughter moved to England; she said she couldn't live in Germany any more. The son came back here to Germany and became a salesman—he was simply uprooted. My grandmother's other relatives died in the meantime because they were all old.

In 1943 we were bombed. I unwillingly ended an apprenticeship in 1943. We didn't have anything to eat after 1945, after my mother was gone, because she was always the one who worried about that. She was gifted that way [in her ability to get food for the family]. I couldn't take any typewriting classes or stenography classes because I always had to say whether or not I was "Aryan"—*until I said that I was.* My father got lucky and was able to get out of his job working in the rubble piles because he met a friend in some position of authority who took him to his office to work. He didn't do anything there, but he didn't have to work in the rubble any more. [She pauses.] Yes, and after the bombing we moved here, until my mother left in 1945. [Margot shows the yellow star.] My mother was only in a concentration camp for four months. She was a very courageous person and got through it. It was 1945, already fairly late. The difficulties before that were worse. Your whole life was full of hardships that you had to come to terms with those twelve long years. There was no part of life where you weren't asked whether or not you were Jewish.

In January she received a so-called *Befehl zum auswartigen Arbeits-einsatz* [Command to foreign/far off work duty]—that's what they called it then. It was horrible and a lie. My father ran his legs off to get to her and told me that I was not allowed to go, but naturally nothing could be done at all. We dropped her off at a school in the neighborhood of the already destroyed synogogue on Rappstrasse in Hamburg.

Old and young people were gathered together, and they left in the night. My mother told us she came back on June 15, 1945, one day after my birthday. The Russians had by that time freed Theresienstadt. Mother saw a lot of emaciated people who came from Auschwitz [an extermination camp] through Theresienstadt—not just pictures, but she saw them herself. My mother didn't necessarily have it too bad in the camp. There were no gas chambers in Theresienstadt at that time. They were being built. Theresienstadt was a so-called *Vorzeigelager,* an exhibition camp, because Hitler showcased the camp to visitors to prove it was "decent." It was all a farce. My mother said that people from the Red Cross came to look at the camps. The children were told that when there were visitors they were supposed to come up to a so-called man named Rahm who was the camp's leader and say "Uncle Rahm, Thank you very much for the chocolate!" Naturally none of it was true. I mean, the camps were manipulated that way. That's why the Red Cross was able to come to the camps. They didn't learn anything about what was really going on. And believe me, it was like that in every camp. My mother said that they were probably there to build gas chambers. One surmised that if they were building showers, they were building gas chambers. One of our aunts came to this same camp in 1941. Our cousin, who was half Jewish like me, sent packages to her mother. There was something amazing about this camp. You will not believe it. The packages were actually given to them! The packages were sent there so that they didn't starve because they got only mini-rations. But the packages were given to them! I have never understood that my entire life. They actually survived because of these packages. When my mother arrived in 1945, she found her aunt who had already been there for two years. As long as one did not starve, one survived Theresienstadt. Mother had it pretty good because many friends, relatives, and acquaintances were already there, and they had everything arranged; one was in the bakery, another was in the kitchen. She was only there four months—one can survive for four months. My mother was forty-nine. [First Margot says forty-five then fifty-one]. She was an age where one is still relatively sturdy. She survived fairly well because of her connections in the camp. She had to work, of course. She said that she never understood what she had to do [what they made her do]. She had to shovel sand in piles and move it from one side to another, and they always watched them while they were working, but beatings or anything of that nature never occurred. The camp was terribly overrun by vermin and pests—roaches, fleas, and bugs. We didn't hear anything from her during her four months in the camp. On her way home she came through Dresden the day after it was bombed.[2] If it had been a day earlier, she probably would have been killed with all those people in Dresden. [She pauses.] Yes, that was Theresienstadt near Prague.

When my mother was taken away, my father broke down because he couldn't do anything. Imagine. He must let his wife go away and he can do nothing about it. They take her away, she is imprisoned by SS [chief police agency] soldiers who treat her as an *Untermensch* [as less than human], and you have to say Good-bye, and you go outside and you see your mother standing in the distance and you wave and you know how dangerous it is and you wonder if you will see her again. Or even more, that she just comes back, right? We had already been bombed out and lived with relatives. We went home. My father lay down in bed and cried.

We had heard about transports to the camps. In 1941 our relatives were already gone. So in this respect we knew what was going on. My mother was in a so-called "privileged mixed marriage" because my mother was Jewish and my father was "Aryan." It's just the opposite in Jewish belief. According to Jewish belief, I am Jewish because my mother was Jewish. While I know that according to the Nazis, and in Western tradition anyway, it depends on the father. When the father was a Jew in Nazi Germany, the family was in a much worse situation. But they treated the most well-known intellectuals, civil servants, professors, and those who owned businesses even worse. They had it especially bad. Think about the Jews who had their businesses taken away. My aunt, my father's sister, had a clothing store here on Mönckebergstraße. It still exists—it's called Altmeier; it used to be called Feldbeck. It was a Jewish business, but it was immediately expropriated. Only when Kristallnacht ["night of broken glass"] occurred did we realize how many Jewish businesses existed. We had no idea!

I vaguely remember Kristallnacht. Because, as I said, we lived here in this outer area, and it happened more so in the inner part of the city. Naturally we were careful about going anywhere where something could happen because we always ran the risk of having something thrown at us from the roofs. I lived on Eilbeker Weg—a bit farther up from here. We were bombed out and then we lived in Eppendorf. [She pauses.] I think it was a lot worse in Berlin.

[Margot shows family photos.] But that is naturally pure Jewish, don't you think? They are true Jewish families, while my mother isn't even in a shawl. I would say they look like typical Jewish women of the time. We didn't eat kosher—we ate matzo and liked it. Do you know matzo? It is bread eaten during Passover. We did not celebrate the Seder. There was no differentiation made between practicing and nonpracticing Jews in Hitler's time. For the Nazis it was not a religion but a race. I think it's like that today, too. People still debate about it, you know. I would say it is a race.

Among my father's "Aryan" family—cousins, nephews, nieces, sisters, brothers—there were one or two civil employees who never had anything more to do with us. I can't tell you whether from fear or because they were convinced not to. It was probably both fear and convincing. But then there were also people who visited more on purpose. So it varied. [Margot begins to recap what she had said earlier about a lot of people that did nothing at all against the Nazis but did nothing for them, either. They simply behaved "like normal people."]

I was a young lady then in the BDM [Nazi youth organization] until I said that I was half Jewish and they threw me out. I had to go to the

Kameradschaftsabend [evening meeting of friends]. It was very hard for me in the early days as a child. I was always an outsider. The kids all sat together. They met somewhere, but I was not invited. It's hard for a kid to understand. I was very sad that I was not allowed to wear the uniform of the Nazis. My father was afraid, and when he met someone he didn't know or who didn't know him, he said "Heil Hitler!" out of pure fear. We couldn't listen to the radio, and my mother could not go into any restaurant or pub. Every restaurant had signs: *"Juden unerwünscht"* ["Jews not allowed." Literally, "Jews not wanted"]. She couldn't even sit on a park bench—even the park bench said: "Not for Jews." She couldn't go to the movies; she couldn't listen to the radio. She listened to it every now and then, but no one could see her. The neighbors controlled you. If someone listened to the radio, he could be turned in. Children, especially in schools, all talked. Everyone was a policeman. It was very dangerous. We were actually scared of our neighbors and afraid of the SS. But we didn't have any personal experiences with the SS. We were just aware of these rules.

Concerning the race laws, it's just as I said. My father lost his job; my mother had to work; I could not go to the upper school. I could not get a teaching job. We couldn't get an apartment—we lost our apartment because of the laws. There was nothing that you wanted to do without being asked whether or not you were Jewish or of Jewish heritage. There was absolutely nothing you could do. Wherever you went you had to fill out questionnaires which always contained such a question. They always asked. They didn't take anything from us. There was nothing to take. We had nothing. There were reasons my parents didn't leave the country. The first point is: They would be leaving their homeland. The second point is: They had no money. What would they have wanted in a foreign country? They could have saved their lives, which everyone had thought about. First they thought: How long would this thing with the Nazis last? They thought that it would end sometime. Second they thought: Maybe they won't do anything to us because we were together [because her father was German]. But my mother's mother and my mother's aunts, my God, they were old, they were over sixty—where were they supposed to go? Where? Holland? There was no escape in all of Europe.

And how to cope overseas [in America] with not a word of English, no money in their pockets? Who wanted the Jews?

My father died very young. I was only twenty-six. I practically lived with my mother until the following year. My mother was a simple, dear woman, but she was not intellectually educated. She was an average woman. She was neither Jewish nor any other label; she was simply a mother. People always said I was more of a Jewish woman than my mother. So my mother was simply like all the others. She was practical. She got along okay in life. She was a salesperson.

My father was much more intelligent, but I would say he was lazy. He was also pretty fat. When he played sports he was skinny like in these pictures but then he stopped playing and got fat and lazy, even though he was very intelligent. I can't understand that even today. He read a lot. When we were bombed in 1943, he had his bookshelves lined all along the walls, and the house burned to the ground as we sat underneath in the cellar, and we heard the bookshelves in flames. I think it broke my father's heart. [She pauses.] You have to imagine—it was hard to know that we would be free eventually through the bombing and nonetheless lose everything. My father was a well-rounded man and very gentle compared to my mother. The fact that he lost his job weakened him and this whole Jewish thing when my mother was taken away. My father died from a heart attack in 1953. He was obese; that's the reason he had a heart attack. Everything weakened him. I got more from my father because of his intelligence. I really depended on him, in my marriage as well. I remember that I asked my dad, "Should I or should I not get married?" And my father said, "You yourself have to decide." And that was a bad answer. [We laugh.] I think I lost my mother too late. She was ninety-seven when she died last year. It was terrible losing her after so many years. I was closer to my mother. Even though we weren't very close intellectually—she couldn't understand me in what I thought or did—she loved me very much. She spoiled me her entire life. She said the reason was because she had a bad childhood. She wanted things to be better for me, as all parents say to their kids. I could hardly cook when she died, because she had done everything for me. Always. Up until about a year before she died, she pretty much took care of everything, although

I helped her. Therefore, if you ask me how I feel, I answer "Like an absolute parasite." I was friends with a man for many years and she always came along. We had a weekend house and when we went to it she was always there with us. In this way I think she also had a wonderful life. I would have liked a child, one like you, but it did not work out. I don't know if I am happy or sad about that.

We were just as poor as everyone else, but everything was always there for me. My mother always thought three times before she bought a pair of hose, but if I wanted some toy, then I got the toy. She was fifty-six when my father died. She never remarried. So they made it together through the whole ordeal. That's good because many times it's not that way. Many people are separated. If I had been married and had children everything would have been harder. My mother never had to wear the Jewish star here in Hamburg; she first received it in the concentration camp. Being married to my father was really protection, but the Nazis had tried many times to get my father to divorce her. He was, to be sure, weak, but he never did that. Here is my mother's concentration camp armband with her number, but it was not tattooed on her. As I said, her childhood was terrible since she was illegitimate. We never learned who her father was—she never told us. It was terrible. An illegitimate child—that was like a nothing child. She told me a lot about her childhood. She was, as I said, moved around, and she was adopted by another family. When she was ten she had to keep house for a cousin—it was also a Jewish family. Finally she said, "I don't like this any more. I've been doing it since I was ten years old. I'm fed up!" [She pauses.] She never had a lot of time to learn, so it was no wonder that she wasn't especially intelligent. She had the household work to do. It was a pretty hard childhood. Intelligence is of high importance in Germany, but it's not only intelligence, but also knowing a lot about many things. You can't just live by saying "I have enough to eat, and I have a TV—before it was a radio—and my husband earns enough, and then world history is taken care of for me." The world is so diverse and so interesting. There is so much in the way of art: music or poetry or novels. The "little life" is just not enough today. How can we understand each other if we just live in a limited world? How are we going to learn tolerance if we don't know how it all fits together? What I am missing today is the *Abitur* [pre-college exam] that I never got. I miss that. When I see my friend, who is super intelligent and got his *Abitur* when he was seventeen, he knows a lot! I don't need a dictionary; I can ask him. He knows everything and how it connects to everything else. He knows the names of kings, which kings there were and how everything goes together. That is so important, not in order to be intelligent. But today that's just not enough. Only eating well is enough, which is also important. It's good and pleasing. And that's why I don't think very much of the German school system. They no longer teach any general knowledge. That's important to me. They only produce people who only know one subject. It was better before. The kings are infrequently taught even in America, and it's not taken seriously here in *Gymnasium*. Just get the *Abitur*. That's how it is. And look at grammar. Since I am learning French there is so much about German grammar that I lack, and since I lack in German grammar, I cannot learn it in French. I admit that having both intelligence and other things to be loved for would be nice. There should be a "mixture" of skills. I would say that many lack that today in their jobs. They get out of school, know everything in theory, but lack in practical skills. They don't know how to project their knowledge. As I said, my mother, although not intellectual, was a practical woman. She was very stable emotionally.

I remember in 1945 there were no more bombs here in Hamburg and the British came into Hamburg on May 8 with their tanks and Father and I went by foot to the store. We lived in Eppendorf. I will never forget the feeling of happiness. There was fraternization. We weren't allowed any contact with the English, but I could have crawled to them behind the tanks. I had no brothers or sisters. I would like to say more, but I can't.

When it all began in 1933, I was six years old. We were so busy trying to survive those twelve years and to move when possible within the loopholes which were given to us. We never came to the point where we would discuss things. We survived. Whenever we went to our relatives before 1941 when they were all here, we ate halfway kosher—that was for the quality, not because of the cook's beliefs. The food was very treasured because of the quality, but positively kosher it wasn't. I don't think any of us were interested. My mother's aunts could cook very well because they all worked, and they had a woman who helped them. It was a normal middle-class household. [She pauses.] But it was okay. My aunts also had the grocery cards with "J" on them, but my mother and my aunts could not shop in the same stores. They could no longer shop together.

You have to remember, in 1945 the mother element was absent in my life. My father's side of the family was wonderful—all of the in-laws were too. When the civil servants were with the in-laws, they sat somewhere else, but my father's brother and sister and others were wonderful. We also lived with my father's relatives in 1943 after the bombing of the house. The family supported each other absolutely.

I wonder now, and I've wondered since 1945, why didn't the British and the Americans just bomb the concentration camps? Can you tell me? Why didn't they bomb the roads to them? No more wagons would have been able to drive into the concentration camps. I can't understand that. Did they want the Jews to die? Was it fair to them? They knew the horror; of course they knew. They had enough information. Everyone knew. If they could just have bombed the cities, like Dresden, where nothing was left, and here in Hamburg, *then* why not the camps? If they were worried about killing the Jews with the bombs, then bombing the roads to the concentration camps would have sufficed. *Die Gleise* [the train tracks] ! When I was in Israel in 1984—it really impressed me—have you been there? What an exciting country. I was there before everything got so bad. I experienced the old part of the city in full bloom. There was a guy who made the trip there with us—naturally a former German who left for Israel as a child. He said, "So that something like this never happens again, so that we must ask people, "Why didn't you do that?" [referring to the British and Americans reacting against Nazis]. Because of that we should never give up arming our army. I can understand. Most people can't answer, "Why weren't the concentration camps bombed?" You really can't say anything to that. Who could answer such questions? It was a sad chapter in history.

But then there was also this problem: Who wanted to have the Jews? No one would let them in. Just think about Switzerland. The Jews went over the mountains into Switzerland. Switzerland didn't let them in.

When one talks about the asylum-seekers today, I think so much of it is about being against what happened at that time. Everybody always thinks that all the Jews were rich. My God, there was an infinite number of poor Jews, and they weren't all intellectual. They were just as dumb as other people. It was also true that even if some had money, they couldn't go anywhere with it. That's how it was. They just couldn't go. They had to pay their passage. They couldn't just say "I'm going abroad." Just getting to the border was an ordeal. If they could get to a boat, they had to pay first, and with what when everything was taken from them? After so much unemployment in 1930, who had money? There was poverty in Germany. For everyone.

I don't know that poverty was the reason for Hitler. I think many factors came together. First we can't forget the Versailles Treaty. It was a shameful treaty for Germany. Then in 1929 the recession was, so to speak, over, and there was once again hope. Then came Hitler. He came in at the beginning of this opportune time when German confidence was low, and their morale was destroyed. Then someone appears who told the people that they were somebody. The work programs—the highway system, the armaments industry—were created. He helped industry. But people also thought, "Let him do something first, then we'll throw him out." But there wasn't anything left to throw out. We had the conflicts of German politics. They destroyed each other. There was nothing there. It was virtually a vacuum into which Hitler came. He was the right man at the right time. There was the currency problem during the Weimar Republic, and think about how the whole right side of the Rhine was taken from us. Politicians did after 1918 what was not done in 1945, thank God. They wanted to destroy a foe, and that meant an entire nation. Naturally the German people were not religious or political either. But how could they be political? By those estranged parties? Every party was eradicated—The Reichsbund (The old German federation), as everybody called it, and the SPD [Social Democratic Party of Germany]. It's not without reason that chaos emerged from the Weimar Republic, from the conflicts of the politicians. Everyone was afraid of that. Then someone came along who had courage. That's how it was. Let's not forget that Hitler was elected by normal means, which helped him, but immediately after he came to power all the laws that governed before were no more and they couldn't get rid of him. The role of industry was not especially good either. That never helped.

Foreign countries should have tried to contain him also. What was Chamberlain's visit here in Germany about? He should have smacked Hitler on the head. But they didn't do anything out of pure fear. They let him annex everything, for instance, the Sudetenland.[3] He could do whatever he wanted. Did other countries do anything about it? No. The Germans are mostly to blame, but other countries are also. Unfortunately, it was a terrible time for us. [She pauses.] The entire twelve years were full of *Nadelstecken* ["pin pricks" that connote suffering]. There was always something new that they thought up. Hitler was known already as being a criminal element; he had been in jail and started all kinds of right-wing activities, and he wrote *Mein Kampf*. Some people knew immediately that the Third Reich was going to be exactly as he said in his book. Everyone could have read it. He said in *Mein Kampf* what he was going to do with the Jews. It was known. And don't forget that anti-Semitism was already rampant. Think about Austria—the Austrians were conceivably even more anti-Semitic than the Germans. They had persecuted the people just as the Germans

We had an exhibit here about two years ago in the Altona Museum, "400 Years of Jews in Hamburg." The exhibit was excellent, but there were so many Jews portrayed who were city officials or part of the judicial system. It was incomprehensible. There were thousands of Jews who were lawyers or city officials or judges. If only they had removed or sent them away during the Hitler years. Why did they simply kill them? I cannot understand that. They could have just forbidden them to be city officials. But they simply killed them. They killed all of the Jewish intelligentsia. Think about the artists—they killed all of the artists. Because of that, Germany has never recovered. The doctors were the first ones squelched. I don't know why. They were not allowed to practice. The Nazis simply took everything away from those who owned anything. They systematically destroyed them, even when they were still here. [She means before they were sent to the concentration camps.] They were already destroyed when they went away. Then the Nazis reduced them in the concentration camps to an even lower level, to vermin. In the films that we saw, it was not difficult to humiliate people. I see at the moment this damned war— I don't know if you've seen it on TV—and how they have reduced the German soldiers to humiliation.[4] They said last night [on the news], "We hadn't eaten anything for weeks and then they gave us fatty soup while we were marching. We had diarrhea. You can destroy people quickly. [In English]: Any questions?

I don't know if I feel more Jewish or Christian. It's a good question to ponder. I am outraged at the inability of the Jews to come to terms with the Arabs. They have had forty-five years to learn to get along with the people who they pushed out of Israel. I have to say that this bothers me. The Jews could have proved how one lives with minorities, and yet they have behaved just the same as people in other countries. They have simply kicked them [referring to the Arabs] out because they didn't want them. It's a shame. That bothers me. [She pauses.] But if you ask me whether or not I feel Jewish, when I see the people at the wailing wall, it seizes me, and I have to say I cannot understand the people who do not like the Jews. I don't like *them* either. [She utters a sound of disgust.] Hah! It's terrible there! Everything begins with "too": "too orthodox" and "too fascist" and I just can't understand it. Why haven't we learned any tolerance in all this time? That's one of the reasons why we're not affiliated with the Jewish community here. I have nothing against foreigners, but there are only foreigners in the Jewish community. There are no more Germans. We were once at an open Seder. My mother wasn't there, but it didn't do much for us. [We discuss various groups in Hamburg that had an open Seder to get to know everyone, and the other group, an Orthodox one, where the women were separated in the kitchen while the men ate.] I believe it's not like that in America, but I've also seen those Orthodox Jews in America—the men with their hats, they all dance around. That's just horrible. [She indicates there are not as many Orthodox there]. I liked the Jews in Israel; I would like to go there again. It really impressed me and I liked being there, even though the food was awful. There was only dried beef or poultry. [She is laughing.] But the Quark—we can't forget the Quark.[5] [She pauses.] When I was in Vienna and I went to where the synagogues were, and if there were restaurants around the synagogues, I went to the restaurants, so it affects me.

I think it's better if there wasn't so much in the papers about the Third Reich. It's better if they would stop. It doesn't promote tolerance; I would say that it promotes anti-Semitism. When one thinks about the asylum-seekers, when one says one must behave in such a way because one has a guilty conscience from the past, one can finally stop it. I'm not sure if people are enthused about this feeling of guilt. In this area I would prefer not to say that I am Jewish or half Jewish. I'd rather keep my mouth shut. My French class that numbers about twelve or fourteen people all know about me. But they are, I would say, more educated. They ask questions and are affected by it, and when there is literature, I take it along. That's all different. But here in our area I would be a little scared to have a Star of David in the house. Although I've heard some houses have a Star of David on them in Eppendorf, I have not seen them. There will always be things like that.

I wanted to say that young people often glorify the past and think that the National Socialistic ideology is for them because they can't find anything else. They have fallen in a hole! Young people want to know the limits. Children need a relatively strong upbringing. They should be told by their parents "You may do that" or "You may not do that." There has to be a foundation in place. [Here we discuss President Clinton, whom Margot thinks is wonderful, but believes he is probably liked more abroad.] The institution of the family has fallen apart in the USA, but that is everywhere. You can go to the East and see it—you can see it in China! With increasing prosperity, the family falls apart because everyone is thinking only of himself.

I didn't get to know something like a generational family closeness for a long time, because, like I said, I didn't know who my grandmother was, and my father's mother kept her distance. I was a very spoiled child, and my grandparents certainly were affected by that. So I never received real caring, but instead people would say "My God, that is a spoiled child!" So I never really had experiences with my grandparents. I had more from my dad's brothers and sisters. Since I was the only kid in the whole family, I was very spoiled by the family, but that was nice. I had an uncle who loved me a lot; and my aunt too. Then I got married in 1951 and divorced in 1953, and my relatives never forgave me for it. Then the family fell apart. [Margot shows pictures of her and her ex-husband.] That's me and that's my ex-husband. [She pauses.] He was a total bore! But then I blame his war relationships also. The soldiers were in those times released in certain cities, and they had to say when they were leaving the army where they wanted to go. And so he went to Hamburg. But his home was in Stuttgart. And when he got to Hamburg there was nothing left! [She laughs.] No apartment! [She pauses.] Then the relationship—it was impossible to live with someone that way. I told you I got divorced because he was boring! [Laughs]. He was a good-looking man, but too big for me. He was 1 meter 86 centimeters (about 6 foot 1 inch).

I have no kids. I had a really good job. I worked in an office for forty-five years. I was a sales lady for twenty years; I bought groceries, and then I was in the management of a business. I was already a supervisor when I was twenty-one. So I went straight into business. I have always earned enough money. Having my mother's reparation money made life comfortable for us, I admit; and today I am doing well too. I don't have to take care of anyone else, only myself. My mother received a lot of money because she was old when she was taken. My mother got over 1,000 Marks a month, I think. You know, actually, as a woman, I'm a bad partner for women. I have always worked with men, and I've always worked well with men. I don't need emancipation. [She laughs.] I have never felt oppressed. However, I am not the most sensitive, I'll admit. Since I have always had a position of leadership, I could always make decisions when it was necessary. I can't understand today's debate over the role of women. You can't deny that when women work and they have a family and children that normally it's worse for them than the men. The men are free!

I had a friend who had a very good position. She then got married and said, "I want to have a child one day." She had a child and didn't take the six months of maternity leave that women get here in Germany, but she took six or eight weeks. Then she got a nanny and came back to her company, Otto Versand [one of the largest mail order houses in the world.] Today she has just as good a position as earlier. You have to have your priorities straight. Then you will not have any problems. If you let yourself be walked all over by men, then I think you have no one to blame but yourself. You simply have to be strong and be with the times. But if a woman takes her six months of pregnancy leave and then has another child and then another, why should a company keep her position for her? Tell me that. It just doesn't work. I myself wouldn't have worked with such women. Other employees do all the work for the absent woman, and then she comes back, and then the kid gets sick, and then she has to go back home! It all sounds really good, but it doesn't work. Therefore I don't think much of these so-called Frauenquotes, women's quotas.[6] If women are competent, then they will get positions. I have friends who are married, but neither work. I have a friend who is not married, and she had just as good a job as I had. Single women are the ones who accomplish something in life, in the United States also, otherwise a woman has to have a light bulb go off. Then she really has to put the children aside and can't run home for every cough. That's hard, I admit, but it's true. Naturally there is something else: When women are married, the men are not as reasonable as the women are with the men. When men have an important position, the women play along. But when the woman has the important position, then the man either does not play along and work with her, or he is jealous. I have had that experience too. I earned more than my husband. It was a point of tension. He was jealous of everything, including my better job. I have to say that I have been very lucky in terms of my career. I could have done it without luck, but I was lucky. I always got important jobs, but I could do them. I did not experience prejudices in my career for being very successful and half Jewish. Actually it was the opposite. When I began in 1952 in the position as a buyer, the owner of the company told me that he had already hired a Jew. In those days we always called them the so-called *Vorzeigejuden* ["showcase" Jews—the company had one so they didn't need another]. The owner told me that actually he had wanted to hire a non-Jewish person. But he hired me anyway, and it was after that time, I would say, no longer an issue. In the job where I was a supervisor, the owner was himself Jewish. So that job was relatively simple. But there was a connection, I would say, independent of being Jewish. The older man liked me and I liked him—even though he was a *Schlitzohr*, a crafty character, a real Jew. [She laughs.] But it was okay. German men are hard to get along with, especially if they're wanting more than just the family and the children, that they want a profession. I believe that, and I believe that it has not gotten any better. It was difficult before and it is difficult today, for different reasons. For one, men don't want to give up their feeling of comfort. If the women are not at home, men lose a bit of their feeling of comfort, and I would say there is a certain amount of jealousy. Oh, please! Whoever is the more competent should work. But that is, I think, very complicated. Perhaps German men are not quite as liberated as men in the States, although I have seen the opposite here in Germany. But I have also seen some men who have these same prejudices that we have been talking about. It also depends in which type of family you grew up.

I have not seen myself as an outsider because of my Jewish heritage, since I had no problems in school. While I was trying to get an education, I may have been an outsider. I felt that I was affected, and it made me angry, but I wouldn't go so far as to say that I felt like an outsider because I had many friends with whom it really wasn't an issue. No, I couldn't say that I felt like an outsider. You have to think, in 1945 I was nineteen. Not that I didn't understand what was going on, but as a fairly young person, you get through such things better. I don't know what I would have thought if I were twenty years older, but I don't even think that my mother felt like an outsider, only that the persecution made us angry. Not that we were pushed to the edge, but the harassment that we had to endure simply made us angry. I think my father felt more "outside" than we did. We always fought against it.

You have to think, I had already met my future husband during the war. He was in the Navy, and he knew that I was half Jewish, but that didn't change anything and didn't matter. If one wasn't too involved, like, for example, a doctor whose practice was taken away, I think we relatively "small" people were passed over, but one might have to leave at some time if one was important. We didn't really experience segregation in that sense. Nothing was taken from us. My father lost his job, but we learned to get along without it. Things were going badly with everyone. Since we did not get together with Jews, I have to say, we didn't experience it. We weren't in Jewish circles where it could be discussed time and again.

Out of the twelve or fifteen people in our family, only three or four split up. Nothing changed. It was not an issue with us. Things were bad, but there was no major effect on the family. The family stayed together. I really cannot say how we felt about the whole racial persecution from the beginning up until my mother went to the camp. It was not a problem. It became a problem because something happened to us. When my mother went away I know that we all cried together. But it was just the same as if she had become a soldier—it wasn't particularly because she was Jewish, but because she was going away, because of the situation. I and my relatives weren't convinced that any person was an *Untermensch*. There were some who were convinced, but we didn't have any contact with them. They said, "We don't want to have anything to do with that. We are public workers, and we don't want to have anything to do with you."

No one in my family was religious. My mother's relatives felt Jewish, to be sure, but they weren't really "religious." No one read the Torah. That's how it was, generally speaking. I would say that they lived like the Jews in Israel today. Well, there are certain things—the man who accompanied us to Israel, his son was circumcised. He said that it was completely logical that his son was, but they lived "Jewish" only minimally. I was never in a synagogue as a child. I didn't even know the synagogue that was destroyed on Bornstrasse. Many "half Jews" were baptized Christian and had never been in a synagogue. Similarly, my uncles were soldiers in the war [World War I]. One of my uncles said, "What can happen to me? I was a soldier!" They couldn't believe what was happening. They only wanted one thing: to be German. I feel badly, I admit, badly, that the Germans were Nazis. I just don't understand that at all. What can we do about it? Nothing at all.

They were afraid. The ones who committed these atrocities were not all SS men. I have been friends with an SS man for many, many years. He had absolutely nothing to do with the atrocities. He went to East

Germany after the war because he was so sure that no one could pin anything on him. Everything is in the *Soldbücher* [military books] that existed then. In these books is recorded exactly where every military person was and where he was assigned. He said he never even saw a concentration camp from the outside. So see, that happened too. He was really in the SS—he was drafted into it. He was in one of the Napola.[7] There were these National Socialist institutions where you went when you were fairly young. He was there. It wasn't all SS people running the concentration camps. It was the so-called *Feldpolizei* [field police] branch of the SS who were there. I know them too. They walked around with these Blackshirts. There were SS men, and then there were these others. We always said they were like so-called guard dogs. It was a very fine distinction. [She pauses.] I mean, we can't forget that when we talk about SS men, they weren't all directly involved. My friend had the blood-type sign on his arm. He was a legitimate soldier. He said that they had only one disadvantage—they were always sent where it was burning. Whenever there was a problem they had to go. From his group of one hundred men, only ten survived. They were against the Nazis from the beginning. It was hard to be a soldier. And there were certainly many of them, and they weren't all enthusiastic soldiers. [She pauses.] It was terrible. The war was terrible.

I believe there are still Nazis in the government. That's how it started in 1945. Globke, who wrote commentary for the Nazi laws, I believe, was Adenauer's closest advisor.[8] Of all the judges, only one was convicted—the others were let off. Those who say they want to reconstruct East Germany's past should first reconstruct the Nazis' past. Nobody was punished when they should have been. It's crazy. I mean, if a Nazi had done something, like Mengele for example, I would say that he has unfortunately lived free for too long. I don't understand that at all. But there is something else that happened in 1945: The British, at least here in Hamburg, wanted to keep the government. If they had thrown out all the judges, it would have collapsed. I mean, with East Germany, we could send people from the West. But what could be done in Germany in 1945? Simply leave the people in their positions. The government had to be maintained—the English knew that. They also knew that they would leave the North Sea waters in the sea.

I would say what happened in Germany could happen anywhere. Think about Cambodia and Pol Pot. It might not happen in the United States, but I don't think it could happen in Germany again either. I would say that we have the youth to thank for that. I don't think that the youth today would let such a thing happen to them. Think about the atomic weapons—it would cause an uprising. Today it would be out ruled in Germany, I think. But basically it could happen anywhere. It depends on how bad things are with people. When times are bad and a "holy speaker" comes along, that's it. All we have to do is think about South America, where someone promises the people something and they always believe it because people are gullible. That's exactly what I wanted to say. It's one of the reasons why it could hardly happen in America. America is too big. Here we are too small—everything is too close together. Such gruesome deeds can happen in small countries, that's how it is. But not in America, although the driving out of the Indians is a terrible chapter for Americans.

In regard to the Polish Jews, the Poles did nothing at all to protect their Jewish counterparts. That was another group of people who were happy to get rid of Jews. Others were persecuted as well, but I don't expect much resistance from the Gypsies either. My parents were not political at all. I have a woman friend whose parents were very involved in the Socialist party. I believe the man was imprisoned in 1933. He was not Jewish. The Socialists were killed first, and then it became the Jews who were centered on. They, of course, lost their jobs and everything and lived on a minimal amount of money. They didn't have a job. You can't determine from birth certificates whether one is Communist or not, but there were, of course, party registers. With the Nazi takeover of power, the Socialists and Communists were immediately eliminated. You have to remember, everything was registered in Germany at that time. That's why they found them immediately. It's still like that with the Protestants and the Catholics concerning church taxes. But that's no longer an issue—whether you are Catholic or Protestant. Germany overcame that, thank God.

There was not any resistance. I would say that people consciously "looked away" because they were all afraid—you can't forget that. The resistance movement was minimal. And something else: The Nazis were carried along with the general public. It's not that the Nazis reacted against the people. Rather, because of the times then, the people were manipulated. We only have to look at the old pictures at how they went along when the Nazis held their speeches. They agreed. And about the atrocities, I would say that the Germans always knew about them but they always looked away, and thought, Just don't have anything to do with it. [We discuss the Swing Youth. Margot mentions Teddy Staufer and her English albums. She sings "A Tisket, A Tasket."]

I do not remember any incidents that happened in the street against Jews, probably because we lived too far from the Jewish part of town. The Jews lived on Rothenbaumchaussee, Rappstraße, Isestraße, Grindel, Grindelberg—they were mostly there. Our relatives also lived there later. I feel lucky that I wasn't affected. Nothing really happened to the "half Jews." If they were brought up Jewish, if they were in the Jewish community and Jewish religion, then the same things happened to them as if they had been Jewish. But basically nothing happened to the "half Jews." More would have happened after 1945 if the war had lasted longer. As far as I know, there weren't many "half Jews" in concentration camps. That would be news to me, unless they were brought up Jewish. The Nazis probably had enough to do already with the Jews [in reference to why the Nazis didn't send all "half Jews" to the concentration camps].

There were people who helped others escape. If I had had to go away, I had a colleague in my company who had offered, and I believe she was serious, that if necessary, she would hide me. Certainly there were people like that. But the whole thing is problematic. We [Germans] had nothing to eat. Whoever hid someone also had to feed him. And who knew how long it would last? You can hide someone when you know how long you're going to be hiding them; but to hide someone for years and feed them at the same time, no one can do that. More would surely have done it if they knew that they were only going to be hiding someone for a couple of months. But who knew? And that would mean that you could not go outside again. [She is referring to the people being hidden.] Even in Hamburg that happened. But I never had to answer that question.

Today Germany is more political and religious than in the past, without question. [She pauses.] I would say there is no comparison. Think about our voter participation and think about America's. We have almost 80 percent voter participation. I would say we are much more political than the Americans. [She pauses.] I think it is better here. The indifference of the Americans bothers me. You can't avoid voting and then complain about who is elected!

I would say, finally, I need to talk about this past and have these tapes and paraphernalia to remember because people start to forget what happened.

CHAPTER TEN

URSULA BOSSELMANN

*"I stood at eighteen
looking into nothingness"*

∼

Ursula Bosselmann was one of my last interviewees. Her apartment was small and plainly decorated, as was the case with most of the women's dwellings. Books lay everywhere; one by Anna Freud and others by various psychologists suggested to me that Ursula was and is searching for answers. Ursula, in her late seventies, was dressed in a simple skirt and blouse. She was large in stature with white hair whose wisps lay haphazardly around her face like thin, curled ribbons on a Christmas present. Her big, crooked teeth, larger, round nose, and the characteristic deep wrinkles that so many of the women possessed contrasted with her small, sagacious eyes. Her soft, reserved voice, graceful long legs, and folded hands

reflected her two professions—minister and dancer. Throughout our talk, she sat up and then back in her chair. She rose
only to pour more tea or to take pictures from the wall.

Ursula contacted me after having read my announcement
in *Die Allgemeine Jüdische Wochenzeitung* [the Jewish weekly] that
stated I was looking for survivors from "mixed marriages."
Ursula explained she had written a short memoir of her life. She
emphasized how she was in a Jewish-Christian organization
where both religions worked together. There she met Pastor
Arnulf Baumann. After she got to know him, he asked her in
1991 to write a section for his book *Ausgegrenzt* about "non-
Aryan" Christians.[1] She mentioned that she and two other
people translated a book by Rabbi Dov Edelstein from English
into German.[2] She met Edelstein in America; he now lives in
Israel. He had been in Auschwitz. He didn't speak German, only
Hungarian, English, and Hebrew, so Ursula had to speak
English with him. She pointed this out because she now struggles with English. The menorah in her apartment was a gift from
him. She prizes this menorah, which symbolized her connection
to the Jewish religion. Although she had no spiritual affiliation
with the Jewish faith and no interest in practicing, she had
studied the faith in depth and had a passion for discovering more
about it. The pictures in her home are the same subjects that
appear in her written and oral autobiography—one is of her and
her two sisters, Gisela and Irmi, together in flowing white cotton
dresses in which it is apparent that Irmi, the youngest, has a
larger head than normal. Clearly, Ursula was protective of her
"slow" sister who caused strain in her parents' marriage. There
is a formal, elegant portrait painting of her mother, to whom she
was irrevocably attached, and her mother's only brother who
disappeared in Auschwitz, and a recent photo of Ursula with
her mother. Both bear facsimiles of the other's nose and mouth.

Ursula spoke English intermittently but then would say
"I must speak in German. It's difficult if I don't speak in
German." Because she is very open about her past as a

Mischling, her story is extensive and detailed, and the headings that she originally chose when writing down her life remain in the final story here. The following is a translated fusion of Ursula's written and oral text.

Ursula's story still stuns me, as did Ruth Wilmschen's, because of the tragic lives of all the women involved. Silence kills. Ursula's Jewish grandmother committed suicide before she could be deported; her mother was deported to Theresienstadt (a work camp), and after the war her sister Gisela committed suicide. Ursula is fascinated with the concept of suicide. Do survivors ever wonder if death might have been more peaceful than carrying on with their memories? On the other hand, it takes incredible courage to kill yourself. Ursula's grandmother felt she would have a better life in the afterworld, as she had fought and was exhausted in Hitler's world. Indeed, many of the Jewish and *Mischling* women did not own their own lives; so by taking their lives, they reclaimed power over them.

Ursula was an "illegal" dancer during the Third Reich and later became a theologian. She managed to work in German congregations in other countries for over forty years. Not until recently did she return to Germany and settle down the street from where she used to live; an unconscious decision, she claims, to forgive, just as her studying to be a theologian was to forget. She spent ten years in psychotherapy with the famous psychiatrist Margarete Mitscherlich after reading the 1967 groundbreaking book *The Inability to Mourn: Principles of Collective Behavior* that Mitscherlich co-authored with her husband.[3] The book discusses the "collective rejection of guilt and its psychic consequences for the individual as well as society." It sold more than 100,000 copies in the original edition. Germans had unresolved conflicts resulting from the collapse of their society. Ursula desired to be healed by this woman. Ursula appears to be one of the few testifiers who has integrated her split selves and overcome her physical ailments. She had migraines for three decades.

Ursula has commemorated her mentor by placing a framed photograph of her in clear view, even though she did not, ultimately, follow Margarite Mitscherlich's suggestion that she not return to Hamburg. Ursula's return to Germany and to "those Germans" who persecuted her and her family in many respects ignores the Mitscherlichs' analysis of the German's chronic "inability to mourn." If, as Mitscherlich points out, innumerable Germans cannot even consciously acknowledge their reverence for and participation in the Third Reich, then certainly they would never solicit Ursula's story nor see her as anything than what she was before Hitler—a German. Thus, Ursula, like some of the other women, remains mute on topics unpleasant to nonpersecuted Germans in order to "fit in." By being forced to conceal her past, she is never again fully German. If Ursula is inside yet outside—German, yet not German—who *are* the Germans?

What struck me about Hamburg were the cast-over, deep shadows, years before we had to darken the windows in the evening because of plane attacks. In spite of that, I have come back to this city after exactly forty years, for I have my roots here. I love my father city. It is, yes, really the city of my father. I love the Alster with the white fleet, the many yachts and swans. And the large old houses between Rabenstraße and Eichen Park. And naturally, Jungfernstieg and the Neuen Wall. I love Uhlenhorst, where we lived in the Overbeckstraße, went on Graumannsweg to the school, and were confirmed in St. Gertrud Church. And I add to that Eppendorfer Landstraße where we survived the war and all of the terror, and where my parents' apartment stood until 1985. In addition, around the corner, not far away from Hamburg, are the Baltic Sea and the North Sea. One sensed the sea wind near us and it was suggested that sometimes you could smell it. I have a special love for the ocean. Already as a small child, I had dug on Timmendorfer beach on the Baltic. Keitum in Sylt became our summer paradise. Berlin is the city of my mother and, above all, the city of my grandmother. Because it was always the autumn holiday in our youth that we spent at our grandmother's in Berlin, the street names—Wilmersdorf, Charlottenburg, Lietzenburger and Emser Straße, Kufürstendamm, Unter den Linden, Brandenburger Tor, Grünewald, Potsdam—sounded like children's melodies that accompanied the falling green and yellow leaves. We traveled a last time in peace on Easter to Berlin. That was in 1933. After that the forthcoming events [of Hitler's Reich] crept up on us children like something eerie and unnamable. We were only aware in part, but not in whole, because everybody's parents remained silent as long as possible.

LIFE IN THE FAMILY

On Easter 1936 I left the private middle school, Mittell und Redlich, in Hamburg's Graumannsweg with an intermediate secondary school certificate. Even belatedly, I cannot say whether and how this school altered under National Socialism. Did we have "party-friendly" teachers? I believe no. I recall there *was* a "flags parade" on the playground. This "flags parade" was probably obligatory for all schoolchildren.[4] One episode occupied our minds for some days, although we really did not grasp its significance. We sat in a school performance of [Friedrich Schiller's] *William Tell* in the Hamburger *Schauspielhaus* [theater]. It was explained to us beforehand that we, in the manner of *Rütli-Schwur*[5] [a Swiss oath] would have to stand up and raise our arm in a Hitler *Gruß*.[6] At the words "We want to be a united people of brothers, no trouble and danger separate us," we stood up solemnly. A girl from my sister's class took a comb out of her pocket, lifted it over her head, and combed her hair. When we reported this at home, my parents exchanged meaningful glances. The recalcitrant girl was kicked out of school. I was fifteen years old.

We were children of our time. On school excursions we sang the Hilter songs. They were easy to sing. We didn't understand the contents at all. What did it mean: "Red front and Reaction?"[7] We were, like everyone else, exposed to propaganda; for example, in the newsreels and films shown at that time. I remember a trip at Pentecost to Dreisacker

near Glücksburg [a town near the Danish border in Schleswig-Holstein].
We rode in an open car of Uncle Diederich D. Gisela and I greeted the
cars driving past us with the Hitler greeting. We had a lot of fun with
that. At the time, we knew nothing about the Nürnberg Laws.

My father was a lawyer. He hailed from an old Hamburg family
that still adhered to formal traditions. Thus, my mother used the formal
Sie (you)[8] with her father-in-law, and he with her. This was a Hanseatic
tradition. Similarly, my father's father probably stood on a pedestal for
him. Although my father was a good lawyer, he had—how do I say it—
not selected his occupation very sensibly. His main interests turned to
literature and theater. In those subjects, he was a walking dictionary to
us children because he knew about all of the operas' and plays' main
figures and he knew which well-known singers and actors had played
in what roles in specific years. The director of the Schauspielhaus and
the Thalia Theater, among others, befriended him, and he was also the
legal advisor of the Thalia Theater for several years. In this function,
he appeared one time as the Thalia Theater's defender in a case. It was
said that an employee had lost his life on a fast, down-moving elevator.
It is the only time that I heard my father deliver a summary in the
courtroom. It made a huge impression on me. My father possessed, as
well, considerable general knowledge, and spoke, like my mother,
fluent French, for he had completed one part of his studies in Lausanne.
Unfortunately, he could not deal with money. As soon as it hit his
hands, he spent it gladly and generously. In 1933 he won a case and to
amuse us bought a small car. However, he was not capable of keeping
money for long.

Before 1933 my father was in *Stahlhelm*.[9] Beginning in 1920, he
managed a practice in the inner city. In 1938 he moved us to an
apartment on Eppendorfer Landstraße. From there we moved to the
Overbeckstraße. My father's father was already dead in 1905. My father's
mother married a second time to the shipbroker, Paul Günther. His firm
still exists today. My grandmother died at seventy-two in 1932 after
being sick for many years. Every time we visited my grandparents in the
old Rabenstraße in the suburb, Harvestehude, we went with a little "fear
and trembling" because of their reserved manners. I can see us on the

steamer that we boarded at the Uhlenhorster ferry stop and rode to the other side. One afternoon comes to mind when the advent candle started a fire on the coffee table. Before we could scream, my mother had courageously gripped it with her hands, pushed open the balcony door, and put it out in the garden. Christmas Eve, our grandparents came to our house with Uncle Walther, my father's brother. There was carp with horseradish. The table was festively laid, and Grete, our house-girl, served. We were always happy to have lived through these ceremonies.

My father was *alt Hamburgerisch,* old Hamburg. He didn't know how to handle kids. When we grew older, we talked about theater. Maybe this is why I had a calling for the theater. One could discuss *that* with him. Of course, when I worked for him I talked with him about legal matters that I had to record. But not a lot. He wrote about divorce, and I didn't understand it. He worked with divorce cases— often they disputed over whether the property was the husband's or the wife's. As a young girl, I found this horrible. It was such a petty matter but, at the time, so important. To me it was silly to get worked up about material items.

Oddly enough, a father figure remained very colorless for me, although I had worked some years in my father's office and we should have been bound by our interest in the theater. However, there was truly no interior relationship. When he died in February 1957, he disappeared without a trace from my life. Ours was not an internalized relationship, intimate. It wasn't evil or malicious; I never hated him, not at all. It was a neutral bond. It had to do with my mother doing so much for my family, taking care of everyone. We traveled in the summer. My mother was there but my father did something else. It was more like a family without a father. When he was there he was on a pedestal—we had to be quiet. We couldn't talk at the table. My parents loved each other despite being different. My father didn't make a mistake in marrying my Jewish mother. In this generation: Once married, not to be discussed. There wasn't a question about it. It was a loving relationship. It was clear that one person would remain faithful to the other. It was deeply rooted for him—Hanseatic that he was. Later my mother had to do everything alone. We couldn't hire anybody. My mother fulfilled this role fantastically well. Never complained. Never said anything. Everything was strange and new and stressful. She had a strong character.

My mother came from a Posener family.[10] I don't think it was difficult that she was Jewish because she was baptized as a child. Her mother and brother were also baptized. Opapa, as we called my grandfather, owned a cannery there that he expanded considerably after the move to Berlin. He had already died in 1923. I was just five years old, yet I can still remember him. I also remember that in my grandparents' bedroom, a big, greenish lion's head hovered over the wash bowl and whenever you pushed a button water flowed out of his mouth.

This grandfather left my maternal grandmother a considerable fortune. According to my mother's statements, her childhood and youth were full of promise and lucky. Many times she spoke proudly about trips that both she and her brother Helmuth took with their parents— trips that many people in those times were not in the position to finance. For a year after finishing school, she stayed and worked in a *Pension* near Paris that she would rave about in her old age. I own her diary written in German script that records this time. Up until her marriage she played violin very well. My parents' marriage took place in summer 1917 in Berlin—my father in "neat uniform," my mother a very beautiful young bride. We three sisters, I, Gisela, and Irmi, were born in 1918, 1920, and 1923 respectively. My parent's marriage was—as only I can arrange in my mind in retrospect—severely burdened by the birth of my youngest sister, Irmi, who made it through a so-called birth trauma and was viewed as physically handicapped. My father could not cope with this "insult" that stained his reputation. Only thirty years later was he really reconciled with his daughter. My mother had a very special love for this child and fought for her like a lioness. Later this was necessary. My mother was absolutely the strongest, the connecting bond, in the family.

Gisela and I grew up like twins and were always dressed alike. For a year we sat next to each other in the same school class. It was the only time that I carried away a 2 [on a scale of 1 to 5] in behavior—otherwise it was always a 1—because Gisela would infect me with her bad habits or I would not be superior to them. Gisela, blonde and strong, was my father's child, and I, dark-haired and slender, was my mother's child.

Gisela always knew what she wanted and knew how to get it. I was very shy. After school, our ways parted.

My sister Irmi possessed a sunny nature. Sister Ilse Henneberg, now in her late eighties, who for over forty years has been a friend of the family, can still remember very well Irmi's "imprisonment" in the hospital nursery and remembers our house in the Overbeckstraße. Sister Ilse worked four years in the so-called reception station and knows to this day that Irmi lay about three months in Crib 7 (occasionally also Crib 5 and 1). Irmi was brought to my parents six weeks after her birth. My father is said to have come seldom to the clinic. My mother mainly visited Irmi alone. Several times we must have been present for I can remember the bed behind a glass wall. The head doctor of the clinic was Professor Bauer, who was the assistant doctor to Walter Giller [the father of the actor] for two years. Irmi was often very sick after her months in the nursery, so Dr. Bauer came to us at home. He also came if Gisela and I were sick. He was a well-loved children's doctor. Because Professor Bauer was a Jewish doctor, he had to leave the clinic when the Nürnberg Laws came out. He immigrated to England where, after a short time, he died of a broken heart.

Sister Ilse said she never heard a word of complaint from my mother in four decades. My mother never despaired and cared lovingly for us day and night. Everything was expected to be orderly.

Irmi was behind developmentally for her age but, in her own fashion, was extremely intelligent. We all grew up together, and you don't notice when you have an ill sister. Irmi wasn't treated as sick but healthy. She was nice and kind, and had a marvelous sense of humor and an incredible head for jokes. No one had negative feelings towards her. During the Hitler years, a great fear sometimes gripped us that she might pass on political jokes to the wrong people. However, she knew instinctively where and when she could tell them. Often I envied Irmi her tanned complexion. In the summer at the ocean she became cocoa brown, and her light hair bleached almost white. Irmi couldn't sit until she was four and couldn't walk until she was six. She had trouble with speaking or with parroting back the teacher's words, but she balanced that out with bouts of humor. In this way she was hard to describe. *Sie hat alles mitbekommen* [she took everything in]. Although she went to the same school as we and even the four prep years [beginning four classes of the six in high school], she had to take each class twice. Job training was not yet available for the handicapped, so she stayed home.

My parents had persuaded us not to do an *Abitur* [pre-college exam]. At first, we did not know the real reason. My parents said taking the *Abitur* served no purpose for a woman. My mother never explicitly told me "You're not allowed to do that because of your Jewish blood," which was really the truth. Gisela participated for a while in the BDM [Nazi youth group] because she insisted on it. We didn't realize that we could not be drafted into "work service" because of our Jewish blood. At my parents' urging, Gisela worked a half-year on an estate in Pomerania. I went to my mother's friend in Dreisacker in order to learn how to keep house, a skill that I didn't learn well then or later. For many years we had been going to Dreisacker for the Pentecost holiday. Fifteen guests listed in Dreisacker's guest book spoke about my mother's visit before her marriage (September 1917) and later with us three (up until 1952). We always had unequaled experiences with the many children of the families. Elle and Christian are still our friends today. Except for some difficult mistakes that I innocently made in the Dreisacker household, I can only remember that at the afternoon rest times I ran to the fields and hid myself there. I memorized the roles of Gretchen, Iphigenie, Thekla, Hamlet, Faust, and others and recited them because life lay before me. I lived in Hamburg, the door to the world. Now it should open for me. I wanted to be in the theater.

ISOLATED

In October 1936 Gisela and I returned home. One afternoon our mother got us together for "a meeting." In my memory, it was horribly dark in the living room where we were supposed to sit together. My mother disclosed that she was of Jewish background, that is, "not Aryan." My mother was baptized together with her brother at the age of three in January 1898 in the Dutch Reformed Church in Hanau and on March 11, 1910, confirmed in Berlin. My grandmother,

Hedwig Moral, was confirmed on February 13, 1903, in Berlin and had declared her resignation from Judaism and her simultaneous conversion to the religious organization of the Protestant church. Grandfather Moral was a dissenter but received his "last rites" at his cremation in 1923. However, after Hitler's Nuremberg race laws of 1935, the facts of the case didn't count. It didn't matter whether or not you were baptized or confirmed. Because of the race laws, which had not been explained earlier to us, we could not do an *Abitur*, be in the BDM or in the "work service," and could also not take up any kind of profession that required a state exit exam. She didn't say that we also were forbidden to marry. My mother told me many years later that I had cried. It was not common to cry in our house. I believe also that I never again shed tears over it. The shock was too great. From one minute to the next everything changed: There was no future, no destination, no joy. Suddenly we were no longer Germans, and according to the official state version we were no longer Christian even though Pastor Speckmann just had confirmed us a year ago. And we hadn't the slightest notion about Jewish culture or religion. Hence, we also didn't belong to that side! Before I knew what was going on, I stood by my mother, but after I knew, I think my relationship with her became more difficult. Perhaps I blamed her for our miserable situation. Of course she was blameless. For young people today it is hard to imagine that at home we asked no questions. It sufficed that indefinability hung in the air. We especially would have never asked about Hitler's Reich. To probe the feelings of others, especially parents, was taboo. The door to the world slammed brutally shut. There I stood at eighteen looking into nothingness.

Yet life continued. After a long search, I found I could take courses in stenography and typing at the business and language school. After that I worked for a year and a half for an acquaintance of my parents in a very small company for agricultural machinery and products. This field was totally uninteresting to me, but at least I earned my first income. At this time I wrote very melancholy poems. A friendly doctor, who visited us one time, said that he had never before seen a young girl at my age that looked as miserable as I. To cure my unhappiness, my mother gave me dissolved glucose in a small bottle daily; however, I poured it out into the Alster on my way back from work. Today I know this action was a protest against life. *I did not want to live.*

In March 1939 I moved over to my father's office. I assumed that he already was ordered not to hire an unknown secretary because of his "mixed marriage." Also, his financial situation had tightened so much that he could not pay for a worker. Therefore, I was the best solution. Someone from the lawyer's chamber had suggested to him that he get a divorce. If he took this step, he could save himself. I know from Käthe Augstein, a distant relative, that my father was completely desperate, but he could not or did not want to take the steps toward a divorce. Had he divorced my mother, he certainly would have delivered her up to death. She would have been treated as a "full Jew" then and would not have survived. Because of her marriage to my father, she counted among those who still enjoyed privileges. During the war, Käthe lived with us, namely from February until the end of May 1940. She did deskwork at the airfield in Blankenese[11]. She told me, among other things, that my mother remained at home in the evenings while my father gladly went out. Käthe accompanied him many times to the theater, about which I speculated in later years. After the performances they sat together with the director of the playhouse, Karl Wüstenhagen, or with the director of the Thalia Theater, Ernst Leudesdorff. Käthe found these hours very amusing.

I also did not like the office work at my father's, although it was not entirely uninteresting. I had acquired such strong typing skills that while I tapped out my father's dictation, I could look out the window and think about other things. And then I had good luck. One day, probably the beginning of 1938, I had gone by the sign "Lola Rogge School for Gymnastics and Dance" (at that time, on Schwanenwik 38). I enrolled in amateur classes and fell in love with dance and the personality of Lola Rogge so much so that I soon participated in other activities apart from this class. For "Faith and Beauty"—a BDM sport and cultural performance—there was a parade through the city. I found it wonderful that we strolled in airy white clothes through the streets. Also, I soon danced in a Christmas fairy tale in the Thalia Theater. I played minor roles as well in the Thalia Theater, for example, in Curt

Goetz's plays. [Goetz is a comic playwright.] We absolutely did not read newspapers or listen to radio. Sometimes at films on the newsreel there'd be "*Jüden 'raus*" [Jews get out] or "*Jüden sind unsere Unglück*" [Jews are our misfortune]. It's odd but I don't recall how I felt at that time. I had feelings of guilt. I think as a young person you try to seek out every possible way to be joyful and to do something interesting. For this reason, I went to the Lola Rogge School and did what I had to at my father's office. I didn't really like office work, but it was tolerable. I was preoccupied with other matters. All day I was busy buying things and running errands. When we didn't have heat, I had to go to the basement. You can't take care of yourself when so preoccupied. You could only just wait and see. Like with my uncle.

In November 1938 my mother's only brother, Helmuth, was denounced and sent to the concentration camp Buchenwald after Kristallnacht ["night of broken glass"]. He was a heart specialist in Bad Kudowa in Schlesien and had his own flourishing practice. At the end of December he surprised us in Hamburg on his way to Holland. He had been fired. He thought perhaps he could secure emigration to Brazil. His head was shaved. In Buchenwald he had to sign a paper that stated he would say nothing about his internment. He remained with us for several hours. When my mother cried at their good-bye, my uncle comforted her: "America is still not out of the picture!" It was still a time when you could pay your way out to get to the United States. He telephoned for a taxi to take him to the main train station; he took me along in order to give me a lift to the Thalia Theater. My uncle was very upset in the taxi, the meaning of which I really could not grasp. In August 1943—almost five years later—we received a postcard from Holland in care of a family Rault in Driebergen, which read: "Don't worry if you hear nothing from me in a long time." I suppose he believed firmly that he would immigrate to America. His wife was Catholic and unable to save him. It was harder when the man rather than the woman was Jewish. He married a Catholic and became Catholic. He was still considered Jewish. It wasn't the case that for all "privileged mixed marriages" it wasn't so bad. That's not true. In the case of my uncle, for instance. It did depend on where you lived; for instance, it was easier to live in Hamburg, a big city, than Schliessien [rural south east Germany]. I strongly suspect envious doctors in Schliesien denounced him early on. It was different in a large city where much goes unnoticed. In Bad Kudowa, my uncle lived in a small community. I suspect it was the other doctors—someone recognized him and turned him in. He was stuck in Holland for about five years until 1943. He studied military medicine. They knew in Holland that he was Jewish. The Dutch accepted many Jewish immigrants. And then came the Germans.

According to an answered request we made to the state president of Köln in 1961, my uncle had pursued tropical medicine in Holland. He did not have an income there. Never again did we receive a sign of life from him. They reported, "In Holland when the persecution of the Jews began, the hunted were living in hiding; however on January 1, 1944, there were deportations from the camp Westerbork in Holland to Auschwitz. From there the persecuted did not come back."

THE FIRST YEAR OF THE WAR

When the war broke out in 1939, all of us shared the same fate. There were air raid warnings and ration cards, the long, unmoving lines before the grocery stores, the first bombs, and the many night hours in the air raid shelter.

My mother had a "J" stamped in her passport. She had to assume the name of "Sara." She now received her ration card from the Jewish community in Schäferskampsallee. However, she was not allowed to use the streetcars in order to get there. She was no longer allowed to attend the theater or cinema. She was also not allowed to vote. During air raids she had to remain upstairs in the apartment. In case of a bombing, she was helpless. During the air raids we were in the basements with neighbors. Twenty to thirty kids. The house in which we lived was magnificent. The husband in one of the families was a Nazi. My mother was concerned about the repercussions if she went to the cellar, so she didn't. The application of the Nürnberg Laws affected her completely. There were always new humiliations. Until about fall 1944 she was protected because of my father—not all the paragraphs of the Nürnberg Laws against the Jews in a "privileged mixed marriage" were put into effect.

It was impossible to go away to any country with five people and my sister handicapped, with no money and no connections to people in America or England, and my father, a lawyer. And the war had begun, which made it was even more difficult. My parents spoke French well. If we had immigrated to France then it would have been the same as with my uncle in Holland: eventual death. It was not possible. My parents never thought the laws could become so heinous. It started with the Nürnberg Laws and worsened little by little. Always a more severe law. We didn't see in the beginning, especially as my father was "Aryan" and a lawyer. What could happen to us? My father *knew* but he didn't know what to do with five people. He never would have immigrated alone. He had the practice and thought life would continue as before. Then came the war, and it was too late. Hitler's book *Mein Kampf* stated his ideology, but who read it? Few people. My father probably knew about the camps, but what should he do? The events wouldn't affect him.

How dangerous our situation was is apparent in the following example: Paris was conquered in June 1940 by the German army and flags had to be raised. It was a magnificent summer day and we had opened the door to the balcony. The street was a sea of flags and *Heil Rufe* [people shouting Heil Hitler] played on the radio. My parents had taken out the flag but they didn't know how to behave. Not being "pure" Germans, we were not allowed to wave a flag. However, we didn't obey. The flag was seen by our fellow lodgers and by everyone who glanced up at our house in the Eppendorfer Landstraße. How would they react? My parents just let the flag fly. We were lucky that nothing happened.

Every violation of the laws at that time could be punishable by work camp. So we fell into permanent conflict. I sometimes thought, If there's a God he wouldn't allow us to be bombed, in addition to all the emotional torment. This belief helped now and then to stave off the fear that had enlarged into a constant dread. We trembled at every knock on the door, at every phone call, at every mail delivery.

GRANDMOTHER

My Berlin grandmother's possessions were confiscated by the state. She was ordered to give up her apartment. So she moved to her son's in Bad Kudowa. She joined the Confessional Church as a baptized Jew in 1934; however, her presence in Kudowa became increasingly dangerous for her son, daughter-in-law, and also for the medical practice. So she came to us in Hamburg one day at the end of 1938, beginning of 1939, around the same time my uncle had been deported. She lived with us in the apartment for several weeks or months, until my mother disclosed to her one day that she couldn't stay with us any longer. Her presence had only brought our family into trouble again. I was told that she had been completely perplexed. Those affected by my grandmother's persecution had their hands bound. Someone would have looked first for my grandmother at her daughter's in Hamburg. What relatives, friends, or acquaintances would have wanted to or could have hidden her? Who would we have asked to take such a risk? Certainly there were underground organizations in Berlin, but my grandmother had no ties to them. Also, the professing church could offer only a limited amount of help. Besides, my grandmother probably wouldn't have wanted to live a life in hiding. I will soon be as old as she was then. I don't really care to hide either.

Grandma was small, fragile, and very smart. She was a doctor's daughter. All of her male relatives had been doctors. Earlier she had been a member of the *Leipzig Gewandhaus Choir* [a famous Berlin choir]. In my memory, I see Grandmother knitting constantly: She was so talented in knitting that she was an artist. We three sisters wore clothes and jackets knitted by her, even when we were adolescents. The most beautiful gifts at Christmas always came from her. Gisela and I each received a genuine Käthe Kruse doll, "little dreamer," a doll about the size of an infant, when we were about twelve. We were enormously pleased. I have a very special memory from a still earlier time of two small black dolls of Gisela's and mine for which Grandma had crocheted both a light blue and pink dress. They stood under the gargantuan Christmas tree that reached from the floor up to the ceiling of the old frame house. Grete, our house-girl, remembered that my grandmother visited us often. She sometimes spent the summer holidays with us. In Spiekeroog [an East Friesian island] she broke her foot in the dunes. I trusted Grandma in particular. At fourteen, I wrote novels that only she was allowed to read.

From Hamburg, she moved again to Berlin to a small *Pension* in the suburb Wilmersdorf that belonged to two Jewish sisters. The Nazi government had forced other Jews to take in their own kind. In fall 1940 I visited my godmother in Berlin and then my grandmother. We had arranged on the telephone beforehand that she would wait for me at the U-bahn train platform. On the way to the *Pension*, I was not allowed to accompany her. She had told me I must go on the other side of the street so that we wouldn't be seen together. She wore a "Jewish yellow star," and we could have been punished because Jews were forbidden to associate with "Aryans." I noted which house she entered, and shortly after I followed her. The picture of her small, dark, ducked figure that I followed from a distance, I will never forget.

Her room on the first floor of the *Pension* was medium sized. On one side near the window was a bed, and we sat at a small table. The room was nearly empty, and no pictures hung on the wall. Next door was a small kitchen. I don't know anymore what we spoke about; however, I certainly talked about Hamburg. The atmosphere was depressing.

My grandmother had tried to obtain an emigration permit through the department of the American Embassy in Berlin. A certificate from March 22, 1941, shows that she was on the "Polish Waiting List" [she resided on the Polish side] under the number 22829. On this paper was a warning: "Make no itineraries—examination only after many years— regulations very harsh—chances extremely small—meanwhile, unfortu- nately, inquiries cannot be regarded." The chances for emigration were equally nil.

Beginning in summer 1941, my mother got more packages from Berlin. My grandmother sent her everything she owned. Either she knew already about her imminent deportation or she suspected it. Her fur coat lay under other items: "It was always too big for me," she wrote in a letter on October 27, "I am sending this with other things that are only in my way, but please don't be sad over anything. I miss nothing and have, above all, still an abundance. The pictures that I'll eventually send are only in my way especially since I have everything in my heart and before my eyes as if the pictures were here."

Except for this letter, I received one last card from her through my mother November 5, 1941:

> My dear child! I pack in haste, therefore, have not looked through any more papers. . . . I have nothing more in the bank or God knows where else? Probably I'll still send a package. . . . I can take hardly anything with me, also no medication, that all will be picked up. Just as all jewels, genuine and fake, clocks, pure soap. Finally, you get the cross necklace, so don't cry! Someone would certainly take it away from me in any case. It was my support in these last difficult weeks. Little Irmi should wear it as often as possible. God protect you all . . .

In the morning, on November 12, my mother received a telegram. I knew nothing about it and after the evening meal practiced my piano. After some time, she said she would like for me to stop playing and come to her. My younger sister was already in bed. Gisela didn't live at home. I see us sitting at the dining room table, my mother to the right and my father to the left of me, when she opened the telegram. A doctor, my grandmother's friend, informed us of her death. His detailed report followed. My mother cried while my father seemed euphoric. Only those who have experienced the terrible pressure of the Nazis as if on their own body can understand. My father believed that now our family was saved. He was mistaken. The doctor's telegram, among other things, contained the following lines:

> And it came as it must come. This past Saturday I spoke with your good mother a long time and repeatedly encouraged her to muster the strength to bear the heaviest burden. But I knew that her decision was already made . . . in the letter I received this morning, she had meticulously written down

in her careful handwriting her last requests—touchingly modest and without a mark of internal distress—and enclosed this letter for you. Death came to her gently and kindly. In her features lay no struggle, no bitterness, and her hands were clasped intricately in prayer. When I saw her, she had already been in eternal sleep for hours.

An excerpt from my grandmother's farewell letter:

> My darling children and grandchildren! I don't want to write you a long letter that would make me soft and make your heart heavier afterward. Above all, I would like to say to you how happy my life was because of your love. . . . I wish for all of you that the Golden Age would quickly come again. But you also shouldn't mourn for me, because I am going, yes, so awfully glad, to eternal rest and I hope later to see you again in a better world. This life is no longer bearable for me, and whoever hasn't experienced suffering and misery, doesn't know what that means. . . . Don't, in any way, mourn for me, and you should all follow your joys as always. Read the wonderful chapter in *Gösta Berling*[12] about the burial of the beloved sons. I bless you all and ask our Lord God that he forgive me for taking my life as I have fought long and would have gladly been a good Christian in that fight. However, now my life must end.

My parents traveled to Berlin although this was very risky, as my mother wasn't permitted to ride on a train. The cremation took place in the Crematorium Wilmersdorf. In a notification from there it said, "A Christian clergyman may speak." He spoke? I don't know. My relative, Käthe Augstein, told me some years ago that at the beginning of November my grandmother's nephew, Günther, Käthe's husband, had visited her. He had gotten my grandmother the sleeping tablets. My grandmother had confided her plans only to him. It is said they also had talked about "Aunt Anna." In my grandmother's last postcard there is talk about this "aunt," but I don't know who she was. Aunt Anna's son lived in Sweden. Anna waited and waited for a permit to be allowed to leave the country to go to him. When she learned the date of her deportation, she walked into the Wannsee. A day later her son's eagerly awaited answer came—too late! How terrible was the fate of each individual.

DOUBLE LIFE

I had trained myself to lead a proper double life—one in dream and one in reality. The dream was called Dance and Theater. These were wonderful experiences: the Lola Rogge School took part in Faust I (Walpurgisnacht) and Faust II, both productions by Karl Wüstenhagen. In Faust II, I performed along with the students of the theater school to which I belonged in the Trojan Choir (Act 3). I also danced as a gardener (Kaiserpfalz, Act I) and "Lamie" (Walpurgisnacht). Finally, I acted as "Angel" in the Apotheoses of the captivating Triptython (Act 5), which took up the entire breadth of the stage. As angels, we had to stay completely quiet for twenty minutes. The iron supports of the heavy wings pressed into our shoulders. During each performance I concentrated anew on the wonderful words that I knew by heart. For the Faust II performance we spent six hours in the theater. We rushed home with our makeup barely removed. Often we were so exhausted that we could only laugh. While we, Inge I., Uile O, and I, waited for the U-bahn, we sat on the steps and doubled up with laughter. Around midnight I arrived at Eppendorfer Landstraße. Often the sirens screamed later, followed by hours in the shelter.

The reality of our daily life became more and more distressful. My father tried his utmost to protect his family from the worst. He tried to have my mother declared a Mischling and not fully Jewish. I found a letter dated January 1941 sent by my father to the Hamburg criminal police precinct, Große Bleichen. It said, in part:

> Regarding my wife, I gave the explanation that her descent
> was not completely accurate because she was born in Posen,

at that time still under Polish rule. On the basis of this information, the state statistical office has undertaken research because it is very important to us, not just in the interest of our three children, to receive definitive information. I write to you today with a similar letter sent to the Reichsstelle für Sippenforschung [government office for bloodline research] in Berlin. If this decision [from them] should be unfavorable to me then I intend to make a request on the basis of the 7th paragraph of the Reichs Citizens' Laws of November 14, 1935, in order to reach, if possible, an understanding that she could at least be declared "Mischling of the first degree" because of the special nature of this case and of my own personal background; I am a pure Aryan of north German descent, and a reserve officer who participated in the war from 1914 to 1918.

The answer was negative, which meant my mother was declared completely Jewish and we children were declared *Mischling ersten Grades*. Additionally, a notice was sent to my father from the president of the Hanseatic state court that states: "I have checked over your case on the basis of your letter dated December 9, 1941. To my regret, I don't see how it's possible to restore your name to the list of public defenders since we must consider that the decision process concerning your request to Hans Frank will still take considerable time."

The so-called public defender practice had the same meaning as public practice for a doctor. My father had only private clients available to him, of whom there were few. After the war, in my father's declaration under oath, September 1, 1946 (probably to a military bureau), he wrote:

I was expelled from the Rechtswahrerbund [league of people who defend rights], once called Juristenbund [league of jurists][13] because of my "relationship," and my right to work as a public defender was taken away from me. Everyday, I had to consider the possibility that I might be forced into retiring from the legal profession. Steps in this regard, as the clerk at the Hanseatic state court had indicated, had already been put into effect. In autumn 1944 because of my "relationship," I was supposed to be called to the death battalions of the Todt organization as shelter worker or something similar. My TB bracelet protected me from this on the basis of doctor's orders.

There was work, however, as a public defender before or after December 1941. At this time, French POWs were around and my father got the job because he was fluent in French. I remember this—and this was a great exception—because we were told about it at dinner. My father said happily, "Today I saved the life of a Frenchman." This POW was supposed to be sentenced to death for pilfering potatoes. It was, as I mentioned, not common at our house to talk about politics or what my father witnessed at work. For quite some time, children spoke at the table only when they were asked a question. We discussed literature, theater, and opera only when we attended student performances in the theater. "Discuss" is not the right expression. My father dished out explanations. My mother didn't like it much because she was afraid these lectures would adversely affect our eating.

We started to speak about unspeakable events at home. The death of Jochen Klepper,[14] the author, was a great shock to us. He, with his wife and daughter, committed suicide. His wife was Jewish. There had already been another trauma before this one. My father's friend, the police official Oswald L.—called Uncle Bübchen by us—was shot in police headquarters at a hearing. The bullet did not kill him. He recovered and was able to immigrate to America.

Around 1938, my mother had to report to the Gestapo [secret state police]. For the most part, we heard nothing about it. However, one time she came back very agitated. Someone had "suggested" that she bring in her daughter, Irmi, for mandatory sterilization, which was part of the Nazi euthanasia program for mentally and physically disabled people, "unworthy of life." She defended herself with all her strength, which succeeded at the time only because she still was protected through my father. She lived in what Hitler called a "privileged mixed marriage." When my mother indicated one time to the Gestapo that she was baptized, the "Master" answered, "When one pours water over a dog, it still remains a dog."

Every once in a while as a family we drove into a land of dreams: Sunday afternoons when Inge Ihnken came. Her sister, Gretel, was also a Lola Rogge schoolgirl. That's how we knew each other. Like us, she also lived on Eppendorfer Landstraße. Inge had a very pretty singing voice. After we drank coffee together she sat at our grand piano and accompanied herself while singing. My mother seemed to forget everything. She was happy to see all her loved ones gathered together around her. Perhaps she also thought about how she had played the violin in her parents' house. On these Sundays, we drank a cocoa drink that you could get without ration cards. We had to stand in line a long time, but it didn't matter because it tasted fabulous.

Inge married on December 23, 1943. In memory of that day she wrote to me two years ago: "My husband slept at your house the night before our wedding because it wasn't proper to be under the same roof with the bride. Your mother lent me her pointed veil and white shoes, a few sizes too big, but they were bound together with a white band so they wouldn't fall off my feet." She explained the following event in another letter:

> When I visited Rudolf in Rosenheim, 1944, I first took a train to Halle. I changed trains there. In the first class compartment I had a window seat and, to my horror, I sat with all "party insignia" men, but I started right away to immerse myself in an opera excerpt (probably I was studying some other new section of it). I noticed that the man sitting next to me had been staring at me for a while. Finally he said I seemed quite familiar to him. He lived on Eppendorfer Landstraße 42. I acted indifferent even though—because I quickly understood the danger—my heart was beating into my throat. "What comes now?" I thought. First I acted as if I knew nothing, but he kept drilling me. In the meantime all the "dear fellow travelers" were interested in both of us. This "*Stück Mensch*" then said, "Don't act like that now. On Sunday afternoons, you always went to Mrs. B's." I remem-

bered my father's frequent warning: *Never sell your character
and never deny your friends.* So I said, "Yes. That's what I
did." "Well," he said, "don't you know?" "*What* don't I
know?" I said. "That Mrs. B. is Jewish." Shortness of breath.
"I know it, but I don't perceive any difference. Also, that
doesn't interest me." The other gentlemen got roused up.
One warned me that every German has to be interested in
politics. All in all I must have come across as harmless because
they let me go. I remained in Halle on the same platform
while "No. 42" suddenly shouted out from the next train
platform: "If you go there again, you should take a good look
at the woman (Mrs. B.) and notice that she's lacking Aryan
qualities." When I told Rudolf he only said (and he was a
career officer), "We don't have the right to win the war."

My mother didn't "look" Jewish, and neither did we. In connection
with this, another "affable" occurrence followed: During the short time
when Gisela was illegally in the BDM she was asked to be photographed
for the BDM newspaper. With her blond hair, blue eyes, and snow-white
teeth, she was the best example of a "German girl." This entire race theory
was grotesque. If they had known she was *Mischling,* we probably would
have been arrested. My parents were distressed until these people finally
dropped the photo project.

Dancing fascinated me the more I learned and began to understand
it. I definitely wanted training. The largest hurdle was my father. Not
only because I was employed at his office but also in our circles one was
allowed to be interested in the theater but not to harbor desires to go on
stage. But Lola Rogge trained not only dancers but also teachers who
used dance for body development, and amateur dancing. With all the
persuasive ability I had at my disposal (and with help from my mother
who always stood by us in difficult situations), I obtained my father's
permission. Obviously, I had to continue working at his office. From my
paternal [step-] grandfather I inherited enough money to pay for my
training. He died at seventy-seven in 1937. I was so convinced of my
plan that the thought of the exam that I wouldn't be permitted to take

didn't occur to me, or else I pushed it aside. Who could predict what would happen in two years?

On Easter 1943 Lola Rogge accepted me illegally into training. Only many years later did I understand it—in doing so she placed her own existence, that of her family, and the entire school, in danger. One time she was confronted with an unpleasant situation. A fellow schoolmate went to her and said, "Do you know I have to turn you in because Ursula is in the school?" Lola replied, "Then you must do it." Afterward Lola spent a sleepless night with her husband. The next day this same schoolgirl burst into tears and apologized. Nothing happened.

In the early morning I went from Eppendorf to Uhlenhorst (in the Adolfstraße) then along the Alster to daily training, which couldn't be strenuous enough for me. When I went away from Eppendorfer Landstraße and into the Lola Rogge School, an iron curtain fell between home and myself. It only raised itself again when I came back. In addition, we were in a state of great tension because of alarms, bombing attacks, reduction of food rations, questions of heating (how much coal), and so on. Lola Rogge recounted that I was always a pupil in a good mood and concentrated very hard. I carried none of the problems from home into my training. Concentration was absolutely vital. The fascination of dancing was the only possibility of survival. Also, I never asked Lola Rogge any questions. The fact that I was able to participate in so many theatrical performances like others depended on the protection that the name Lola Rogge provided. It hadn't occurred to any government agency to research the ancestry of the dance group participants. What a magnificent feeling it was to stand at the barre in the large ballet hall with others who wanted to learn the same thing. Sometimes we received instruction in the garden where the hedge extended all the way to the Alster. Middays I went home the same way. In the afternoon I sat at the typewriter. This good fortune didn't last long.

IN THE BOMBING WAR

It was summer vacation. My knees were somewhat sore from training. A "cure" would be good, the orthopedist said. What would be more appropriate than to go to Bad Kudowa, where my uncle's wife still lived in the Count Gotzen House? I bathed for three weeks in mud, took long walks, and spent evenings at Aunt Lotte's house. My grandma was no longer alive and we guessed that my uncle was in Holland. Whether or not we spoke about these topics, I don't know. On a wonderful sunny day I sat on a bench in the spa park. From the radio came news of a heavy air attack on Hamburg. More attacks followed in the next few days.

My fear was great. Because the vacation was coming to an end, I left. The ticket was via Berlin. I lived there with my godmother. I discovered my sister Gisela was also in Berlin. We met each other daily. Because it was known Berlin was the next target for attack, my godmother didn't want to take responsibility for me and forced me to travel on. She didn't receive any ration cards for me. Information posted at the main station stated "No possibility of travel to Hamburg." What should I do? I finally telegraphed a friend of my father's, the mayor in Wernigerode, and asked him to take me in. The telegram never arrived, but I did. Although the house was fully occupied by fellow refugees, they welcomed me.

I am entirely convinced that guardian angels exist. I have come across them many times in my life, especially at critical moments. Such a moment was here in Berlin. I was in an overcrowded train and I found a place to sit. Refugees who'd fled Hamburg reported over and over: "Hamburg is burning. No stone remains on another." Consequently I had to contend with the thought that my parents and Irmi might not be alive. I was alive, of course, but the future was dark and unknown, if there was a future at all. In this frame of mind I sat in my narrow seat. Through the window, I suddenly recognized a familiar figure on the train platform. I jumped up and yelled. It was Gretel Ihnken from Hamburg, the sister of Inge. She wanted to go to Helmstedt. We were headed the same way. Not only that, but Gretel told me that she, with her parents and mine, had left Hamburg on foot after the third heavy attack, and had found refuge in their summer house in Poppenbüttel. I had encountered this sole witness from Hamburg in the middle of Berlin's chaos.

From August 12 to September 11, 1943, I worked temporarily at the Wernigerode city administration. When I left, I received a certificate that said ". . . she was employed in the division of 'support for family evacuation' that takes care of financial losses of those injured by bombs, and proved herself first-rate from day one. I'm sorry to see her leave and I wish her the best for the future. The Mayor."

My father picked me up from the Hartz. Our apartment in Hamburg was still intact. Lola Rogge, who was expecting a child, had moved to Stade near Hamburg after the bombings. A small group of students rode there each morning where we continued training in the guest house Birnbaum. In 1944 the call-up for total war operations was decreed. The school children had to work in the armaments factories. I was excluded from that and remained at my father's. Afternoons and evenings, I taught beginners in the Lola Rogge School. The class often ended with air raid warnings.

Around 1937 Gisela was admitted illegally into a Protestant nursing order to study nursing, but she couldn't get a diploma. She then could continue training on Mittelweg in Dr. Burmester's "lying-in" [maternity] hospital. She studied there at the beginning of the war for one to two years. Then the Nazis took over the house and Gisela had to go. The new officiating doctor arranged for Gisela to go to Berlin to work for his colleague in a private clinic. This clinic was bombed out, so Gisela came back to Hamburg and took over weekly duties at the homes of acquaintance and friend's who were expecting babies.

In October 1944 our house seamstress, Frau Becker, sat in one of the back rooms of the apartment at her sewing machine. Frau Becker's mother, Frau Sorgenfrei, had been our seamstress formerly. When she became too old, her daughter took over. Frau Becker had been coming to us for at least fifteen years. Earlier she had sewn all of our clothes— school clothes and so-called dress clothes worn at dance school and formal balls. There was nothing more to sew but much to mend. Frau Becker had become a friend. Later she and her husband lived with us for a while after they were bombed out.

After drinking coffee one afternoon I wanted to demonstrate a movement from a dance so I cleared away the chairs on one side of the room. I had already changed clothes to dance when the bell rang. At the door stood an SS [chief police agency] man who wanted to speak with my mother and inspect the apartment. When he set foot in the living room that now functioned as my dance space, he became irritated. He found it unheard of that we still possessed such beautiful rooms—genuine carpets, oil paintings, and the Bechstein piano. With my mother he also inspected the back rooms and detected Frau Becker at the sewing machine. He rebuked her: "You should know that you are not permitted to work for a 'Jewess.'" My mother, in order to protect Frau Becker, said, "Not true. Frau Becker knew nothing about me!" With that, the SS man screamed at my mother, enraged: "You will hear from me!" The door slammed shut. Horror paralyzed us. We stood petrified like stone. Naturally I didn't feel like dancing anymore, but my mother didn't want to rise to the panic, so she implored me to stick to the program. I performed the dance.

How Christmas time and the beginning of the year 1944-45 looked, I don't know. Probably my parents tried to make the best of it. But Damokles' sword[15] hung directly over our heads.

MOTHER'S DEPORTATION

On a Friday morning around 8:00 A.M. I fainted in the bathroom. There was no predictable reason for it. Never before and never again in my life did it happen to me. I believe I called out. In any case my mother caught me. I could hear her yell to Irmi for help to carry me to bed. Around 10:00 a postal message came for my mother. But only in the afternoon around 4:00 did she inform me about it. It was her "summons" to the work camp. Maybe subconsciously I had anticipated this in the morning when I fainted. On Wednesday, February 14, 1945, she was ordered to appear at the main train station with backpack and blanket. What did "work camp" mean? I couldn't imagine it. Inge Ihnken told me: "Irmi came to us at that time with this letter. Your father was at a meeting in Bremen. In the afternoon he came to our house. He was chalk white. He said to my father: 'In this case, we have to take precautions. We are coming to an end!' My father fiercely contradicted: 'By no means—the war will be over soon. The Nazis will not be at the helm much longer. Your wife is coming back!'" Inge maintained that my father went away less crestfallen.

I lay on the couch at home incapable of standing up. I don't know what we thought or said. Nobody cried. If it was possible to feel, the feeling was fear. On Saturday morning my mother sat on the edge of my bed. She told me I had "blacked out." I was sick. Really strange: "We want to conclude things tonight," she said. "For your sake I'll go. Both of you [Ursula and Gisela] will probably come through, but not Irmi." The Nazis would immediately put her in an euthanasia program.[16] We also, really, did not come through. My mother didn't foresee that at the time. Later on they not only tormented the Jewish families but also the mixed. Every night we slept in a different place. This wouldn't have been sufficient had it lasted a few months more. We would also have been deported as "half-breeds of the first degree." I couldn't react. My sister Gisela, who was taking care of her friend Irene and her baby, arrived. She packed the backpack with my mother. As I learned later, my mother sewed a tablet of Zyankali (poison) in her coat. In the early afternoon of the fourteenth, my father, mother, and Gisela left by way of the back stairs. Irmi and I remained home. A friend of my mother's was there. Time seemed endless to me until my father and Gisela returned. I believe I had assumed fervently that my mother would also be with them. My father, very horrified, informed me that the name "Theresienstadt" was visible on the train's side. Mother was taken to Theresienstadt.[17] It was insanity. He knew what Theresienstadt meant. We didn't. He knew it was a concentration camp, not a labor camp. The term "labor" was just a camouflage. Above the entrance was a sign "Labor Camp." He never talked about it. He thought we should be protected. Then he said my mother had gone once again to the SS man who had been in our apartment and she said he certainly should leave her in Hamburg as she has three children. His answer to her was: "You have been so impudent. You go along."

LAST MONTHS OF THE WAR

I couldn't get back on my feet. Through my father's doctor friend, I got a bed in the hospital. Next to me lay an amusing patient. Was she given the assignment to cheer me up? She always possessed a bottle of red wine hidden under her bed. At night I was granted a glass. Except for a high temperature, I lacked nothing. It's just that I was so weak that only with incredible effort could I get to the bomb shelter. We experienced various attacks. One time a woman gave birth behind a small curtain. After three weeks I was released because the bed was needed. From the doctor I got a few Pervitin, a stimulant, so that I could walk and carry my suitcase. I went for a week to the Baltic coast. On the way low-flying planes shot at the train. We looked along the slope for needed cover. When we climbed back in I couldn't find the compartment with my suitcase. At each of the stations along the way I climbed in and out of compartments looking for my case. What was I supposed to do without my things? Right before Lübeck, I found my "*gute Stück*" [my trusty suitcase].

Along the coast I was able to take walks. In my memory the sky and the sea remained disconsolately gray. Having returned to Hamburg, I could see how Gisela worked so hard to take care of everyday concerns. For example, the gas pressure was so bad that she set the alarm for 5:00 A.M. so that the coffee water would be boiling at eight. I told her, "I will now relieve you so you can sleep longer." This way my strength came back. From my father's aforementioned declaration under oath from September 1, 1946, I read: ". . . in the last weeks before the collapse of the Nazi government it became the policy that the Gestapo went out hunting for 'mixed race' people. In order to escape, my daughters had to hide for a while, and spent the night at their friends' houses."

One evening around midnight when Gisela and Irmi had left and I stayed in my father's house, the doorbell rang. I pondered whether or not I should save myself by running onto the balcony. But someone would notice that I had just left the bed because it was unmade. The next thought: "Should I jump from the balcony?" Soon I realized that whoever was at the door didn't want to get into my place, but rather into the apartment of the subtenant, Herr Bruno Schmidt, below me.

The events of the *Kriegsschauplatz* (theater of war) followed in rapid succession. Our fate was a race with death. How we experienced the collapse of Germany, I can't really say. On the one hand, it was exciting and liberating, but on the other hand, we didn't know the fate of our mother. Once again, we were human beings like all the others (after twelve years!) but we could only take this in very slowly. There was no celebration.

MOTHER'S RETURN HOME

We slept without air raid alarms. In the evenings there was a curfew. We constantly ran into difficulties taking care of daily needs. My father lost a lot of weight and spent time running around. He arranged things with the military bureau and probably also with the attorneys' association. He learned very quickly that the Jewish couple who was forcibly quartered in our house (while my mother had to go to the camp) moved into the apartment that they'd earlier owned. My father was in touch with families of people who had been deported with my mother. At the beginning of June there was hope that the inmates would return from Theresienstadt. Gisela baked a cake, but the transport was cancelled. On June thirtieth my mother called. My dad went to the phone. The transport would arrive at the Eppendorfer train station. We went. They came in an open truck—all with the Jewish star on their coats (presumably as protection this time for the trip through chaotic Germany). In my memory, greetings with the transportees were short. Mrs. K., who was picked up by her daughter, cried out because she learned that her husband had died in a bombing attack. Each had only one wish: to go home as quickly as possible.

My mother had lost twenty pounds. She told us next to nothing. We didn't ask any questions. Gisela prepared a bath. We drank coffee. The next day, my mother took over the household care. I loved my mother much more than my father. When you're a young girl you think all difficulties come from your mother, and you blame your mother for having the Jewish background. I was ambivalent. It was more than *das ist Blut*—deeper than just a "dumb" situation. Gisela, years later, criticized our mother for not telling us anything, although not angrily. Mother never talked about the camps. Today I ask myself about that. We did ask her questions and got abrupt answers. She'd change the subject and say something like "Where do you need to go?" Then I never asked again. Maybe she told Gisela more. Because I left in 1947, I didn't have the opportunity. When she visited me in England, I didn't ask because so many years had passed. She gave short answers. She might have said, "Better to forget it." I was not that interested in knowing details. I thought it was better to suppress the past. Forty years later I wrote down her story. Perhaps I had sometimes thought, "If my parents divorced it might be easier." I don't know what I thought. [She slaps her legs.] Without my mother at home, it would have been horrible.

Gisela soon attended evening school in order to complete her high school studies. Later she began to study medicine but soon married and gave it up. I reacted to all the upsetting events with a case of shingles. In fall, the Lola Rogge School began again with training. I could finally continue, officially.

In January 1946 I passed my pedagogy exam. My study of children for this exam was called "How the Little Angel Seeks His Mother,"[18] after the same title as the children's book. With forty children I had studied the dance. Rehearsals took place under severe conditions. The ballet hall wasn't heated, and the children had to dance barefoot. The youngest performer, "the little angel" was three years old. For the test, the examination panel had covered themselves in thick blankets. In 1947 I passed the dance exam with "God and the Bajadere," named after the Goethe poem. I had music composed according to my specifications. I passed the exam with distinction.

Gradually, my mother reported a few things about her transport. On February 14, 1945, the train had stood for twenty-four hours on a side track of Hamburg's main station. The severely cold weather had caused technical difficulties so it couldn't depart. On one of the first nights, my mother actually fell when falling asleep and struck an iron oven in the car. A veterinarian, who was among the deportees, bound the wound. During the journey they saw Dresden burning in the last leg of the war. The trip lasted nine days. Again and again the train stood somewhere on a station's siding. After she arrived in Theresienstadt, my mother's head wound was stitched without local anesthesia. Her only commentary was: "All the things we endured!" Because of the accident she had, my mother was the only one who was allowed to take a bath. She said, "The blankets (which she was allowed to take with the backpack) were our salvation." In my father's aforementioned declaration under oath, it states: "In this place [Theresienstadt], they were placed under a daily threat to body and life because of the degrading and hard work, and the bad food and lodging. At the beginning of May 1945, after Theresienstadt had been freed by the Russians from the Nazis' oppressive government, the concentration camp inmates had to stay a few weeks because of spot typhus."

My mother described how they had been brought in groups of six into a room. Compared to some others that was preferential treatment. Five women from Hamburg and a "little farmer," a woman from Kiel, lived together. Every year she met with this group of five women who were with her in the camp. Later this group met for many years every February 14th at my mother's house in Eppendorferlandstraße. She maintained contact with this small circle. She invited them every February to her home. Many experiences were collected in one room. Today it's incomprehensible. On June 23, 1945, my mother baked a rhubarb cake in the liberated Theresienstadt for the woman from Kiel. That was mentioned every year for forty years. My mother met the sister of her mother, "Aunt Trudchen," in Theresienstadt. She had been deported a year earlier from Elbing. This reunion must have been harrowing. Every midday, my mother brought her aunt a portion of her own ration.[19]

RESULTS AND CONCLUSIONS

My father was a well-liked Hamburg lawyer before 1938. His practice did very well and he had many friends. But from 1938 on, his activity decreased. Because of this, the financial situation of the family became increasingly strenuous. I never wanted to recognize my father as a father. As children, we hardly saw him because until 1938 he was working in his practice in the city and only came home in the evenings. We then went to bed. During summer vacations we traveled only with our mother. My father felt shame because I had to work with him. But it wasn't his fault at all. Perhaps unconsciously I rejected the "Aryan" in him, the one who remained "unsheared." But he *didn't* remain "unsheared." That's exactly what I didn't see—that already before 1945 he was a broken man. His reason for existence—the law practice—was destroyed. He didn't have the strength to build up his practice again. After the war he couldn't work again successfully. Refugee lawyers from the East [11 million Germans] who had settled in Hamburg could work simultaneously as notaries. In the East they were tested as both lawyers and notaries. The notaries found work more quickly and were needed more often. The Hamburger lawyers, on the other hand, were either lawyers or notaries. My father couldn't obtain a passport and the small number of clients he had weren't enough to support a family. We had a larger apartment for the practice, which we separated into parts. We had a nice neighbor who moved in and mentioned to me that she was able to move in because she made three rental payments for my father. This was 1950. My mother was insured. My father didn't have any insurance. He couldn't rebuild his life. My father had few sources of revenue. I have a letter from August 26, 1945, that reads as follows:

> Dear Colleague. In my personal case of emergency in which I had written on July 22 this year to the Hanseatic chamber of lawyers, I take the liberty now with the close of this month to come back to this matter and to ask you whether I can work out a monthly subsidy of DM 150 to be paid to me from now on. My suffering has in no way improved, and my economic position is worse than ever. I have striven in the meantime to find a colleague who perhaps would be prepared to practice his profession in my office with me. However, all attempts up to now have miscarried.

I also have before me more of my father's letters, one from April 18, 1950, to the social welfare office: "... My economic relationships, as it's been shown, have turned out so catastrophic that my spouse has had to seek compensation as a prison inmate." There is also a "distress resolution" from 1955. The pledge, of course, could be cancelled (as far as I can tell). We got an *Auszahlung* [payoff]. Altogether, it took eleven years until my mother received compensation, her *Wiedergutmachung*, reparations, in the form of a pension. That was very good. It was no fabulous payoff; we had to give it away immediately because we were in debt. My mother got a pension and it increased. It wasn't much but it grew. My father left nothing behind, just debts. It lasted four horrible years. I was working. I couldn't help my mother. It wasn't enough. In the meantime, my parents took in a sister of my grandmother's who had survived in Brazil. Other rooms were sublet. Finally, my parents sold the grand piano, one or two paintings, the last of my mother's jewelry, and the remaining silver.

A few days before he was taken to the hospital, my father's last words to my mother were: "How good that you now got the money for yourself." He died on February 24, 1957, without leaving a penny behind. A minister of the Johannes Church in Eppendorf had come across my father in the empty church one time shortly before his death. When the minister asked, "What are you doing here?" my father is said to have answered, "I am seeking peace."

In spring 1986 I traveled to Israel with a tourist group. We visited the Wailing Wall in Jerusalem and the large concentration camp memorial. In the "Room of Names" I discovered the name of my uncle, Dr. Helmuth Moral, in a register of the deported Jewish people from Holland. This clarified definitively that he had been murdered in Auschwitz. I was thunderstruck. I picked up the precise dates from information that I obtained from the International Search Service in Arolsen: On January 12, 1944 (he lived almost five years in Holland in the underground and had waited in vain for the journey to America), he was dispatched to the concentration camp Westerbork in Holland and on March 3, 1944, was deported from there to Auschwitz (probably by way of Theresienstadt). He was considered dead on July 31, 1944.

My uncle had forwarded his entire medical practice (thirty cases with very valuable contents) before leaving Germany to Holland. These cases arrived then disappeared in a mysterious way. The reestablishing of contact to a Holland family whose address my father had discovered provided no sort of information. In many places, with the end of the war, a great silence and a keeping of secrets prevailed.

My sister Irmi died in 1969 from muscle deterioration. The last half of the year my mother pushed her in a wheelchair. Gisela took her life in 1971 after a harsh skin disease. It had nothing to do with the Nazi time. She was fifty. She was just sick. She started to study medicine and she wrote about her illness—that it was hopeless. [She sighs.] I witnessed her illness. What should one think or say? I could understand it [her suicide]. What do you do if you have a disease and read about it and know it will end in death anyway? She was sick about two years. She was born in 1920. Her husband married again. He doesn't call much at all. My mother was alive then. I was in Hamburg at that time, for a short time. Gisela had *Pemphigus vulgaris,* when the skin is detached from its basic layers. Bubbles are in between and infected. She had it in the throat and mouth, in all cavities of the body. Bubbles on her cheeks. They did not diagnose her early enough. It took a long time until they did. They released her from the hospital, and she read about it. She was married and had her own family, and I wasn't in Hamburg so we'd lost contact. It was hard for my mother—two children dying before her own death. It *must* have been very hard. My mother refused to take poison because of Irmi. Now she had to deal with her daughter doing what she didn't do earlier, which would have left her children alone.

Out of Gisela's marriage came a son and daughter. He is married and lives in Moscow, actually Estonia in Tallinn [the capital of Estonia]. He married a Russian and they both went to Estonia. At eighty-five, my mother flew with me to Moscow to see her grandson. I don't know my nephew well in Estonia; they're too far away and he doesn't have much interest in me. Since my mother died we're not as close. Until 1985 the family held together—even with the new daughter-in-law. My mother held it all together. Gisela's daughter, Andrea Craft, lives in Hamburg; she is in the Jewish community. My niece tried to get more information out of my mother but she couldn't get much. She's difficult in every way. Not really in trouble, she just doesn't communicate, doesn't stick with any job. Her dad gave her an apartment as a gift so she can live. She doesn't have a relationship with her brother and father. Andrea has asked me questions but I tell her to read what I've written. [She laughs.] Naturally she's asked me questions. But I also can't say much. I can tell you what I think as a theologian about all these women who took their lives, all these things that weren't spoken about. What should I say? Self-murder is not punishable. It's not possible that a God would punish a person who *is* punished. The idea that those who commit suicide won't get a place in the cemetery is passé. I think people who suffer so much shouldn't be punished. How can another person be an authority judging another's life? No one should argue about a suicide's life. Perhaps I studied religion because of the Hitler era, to understand something.

My mother was granted and lived out many fulfilling years. After the war she enjoyed life immensely, now that it was normal. After my father died and Irmi died, she visited me in all those countries and relished it. While I was living abroad for sixteen years she visited me everywhere. She really didn't want others to speak about the Nazi regime and her time in Theresienstadt. She was not embittered and never complained. Up until her last days she remained constantly busy doing things for others. With a mind that hadn't clouded over, she died in 1985 shortly before her ninety-first birthday.

From 1946 to 1949 I was involved in the small city theaters in Essen. I always visited home, but then Gisela married. Our relationship wasn't as close. Of course, when I came home for visits, everything was beautiful. I never talked with my father after the war because I was only home occasionally. It certainly seems strange to others that we never discussed such things. I had two accidents at work, once going out of the theater and once during rehearsal. I broke my right foot each time. I had to stop dancing. I began soul-searching the second time I broke my foot. I thought it was the way it should be, and I needed to stop. I had intense contact with a church community in Essen. I was eating meals with a very devout family. The son was a theology student with whom I spent time. Internal and external concerns eventually drove me to step out of my profession and allowed me to study in a theological seminary in Wuppertal-Elberfeld in Rhineland, and to work as parish helper in Leverkusen. It wasn't possible to take all the exams in theology and dance. Sometimes I danced for a birthday party and, in Sweden, for a wedding. It was a real break between two differing paths.

In 1956 the "Gateway to the World"[20] opened for me, although not in Hamburg. The Foreign Relations Bureau of the Protestant Church in Germany dispatched me for six years to Boras, Sweden, then for two years to Lisbon, Portugal, and finally for another three years to Leeds, England. Gisela spent two years with her family in Sweden. I had already been there and helped my sister move. I understood Swedish but she did not. After eleven years of foreign experience I came back to Hamburg, lived in Mission Academy, and studied theology for four semesters at the university where I got my diploma. I'm a diploma theologian. Once again in the Rhine church I was ordained and was sent out again by the church "outreach" as pastor of the German congregation in Manchester (six-year contract). I worked with the church and often was sent out to various places—six years in Portugal, three years in England, and later six years again in England. [Switches from German to English.] My English is not good. I was always in a German community and we always spoke German except when we were shopping. I gave seminars in English, but not with a discussion afterward. But when I did baptisms, I spoke English. [Switches back to German.] I could talk ad nauseum about my sixteen years away and about the time in Germany (the last six years as hospital chaplain in Wiesbaden), but that doesn't belong in this context. After thirty-five years in church service, I have now come back—through the large "Gateway to the World"—to Hamburg.

I wanted to be out of Germany. It wasn't very conscious, rather unconscious, that I went to several other countries. I wanted to stay in Sweden and then many times I thought I'd like to stay in England. [Switches to English.] I didn't realize it was like an emigration—an inner emigration. I think I know it now but I didn't at that time. [Switches back to German.] This foreign ministry didn't like it when their people went away and stayed away. They were peeved when a German pastor said, "I'll stay in this other country." They wanted them back with all they had learned to live *here* and teach others. They didn't say, "You definitely can't do that," but said they'd offer something else to me.

I can't really say with what or whom I identify. I'm German and Christian. What I *really* am, I don't know. *Ich wäre lieber kein Deutscher.* I would prefer not to be German. [She repeats this twice.] If the neo-Nazis get even stronger, I won't stay. Now that they *are* strong, I wonder if I should go to another country. Yet German is my own language. I mean, no one can 100 percent adopt a new language and culture. Not 100 percent. Ah, I love Faust and Goethe. I have always been homeless. I've never been truly here when I gladly was in other countries. And when

I would stay in other countries, then I wasn't 100 percent. There were problems with Germans whom I got to know in Sweden, Portugal, and England. I always had work to do with Germans in foreign countries, and I saw how hard it was when they suddenly became old and alone, and had lived for forty or fifty years in England and were in a hospital and could no longer seem to understand English and no one around spoke German. They reverted to German because English was an "inherited" language. A strange idea. I saw all that. It's hard to live in a different land, to emigrate. You are never 100 percent. I closed the circle by going back to Hamburg. When I lived in Wiesbaden, I thought I'd live there forever. One day I called Lola Rogge, and she asked me when was I coming back for good and not just for vacation. And a spark went off in my brain. My mother was no longer alive; she died in 1985. In spite of that, I had a feeling I needed to return to Hamburg. Strange to say, I found an apartment quickly. Very strange. It was near the Gertrud Church where I was confirmed and near where we'd lived in Overbeckstraße. The circle was closing. But the thoughts never go away. In any kind of political difficulty, I think about old times and just want to leave, take a flight to Sweden or England. It always comes back. I'm more left politically but not active. I do vote Social Democratic. I don't like Kohl, the chancellor. There are lots of political mistakes. My niece, Andrea, is political. My dad was considered intellectual. It was a generation when women didn't have a profession. I never married. As a woman, I had no difficulty. I do what I like. In the communities where I worked you couldn't do what you wanted all the time. It's a profession in which you get much criticism. I really can't answer the question about my role as a woman. I talked to students when I was at the university. I can't understand how today young people want to get married, have kids, and a career. It would be impossible for me. Something will suffer. It's not in your power to do it all.

Earlier I felt like an outsider. I was silent. Whenever people talked about the war or what happened, I said nothing. I tried to be friendly and agreeable to others, say "yes." Today I don't feel like an outsider. I don't talk to people who thought the Nazi time was good. It is terrible when someone says, "He [Hitler] did great things—he built the high-ways." I can't bear to hear it. I wouldn't talk about my difficulties. The school friendships ended. Also the ones in the dance school. Then I studied theology. I had trouble sustaining contact when I moved around. I kept in touch with Lola Rogge. Even in the congregations outside Germany no one talked about it. In Lisbon there were émigrés who never mentioned it. People who were directly affected by it remain silent or, in any event, did so for a long time. All the books about the Third Reich were written forty years later. I've read a lot about it. When the *Holocaust* film came out in the late 1970s I began to comprehend what had happened. After fifty years, the remembrance ceremonies are too much. [Switches to English.] Again and again. All these terrible things to hear again and again. Sometimes I couldn't watch it or read it. [Switches to German]. Up until the 1970s, it was not possible for me to talk about experiences of the Nazi era.

Approximately 1974, I read *The Inability to Mourn* by Alexander and Margarete Mitscherlich, a book that greatly impressed me. I saw the book in a book announcement, so I ordered it, read it, and found it so marvelous that I thought *I must talk to this woman*. I had to go to her in Frankfurt. When I visited Frankfurt from England for Kirchentag[21] in 1975 I made an appointment with Dr. Margarete Mitscherlich. She said, "There's also good people in England. Do you know anyone there?" I said, "No. I'll come back after a day." I flew twice or three times from England to Wiesbaden near Frankfurt. I could take the train. For over ten years this woman accompanied me in her loving way and with unending patience as I tried to make sense of my past. I have her to thank that I can now speak and write about the events of the years 1933 to 1945. I've written down my ideas through analysis with the Mitscherlichs. It's my opinion today that we—the witnesses—must speak. Above all, the youth should hear about what they didn't experience. I can only think that the Nazis wanted us to keep it secret. That was the idea. Children must keep secrets above all. I heard from my generation—that it was understood and also true in their families—about this not speaking and not asking. So, some understand in our generation that it wasn't proper. It would have been better for me if we had talked about it. I think, on the other side, we were somewhat a little bit too carefree. What I did not know wasn't a hot topic for me. I don't know if I could have gone to the Lola Rogge School if I had known it meant danger for her. I was just trying to be carefree. I didn't know any better.

I was in psychoanalysis from 1977 to 1987. It was only one time per week with long vacations in between. She did many lectures in other cities and was often away. Ten years sounds like an enormous time, but the therapy wasn't constant. We always had solutions to clarify. We talked about this entire Hitler time. It was hard work to write it down because nobody in our family talked about it. It was hard to find documents and to make a logical story out of it. I found dates in papers and reparation documents when my grandmother had left the Jewish religion and was baptized. I had to put effort into figuring out the dates. I stopped therapy when I came to Hamburg in 1987. It's very expensive. But healthcare takes care of these things—for psychiatrists but not psychologists. Mitscherlich was a fine woman—very patient, and always listened. I had a very good relationship with her. She was very loving in our sessions; otherwise, I had absolutely no contact with her. That's her [points to a picture, then gets up and brings it over]. She is Danish, or half Danish. Her husband is no longer alive. I happily went to see her every week and gladly paid the fees; it was so positive for me to talk to someone about the past. It was the first time I'd talked about it to anyone. In America it's entirely normal to go to therapy. If you break your foot you also go to the doctor or for your teeth you go. And so it should be for mental sickness—not just if you're crazy. I don't think I'm as imbalanced now.

I had migraines for thirty-five years. I looked everywhere in England to get free from migraines. Nothing helped. I pursued all possibilities in England—*Urschrei* (primal scream) therapy and rebirth, many things. Nothing helped. Then I read this book *[Inability to Mourn]* and I said I must seek this out. Mitscherlich said, "It's already sunken into you. Naturally it is a sickness and it's okay that you feel unable to talk about it." She couldn't promise rectification. Nevertheless, it turned out well. It had to do with the repression. I very seldom have headaches now. The therapy was a mix. Mitscherlich asked questions and I answered, more or less. She brought up a point and I had to associate with it and go with it, similar to Freudian analysis especially when I talked about my dreams, which brought me to talk about the past. I worked with dreams a lot. Why do you act in a certain way right now? It must be associated with your past. I didn't write a diary—no time—and I was stressed in my profession. I talked about everything with Mitscherlich, about how Irmi was difficult on the marriage, but they didn't talk about that. My mother said once, "Everything that was difficult I had to survive myself." With Irmi, with her mother, her brother. My mother in Theresienstadt alone. Always *she* alone. You can't grasp that my own father took my mother to the train station for deportation. What could he have done? Should he have left her alone? Hide her? We didn't know where to hide her. For Giordano, maybe.[22] For us, hiding wasn't possible. The war had progressed and so my father thought it couldn't last that long. My mother was deported late, thank God.

Mitscherlich also had victims of the war coming to her, not former Nazis. I am still nervous that people are alive who were a part of the Third Reich. I feel creepy that many lawyers came through it and again secured high positions. Who was the judge who gave out death sentences? The main judge in Berlin? I heard about it afterward. The wife got a golden pension because her husband was a judge. He had pronounced death sentences. That angered me! I also wrote in my book about an SS man who lived in our apartment building. Once he moved in, things were awful. Later I asked my mother what became of this man. She said she'd met him out shopping. I thought, It can't be true. He should be dead. I'd like to shoot him. My mother said—also impossible to believe—that Jewish people who weren't sent away gave him money to bribe him. So now they won't mention his name. Twenty or thirty years later I found this out. Then there were those Nazis who went to Latin America—Himmler or Hess or Eichmann? Eichmann. The Germans didn't care about it.

Hitler and the government naturally horrified my father. We were all against Hitler, but we were always between mother and father, between Nazi Germany and resistance. We were always in between. To a young person, none of this is understandable. I think more passive resistance was offered than we realize. The ones who in fact staged resistance were killed. In addition, we must always remember that opposition in a democracy is not the same resistance as in a dictatorship. For resistance in a democracy, courage isn't a prerequisite. Resistance in a dictatorship is a matter of life and death. Today we're saturated with news and reports, and it wasn't that way then.

Before Hitler, I had absolutely no knowledge of Jewish religion. If someone had said *"schabbot"* I wouldn't have known what it was. My grandmother had been baptized, which was our break from Judaism. Later, as a theology student, I was interested in the Old Testament more so than the New. I gave many sermons about the Old Testament. I had difficulty with Christology [idea of Christ] but I wouldn't change. Gisela's daughter is now in the Jewish community returning to our roots—I think more for political than religious reasons. She is against the Nazis—even though she was born after the war—and everything related to it. The Jewish tradition is too foreign to me but fascinating. I'm in the Jewish-Christian Society that holds dialogues between the religions. I couldn't be Jewish in that tradition. My mother wasn't into it, but when I began to study theology after the war, she became interested. She took a Bible to Theresienstadt. But I never asked her why. [Says next sentence in English]: My father was nearly nothing—nothing in that way. He was a good lawyer but not into religion. I also didn't know as much about law. I never was into being a lawyer, but now I'm interested in documentaries on television if they are related to court. In the 1950s and 1960s, no one asked any questions about the German past. The congregations outside of Germany and the individuals in the congregations had completely different problems. Even for myself, the past had entirely disappeared. In the 1970s in England, German women made occasional references to the past because in England there were war films and the Germans in the films were often portrayed negatively, which made people angry. One could often hear comments: "The POWs in Germany had it very good." I never got involved in the discussion. I had negative experiences with the few friends to whom I'd disclosed my past. I then regretted that I'd broken my silence and withdrew internally even further.

In the 1980s many things changed in the Federal Republic. On television there were discussions and reports from contemporary witnesses;

there were films about the time from 1933 to 1945; there was a flood of literature and the so-called historian's dispute [Historikerstreit]. A part of the student body is very interested. For others this time is an epoch over which it's not worth occupying your mind. To this very day, the dialogue with my own generation is the most difficult. There are many attempts at justification and very unrealistic thinking. People like to put it out of their minds—that the Germans began the war and we have to accept the consequences. Regarding the Jewish destruction, people say, "Oh, that was such a long time ago." Today I can respond to that.

I have had many thoughts about and have continually looked for the factors that made the happenings in the Third Reich possible, that created this race obsession and xenophobia. I came to one of these conclusions: If only it were possible for parents to sense and direct their children's aggression and guide them in correct behavior, then it would not be necessary for these children later in life to form images of an enemy in order to carry out the struggle externally that fundamentally occurs internally.

Just as important: If parents understand the disorderly impulses of their children so as to guide them in a proper way, then these children must not unrestrainedly relinquish their impulses, so that later they will not be enraged and strike at random. Those who seek an external enemy will always find one. The recognition begins with ourselves. No one has done anything to determine whether his body color is back or white, or that he was born into one or the other country, culture, or religion. We've done nothing to determine our skin color or place. In the same way, we need to recognize that good and evil are not found only in the external world but also within ourselves—all of us have negative aspects that are brought out, for example, by jealousy and envy. Already the first pages of the Bible, Genesis 4:8, tell about a fratricide and in Genesis 8:21, it says: ". . . the statements and strivings of the human heart are evil from youth on." Wherever ideology and fanaticism form an alliance—as in Hitler's time—all of the evil elements in a human being come forth out of the depths and corrupt the human being into acts of brutality and contempt for humanity.

I am sometimes asked if I can forget and forgive. I think forgetting is impossible but I can accept the way my life's turned out and it definitely was a very rich life. Forgiving, I would say, is not permitted to us, the survivors, because we "came out of it." I would like to ask my grandmother and uncle. We all would have to ask the millions of those murdered for an answer to that. But they are silent.

NOTES

PART I: THE SPIRIT

1. See Frank Bajohr, *"Arisierung" in Hamburg. Die Verdrängung der jüdischen Unternehmer 1933-45* (Hamburg: Christians Verlag, 1997). Bajohr analyzed hundreds of files and came to the conclusion that 1,500 Jewish businesses in Hamburg had to be sold under pressure. This process of exploitation has been well documented for Hamburg. Most Jewish businesses in other cities were "Aryanized" as well, since it was a nationwide law.

2. My great grandfather, Senator Carl Johann Cohn (1857-1931), decided to locate his business in Hamburg because that is where he had the most contacts, an obvious choice for him since he had apprenticed in the African trade with the Lippert firm and needed a big port city for his headquarters. He and Oscar Arndt founded Arndt and Cohn in 1883. When his father, August Cohn, died in 1893, his widow, Charlotte Cohn, née Hahn, moved to Hamburg with her unmarried daughter, Clara. They lived together in a home in the Hagedorn Strasse until Charlotte's death in 1924. Clara, a distinguished and intelligent woman, is said to be the only one of the family who could have perished in the Holocaust, not in a camp, but in a crowded retirement home where she was much neglected.

3. The actual decree prohibiting Jewish doctors from practicing medicine was July 25, 1938. As early as April 1933, non-Aryan doctors were not permitted to have patients who had public insurance. They could treat only people who had private insurance. These patients usually had more money. According to this law, my grandfather could no longer treat worker patients, although it is likely that he continued to do so.

4. The events conducted in Germany, Austria, and the Sudetenland on November 9 and 10, 1938, were coined "Kristallnacht" (night of broken glass) by journalists, in reference to when the Nazis ravaged, burned, and looted Jewish synagogues, stores, and homes. The Nazis claimed their actions were spontaneous when in fact orders had been given to act against the Jews, and crowds were incited to attack any Jews. Many Jewish people and organizations refer to this night as the November pogrom. After this pogrom, 30,000 Jews were rounded up and incarcerated.

5. Lucy Dawidowicz, *The War Against the Jews 1933-1945,* Tenth Anniversary Edition. (New York: Bantam, 1986), p. 65.

6. Supposedly, Carl is the enigmatic "Dr. Cohn" mentioned in *The Warburgs* (pp. 475-476). Fritz Warburg and Carl August Cohn knew each other and Carl is almost certainly the man who was paired up with Fritz by the prison guard. See Ron Chernow, *The Warburgs : The Twentieth-Century Odyssey of a Remarkable Jewish Family* (New York: Vintage, 1994).

7. See Herta Bahlsen-Cohn. *My German Lessons, 1915-1939.* (New York: Vantage Press, Inc., 1995).

8. He was in the Senatskanzlei, the official government office for Hamburg. Being a "Stadtstaat," having the status of a federal state, Hamburg has senators, not ministers, as in Bavaria or Lower Saxony.

9. Claudia Koonz. *Mothers in the Fatherland. Women, Family Life, and Nazi Politics* (New York: St. Martin's Press, 1987), p. 259.

10. 10. Maria Lugones. "Playfulness, 'World'-Travelling, and Loving Perception." In *Feminist Social Thought: A Reader.* Diana Tietjens Meyers, ed. (New York: Routledge, 1997), pp. 148-159. Quote from p. 156.

11. The Nazis had approximately forty-three *Konzentrationslager (KZ)* (concentration camp) categories. The terms "*Vernichtungslager*" (extermination camp), such as Auschwitz, and "*Arbeitslager*" (labor camp), such as Theresienstadt, appear repeatedly in the interviews. Also mentioned are Sachsenhausen, Buchenwald, Westerbork, and Bergen-Belsen or Belsen, all of which were designated as "work" camps.

12. Primo Levi, *The Drowned and the Saved.* Trans. Raymond Rosenthal. (New York: Summit Books, 1988), p. 21.

13. Paul John Eakin, *Fictions in Autobiography: Studies in the Art of Self-Invention* (NJ: Princeton UP, 1985), p. 252.

PART II: THE LAW

1. In Germany, one may decorate walls with the swastika, and it is permissible to use historical photos with a swastika on it, or it may be used in pieces of art, but it must be critical, not propaganda art. If a publisher wants to use a swastika on a book cover, it must be relevant to the book's content. It would not be acceptable to use merely to trigger the interest of potential customers. Any sensitive designer/publisher would try to avoid using it. The swastika was used in India many centuries ago, and you can find Buddha statues with a swastika on the forehead. Of course it would be legal to publish those photos in a book and on the cover of it as well.

2. Libraries can buy this book for research; specifically, booksellers are allowed to sell it to only those customers who give proof that they need it for research. Libraries are not allowed to lend it to people who have no proof of serious interest. However, anyone can own *Mein Kampf.* Some people have three or four copies from Nazi relatives. This book and other Nazi books tend to be kept in a so-called poison cabinet. Many Germans, especially those in younger generations, do not want visitors to browse the bookshelf and get the wrong impression. Thanks to K. Dohnke for this information.

3. *Der Stürmer* [The Stormer], a weekly newspaper published by the vicious anti-Semite, Julius Streicher, between 1923 and 1945. It became known worldwide as an anti-Semitic publication. Streicher printed repugnant, nearly pornographic photographs, cartoons, slogans, and articles about Jews. Streicher gave speeches and set up nationwide display cases that further popularized his paper.

4. Two racial laws issued on September 15, 1935. The Reichsbürgergesetz (State citizenship law) declared that Jews were not citizens of the German state. The Gesetz zum Schutze des deutschen Blutes und der deutschen Ehre (Law for the protection of German blood and honor) prohibited relations between Jews and Aryans and created categories and definitions for who was a Jew, Aryan, and Mischlinge. This legislation was the foundation for all anti-Semitic laws that followed.

5. Ursula Büttner, "The Persecution of Christian-Jewish Families in the Third Reich," *Leo Baeck Institute Year Book* 34 (1989): pp. 267-289. Quote from p. 271.

6. Nathan Stoltzfus, *Resistance of the Heart: Intermarriage and the Rosenstrasse Protest in Nazi Germany* (New York: W. W. Norton, 1996), p. 71.

7. Named after Fritz Todt, SS General and Reich Minister for Armaments and Munitions. Todt is known for building the Autobahn. Todt put together a group of his own laborers forming the Todt Organization to construct the Western Wall, the Siegfried

Line. The project began in 1939. Todt used slave labor, including *Mischlinge*, for his various projects.

8. Shari, Benstock, "Authorizing the Autobiographical," in *The Private Self: Theory and Practice of Women's Autobiographical Writings.* Ed. Shari Benstock (Chapel Hill, NC: U of North Carolina P, 1988), p. 29.

9. Shoshana Felman and Dori Laub, *Testimony: Crises of Witnessing in Literature, Psychoanalysis, and History* (New York: Routledge, 1992), p. 71.

10. Ingeborg Hecht, *Invisible Walls: A German Family Under the Nuremberg Laws* (New York: Harcourt Brace Jovanovich, 1985), p. 136.

11. Louise J. Kaplan, *No Voice Is Ever Wholly Lost* (New York: Simon & Schuster, 1995), pp. 225, 222

12. Aharon Appelfeld, *Beyond Despair: Three Lectures and a Conversation with Philip Roth.* Trans. Jeffrey M. Green (New York: Fromm International Publishing Corp, 1994), p. viii.

13. Laub in Felman and Laub, *Testimony,* p. 69, emphasis added.

14. Büttner, "The Persecution of Christian-Jewish Families in the Third Reich," p. 270.

15. Raul Hilberg, *The Destruction of the European Jews* (New York: Harper and Row, 1961), p. 268.

16. Büttner, "The Persecution of Christian-Jewish Families in the Third Reich," p. 279.

CHAPTER 1

1. Ingeborg Hecht, *Invisible Walls: A German Family Under the Nuremberg Laws* (San Diego: Harcourt Brace Jovanovich, 1985), p. 66.

2. Louise J. Kaplan, *No Voice Is Ever Wholly Lost* (New York: Simon and Schuster, 1995), p. 222.

3. Hecht, *Invisible Walls,* p. 87.

4. Ibid., p. 95.

5. Ibid., p. 37.

6. Ibid., p. 42.

7. Ibid, p. 101.

8. Ibid., p. 101.

9. Ibid., p. 71.

10. Ibid., p. 72.

11. Ibid., p. 73.

12. Ibid., p. 75.

13. Ibid., p. 76.

14. Ibid., pp. 76-77.

15. Ibid., p. 85.

16. Ibid., p.108.

17. Aharon Appelfeld, *Beyond Despair: Three Lectures and a Conversation with Philip Roth.* Trans. Jeffrey M. Green (New York: Fromm International Publishing Corp, 1994), p. 14.

18. Ibid., p. 18.

19. Hanns Studniczka, *Saturnische Erde: Stätten, Männer und Mächte Italiens* [Saturnian Earth: Places, Men and Powers of Italy] (Berlin: Verlag die Runde, 1941; 3rd ed. Frankfurt am Main, 1949).

20. Ingeborg Hecht, *To Remember Is to Heal: Encounters between Victims of the Nuremberg Laws.* Trans. John A. Broadwin (Evanston, IL: Northwestern UP, 1999).

21. Ralph Giordano (1923 -). *Die Bertinis* (Frankfurt am Main: S. Fischer, 1988, [1985]). Giordano is mentioned frequently in subsequent interviews. He is a *Mischling*. His

mother was Jewish, his father of Italian descent ("Aryan") from a family of musicians. His family survived first in a village after Hamburg was bombed in 1943 and finally in hiding in the cellar of a ruin in Hamburg. The story continues until May 1946 to show what happened after the war. The love for his hometown, Hamburg, plays an important part in his book. The story has the form of a novel, a fictional family-saga starting with the grandparents, but it is mostly autobiographical. It was first published in 1982 and was a great success. It was also a TV film.

22. Inge Hutton or "Kleine Inge" is a close friend of Hecht's. Inge did not want to meet at the time because of scheduling overload. She has been featured in a film and has conducted numerous interviews relating to her former *Mischling* status.

23. I got the impression that she enjoys being one of the few "half Jews" around. The success of her books has confirmed her claim to this territory.

24. *Das Sonderrecht für die Juden im NS- Staat : eine Sammlung der gesetzlichen Massnahmen und Richtlinien, Inhalt und Bedeutung* (Heidelberg; Karlsruhe: Müller Juristischer Verlag, 1981).

25. This is an honorary prize. The real Anne-Frank Award was given to Ida Fink in Israel. See Hecht, *To Remember Is to Heal*, pp. 221-229.

26. The name of the oldest *Gymnasium* in Hamburg. For many people still the best school in which to make your *Abitur* (pre-college exams). Old schools are often named after a churchly saint (Johannes = St. John), or after the prince of the land, i.e., the Leopoldinum in Detmold where the prince who founded the school was Leopold.

27. Lotte Paepcke, *Ein kleiner Händler, der mein Vater war* (Karlsruhe: G. Braun, 1998).

28. Because she used an incorrect pronoun, Hecht actually said, when translated correctly, that she "cross-sections the children." Hecht's German is a flavorful mixture of Hochdeutsch and Southern dialect.

29. In 1979 the American movie *Holocaust* (with Meryl Streep as an "Aryan" wife of a Jew who was sent to Theresienstadt/Auschwitz) ran on German TV. Almost everyone there watched it. It was a success precisely because it was like a fictitious television show. *Holocaust* focused on a Jewish family called Weiss who originally came from Poland. Their fates mirrored the different fates of Jews during the war: The father was in the Warsaw ghetto, one daughter fought with Russian partisans, one was an artist in Theresienstadt. People were more moved by that film than by all the documentaries because it was easier to identify and sympathize with this Jewish family. *Holocaust* caused the second wave of questions—What did you know about this?—from children to parents and grandparents. The first wave was in the course of the student "revolution" in 1968, which was a movement motivated partly by anger at the secrecy and silence about the past. This generation actively sought to confront their parents' generation.

30. Because Hecht's husband was a diplomat, he would not have been pressured to be in the army. At that time, there were special rules and regulations. Soldiers holding certain ranks were excluded from party membership; the military leaders had their own strategies and were not always purely Nazis.

31. Literally, it means the dot on the letter "i," the final or ultimate thing to happen.

32. See Hecht, *To Remember Is to Heal*, p. 128.

33. Josef Mengele (1911 - 1979?). A Nazi very early on, he was the notorious camp doctor at Auschwitz, in charge of selections for extermination and abominable medical experiments on humans.

34. Hecht is bothered by this phrase because many concentration camp prisoners died from over-exhaustion or were gassed in the gas chambers. She thinks the phrase is insensitive, in particular, to survivors of the Holocaust. The word *Vergasen* and the phrase to do something, "bis zum Vergasung," is older than the Third Reich. *Vergasen*

can mean to kill with gas, but also it denotes in chemistry the process of *Vergasung*—carbonation/gassification. Originally, it meant to perform with so much energy that finally you dissolve/disintegrate into a gas. Today, of course, the word reminds one of the concentration camps.

35. Movie director Veit Harlan (1899–1964). *Jud Süß* (1940) was an anti-Semitic film based on a historical Jew who was financial consultant to a German prince/count in the eighteenth century. Harlan also directed other films that served the Nazi-propaganda machine, such as *Kolberg* (1944/45), a so-called *Durchhaltefilm*, a film motivating the German people *zum Durchhalten*, to hold out and not give up although the war seemed lost. Actress Kristina Söderbaum was born in Stockholm, married Harlan in 1939, and played mainly in his (melodramatic) films. She was one of the stars of so-called *Tendenzfilme*, films with a political purpose. Her nickname "Reichswasserleiche," which also can be translated as "national drowned woman," was given to her not especially by Jews but was part of the whispered jokes common among some Germans who liked to make fun of the Nazis' pompous ways.

36. A short-lived, anti-Nazi student group founded at the University of Munich in February 1943. The group attempted an anti-Nazi campaign but were thwarted by the Gestapo. Most of the group's leaders were executed.

37. Andersch's *Sansibar oder der letzte Grund* (Olten: Walter, 1957) is still read in German schools. It is about an escape from Nazi-Germany. Andersch was an anti-Fascist.

CHAPTER 2

1. Louise Kaplan, *No Voice Is Ever Wholly Lost* (New York: Simon and Schuster, 1995), p. 240.

2. An irony to note: When the Jews left Egypt with Moses, the Egyptians gave the Israelites all their jewelry. Exodus 12: 35-36.

3. Her interest in facts and laws reminded me of Beate Meyer and Ursula Büttner, two researchers of *Mischlinge* in Hamburg. Meyer and Büttner had interviewed Ingrid, and Meyer did a video production of Ingrid's extended family entitled *Familie Riemann-Blumenthal. Grindelallee 139.*

4. Ursula Büttner and Werner Jochmann, *Hamburg auf dem Weg ins Dritte Reich. Entscheidungsjahre 1931-1933,* 4th ed. (Hamburg: Landeszentrale für politische Bildung, 1993).

5. The black-white-red flag was the old Reichs flag from the Kaiser era, which ended in 1918. Very conservative people, German nationals, Kaiser-true (those who still hoped the emperor would come back) still showed this flag during the Weimar Republic. In case those Conservatives did not like the Nazis either (which was often the case), they tried to show this old flag instead of the swastika flag. But then the Nazis made the swastika flag obligatory to show on flag days. The Communist flag was red with a hammer and sickle.

6. Psychiatrist Hans Bürger-Prinz, military district doctor in Paris and Hamburg, conducted experiments on humans considered to be mentally ill. There was strong evidence that he was trained in killing activities, such as were carried out at Burg Sonnenstein, and tried to make money from it. After the war, he denied his activities and served as President of the German Society of Psychiatrists and Neurologists (GSPN) from 1959 to 1960.

7. This was her father's final destination. It was one of six euthanasia centers opened April 1940 and closed May 1943. There were 20,000 victims. At first it was a sanatorium but the Nazis made it a killing center.

8. "Within the context of Nazi eugenics, euthanasia became a term for the systematic murder of those deemed "unworthy of life." Initially, the plan was to sterilize the physically and mentally disabled. After the war began, however, the Nazis converted from sterilization to murder to speed up the eugenic benefits of the program. In August 1941 the Euthanasia Program was officially terminated, due to the resistance of the German people and Church. In practice, however, killings on eugenic grounds—as well as medical experiments on concentration camp inmates—continued to the end of the war. . . . Throughout its existence (1939 - 1945) at least 100,000 people fell victim to the Euthanasia Program." Abraham J. Edelheit and Hershel Edelheit, *History of the Holocaust: A Handbook and Dictionary* (Boulder, CO: Westview Press, 1994), p. 229.

9. This was a Nazi organization, so the term was used only between 1933 and 1945. In a law from September 22, 1933, it states that everybody working in the field of art or culture had to join this organization. It was subdivided into the Reichsschrifttumskammer for writers; Reichspressekammer for journalists; Reichstheaterkammer for actors, performers, and theater people; Reichsmusikkammer for musicians, composers, and the like, and an intermediate Filmkammer for movie directors, film actors, and people working in studios; later it became an official Kammer. By expelling people from the Kammer, the Nazis made it difficult for these artists to do their work. They could be dismissed for political, racial, or simply personal reasons.

10. Actually called "Bund deutscher Mädel in der HJ," League of German Girls. Female sector of HJ/Hitlerjugend, Hitler Youth, an organization for fourteen- to eighteen-year-old girls. After 1939, membership was obligatory for "Aryans." Both the BDM and HJ, seemingly innocent youth groups (like the Boy Scouts) on the exterior, were main balusters of Hitler's propaganda. Many former members, especially those in the BDM, claim today that they did not realize the political aspects of these groups (inherent in their songs, rhetoric, slogans, pledges).

11. Education in Germany is not centralized. There is a different system in each German state. *Grundschule* (term after the war) or *Volksschule* (term before the war): elementary school. All children must attend this level together, after which they split and follow particular paths. The following schools are secondary schools: *Hauptschule* has a vocational training emphasis; *Realschule* has a commercially oriented curriculum; *Gymnasium* or *Lyzeum* (girls only) is college preparatory.

12. From the Nazi Party newspaper *Der Stürmer.* A lot of ugly caricatures of Jews, usually on the front page, depicted them with big hooked noses and fat lips. "*Ponem*" is a Yiddish word for head. So this is a Jewish way to describe his looks.

13. See Heinz Rosenberg, *Jahre des Schreckens: . . . und ich blieb ubrig, dass ich Dirs ansage* (Gottingen: Steidl Verlag, 1985).

14. Kronprinzenkoog is an area in the very west of Schleswig-Holstein. "Koog" means an area where land is gained from the sea. The technique of gaining land started in medieval times. The Nazis were big with these projects, and the first Nazi Koog (plural Köge) was called Adolf-Hitler-Koog; the name was changed after 1945.

15. K. Ernst Dohnke mentioned, "You cannot blame it only on the Jews. The worship services are open, but nobody wants to come in. I think that people are not interested in this time of World War II. You could write more and more books about it, like I try to do as an independent publicist, but nobody would buy a book. Even today, if anybody hears the word "sect" in connection with a religious group, immediately people work against this group since they could influence young children. But the problem is, most of these groups are not dangerous sects, but are all thrown into one pot without any effort of distinguishing. That is why even the Jewish church has difficulty establishing itself in today's Germany."

16. Flak stands for Flugabwehrkanone, anti-air raid gun. *Heimatflak* were the guns in the neighborhoods manned by people from the area. Flak is more common usage. Many women served this job [see the Erna Tietz chapter in Alison Owings, *Frauen: German Women Recall the 3rd Reich* (New Jersey: Rutgers UP, 1994), pp. 266-283].

17. The German reading and other systems are based on a 1 to 5 or 1 to 6 scale, the higher number being the worst.

18. Käthe Starke, *Der Führer schenkt den Juden eine Stadt. Bilder, Impressionen, Reportagen, Dokumente* (Berlin: Haude und Spenersche Verlagsbuchhandlung, 1975).

19. Henny Porten was a famous actress in successful movies. Günter Hagen was a comedian who performed in cabarets in Berlin. He died in Theresienstadt. The connection with theater was through Ingrid's uncle, Felix Rodemund.

20. House of the Freemasons where Jews were gathered before the Nazis drove them to the train station to deport them to Theresienstadt and other ghettos/concentration camps. Some had to stay there for several days in appalling living conditions.

CHAPTER 3

1. Susan Neiman, *Slow Fire: Jewish Notes from Berlin* (New York: Schocken Books Inc., 1992), p. 16.

2. By Eugen Roth (1895-1976). He wrote "Ein Mensch." Often he takes little snapshots from people's lives that are light and humorous and display the fullness of humanity.

3. One Nazi idea was that bread comes from the pure, German soil and thus is sacred. Her father had internalized the *Brot* idea—the Nazi logic that German soil stood for something sacred. These and other ideas were extracted from the Bible and twisted into Nazi slogans.

4. Foreman. Term used in Nazi concentration camps to designate an inmate appointed by the SS to head a labor group of other prisoners. Sometimes a Jewish man or woman was chosen, which, at the least, bought them time. These *Kapos* were known for their brutality toward fellow prisoners and often were more feared than the SS.

5. It is debatable whether Ruth could have known at such an early age of these atrocities. They were well documented in published accounts *after* the war; she may have read them and confused them with an earlier memory. Because of her connection to the Jewish community, it is possible that she had heard stories.

6. According to Paul Johnson's *A History of the Jews* (New York: Harper and Row, 1987), p. 590, "The non-legal part of the Talmud and midrash, tales, folklore, legends, etc., as opposed to the Law itself *(halakhah)*."

7. Ration cards, called *Lebensmittelkarten*, were issued on August 27, 1939. The amount of rations one received depended on one's ethnicity. Jews received the smallest allotment, averaging under 500 calories per day.

8. She probably meant Häscher, myrmidons, people who carry out orders without question. Today it still refers to human bloodhounds.

9. Friedrich Gottlieb Klopstock (1724-1803). A celebrated poet. He wrote the first large epic of modern German literature "Der Messias." His odes were published in 1771; they were influenced by the Bible and Horace, Pindar, and Milton. His topics were love, friendship, and fatherland. He is situated somewhere between late Baroque and Classicism. (Goethe and Schiller are younger). He was a forerunner of Sturm und Drang, Irrationalism, and *Empfindsamkeit* (sentimentality). He died in Hamburg, and was buried in Altona. Klopstock was a bourgeois poet, a man who had written an epoch on a Christian theme, whose original sympathies for the French revolution had turned into criticism and condemnation when the terror mounted. In East Germany only eighteenth-century writers were favored who could be shown as a forerunner of

Communism. Klopstock was old-fashioned and out of date. Johann Gottfried Herder (1744-1803), philosopher, in contrast, was a more modern, politically engaged author and pragmatic thinker.

10. Freie Deutsche Jugend (Free German Youth). A socialist organization whose member-ship was mandatory for all boys and girls in Eastern Germany after 1946. Uniforms were required and, like the Hitler Youth, there was strong political indoctrination.

11. Friedrich Nietzsche in *Thus Spoke Zarathustra* (1883-1884) stressed importance of social arrangements and that some exceptional human beings, the "overmen" *(Über-menschen),* could rise to a higher level of creativity and independence, elevating them above the normal "herd" *(Untermenschen).* Hitler perverted and used Nietzsche's terms to further bolster his own "ruling Aryan" ideology. [Trans. Walter Kaufmann (New York: The Viking Press, 1966 [1954])].

12. *Persilschein,* meaning an "ivory snow" certificate, is a colloquialism for a certificate of your innocence, a new word coined after 1945 when the de-Nazification started. Persil was (and is) the best-known detergent in Germany—it makes everything white/ innocent again. Those suspected of Nazi activity had to obtain signatures from witnesses as proof they had acted humanely during the Third Reich.

13. The Russians arrived in May 1945 and raped German women whenever they found them; this continued for months. German women were hiding in lofts or basements for long periods of time. Other women who were in Berlin at the end of the war experienced similar atrocities. Rapes also occurred in all other places in East Germany that were liberated by the Soviet Army. It is not surprising that the majority of Germans never refer to 1945 as the liberation, but say they were defeated or conquered in 1945. In the DDR people were not allowed to say this, but had to refer to the Russians as the power they were grateful to. There are stories about Jewish women at the time who said they were Jewish and they were not raped. Ruth's mixed identity was what forced her to hide like all the others. After being a Jew up to age ten and then having become a strict Lutheran, with an atheistic stepfather, she probably was not able to go out and say "I am Jewish" because she did not feel like that any more after such a 180 degree turnaround. In her mind it had become too dangerous to ever acknowledge this fully.

14. Ruth is arguing against centuries of anti-Semitic laws that said Jews could be business people but that working with money was not honorable. Hitler equated Jews to rats— gluttonous, base vermin. They were rats who dirtied their hands with money.

15. Not translatable. Generally, the inhabitants of Hamburg who spoke the Low German dialect (Plattdeutsch) used this term to refer to somebody who spoke standard or High German. According to Ruth, it is ingrained in much of Hamburg thinking that the city has walls around it and people who come from outside do not really belong.

16. Official newspaper published by the National Socialist Party from 1921 to 1945. In 1923 it became a daily paper. Several libraries have holdings of the paper.

17. Short for *Zigeuner,* Gypsy. This is an old German term now discredited as prejudicial; the Nazis used it.

18. The two main "tribes" of Gypsies. They make up about 90 percent of all Gypsies in Germany. Both terms are always used together, as a non-Gypsy can not distinguish one from another, and the Gypsies' feel this is a neutral expression as compared to *Zigeuner.* On numerous occasions the Sinti and Roma have staged protests in an attempt to force politicians into negotiations.

19. "*Sich fettfressen*" means gluttony. This is a common expression.

20. "*Land der unbegrenzten Möglichkeiten*" means land of unlimited possibilities. This is a common expression.

21. "*Was mir in der Fremde blühte*"—literally what would blossom in strangeness, what was in store for me, what I was in for. This is a common expression.

22. Ruth said "*Marder*," which is marten fur. Probably she is referring to furs from their former shop.

CHAPTER 4

1. For example, Abba Solomon Eban, *Dies ist mein Volk; die Geschichte der Juden* (Zürich: Droemer, 1970); Clara Eisenkraft, *Damals in Theresienstadt: Erlebnisse einer Juden-Christen* (Wuppertal: Aussaat Verlag, 1977); Simon Wiesenthal, *Die Sonnenblume: Eine Erzählung mit Kommentaren* (Frankfurt am Main: Ullstein, 1984); Bernt Engelman, *Deutschland ohne Juden. Eine Bilanz* (München: Schneekluth, 1970); Ralph Giordano, ed., *Narben, Spuren, Zeugen: 15 Jahre Allgemeine Wochenzeitung der Juden in Deutschland* (Düsseldorf: Verlag Allgemeine Wochenzeitung der Juden in Deutschland, 1961).

2. Masuren is a part of East Prussia that now belongs to Poland.

3. Hermann Goering (1894-1946). President of the Reichstag, Chief Commander of the Luftwaffe, originator of the Gestapo, and Hitler's successor. He was a blustering extrovert, which caused many Germans to mistakenly think he was good-natured and accessible. In actuality, he was a depraved egomaniac. See John E. Dolibois, *Pattern of Circles: An Ambassador's Story* (Kent, OH: Kent State UP, 1989), especially pp. 110-237.

4. Adolph Menzel (1815-1905). A self-taught man who was one of the forerunners of the Impressionists in his use of color and light, he is famous for his drawings and paintings. He was favored by the bourgeoisie for his paintings of historical subjects, especially the life of the eighteenth-century Prussian king Friedrich the Great. He also painted factories, nineteenth-century industry, when that was not yet considered a worthy topic.

5. Werner Höfer was the host of one of the longest-running TV talk shows, called *Der Internationale Frühschoppen* ("Frühschoppen" is a German habit of having a glass of wine at noon on Sundays). It was broadcast Sundays at noon not only in Germany but also on Swiss and Austrian TV and on German public radio. Journalists—correspondents for foreign newspapers working in Germany as well as one or two German journalists—discussed international and national politics (and a hostess ran around and refilled the wine glasses). The show's motto could have been "Discussing the Headlines of the Week." The show had top ratings. Then the media revealed that Höfer had been a Nazi journalist (he wrote Nazi material, although not purely ideological). Although his show had a democratic touch, he had to resign, and the show terminated. Its successor, *Der Presseclub*, still runs every Sunday at noon.

6. Deutschkron spoke on many programs about the Jewish situation. She has written many books including her memoir, *Ich trug den gelben Stern* [*Outcast: A Jewish Girl in Wartime Berlin*, trans. Jean Steinberg (New York : Fromm International Pub. Corp., 1989)], *Unbequem—: mein Leben nach dem Überleben* (Köln: Wissenschaft und Politik, 1992); and . . . *denn ihrer war die Hölle. Kinder in Gettos und Lagern* (Köln, Verlag Wissenschaft und Politik, 1965). The play *Ab heute heißt du Sara* is based on her memoir.

7. National Socialist German Workers' Party. The Nazi Party. Originally founded as the *Deutsche Arbeiterpartei* (German Workers' Party) in 1919, it developed into a power-house a decade later. The employment of "socialist" in its title is misleading: Hitler's party was not a socialist party in the Marxist sense of the word. He did not advocate class struggle; rather, racial conflict between "Aryans" and Jews.

8. Part of the Western Front; namely, a huge fortification with hundreds of concrete shelters along the French coast. The Nazis expected an invasion and wanted to protect

the coast from troops coming in from Great Britain. Many German men, older soldiers who were not fit for fighting, were drafted and sent as laborers.

9. Düsseldorf was bombed by the British numerous times: between July and September, 1942; between January and April, 1943; into the summer, 1943; and on April 22-23, 1944. Dudley Saward, *Bomber Harris* (New York: Doubleday & Company, Inc., 1985), pp. 148, 196-197, 232.

10. This is a term used to denote Russian female soldiers or any harsh, heartless, masculine uniformed women.

11. The well-known Leuna-Werke, a chemical factory producing synthetics, artificial fuel/ propellant for war efforts, was in Leuna. In 1944 the Leuna-Werke were nearly destroyed. Halle was severely bombed, so slave workers were no longer needed. The workers were sent to Theresienstadt in January 1945. After the war, Halle became the most important industrial region of East Germany.

12. The Red Army liberated Auschwitz on January 27, 1945.

13. At the end of the ninth year, students take this series of exams. These exams must be taken in order for a student to study at a university. Most *Mischlinge* were unable to take them.

14. An exam based on aptitude and experience. After the war and in the early 1950s there were people who did not have qualifications for university study because the war had forced them to leave school for various reasons, so this exam was instated to fill an immense demand for teachers. In Hessen the education minister, Miekatz, publicized a search for former elementary teachers who had retired to get married and have families. He wanted them to come back to the schools. These women were called *Miekätzchen* (pun on *Maikätzchen,* kitten born in May).

15. Ruth Klüger, *weiter leben. Eine Jugend* (Gottingen: Wallstein Verlag, 1992).

16. Successful German writer. Germans make a distinction between highly regarded literature and what they call *Unterhaltungs,* or *Trivial- literatur.* Simmel's books are best-sellers, but he is not read or taught at universities because his novels are considered *Trivial.* Simmel writes about issues that are currently being discussed; he was one of the first writers to include show business, terrorism, cancer, and foreign policy in popular novels (a break from the usual subject of *Weltanschauung* [world view] that German writers tend to write about). He seeks out trends and used to put out a book a year.

17. See Yost interview, chapter 3.

18. Ralph Giordano, *Die zweite Schuld, oder, Von der last Deutscher zu sein* (München: Knaur, 1990 [1987]). In addition to the *Die Bertinis* (Frankfurt am Main: S. Fischer, 1988, [1985]), (see Hecht interview, chapter 1), he wrote numerous books about the Nazi time.

CHAPTER 5

1. Randt, Ursula, *Carolinestraße 35. Geschichte der Mädchenschule der Deutsch-Israelitis-chen Gemeinde in Hamburg 1884-1942* (Hamburg: Selbstverlag Verein für Hamburgische Geschichte, 1984).

2. Although this was not the case with Ursula, according to Alexander and Margarete Mitscherlich, "An unusually fateful historical moment was at hand. Parents grew notoriously afraid of their [usually older] children, who were being urged by the Nazi youth organizations to interrogate and if necessary denounce them to the super-father or big brother. Suddenly, it was possible to act out Oedipal wishes directly." *The Inability to Mourn: Principles of Collective Behavior,* trans. Beverley R. Placzek (New York: Grove Press, Inc., 1975), p. 47.

3. Actual decree, July 25, 1938, prohibiting Jewish doctors from practicing medicine. The law did not go into effect until October.
4. In "Jewish Women in Nazi Germany: Daily Life, Daily Struggles, 1933-1939," p.197, Marion A. Kaplan states, "The pain of their children—who often faced anti-Semitism more immediately than their parents from classmates and teachers in German public schools—disturbed both women and men profoundly as parents, but women learned of and dealt with the children's distress more directly than men. When children came home from school, their mothers heard the stories first and had to respond." In *Different Voices: Women and the Holocaust,* Carol Rittner and John K. Roth, ed. (New York: Paragon House, 1993), pp. 187-212.
5. Adrienne Thomas, *Die Katrin wird Soldat : ein Roman aus Elsass-Lothringen* (Frankfurt am Main: Fischer Taschenbuch Verlag, 1987). English translation: *Katrin Becomes a Soldier,* trans. Margaret L Goldsmith (Boston: Little, Brown, 1931). First published in Germany, 1930. It has been translated into fourteen languages. It is written in the form of a diary of a young girl, Catherine Lentz, starting in 1911 with her fourteenth birthday and ending with her death in 1915. She lives in Metz in Lothringen, which at the time was German and became French again after 1918. She wants to be a singer, but in the war she is a nurse for the Red Cross.
6. These classes were home economics (needlepoint and cooking) for girls and "shop" (carpentry and mechanics) for boys.
7. Starting on February 15, 1938, all unmarried females under the age of twenty-five were compelled to serve for one year in housekeeping or farming. Exempted were only women who were working there anyway. A person's *Pflichtjahr* was written down in a work book. If there was no entry, a woman was not permitted to find other work outside of farming and housekeeping. The goal of the *Pflichtjahr* was vocational guidance and to satisfy the need for labor. At the time there were still a lot of large families, so the mothers really needed help. It also had to do with the idea that social classes should become unimportant and everyone feel equal as a German Volksgenosse (member of the people) whether poor or rich. Women who made *Abitur* had to do their *Pflichtjahr* before they could go to a university. These workers did gain insights into other social classes, but also were exploited quite a bit, made to work from morning to night. At the time it was not unusual for girls from a well-off background not to have an occupation but to stay in the family until they found a husband. Married women did not work, even when there were no children. They had to do housekeeping for their husbands. In 1940 there were about 200,000 women doing their *Pflichtjahr.* (Thanks to Almuth Ditmar-Kolb for this information.)
8. Riga was a ghetto with a work camp nearby. There Jews starved or were worked to death.
9. All Jews in the German Reich had to wear the star beginning September 19, 1941. The deportations to the East (the Hamburg Jews were sent to Riga, Lodz, Minsk, Theresienstadt, or Auschwitz) from the Altreich started on October 14, 1941. These events are what made Randt so sick in late 1941.
10. July 2, 1942. Decree against *Mischlinge* in public schools. The laws were named after Bernhard Rust, the minister of education who devoted himself to expelling Jews from schools. Rust committed suicide in 1945.
11. KLV for short. Literally, evacuation of children to the country. The KLV started before the war with the idea to send "Aryan" children whose health was bad from the bigger cities to the country so they could get better. Jewish children, even if their health was bad, could not be sent to the country. When the aerial warfare became worse in 1942, all the young students in endangered places were sent to rural areas in East and South Germany and also in the Protektorat Böhmen und Mähren (the former Czechoslova-

kia). From 1941 to 1944 about 800,000 children altogether were sent away from home with the KLV to camps organized by the Hitler Youth. There the Nazis had an opportunity to bring up children to become Nazis, to indoctrinate them. Parents could not be forced to send their children away, but in the big cities, where there were air raids all the time, there was no school and parents did not really have any choice.

12. When asked by author Alison Owings what her first impression of the American soldiers was, Frau Martha Brixius replied, "They looked very healthy and red-cheeked. Well dressed, the uniforms still in one piece and new. From our point of view, they looked fantastic. Ach, to us they looked like gods." Cited in *Frauen: German Women Recall The Third Reich* (New Brunswick, NJ: Rutgers UP, 1994), p. 209.

CHAPTER 6

1. After Kristallnacht, you could still buy someone free *(freikaufen)* from the camps when, in addition, you could prove that the person had a visa.

2. A town in Lower Saxony between Hannover and Braunschweig.

3. Ahrensburg is a suburb of Hamburg in the northeast, but there was no real camp there, only a place where forced laborers were kept. On the other hand, Neuengamme had so many outposts in the Hamburg area that it is hard to tell which were camps and which not.

4. The mother's sisters were taken to ghettos or camps later, when the deportations from the Altreich started on October 14, 1941.

5. In Poland, where on September 7, 1942, an *Aktion* took place; 6,000 victims were murdered at Belzec.

6. A camp near the villages of Bergen and Belsen in Prussian Hanover, Germany, established in 1943 as a prisoner-of-war camp and Jewish transit camp. Around 35,000 prisoners died from disease, starvation, and overwork. Known as one of the most squalid of Germany's camps and where Anne Frank, author of the world-renowned diary, died.

7. The Jews were not kept and harassed in the city hall. They were gathered in a place at the Moorweide close to Dammtor train station that belonged to the Freemasons. It's a very impressive building purported to have a *Spiegelsaal,* a room with mirrors.

8. Buchholz is a little town southwest of Hamburg.

9. "*Fragt mich noch ein Loch in den Bauch,*" means "asks me a hole into my belly." A German expression for somebody, especially a child, who relentlessly asks questions.

10. *Swing-Jugend* were kids who listened to American swing music. They dressed differently, did not join the Hitler Youth, and did not follow rules. Some of them were sent to a concentration camp for youth in Moringen/Lower Saxony; others were not caught.

CHAPTER 7

1. See Sigrid Lorenzen interview, chapter 8, for clarification.

CHAPTER 8

1. During the war it was rumored that King Christian X threatened to wear the star of David to protest anti-Semitic laws that the Germans were putting in place.

CHAPTER 9

1. A part of Hamburg east of Uhlenhorst and south of Barmbek, so the so-called Jewish living quarters around Grindel and Emsbüttel were on the other side of the Außenalster.
2. This could not be. Dresden was bombed on February 13 and 14, 1945, by British bombers at night, and for the following six days by American bombers by day.
3. The part of Czechoslovakia where mostly Germans lived (the Sudeten are the Sudetic Mountains or Sudetes) that was taken from Czechoslovakia in 1938.
4. She may be referring to a TV documentary series on the German army in World War II; in particular, what the Russians did to the German prisoners of war. They gave them food that gave them diarrhea before they were marched through Moscow in 1945. So the losing army made a very bad impression on the Russians who watched their long march through the city. Here Margot empathizes with the Germans.
5. Quark is a dairy product, similar to cottage cheese that is mixed with sour cream.
6. If there are two people looking for the same job, it is given to the woman so she finally has a chance. In Germany now, the word "Quotenfrau" is nearly an invective.
7. *Nationalpolitische Erziehungsanstalt.* Motto: believe, obey and fight. These were boarding schools where the Nazis raised young boys (a few were for girls too) from the age of ten to precollege exams to become good Nazis. They had to do a lot of sports and paramilitary education, but in some they also got a good school education. In the 1940s there were more than forty Napolas. It is a rarely mentioned topic, but as people who were sent to these schools by their Nazi (more or less) parents are retired now, they finally feel free to talk about the topic. Most of them were not allowed to go to the university after 1945. Many well-known people went to Napolas: the actor Hardy Kruger, artist Horst Janssen, book critic Hellmuth Karasek, diplomats like Rüdiger von Wechmar. See Johannes Leeb, "Wir waren Hitlers Eliteschüler": ehemalige Zöglinge der NS-Ausleseschulen brechen ihr Schweigen (Hamburg : Rasch und Röhring, 1998).
8. Hans Globke (1898-1973). Authored numerous commentaries and legislation during the Nazi period. He was never a member of the NSDAP (the Nazi party). After the war he served as State Secretary of the Chancellery, and Federal Chancellor Konrad Adenauer, an avid anti-Nazi, stood by Globke despite his past record.

CHAPTER 10

1. Ursula Bosselmann, "Plötzlich waren wir keine Deutschen und keine Christen mehr:Ein Zeitzeugnis der Jahre 1933-1945." ["Suddenly we were no longer German or Christian. A Report of the years 1933 to 1945"] in *Ausgegrenzt: Schicksalswege "nichtarischer" Christen in der Hitlerzeit* [Isolated: The destiny of "non-Aryan" Christians in the time of Hitler], Arnulf H. Baumann, ed. (Hannover: Lutherisches Verlagshaus, 1992). Translated here by Cynthia Crane.
2. Dov Edelstein, *Worlds Torn Asunder.* Although Bosselmann and her friends translated his book, it was never published. Bosselmann gave the German manuscript, *Welten zerbrachen,* to him as a present
3. The book was also known in the United States. In 1996, Mitscherlich appeared on the TV news program *Dateline* and discussed aspects of her book.
4. This ceremony, before school started, was obligatory at some schools. It was not regularly done. There *was* a "flags parade" when you were in a camp of the Hitler Youth.
5. An oath the Swiss originally recited when Switzerland was founded. Rütli is an alpine meadow/hill on which the oath took place, and the oath is the founding legend of

Switzerland. (Schiller based his play Wilhelm Tell on it.) The term "Rütli-Schwur" is used for any kind of very special, honest oath. Bosselmann uses it ironically here.

6. The Hitler-Gruß was also called Deutscher Gruß. You raised your outstretched right arm about eye-level with your left arm at your side like a soldier. Only Hitler and some of his leading men greeted with their arm at an angle. It was probably used around 1925 and was mandated after 1933 as the German greeting.

7. Lines from "The Horst Wessel Song." Wessel was a Berlin SA (stormtrooper) leader. After his death, this tune became the NSDAP's (the Nazi party's) anthem, and he was canonized through Nazi propaganda. He was killed in 1930 in a brawl. He was amoral, which Goebbels cleverly kept quiet. Wessel had been a (Nazi) pimp fighting for prostitutes in the streets. The line from the song here refers to the Communists (Rotfront) and the ultra-conservative party (Reaktion).

8. Two forms of address in German: familiar you (between friends), "*du*"; and formal you (to superiors, elders, or acquaintances), "*Sie*." Today, addressing an in-law as "*Sie*" is rare.

9. Literally "steel helmets." A group of German veterans with nationalist leanings who had served in World War I. After 1933 this group was a part of the Sturmabteilungen (SA) (stormtroopers). At that time, some members left.

10. Posen was an originally Polish land, south of West Prussia, that belonged to Prussia from 1815 to 1918; then it became Polish again. The population was mixed, German, Polish, and Jewish. Many Germans and Jews left Posen after the end of World War I, in 1918, to live in Germany.

11. Although "Blankenese" was written in the original text, apparently during the war the airfield was in Ütersen between Wedel und Elmshorn, west of Hamburg, not in Blankenese.

12. *Gösta Berling* is a famous novel by Swedish Nobel Prize winner Selma Lagerlöf.

13. Assistance to the poor. Hitler renamed this league.

14. Jochen Klepper (1903 - 1942) was a Christian writer married to a Jewish woman who had a Jewish daughter. He is now famous primarily for the fact that he, his wife, and his stepdaughter committed suicide under Nazi pressure. His diaries were published in 1956 and 1958; they are moving documents of the times.

15. Damokles' sword comes via poet Friedrich Schiller from Greek mythology. The sword was held by a horse's hair. If it fell your life was lost. It is a common phrase among Germans. When Damokles' Sword hovers over a situation, very important issues are at stake. If fate is in your favor, the sword will not fall.

16. Carol Rittner and John K. Roth, *Different Voices: Women and the Holocaust* (New York: Paragon House, 1993), p. 9. "Already laws decreed in 1933, during the earliest months of the Nazi regime, legalized race-hygiene sterilization to prevent the propagation of *lebensunwertes Leben* (lives unworthy of life)."

17. See Ursula Büttner, "The Persecution of Christian-Jewish Families in the Third Reich." *Leo Baeck Institute Year Book* 34 (1989): 289. "[February 1945] . . . Jewish husbands and wives up to now defined as living in 'privileged mixed marriages,' were deported to Theresienstadt. . . . The Jews living in 'mixed marriages' and probably the half Jews as well owed their survival only to the ultimately rapid collapse of Hitler's regime."

18. Magdalene Wanske, *Wie Engelchen seine Mutter suchte. Ein Märchen in Versen*, 16th ed. (Esslingen: Gebundene Ausgabe Hahns, 1930). First published in 1927. Successful children's book.

19. Ursula stated, "One should read about what all that meant in *Der Führer schenkt den Juden eine Stadt* (The Führer gives the Jews a city) by Käthe Starke or in *Theresienstadt 1941-1945* by Hans G. Adler."

20. Hamburg, because it is a port city, is known as "the gateway to the world."

21. "Church day." This is an annual tradition featuring speakers, workshops, music, and so on that began after 1945. Originally initiated by the Lutheran Church, today it has turned into more of an ecumenical gathering (sign of tolerance), but it remains primarily a Lutheran concern. A *Katholischer Kirchentag* is now being held annually as well. Both run for a week.

22. Ralph Giordano is a well-known *Mischling* and German author whose mother was German Jewish and whose father was Italian Christian. See also Hecht and Wilmschen interviews, chapters 1 and 4 respectively.

WORKS CONSULTED

Adler, H. G. *Theresienstadt, 1941-1945; das Antlitz einer Zwangsgemeinschaft. Geschichte, Soziologie, Psychologie.* Tübingen: Mohr, 1960.

Appelfeld, Aharon. *Beyond Despair: Three Lectures and a Conversation with Philip Roth.* Trans. Jeffrey M. Green. New York: Fromm International Publishing Corp, 1994.

Baumann, Arnulf H., ed. *Schicksalswege "nichtarischer" Christen in der Hitlerzeit: Mario Sello, Ursula Bosselmann, Werner Steinberg.* Hannover: Lutherisches Verlagshaus, 1992.

Baumbach, Sybille et al. *"Wo Wurzeln Waren". . . Juden in Hamburg-Eimsbuettel 1933 bis 1945.* Hamburg: Doelling and Galitz, 1993.

Baumeister, Dr. Roy F. *Escaping the Self: Alcoholism, Spirituality, Masochism, and Other Flights from the Burden of Selfhood.* New York: Basic Books, 1991.

Begley, Louis. *Wartime Lies.* New York: Ballantine Books, 1991.

Bettelheim, Bruno. *"Surviving" and Other Essays.* New York: Alfred A. Knopf, 1979.

Braham, Randolph L., ed. *Reflections of the Holocaust in Art and Literature.* New York: Columbia UP, 1990.

Braun-Vogelstein, Julie. *Was niemals stirbt: Gestalten und Errinerungen.* Stuttgart: Deutsche Verlags Anstalt, 1966.

Bridenthal, Renate, Atina Grossmann, and Marion Kaplan, eds. *When Biology Became Destiny: Women in Weimar & Nazi Germany.* New York: Monthly Review Press, 1984

Bullock, Alan. *Hitler: A Study in Tyranny.* New York: Harper and Row, 1964.

Büttner, Ursula. *Die verlassenen Kinder der Kirche: der Umgang Mit Christen jüdischer Herkunft im "Dritten Reich."* Göttingen: Vandenhoeck + RUP, 1998.

Büttner, Ursula. "The Persecution of Christian-Jewish Families in the Third Reich." *Leo Baeck Institute Year Book* XXXIV (1989): 267-289.

Chernow, Ron. *The Warburgs : The Twentieth-Century Odyssey of a Remarkable Jewish Family.* New York: Vintage, 1994.

Davidowicz, Lucy. *The War Against the Jews 1933-1945.* Tenth Anniversary Edition. New York: Bantam, 1986.

De Beauvoir, Simone. *The Prime of Life.* Trans. Peter Green. New York: World Publishing Co., 1962.

Delbo, Charlotte. *After Auschwitz.* Trans. Rosette C. Lamont. New Haven: Yale UP, 1995.

Deutschkron, Inge. *Ich trug den gelben Stern.* Cologne: Verlag Wissenschaft und Politik, 1978; Munich: Deutscher Taschenbuch Verlag, 1985.

———. *Outcast: A Jewish Girl in Wartime Berlin.* Trans. Jean Steinberg. New York : Fromm International Pub. Corp., 1989.

Dolibois, John E. *Pattern of Circles: An Ambassador's Story.* Kent, OH: Kent State UP, 1989.

Drewitz, Ingeborg. *Gestern war Heute: Hundert Jahre Gegenwart.* Stuttgart: E. Klett, 1980.

Dworkin, Andrea. "The Unremembered: Searching for Women at the Holocaust Memorial Museum." *Ms.* (November/December 1994): 52-58.

Edelheit, Abraham J. and Hershel Edelheit. *The History of the Holocaust: A Handbook and Dictionary.* Boulder, CO: Westview Press, 1994.

Edvardson, Cordelia. *Gebranntes Kind sucht das Feuer.* Trans. Anna-Liese Kornitzky. Munich: Carl Hanser Publishing, 1987.

Ehre, Ida. *Gott hat einen grossen Kopf, mein Kind.* Hamburg: Rowohlt Taschenbuch, 1988.

Eisenberg, Azriel. *The Lost Generation: Children of the Holocaust.* New York: Pilgrim, 1982

Eisenkraft, Clara. *Damals in Theresienstadt: Erlebnisse einer JudinChristen.* Wuppertal: Aussaat Verlag, 1977.

Engelmann, Bernt. *Deutschland ohne Juden.* München: Schneekluth, 1970.

———. *Germany without Jews.* Trans. D. J. Beer. New York: Bantam, 1984.

———. *In Hitler's Germany: Everyday Life in the 3rd Reich.* New York: Random House, 1986.

Epstein, Helen. *Children of the Holocaust: Conversations with Sons and Daughters of Survivors.* New York: G.P. Putnam's Sons, 1979.

Felman, Shoshana and Dori Laub. *Testimony: Crises of Witnessing in Literature, Psychoanalysis, and History.* New York: Routledge, 1992.

Fleischmann, Lea. *Dies ist nicht mein Land.* Hamburg: Hoffmann & Campe, 1980.

Friedlander, Henry, and Sybil Milton, eds. *The Holocaust: Ideology, Bureaucracy, and Genocide.* New York: Kraus International Publications, 1980.

Gay, Peter. *Weimar Culture: The Outsider as Insider.* New York: Harper & Row, 1968.

Golsan, Richard J., ed. *Fascism, Aesthetics, and Culture.* Hanover, NH: UP of New England, 1992.

Guide to Yale University Library Holocaust Video Testimonies. Vol. I. Fortunoff Video Archive for Holocaust Testimonies. New York: Garland, 1990. (*Mischlinge* testimonies: HVT-171, HVT-177, HVT-227).

Haas, Peter. *Morality After Auschwitz: The Radical Challenge of the Nazi Ethic.* Philadelphia: Fortress, 1988.

Harrelson, Walter and Randall M. Falk. *Jews & Christians: A Troubled Family.* Nashville, TN: Abingdon Press, 1990.

Hecht, Ingeborg. *Invisible Walls: A German Family Under the Nuremberg Laws.* New York: Harcourt Brace Jovanovich, 1985. Trans. of *Als unsichtbare Mauern Wuchsen.* Hamburg: Doelling & Galitz Verlag, 1984.

———. *To Remember Is to Heal: Encounters between Victims of the Nuremberg Laws.* Trans. John A. Broadwin. Evanston, IL: Northwestern UP, 1999. Trans. of *Von der Heilsamkeit des Erinnerns: Opfer der Nürnberger Gesetze begegnen sich.* Hamburg: Hoffmann und Campe Verlag, 1991

Hegi, Ursula. *Floating in My Mother's Palm.* New York: Simon and Schuster, Inc., 1990; rpt. New York: Vintage Books, 1991.

Heilers, Margarete B. *Lebensrations: Tagebuch einer Ehe 1933-1945.* Frankfurt: Tende, 1985.

Heinemann, Marlene E. *Gender and Destiny: Women Writers and the Holocaust.* New York: Greenwood Press, 1986.

Hershman, Marcie. *Tales of the Master Race.* New York: HarperCollins, 1991

Hilberg, Raul. *The Destruction of the European Jews.* New York: Harper and Row, 1961.

Hirsch, Robert. *Genocide and the Politics of Memory: Studying Death to Preserve Life.* Chapel Hill, NC: U of North Carolina P, 1995.

Hitler, Adolf. *Mein Kampf.* Trans. Ralph Mannheim. Boston: Houghton-Mifflin,1962.

hooks, bell. *Yearning: race, gender, and cultural politics.* Boston, MA: South End Press, 1990.

Humanities Press International. *Forever in the Shadow of Hitler? Original Documents of the Historikerstreit, the controversy concerning the singularity of the Holocaust.* Trans. James Knowlton and Truett Cates. New Jersey: Humanities Press, 1993. Trans. of *Historikerstreit: Die Dokumentation der Kontroverse um die Einzigartigkeit der nationalsozialistischen Judenvernichtung.* Munich: R. Piper GmbH & Co., n.d.

Johnson, Paul. *A History of the Jews.* New York: Harper & Row, 1987.

Kakutani, Michiko. "When History and Memory Are Casualties: Holocaust Denial." *New York Times,* 30 April 1993, 4B1.

Kaplan, Louise J. *No Voice Is Ever Wholly Lost.* New York: Simon and Schuster, 1995.

Kaplan, Marion A. "Jewish Women in Nazi Germany: Daily Life, Daily Struggles, 1933-1939." In *Different Voices: Women and the Holocaust.* Carol Rittner and John K. Roth, eds. New York: Paragon House, 1993, pp. 187-212. Rpt. from *Feminist Studies* 16 (1990): 579-606.

———. *Between Dignity and Despair: Jewish Life in Nazi Germany.* New York: Oxford University Press, 1998.

Kent, George O. "Research Opportunities in West & East German Archives for the Weimar Period & the 3rd Reich." *Central European History* 3.1 (1979): 38-67

Kershaw, Ian. "The Persecution of the Jews and German Popular Opinion in the Third Reich." *Leo Baeck Institute Yearbook* 26 (1981): 264-274.

Klueger, Ruth. *weiter leben. Eine Jugend.* Gottingen: Wallstein Verlag, 1992.

Koehn, Ilse. *Mischling Second Degree: My Childhood in Nazi Germany.* New York: Greenwillow Books, 1977.

Koonz, Claudia. *Mothers in the Fatherland: Women, the Family, and Nazi Politics.* New York: St. Martin's Press, 1987.

Kramer, Jane. "The Politics of Memory." *The New Yorker* (14 August 1995): 48-65.

Kritzman, Lawrence, ed. *Auschwitz and After: Race, Culture, and "the Jewish Question" in France.* New York: Routledge, 1995.

Kuehn, Heinz R. *Mixed Blessings: An Almost Ordinary Life in Hitler's Germany.* Athens: U of Georgia P, 1988.

Lang, Berel, ed. *Writing and the Holocaust.* New York: Holmes & Meier, 1988.

Langer, Lawrence L. *The Holocaust and the Literary Imagination.* New Haven, CT: Yale UP, 1975.

———. "The Writer and The Holocaust Experience." In *The Holocaust: Ideology, Bureaucracy, and Genocide.* Friedlander and Milton, eds., pp. 309-322.

Laqueur, Walter. *Fascism: Past, Present, Future.* New York & Oxford: Oxford UP, 1996.

Leitner, Isabella. *Fragments of Isabella: A Memoir of Auschwitz.* Ed. Irving A. Leitner. New York: Thomas Y. Crowell Publishers, 1978.

Levi, Primo. *Survival in Auschwitz, The Nazi Assault on Humanity.* Trans. Stuart Woolf. New York: Collier, 1961.

———. *The Drowned and the Saved.* Trans. Raymond Rosenthal. New York: Summit Books, 1988.

Lewis, Helen. *A Time to Speak.* Belfast, Ireland: The Blackstaff Press Ltd., 1992.

Lifton, Robert Jay. *The Nazi Doctors: Medical Killing and the Psychology of Genocide.* New York: Basic Books, 1986.

Loewenberg, P. "Psychoanalytic Perspectives on Modern German History." *Journal of Modern History* 47.2 (June 1975): 229-279.

Lorenz, Dagmar C. G., and Gabriele Weinberger, eds. *Insiders and Outsiders: Jewish and Gentile Culture in Germany and Austria.* Detroit: Wayne State UP, 1994.

Lorenz, Ina. *Die Juden in Hamburg zur Zeit der Weimarer Republic. Band 1&2.* Hamburg: Christians Verlag, 1987.

Maller, Allen S. "Religious Identity of Children in Jewish-Christian Marriages." *Journal of Reform Judaism* 36.1 (Winter 1989): 25-30.

Meyer, Beate. *"Judische Mischlinge" Rassenpolitik und Verfolgungserfahrung 1933-1945.* Hamburg: Dölling und Galitz Verlag, 1999.

Milton, Sybil. "Women and the Holocaust: The Case of German and German-Jewish Women." In *When Biology Became Destiny.* Bridenthal, Grossman, and Kaplan, eds.

Mitscherlich, Alexander and Margarete. *The Inability to Mourn: Principles of Collective Behavior.* Trans. Beverley R. Placzek. New York: Grove Press, 1975. Trans. of *Die Unfaehigkeit zu Trauern, Grundlagen Kollektiven Verhaltens.* Munich: R. Piper & Co Verlag, 1967.

Morrissey, Charles T. "Oral History and the Boundaries of Fiction." *The Public Historian* 7.2 (Spring 1985): 41-45.

Neiman, Susan. *Slow Fire: Jewish Notes from Berlin.* New York: Schocken Books, 1992.

Noakes, Jeremy. "The Development of Nazi Policy towards the German-Jewish 'Mischlinge' 1833-1945." *Leo Baeck Institute Yearbook* 34 (1989): 291-354.

———. "Social Outcasts in the Third Reich." In *Life in the Third Reich.* Richard Bessel, ed. New York: Oxford UP, 1987.

Noren, Catherine Hanf. *The Camera of My Family.* New York: Alfred A. Knopf, 1976.

Oliner, Samuel P. and Pearl M. *The Altruistic Personality: Rescuers of Jews in Nazi Europe.* New York: The Free Press, 1988.

Owings, Alison. *Frauen: German Women Recall the 3rd Reich.* New Brunswick, NJ: Rutgers UP, 1994

Paepke, Lotte. *Ich wurde vergessen. Bericht einer Judin, die das Dritte Reich ueberlebte.* Freiburg I. Br.: Herder, 1979.

Parnass, Peggy. *Suchtig nach Leben.* Hamburg: Konkret Literatur Verlag, 1990.

Pinkus, Lily. Verloren-Gewonnen: *Mein Weg von Berlin nach London.* Stuttgart: Deutsche Verlags Anstalt, 1980.

Pogrebin, Letty Cottin. *Deborah Golda & Me.* New York: Bantam Doubleday, 1991.

Pschorr, Elizabeth. *A Privileged Marriage.* Sausalito, CA: Windgate Press, 1994.

Pollack, Harriet. *Having Our Way: Women Rewriting Tradition in Twentieth-Century America.* Lewisburg, PA: Bucknell UP, 1995.

Read, Anthony, and David Fisher. *Berlin Rising: Biography of a City.* New York: W.W. Norton, 1994.

Reinharz, Yehuda, and Walter Schatzberg, eds. *The Jewish Response to German Culture: From the Enlightenment to the Second World War.* Hanover, NH: UP of New England for Clark University, 1985.

Richarz, Monika, ed. *Jewish Life in Germany: Memoirs from Three Centuries.* Trans. Stella P. Rosenfeld & Sidney Rosenfeld. Bloomington, IN: Indiana UP, 1991. Trans. of *Judisches Leben in Deutschland: Selbstzeugnisse zur Sozialgeschichte, 1918-1945.* Stuttgart: Deutsche Verlags-Austalt, 1976.

Rittner, Carol, and John K. Roth. *Different Voices: Women and the Holocaust.* New York: Paragon House, 1993.

Rosenbaum, Alan S., ed. *Is the Holocaust Unique? Perspectives on Comparative Genocide.* Boulder, CO: Westview Press, 1996.

Rothchild, Sylvia, ed. *Voices from the Holocaust.* New York: New American Library, 1981.

Salamon, Julie. *The Net of Dreams: A Family's Search for a Rightful Place.* New York: Random House, 1996.

Schindler, Roslyn Abt. "The Writings of Ralph Giordano and Ingeborg Hecht: Toward a New Enlightenment." In *The Enlightenment and Its Legacy: Studies in German Literature in Honor of Helga Slessarev.* Sara Friedrichsmeyer and Barbara Becker-Cantarino, eds. Bonn: Bouvier Verlag, 1991, pp. 195-207.

———. "Bezwingt des Herzens Bitterkeit: Hilde Bürger's Return from 'Paradise.'" In *Insiders and Outsiders: Jewish and Gentile Culture in Germany and Austria.* Dagmar C. G. Lorenz and Gabriele Weinberger, eds. Detroit, MI: Wayne State UP, 1994, pp. 175-185.

Schneider, Peter. "The Sins of the Grandfathers: How German Teen-agers Confront the Holocaust, and How They Don't." Trans. Joel Agee. *New York Times Magazine,* December 3, 1995: 74-80.

Seltzer, Sanford. "The Psychological Implications of Mixed Marriage." *Journal of Reform Judaism* 32.3 (Summer 1985): 21-36.

Spiel, Hilde. *Die hellen und die finsteren Zeiten: Errinnerungen 1911-1946.* Munich: Paul List Verlag, 1989.

Stoltzfus, Nathan. *Resistance of the Heart: Intermarriage and the Rosenstrasse Protest in Nazi Germany.* New York & London: W.W. Norton, 1996.

Sutin, Jack. J*ack and Rochelle: A Holocaust Story of Love and Resistance.* Ed. Lawrence Sutin. St. Paul, MN: Graywolf Press, 1996.

Szeman, Sherri. *The Commandant's Mistress.* New York: HarperCollins Publishers, 1993

Varnhagen, Rahel. *Varnhagen, Rahel: The Life of a Jewish Woman.* Ed. Hannah Arendt. Trans. Richard and Clara Winston. New York: Harcourt Brace Jovanovich, 1974.

Vegh, Claudine. *I Didn't Say Good-bye.* Trans. Ros Schwartz. New York: E.P. Dutton, 1984.

Whiteman, Dorit Bader. *The Uprooted: A Hitler Legacy: Voices of Those Who Escaped Before the "Final Solution."* New York: Insight Books, 1993.

Wiesel, Elie. *Night.* Trans. Stella Rodway. New York: Bantam, 1982.

Wiesenthal, Simon. *The Sunflower, With A Symposium.* New York: Schocken Books, 1970.

Wolf, Christa. *Patterns of Childhood.* Trans. Ursule Molianaro and Hedwig Rappolt. New York: Farrar, Straus and Giroux, 1980.

Wolff-Monckeberg, Mathilde. *On the Other Side. To My Children: From Germany 1940-1945.* Trans. and ed. Ruth Evans. London: Peter Owens Limited, 1979. Trans. of *Briefe, die sie nicht erreichten. Briefe einer Mutter an ihre fernen Kinder in den Jahren 1940-1946.* Hamburg: Hoffmann und Campe Verlag, 1980.

AUTOBIOGRAPHY

Alcoff, Linda Martin. "The Problem of Speaking for Others." In *Who Can Speak? Authority and Critical Identity.* Judith Roof and Robyn Wiegman, eds. Chicago: U of Illinois P, 1995, pp. 97-119.

Anderson, Linda. "At the Threshold of the Self: Women and Autobiography." *Women's Writings: A Challenge to Theory,* 54-71. Moira Monteith, ed. New York: St. Martin's Press, 1986.

Barbre, Joy Webster et al. The Personal Narratives Group (eds.) *Interpreting Women's Lives: Feminist Theory and Personal Narratives.* Bloomington: Indiana UP, 1989.

Benstock, Shari, ed. *The Private Self: Theory and Practice of Women's Autobiographical Writings.* Chapel Hill, NC: U of North Carolina P, 1988.

———. "Authorizing the Autobiographical." In *The Private Self: Theory and Practice of Women's Autobiographical Writings.* Shari Benstock, ed. Chapel Hill, NC: U of North Carolina P, 1988, pp. 10-33.

Brodzki, Bella and Celeste Schenck, eds. *Life/Lines: Theorizing Women's Autobiography.* Ithaca, NY: Cornell UP, 1988.

Fox-Genovese, Elizabeth. "My Statue, My Self: Autobiographical Writings of Afro-American Women." In *The Private Self.* Shari Benstock, ed. Chapel Hill, NC: U of North Carolina P, 1988, pp. 63-89

Gusdorf, Georges. "Conditions and Limits of Autobiography." Trans. James Olney. In *Autobiography: Essays Theoretical and Critical,* James Olney, ed. Princeton, NJ: Princeton UP, 1980, pp. 28-48.

Heilbrun, Carolyn G. *Writing A Woman's Life.* New York: Ballantine Books, 1988.

Hewitt, Lea. *Autobiographical Tightropes.* Lincoln: U of Nebraska P, 1990.

Kristeva, Julia. *The Powers of Horror: An Essay on Abjection.* Trans. Leon S. Roudiez. New York: Columbia UP, 1982, pp. 1-17.

Miller, Nancy K. "Women's Autobiography in France: For A Dialectics of Identification." In *Women and Language in Literature and Society*. Sally McConnell-Ginet et al, eds. New York: Praeger, 1980, pp. 258-273.

Moers, Ellen. *Literary Women*. New York: Doubleday & Co., 1976.

Morgan, Janice, and Colette T. Hall, eds. *Redefining Autobiography in 20th Century Women's Fiction: An Essay Collection*. New York: Garland, 1991.

Olney, James. "Autobiography and the Cultural Moment: A Thematic, Historical, and Bibliographical Introduction." In *Autobiography: Essays Theoretical and Critical*. James Olney, ed. Princeton, NJ: Princeton UP, 1980, pp. 1-27.

Smith, Sidonie. *Subjectivity, Identity, and the Body: Women's Autobiographical Practices in the 20th Century*. Bloomington, IN: Indiana UP, 1991.

Spender, Stephen. "Confessions and Autobiography." In *Autobiography: Essays Theoretical and Critical*. James Olney, ed. Princeton, NJ: Princeton UP, 1980, pp. 115-122.

Titon, Jeff Todd. "The Life Story." *Journal of American Folklore* 93 (1980): 276-292.

Witherell, Carol, and Nel Noddings. *Stories Lives Tell: Narrative and Dialogue in Education*. New York: Teacher's College Press, 1991.

INDEX